History and Neorealism

D0879812

Neorealists argue that all states aim to acquire power and that state cooperation can therefore only be temporary, based on a common opposition to a third country. This view condemns the world to endless conflict for the indefinite future. Based upon careful attention to actual historical outcomes, this book contends that while some countries and leaders have demonstrated excessive power drives, others have essentially underplayed their power and sought less position and influence than their comparative strength might have justified. Featuring case studies from across the globe, *History and Neorealism* examines how states have actually acted. The authors conclude that leadership, domestic politics, and the domain (of gain or loss) in which they reside play an important role along with international factors in raising the possibility of a world in which conflict does not remain constant and, though not eliminated, can be progressively reduced.

ERNEST R. MAY was Charles Warren Professor of History at Harvard University and a renowned historian of international relations and foreign policy.

RICHARD ROSECRANCE is Adjunct Professor in the Kennedy School of Government and Director of the Project on US–Chinese Relations at the Belfer Center, Harvard University. He is also Research Professor in the Department of Political Science, University of California, Los Angeles (UCLA).

ZARA STEINER is Senior Fellow of the British Academy and Emeritus Fellow of Murray-Edwards College, University of Cambridge.

History and Neorealism

Edited by

Ernest R. May,

Richard Rosecrance,

and

Zara Steiner

CAMBRIDGE
UNIVERSITY PRESS

JZ
1307
.H57
2010

CAMBRIDGE UNIVERSITY PRESS
Cambridge, New York, Melbourne, Madrid, Cape Town, Singapore,
São Paulo, Delhi, Dubai, Tokyo, Mexico City

Cambridge University Press
The Edinburgh Building, Cambridge CB2 8RU, UK

Published in the United States of America by Cambridge University Press,
New York

www.cambridge.org
Information on this title: www.cambridge.org/9780521132244

First published 2010

Printed in the United Kingdom at the University Press, Cambridge

A catalogue record for this publication is available from the British Library

Library of Congress Cataloguing in Publication data
History and neorealism / [edited by] Ernest R. May, Richard Rosecrance,
Zara Steiner.
    p. cm.
Includes bibliographical references and index.
ISBN 978-0-521-76134-5 – ISBN 978-0-521-13224-4 (pbk.)
1. Realism–Political aspects.   2. World politics–20th century.
3. World politics–20th century–Case studies.   4. World politics–
Philosophy.   5. Power (Social sciences)–History–20th century.
I. May, Ernest R.   II. Rosecrance, Richard N.   III. Steiner, Zara S.
JZ1307.H57 2010
327.101–dc22
                              2010021891

ISBN 978-0-521-76134-5 Hardback
ISBN 978-0-521-13224-4 Paperback

This book is dedicated to the late Ernest R. May, co-author, colleague, and friend. Scholar and teacher, adviser to several American presidents, Ernest May represented the very best in the academic pantheon. With intense intellectual curiosity and respect for its complexity, he questioned history and sought alternative avenues to the so-called inevitability of outcomes. Policy-makers, he often remarked, know too little history and worse, misuse the history they do know. Those who knew Ernest May will always miss his brilliance and gentleness, humility and humor, and his capacity to see around corners and show the way.

Contents

Tables

Contributors

MICHAEL BARNHART, Distinguished Teaching Professor, Department of History, State University of New York, Stony Brook.

SHERRILL BROWN WELLS, Professorial Lecturer in History and International Affairs, Elliott School of International Affairs, George Washington University.

NIALL FERGUSON, Laurence A. Tisch Professor of History, Harvard University.

JONATHAN HASLAM, Fellow of the British Academy and Professor of the History of International Relations, University of Cambridge.

ANDREW B. KENNEDY, Lecturer, Crawford School of Economics and Government, The Australian National University.

ROBERT O. KEOHANE, Professor of International Affairs, Woodrow Wilson School, Princeton University.

ROBERT S. LITWAK, Vice President for Programs, Woodrow Wilson International Center for Scholars, Washington, DC.

LISA MARTIN, Professor of Political Science, University of Wisconsin, Madison.

ERNEST R. MAY †, late Charles Warren Professor of History, Harvard University.

JOHN M. OWEN, IV, Associate Professor of Politics, University of Virginia.

RICHARD ROSECRANCE, Adjunct Professor, Kennedy School of Government, Harvard University and Research Professor of Political Science, University of California, Los Angeles (UCLA).

PAUL W. SCHROEDER, Emeritus Professor of History, University of Illinois, Champaign-Urbana.

x

ALEXEI SHEVCHENKO, Assistant Professor of Political Science, California State University, Fullerton.

ZARA STEINER, Fellow of the British Academy and Emeritus Fellow, Murray-Edwards College, University of Cambridge.

DEBORAH WELCH LARSON, Professor of Political Science, University of California, Los Angeles.

SAMUEL F. WELLS, JR., Senior Scholar, Woodrow Wilson International Center for Scholars, Washington, DC.

SAMUEL R. WILLIAMSON, JR., President and Professor of History Emeritus, Sewanee: The University of the South.

Acknowledgments

The editors are indebted to the Woodrow Wilson International Center for Scholars, Lee Hamilton, Director, and Sam Wells, Associate Director, for supporting our 2003 conference of participants when we were in the early stages of formulating the outlines of this volume. We have been assisted by the Belfer Center for Science and International Affairs at Harvard University and a number of research assistants and data processors including Emily Wood, Sally Makacynas, Michael Johnson, and Dr. Tom Neuhaus. MIT Press kindly allowed us to reprint the Keohane-Martin chapter. We are indebted to all the thoughtful, stimulating, and patient chapter writers, but particularly to John Owen who helped us formulate the focus of the final chapter. We also acknowledge Ernest May's essential role in setting us on this course in the first instance.

RICHARD ROSECRANCE and
ZARA STEINER

1 Theory and international history

Ernest R. May, Richard Rosecrance, and Zara Steiner

Introduction

When a major power acts aggressively and unpredictably, opponents often are nonplussed. The targets of aggressive action first interpret the move as a deliberate challenge, and are tempted to adopt an offensive response. But, they hesitate to respond until they understand why the opponent felt impelled to issue the challenge. Chairman Nikita Khrushchev of the Soviet Union placed "offensive" missiles in Cuba, although President John F. Kennedy had explicitly warned him not to do so. When the missiles were detected and the president informed on October 16, 1962, JFK reacted explosively. "He can't do this to me," Kennedy said (in more graphic terms than reproduced here). Kennedy's advisers initially interpreted Khrushchev's move as a completely illegitimate and unparalleled action in terms of Soviet foreign policy. No Soviet leader had ever placed such missiles in the Eastern European satellite countries – how could they station them ninety miles off the coast of the United States? From Khrushchev's point of view, however, while the placement was abrupt and unprecedented, it was also a symmetrical response to American stationing of Jupiter missiles in Turkey near the southern border of the Soviet Union. The Soviet missiles were also sent in reaction to US threats to Cuba which were even more compelling than any Russian pressure on Turkey. "What was sauce for the goose was sauce for the gander," Khrushchev reasoned. The Soviet leader also believed that, since the missiles were to be installed in secret, they could be made operational before the United States could react, and then it would be too late. He did not reckon with the pressures of American politics which made any Soviet build-up in Cuba very sensitive, and a nuclear missile emplacement doubly so. Kennedy could not rationalize Russian missiles in Cuba and continue with business as usual at home. He had to respond, and the crisis was on.

The first reactions which Kennedy and his advisers discussed were belligerent ones, designed to block a general Soviet thrust against

Berlin as well as in the Caribbean. Advisers talked of strikes on the missiles and storage sites (as well as on Soviet aircraft), and began to plan an invasion of Cuba. Later, however, the Americans formulated a cooler response. However unjustified the Soviet move, Americans reasoned, Khrushchev would not be able simply to back down without a rationale. He had to get something out of the crisis to please his Kremlin colleagues and bureaucratic constituents even if it could not be a nuclear missile base in Cuba. A US pledge not to invade Cuba might suffice, if the Russians were convinced that the United States was ready to act militarily and would do so if the Soviets did not remove the missiles and warheads. Such a deal was worked out between Robert Kennedy and KGB representative Alexander Fomin, closely monitored by the president. The US missiles in Turkey were also to be withdrawn, but only later and out of the glare of world publicity. In the Cuban crisis, the proposed US response was moderated to a "quarantine" of Russian shipments to Cuba which gave Khrushchev time to find a way to back down. He wrote Kennedy on Friday October 26, suggesting a compromise, and the way was cleared for a settlement two days later.

Decision-makers initially went wrong in the Cuban crisis because they were too influenced by international theorists who sought to understand world politics through the prism of realist theory. According to realist reasoning, states do only what they are permitted to do in terms of their strength vis-à-vis other states, and the Russians did not have the local or strategic strength to prevail in a contest over Cuba. But Moscow acted anyway. Realist theory could not explain why.

In ancient Greece, the outbreak of the Peloponnesian War was more comprehensible in realist terms. According to Thucydides, the Spartans made war on Athens because "they were afraid the Athenians might become too powerful, seeing that the greater part of Greece was already in their hands." But though the shift in power might have dictated war, Athenian intentions did not. Athens had been peaceful for twelve years, and the only growth in its power had come as a result of the alliance with Corcyra, which was in turn caused by Corinthian pressure on Corcyra which Sparta had actually deplored and tried to prevent. When Spartans went to war against Athens, therefore, they acted to serve the interest of their ally, Corinth, whose support they deemed critical, and not because of any grievance against Athens. Neglecting Athens' intentions, Sparta responded purely to Athenian power in ways realists could understand.

Thus, international history presents two different kinds of cases. In some instances countries calibrate their actions in terms of the power they possess, no more and no less. However, there are also instances in which countries act more aggressively or more modestly than their relative "power line" (i.e. their actual military and economic strength) would justify. They may be overambitious or too constrained in their demonstration or use of the power they enjoy. Violating the strictures of John Stuart Mill, realist theory does not account for the different actions which states take in similar circumstances, or for the same actions in different circumstances.

The writers of this volume contend that such "exceptions" to realism are not occasional but chronic. Some of the most important events in world history have occurred as a result of nations overexercising or underusing their power. When the two are juxtaposed in one episode, outcomes are even harder to predict. There is no evidence that these "exceptions" will not continue in the future. China and/or the United States may overstate or underuse their power in the next decade. It is terribly important therefore to account for these deviations and to explain them in theoretical terms. That is precisely what this volume seeks to do.

Realist approaches

The theory of "realism" asserts that all states (certainly great powers) seek power and sometimes as much as is available.[1] As a result, the only means of disciplining the forward thrust of major states is to create a "balance of power" against them. Threatened nations form alliances or rearm to protect themselves. Such cooperation as emerges is only tactical and temporary, because nations do not have permanent allies, only permanent interests. One version of realism – "offensive realism" – contends that great powers must seek regional hegemony and possibly world hegemony; otherwise they will be overmatched by others nearby or overseas. The United States and China, therefore, will be in conflict as Chinese power rises and as it seeks to dominate Asia. The United States cannot be indifferent to China's gain because it threatens the American position both more generally and ultimately even in the Western Hemisphere. As a result, the United States should today move to cut the Chinese growth rate, through tariffs and other restrictions. "Defensive realism," in contrast, is less certain that nations have to expand "offensively." They may find the status quo acceptable for short periods of time. But they can never reach a lasting accommodation.

---

[1] There is a difference here between offensive and defensive realism (the latter does not predicate a continuing attempt to increase power).

The amount of cooperation in the system is a constant, which can never structurally be increased.[2] It can only be redistributed. If A and B form a cooperative coalition, C is automatically worse off.

This volume attempts to look at the general weaknesses of realist theories both analytically and in terms of specific case histories. It combines essays by theorists with studies of crises or longer-term historical developments in an attempt to outline what were and are the decisive ingredients that determine national action. Why do nations sometimes act realistically and why do they often aim at goals that are far in excess of what their limited power will permit? Why, also, do great nations sometimes minimize their participation in international politics and fail to exercise their power? We conclude that domestic factors and leadership ideology, along with systemic considerations, institutional, economic, and technological, affect the behavior of states. The United States did not have to adopt "isolation" as a policy after 1920. It possessed as much power, relative to the rest of the world, as it enjoyed in 1945. Yet both internal politics and domestic Republican leaders pressed America to stay out of entanglements with Europe save for episodic attempts to bolster the world economy or to encourage disarmament. When Japanese nationalists and National Socialists in Germany came to power, the United States remained on the sidelines. It did not exert its manifest naval and potential military might to curb their ambitions.

Britain was similarly constricted. It failed to support France's desire to restrain Germany and instituted a pervasive "appeasement" policy of the German dictator. But when Poland was threatened by Hitler in August 1939, an unready Britain pledged itself to make war on Germany even though the immediate power situation was weighted against it. The decisive factors were domestic as well as external, and had much to do with a change in both official and popular perceptions of Germany rather than purely balance-of-power considerations.

Germany and Japan, in contrast, were guilty of hubris and overweening ambitions. They believed their European and American opponents were decadent and could not stand in their way as they asserted their rights to expansion. Fanaticism and unfulfilled nationalism pressed them forward in ways that their slender power resources could not possibly sustain. The wars in which the attacking countries engaged were not brought on by aggression or expansion by their foes. Germany and Japan resolved upon them coolly in the rarefied confines of the Reich Chancellery in Berlin and the Imperial Palace in Tokyo. Neither

---

[2] It is, of course, true that two nations moving to defense-dominant postures (from offense-dominant ones) can both improve their position.

country was "forced" into war. They both initiated conflicts they could not possibly win as the Cassandras in their own countries had warned. How do we explain such blunders (and their associated moral crimes)? Militant ideological leadership and domestic acquiescence, cooperation, or enthusiasm dictated the result. Although the two cases were obviously different, in both instances the international power balance did not facilitate their ideologically driven quests for territorial gain.

Such behavior is not exceptional in international politics or limited to marginal cases. For long periods the United States has hesitated to use its great power. Britain has combined restraint with overexercise. Germany and Japan, in the 1930s, moved well beyond their economic and military limits. Our case studies, which deal with different states in different periods of time, speak to some of the weaknesses of prevailing theory. Realism errs both in its treatment of the domestic factors which may determine state behavior and in its depiction of the restraints applied by the international system. Realists see "power" and "power perceptions" as the single key to understanding what will take place in international relations. In dismissing papal influence, Stalin once asked: "How many divisions does the Pope have?" Yet the Polish pope, John Paul II (Karol Wojtyła), helped to sustain the Polish resistance which in turn led to Soviet concessions and an end to the Cold War in 1989. Further in the past, international restraints and incentives – not related to the balance of power – caused countries to limit their depredations upon the European body politic. Even during the retrograde seventeenth century, traditional usages and notions of hierarchy restrained state behavior, though hierarchy was deposed as an organizing principle by its end. Later in the nineteenth century, international conferences and the concert of great powers filed down the sharp edges of political disputes and offered an ameliorative and restorative diplomacy to keep Europe together. Wars themselves, paradoxically, often led to periods of peace as nations and peoples resolved that they should not recur.

International history is as much a chronicle of change as it is of "realist" constancy. Exceptions, therefore, will always emerge to contradict static theory. Sometimes the economic and military failure of empire emboldened a few hardy decision-makers to renounce it as a policy. Territorial gain went, at least temporarily, into the discard. Institutions created after 1945 enabled the rebuilding of the international economy and the construction of a united Europe. Both continued to draw in new members and adherents in the twenty-first century, even though the unification of Europe should have led excluded nations to balance against it. Equally if not more important, the United States amassed more military force than the rest of the world combined, but multiple factors, both domestic and systemic, have so far prevented attempts to balance against it. Meanwhile the globalization of the world economy knit the great powers together in a way that had not been possible in 1914. It might be that the ubiquitous threat of terrorism, unlike past "isms," will act, not to divide the major powers, but to bring them together.

Tasks of this volume

We hope to show, through the use of case histories addressing different countries and covering different periods, that, even in those episodes where power is centrally involved, "realism" characteristically fails to explain what is happening. In some of these, leadership, ideology, and domestic politics as well as non-power international impulses and restraints enter the equation. Some of these illustrations show the change that has occurred in the way that nations and statesmen behave. In international history, nations focusing on economic growth have come to adopt a much longer-term perspective than nations which in the seventeenth to eighteenth centuries were focused on military strength. The very attitude toward war has altered and this in turn affects the timescale adopted by decision-makers. Some powers are more likely to seek long-term gains; for them, no short-term reverse proves necessarily decisive. The quadrille of international politics continues without a necessary resolution and major powers can persevere without issuing external challenges. The very pervasiveness of change contributes to judicious restraint. Powers and regions rise and decline unpredictably. A country or region may gain in one element of power while losing in another. Domestic upheavals can reinforce or transform international relationships. They certainly cannot be omitted from narrow considerations of power.

Conclusion

The authors of this investigation do not seek to overthrow the "baseline" perspective which realism has historically provided. But they are convinced that in attempts to find "regularity" in historical outcomes, realists have seriously misunderstood what actually transpires in international politics. Realists and neorealists have neglected "change," disregarded ideological, economic, and social constraints, and understated the role of ideological leadership. They have ignored the key factor of geography, in itself a changing circumstance; they have omitted transnational ties and institutional, economic, and social factors which affect the international environment in which states operate and indeed alter the balance between the state and the international order. Smaller powers sometimes challenge large and established nations and succeed in their aims. Great powers have been and are sometimes circumscribed by reigning institutionalism. Countries do not attack one another simply because they can.

While offensive realism dictates a univocal concentration upon power, statesmen and women are devising non-political and non-military means, including economic, technological, and propaganda tools, to change attitudes and behavior and to persuade others to cooperate rather than to fight. This does not mean that conflicts will not occur or that war among great powers can now be dismissed as a realistic possibility. But it does suggest that the levers of influence which statesmen use (and in some cases, have used in the past) are much more various than traditional military instruments. More malleable tools have become available than pure resorts to force. The use of these will determine outcomes even more effectively than the hierarchy of state-power relations. Realism suggests that the quantity of cooperation among nations is fixed and cannot be increased.[3] Pervasive change, both within and outside the state, suggests that an enlarged and multilayered approach to the study of international relations would provide a greater insight into the behavior of states than the existing variants of realism.

---

[3] Technically, however, if great powers moved from offense-dominant to defense-dominant strategies, both sides could benefit.

2 Transformations in power

Richard Rosecrance

Summary introduction

Contributors to this volume contend that countries act in ways that sometimes violate established patterns of power among them. Countries with less power are sometimes egregiously ambitious and aggressive; countries with more power sometimes do not assert it politically. In the chapters which follow, authors explain that domestic politics, particular tendencies of leadership, or feelings of national dissatisfaction (or satisfaction) may account for the deviation from expected power outcomes. The present chapter offers another reason for this discontinuity: the very notion of what constitutes "power" may have been in flux and transformation. In very general terms it appears that major nations have changed short-term into long-term time horizons – territorial objectives into economic ones, tangible into less tangible ones, extensive development strategies into intensive ones. Normative transformations have occurred as well. These have permitted states to derive the benefits of cooperation within institutional frameworks and regimes – benefits that would not accrue outside such institutions. Participants in such regimes have been able to save on defense and security costs, attaining rates of growth not permitted to heavily armed states incurring large defense burdens.

Analysts and historians agree that some states act – use their power – differently from others. Yet, traditional realists cannot explain why certain countries apparently exercise more power than they possess, taking excessive risks, while others use much less of their power, becoming hesitant or even isolationist. As a result, one cannot predict a country's course of action by knowing the amount of power it possesses. American President Calvin Coolidge continued his predecessor's isolationist policies even though the United States in the mid-1920s possessed about 30 percent of world gross domestic product (GDP). It had a very large stock of gold. America could have sent troops to Europe, maintained a vast network of military bases overseas and provided large amounts of economic aid to other nations. It perhaps should have done so because its economic and political interests were tied to maintaining the balance of power in Europe. But it did not. When Nazi Germany overthrew the Versailles peace settlement in the mid-1930s, Washington decision-makers were slow to react despite their all-powerful mobilization capability. Equally, early Victorian Great Britain was the first and for a while the only industrialized nation in world politics. In the 1830s and 1840s it might have harnessed that strength to a policy of expansion on the European continent, but it did not do so. American and British patterns of domestic politics may be involved in an explanation of the two countries' hesitancy to exert power overseas.

At the opposite extreme, some countries with a slender base of power behave extremely aggressively. Eighteenth-century Prussia undertook to redraw the boundaries of central Europe even though Prussia was the weakest of the great powers. Frederick the Great – Prussia's king – not only seized territory (Silesia) from Austria, he defended it against a coalition which included three greater powers – Russia, France, and Austria. With English financial aid, he escaped unscathed even though the Seven Years War which ensued involved an estimated 500,000 deaths in Prussia. He was very lucky. Operating on a slender base of power, German dictator Adolf Hitler aimed to attack the "liberties" of Europe. In 1939 he mounted a well-nigh impossible program of expansion which involved making war against France, Britain, the Soviet Union, and the United States, under conditions in which Germany's economic strength had become lower relative to opponents than it was in 1914. Of course, Hitler initially planned to eliminate his enemies one by one (as one peels an artichoke), but he later discarded this policy and waged war with the Soviet Union and the United States at the same time. Hitler believed that dynamic military victories would paralyze his enemies' will, giving him the political triumphs he wanted. Finally, Imperial (interwar) Japan chose an expansionist policy in Asia which could not possibly be sustained, given the opponents it would certainly confront. Japan might have taken territory from north China and perhaps occupied colonies owned by Britain, France, and the Netherlands – who were then totally absorbed by Hitler's threat in Europe. But it could not possibly have prevailed against the naval and military might of the United States. In addition, Japan declined to be drawn into a German–Japanese war before the United States cut off raw materials and oil supplies, even though defeating the Russians would have opened the door to expansion further south and also forced the United States to send most of its troops to Europe. Would America have entered a war with Japan if Russia had already been defeated and if there was no attack on Pearl Harbor? We don't know the answer. We do know, however, that the course the Japanese chose was disastrous for themselves and for the world.

These examples appear to conflict with normal realist assumptions, where power balancing should be as characteristic in international relations as corporate price adjustments are in economics. If countries (or firms) expand too far, rivals will supposedly chip away at their position, preempting territories or markets for their own use. As we know, however, countries do not always act in this way. Balancers sometimes hesitate for reasons of domestic politics, international norms, or institutions.[1] Countries would prefer to be free riders rather than balance against apparent aggressors. Ideologies shape state response. States are impressed by apparently successful strategies of others and they often emulate them, irrespective of broader political and economic realities. Persistent ideas or intellectual fashions may govern policy even when they may not be appropriate to a given situation. Dissatisfied countries may exist in what Kahneman and Tversky have called the "domain of loss"[2] and be accordingly more disposed to take risks. For these and other reasons nations do not respond smoothly to power incentives, taking the appropriate measures prescribed by the extant power balance. To put the matter most baldly: (1) some states underuse their power; (2) others overuse it. Analysts have difficulty predicting what states will do under these circumstances. In fact it is partly because of the first possibility that the second is allowed to occur.

Realists respond that if power balancing adjusts too slowly to changes in threat, or if nations do not seize their power opportunities, they will simply suffer the consequences.[3] Countries will be attacked or eliminated if they do not defend themselves. Highly aggressive states – operating on narrow power resources – will not succeed. Thus countries should be constrained to respond more promptly to power incentives and challenges. But, as history shows, they aren't.

There remain continuing differences in the perception of what constitutes power. The definition of power for one state may be different from the definition of power entertained by another. Who is right may not be determined until a military clash occurs between them. A state located in the heart of Europe may worry greatly about the land

---

[1] The collective action problem involved in maintaining a balance of power also led to free-riding and non-balancing.

[2] D. Kanneman and A. Tversky, "Prospect Theory: An Analysis of Decisions under Risk," *ECONOMICA* March (1979), 263–92.

[3] See Kenneth Waltz, *Theory of International Politics* (Reading, MA: McGraw-Hill, 1979).

power of nearby states. An island state or one situated on the coast may be more concerned with the sea power of its neighbors and the dangers of an amphibious invasion. Some countries will be particularly concerned about short-term threats; others may set policy according to longer-term considerations. Some states may seek to advance their position through internal growth and expansion, others through external aggrandizement.

Equally, concepts of power undergo transformation. For many years, states engaged in military expansion because the amount of territory a nation possessed represented the primary objective in economic terms. Land was the most important factor of production. By conquering peasants, grain supplies, and more defensible frontiers, a ruler could achieve power and grandeur without causing dissatisfaction among his people. Throughout most of the eighteenth century, subjects passively endured royal wars of conquest.[4] Paul Schroeder shows, in Chapter 5, that the eighteenth-century state was incomplete. Given the lack of popular sovereignty and nationalism, peoples expected a ruler to symbolize strength and legitimacy. Kings received legitimacy by ruling their church, and also by winning power and glory through foreign conquest. At a certain point, however, the seizure of new territory became more difficult and costly.[5] As nationalism developed among countries and peoples, an invader would meet resistance from occupied populations.[6] Then the benefits of conquest would decline relative to the costs. In addition, as the Industrial Revolution proceeded, countries could gain strength from internal industrialization and trade without attacking other nations. As long as commercial barriers were low, countries might trade freely with other independent national units for the goods they needed. They did not have to incorporate other nations physically or militarily. Great Britain continued to trade actively with the United States even after America had ceased to be a colony. If countries could grow rich from economic development and trade, they did not have to expand militarily. Thus power could be accumulated in a

---

[4] See Immanuel Kant, "Perpetual Peace," in Ted Humphrey (ed.), *Perpetual Peace and Other Essays on Politics, History, and Morals* (Indianapolis: Hackett Press, 1983); Michael Doyle, *Ways of War and Peace: Realism, Liberalism, and Socialism* (New York: W. W. Norton & Company, 1997); Bruce Russett and John Oneal, *Triangulating Peace: Democracy, Interdependence, and International Organizations* (New York: W. W. Norton & Company, 2001).

[5] See Richard Rosecrance, *The Rise of the Trading State* (New York: Basic Books, 1986) and Carl Kaysen, "Is War Obsolete? A Review Essay," *International Security* 14 (1990), 42–64.

[6] Spanish resistance to Napoleonic conquests is an important case in point here.

novel way. Then capital, not land, could become the paramount factor in the power equation.

Peace, of course, allowed unfettered economic development and trade to proceed. If peace broke out,[7] countries could spend less on the military and devote more resources to civilian investment, thereby increasing their growth. Thus countries with great economic potential would not necessarily turn it into military manpower and weapons, at least in the short run. Under peaceful conditions, states could embrace long-term strategies, saving on military costs.

Thus transformations in power and its perception have helped to account for differences in its use. If countries act on different definitions of power, they will sometimes get into conflicts with one another. Long-term maximizers will be thrown off guard when they confront short-term maximizers. Sea powers will not always know how to deal with land powers. Countries that believe in internal (economic) expansion may not get along with those who seek external (military) expansion. When states have different understandings of what power permits or of the elements of which it is composed, they are particularly likely to overuse or underuse their power.[8] The correct conception of power does not emerge until the different definitions are tested against each other.

Let us take one salient example. The Soviet Union believed that the amount of territory a nation possessed was the measure of its power, and Stalin wished to acquire more.[9] After 1945, the Russians spent a great deal of time and money carving out a "Soviet Empire"[10] in Africa and to some degree in the Middle East, as well as occasionally threatening to take more territory in Europe. Democratic Japan, however, was content to exist within the frontiers established at the end of the Second World War. In physical power terms, Tokyo might have become a nuclear weapons state or resumed a policy of expansion. Instead, it chose to operate on a long-term strategy of economic development and trade and as a result its economic strength rose to surpass the Soviet Union's in 1983. The Japanese concept of power has turned out to be more accurate than the erstwhile Russian definition. Japan has become

---

[7] See Stephen Rock, *Why Peace Breaks Out: Great Power Rapprochement in Historical Perspective* (Chapel Hill: University of North Carolina Press, 1989).

[8] See Paul Schroeder, "The Cold War and Its Ending in 'Long-Duration' International History," in John Mueller (ed.), *Peace, Prosperity, and Politics* (Boulder: Westview Press, 1999).

[9] See V. M. Molotov memoirs, cited in David Holloway, *Stalin and the Bomb: The Soviet Union and Atomic Energy 1939–1956* (New Haven: Yale University Press, 1994).

[10] See Charles Wolf, Jr. (ed.), *The Costs of the Soviet Empire* (Cambridge: RAND Corporation, 1984).

the second greatest economic power in the world, and Russia has been downgraded to middle-power status. Now Russian leaders operate on a different notion of power, though they occasionally burnish older views in hoping that rising raw material prices will restore their former grandeur.

Normative and institutional restraints enter into this calculation as well. If decision-makers are constrained by norms or institutions, they may be less likely to use force internationally, relying instead on long-term growth. If, on the other hand, aggressive countries perceive that democracies are preoccupied with domestic problems or are too dependent on international institutions, they may take advantage. Again, different maximization strategies may result in an inappropriate use of power.

Since the actual use of power may not conform to the appropriate theoretical definition, state intentions and capabilities will vary independently.[11] Ideologies may help to determine a course of action equally with a nation's power. Power will not entirely determine intentions – which may be either excessive or modest by comparison. Two reasons help to account for this divergence. The first is that countries simply entertain different notions of power or maximization strategies. If these were eliminated, states would be back on the same plane and would respond appropriately to one another. There would be no under- or overuse of power. (This disjunction is stressed particularly by Paul Schroeder.) Thus, providing greater information and preventing intelligence failures might help solve the problem. This perhaps cannot be done in all concrete circumstances,[12] but it would help to remedy inappropriate action. A second possibility, however, is that changes in world politics, economics, and technology have actually shifted the currency of power in secular fashion. What used to be power, such as territory or real estate, has now metamorphosed into something else – capital, labor, or technology – perceptions aside. If this is true, nations need to modify their conceptions of power to conform to the new realities. If they or some of them do not do so, they will respond inappropriately and there will be under- or overuse of power.

Suppose, for example, that high technology proved to be the single most important element in power. In that case a country with a large and highly educated population could or would become the strongest nation in world politics, and a measure of its strength would be the

[11] See Stephen Walt, *The Origins of Alliances* (Ithaca: Cornell University Press, 1987).
[12] See James Fearon, "Rationalist Explanations for War," *International Organization* 49 (1995), 379–414.

quality of its education system.[13] Rather than seeking directly to increase GDP, countries would, other things being equal, strive to improve their education and to bring new students to their shores. Since students frequently work in the country that educates them, this would add a high-technological labor force to the country with superior education, generating economic and potentially military power. Computers, internet use, and artificial intelligence of all kinds would compensate for any deficiency in population.[14] As one possible example, China in the years ahead will likely become the largest economy in the world in terms of GDP, but the high-technology sector of East Asia, Japan, Europe, and the United States might still tell the tale in terms of a new definition of power. In such an event, Japan and Europe might be thought to be "underusing" their power as compared to China's, but actually the definition of power would be in the process of transformation.

In another possible example, the European Union has pioneered the notion of "peaceful power" as an objective of the increasingly integrated states of Western and Central Europe.[15] As Europe integrates and enlarges, it seeks to create new norms which will guide not only its own practice but which can be exported to the world at large.[16] The norms which countries seeking to join the euro area are constrained to accept are now being applied to East Asia and elsewhere and are used to judge national practice there. If this trend continued, the world would witness the creation of "normative" power, an entirely new currency of authority and power.[17] Those following the norms would benefit; those neglecting them would suffer accordingly. Again, those adhering to the new norms might appear to be "underusing" power according to prior definitions of the term.

Game theorists have demonstrated in a variety of simulations that persistent cooperators over time surpass the apostles of conflict in cost/benefit outcomes.[18] That is because cooperation leads to Pareto optimality and conflict only to Nash solutions.

---

[13] See Richard Rosecrance's speech at SACLANT, Norfolk (1998); National Intelligence Council, "Mapping the Global Future: Report of the National Intelligence Council's 2020 Project" (Washington, DC: US Government Printing Office, 2004), p. 112.

[14] See KurzweilAI.net.

[15] See François Duchêne, "Europe's Role in World Peace," in Richard Mayne (ed.), *Europe Tomorrow: Sixteen Europeans Look Ahead* (London: Fontana Press, 1972); Jan Zielonka (ed.), *Paradoxes of European Foreign Policy* (New York: Springer Publishing, 1998).

[16] See Peter Katzenstein (ed.), *Tamed Power: Germany in Europe* (Ithaca: Cornell University Press, 1997).

[17] See David Lake, "Escape from the State of Nature: Authority and Hierarchy in World Politics," *International Security* 32 (2007), 47–79.

[18] See Bjørn Lomborg, "Nucleus and Shield: The Evolution of Social Structure in the Iterated Prisoner's Dilemma," *American Sociological Review* 61 (1996), 278–307;

None of these arguments, of course, is taken seriously by present-day realist thinkers. They do not admit to any change in the nature of power or in the need to balance. They do not accept the possibility of long-term peace among great powers, but instead see restless probing for advantage. In one theorist's judgment, "the rise of China will not be peaceful."[19] [20] The errors of the past, as expressed in World Wars I and II and the Napoleonic Wars, will continue in the future. Indeed, from the realist standpoint these are not "errors," for each great power will seek to improve its position, through force if need be, as far ahead as the eye can see or the mind contemplate. Wars will continue as new great powers – China, India, and Russia – rise to primacy. The horrendous calamity of violence is ever to be repeated, and Polybian cycles are all that can be expected.

Yet, this is not the perspective of this volume. Despite dominant power theories, the present collaborators see the under- or overuse of power as characteristic in the international system. The amount of power does not determine what a state does. Norms and institutions matter. Regnant ideas and styles of analysis affect action. There is secular as well as cyclical change. Countries are not predestined to make the same mistakes as their predecessors. Learning can take place. While institutions were weak in the past, they are stronger now.[21] While economic development strategies were neglected 200 years ago, they are the rule among great powers today. In the past a hegemonic transition among great powers usually involved hegemonic war.[22] But there is no necessity of this today or in the future.

In what follows, I shall examine the attempts to transform international politics, to move to a new system of international relations. Technically speaking, these always failed. But the reasons for failure are instructive. And some periods of history enshrined at least a temporary success, a success which can be recaptured in the years ahead. In each case of failure, the tumblers unlocking the safe which held "peace"

Jack Hirshleifer and Juan Carlos Martinez Coll, "What Strategies Can Support the Evolutionary Emergence of Cooperation?" *Journal of Conflict Resolution* 32 (1988), 367–98.

[19] John Mearsheimer, *The Tragedy of Great Power Politics* (New York: W. W. Norton & Company, 2001), pp. 401–02.

[20] Others might rejoin, however, that if the rise of China is *not* peaceful, there will be no rise.

[21] G. John Ikenberry, *After Victory: Institutions, Strategic Restraint, and the Rebuilding of Order after Major Wars* (Princeton University Press, 2001).

[22] See, inter alia, Robert Gilpin, *War and Change in World Politics* (Cambridge University Press, 1983); A. F. K. Organski, *World Politics* (New York: Alfred A. Knopf, 1958).

were misaligned. Understanding the near-misses can help policy analysis today.

In terms of analytic categories, I shall focus on: (1) short-term vs. long-term maximization; (2) intensive vs. extensive expansion; (3) constant-sum vs. variable or increasing-sum games as elements in the explanation of conflict, the misconception of power and peace. These in turn will be applied to (a) failures of war; (b) failures of peace; (c) successes of peace.

Failures of war: resulting from excessive or inappropriate notions of power

Frederick the Great of Prussia, Adolf Hitler, and the Japanese elite in the 1930s and early 1940s resolved upon excessive uses of their (limited) power. One succeeded (Frederick), and the other two failed (Hitler and Tojo). Frederick took advantage of the "Pragmatic Sanction," a document accepted by the great powers that was designed to legitimize Maria Theresa's rise to power in Austria. Yet it did not fully do so. And the first female emperor sat uneasily on the Hapsburg throne. When Frederick decided on a program of Prussian expansion to take Silesia from Austria, he recognized that the other powers (France, Russia, and England) might not go to great lengths to defend Maria Theresa's accession. In the 1740s he succeeded in taking territory away from Austria who had little assistance from the other states. In the 1750s, however, Frederick faced the choice between compromising with the Kaunitz coalition (an overpowering grouping which included France as well as Austria and Russia) or continuing to hold Silesia against all-comers. He chose the latter course and was nearly humiliated in the Seven Years War (1756–63) which followed. Despite huge losses, Frederick held on to his throne and to his territorial gains because Emperor Paul and then Catherine the Great – who liked Frederick and his ideas – came to power in Russia. Thus his potential losses of 1761 were redeemed by great-power acknowledgment of his gains at the 1763 Peace of Paris. He emerged a very lucky (though chastened) man.

In this episode we see Frederick's short-term mentality contrasting with the longer-term maximization strategies of other powers. Preoccupied by the American colonies and the overseas war with France, England did not participate in the continental conflict except for providing financial aid to the Prussian monarch. In addition, Maria Theresa's partially "illegitimate" reign initially stayed the hand of possible balancers against Frederick. Frederick's enlightened military

strategies were relevant to his ultimate success, but it was the sudden
change in Russian policy which proved decisive to the outcome.

Nazi Germany also presents a case of "overuse" of power. Hitler
had contempt for his weak and democratic colleagues. He recognized
that they were trying to rebuild from the First World War and did not
want to repeat that carnage. He also understood the effect of "ideology" and "norms" on Chamberlain and Daladier. As long as Hitler
did not violate the norm of self-determination exercised by German
populations located in other countries, Britain and France would find
it difficult to resist Germany's revisions of the Versailles Treaty. He
undoubtedly hoped that when he crossed that normative line (as he
did on March 15, 1939) the democracies would not act. Initially, they
did not do so, despite their guarantees to Poland and Romania. When
Hitler signed the non-aggression pact with Stalin on August 23, 1939,
he believed the democracies could not act, even if they wanted to.
They had no offensive strategy with which to threaten Germany and
in fact depended on Stalin to do their fighting for them. Thus, in theory, they would have to hesitate even as Hitler ramped up the pressure
on Poland and Colonel Beck. In a heroic act, however, Britain and
France declared war on Germany without any idea of how Germany
would be defeated. The two western allies would not aid Poland, and
they were waiting for Germany to attack them. Unless Hitler had
done so, the "phony war" might have been prolonged. The record to
this point demonstrated the power "irrationalities" of Britain and the
return to the "bulldog spirit" as much as any misconception on the
part of Adolf Hitler.[23]

But Hitler went on to more egregious blunders as defined by the
reigning power constellation. Germany had no more economic and
military power than the Soviet Union. It had fewer economic resources
and population than Russia, even though its mobilized military strength
was initially superior. Possibly Hitler might have prevailed against the
Soviet Union if no others were involved. At least, the chance of succeed-
ing was not much less than 50–50. But when Hitler decided to declare
war on the United States as well, he sealed his own fate. Ian Kershaw
depicts Hitler as believing war with the United States was inevitable in
any case, and if so, he wished to use German initiative to bring it on.
Perhaps this response is understandable on the assumption that the
Soviet Union had already been defeated, but it still was not a rational
decision, and in any event could have been delayed until the situation on
the Russian front clarified. And Stalin undermined Hitler's assumption

---

[23] For more analysis see Steiner and Ferguson chapters in this volume.

by launching his first counteroffensive on December 5, 1941. Japan – Germany's eastern ally – did not support Germany against Russia, and yet Hitler declared war on America on December 11, 1941. After Pearl Harbor, the German dictator spent four days deciding whether to support his Japanese ally with a declaration of war on the United States. When he did so, he committed the most fateful blunder in German military history. The economics did not support his decision. Measured in terms of proportions of world industrial production, Germany's power was no match for Russia plus America. Richard Overy rightly says that German conquests might have helped to make up the difference – if they could have been properly organized – but he also shows that Hitler, Göring, and Speer did not organize German production at home on a rational basis.[24] If Germany could not rearm properly at home, how could it be expected to rearm German-occupied Europe and turn it into an arsenal for German dominance? Moreover, Hitler's plans did not expect the opposition of conquered peoples which he encountered in Russia, Eastern Europe, and to some degree even in France. Even more than Frederick's calculations in 1756, Hitler's notions of power had lost touch with reality.

In each of these cases we observe differences of time horizon, on internal versus external expansion, and on assumptions about the "game" of international politics. Hitler and the Japanese adopted short-term horizons because they recognized that their enemies might grow stronger over time. Chamberlain and Stalin thought that economic modernization might eventually bring them greater power and were willing to delay their response. Chamberlain temporized in 1938 and Stalin did so as late as 1941. However much Stalin believed that a conflict with Hitler was inevitable, he would never have sought to bring it on through Soviet action. Chamberlain (finally) did act but only when British public opinion had shifted, and he was faced with a parliamentary revolt. Frederick the Great also availed himself of the short period in which Austrian legitimacy would remain in question.

There were equivalent differences over internal and external expansion. Hitler knew that the Versailles boundaries were deemed illegitimate by many parties to the settlement. They could be overthrown with bourgeois-democratic help, legitimizing external expansion. Japan – equally with the Europeans – wanted its place in the sun. The militarist

---

[24] See Richard Overy, *Why the Allies Won* (New York: W. W. Norton & Company, 1996).

elite in Tokyo did not regard China as an organized nation-state.[25] It was *terra incognita* (or *nullita*) like Africa and could be seized by a resolute imperialist using the same means Great Britain had employed in India and Africa. Japan's disadvantage, however, was that it attacked other countries after the League of Nations had been created to maintain the territorial integrity of parties to the League of Nations Covenant. What Japan did therefore constituted "aggression" while Britain had operated on imperial necessity (*leges imperii*) to invade Egypt, the Sudan, the Cape, and other places. Certainly Japan conceived of her position as requiring territorial acquisition for both economic and political reasons.[26] Stalin and Chamberlain had longer-term perspectives. They each wanted to be left alone to pursue a strategy of economic modernization and growth. Chamberlain was furious that Hitler had disrupted his longer-term plans to revitalize British industry and to make it more competitive. Stalin knew that the Soviet Five Year Plans were making the Soviet Union stronger and stronger, and he may even have been dimly aware that Russia's industrialization was beginning to surpass Germany's. Stalin would not have precipitated war.

The game of international politics was also perceived differently by the great-power participants. In the mid eighteenth century, power was determined by the amount of territory a country possessed, and it was fixed in amount. Any gain for one was a loss for another. Frederick knew he was acting to undermine Austrian power, and he did not hesitate. By the twentieth century, the question had become more complicated. The economics of Adam Smith had shown that the wealth of nations equaled stocks of goods. Unlike the (gold) "bullionist" theory which previously dominated calculations, these stocks could increase without apparent limit. Thus countries in the 1930s were under no illusion that one state's economic growth would necessarily take place at the expense of another's. But again in the 1930s, the reimposition of high protective tariffs in the aftermath of the Great Depression meant that the gains from trade would not be apportioned equally. Great-power competitors installed "beggar thy neighbor" policies as one country (through tariffs or competitive devaluation) sought to export its unemployment to another state. In 1935 few believed that – in practice – all countries would be able to grow together in economic terms. One's gain would

[25] See Sally Marks, *The Ebbing of European Ascendancy: An International History of the World, 1914–1945* (London: Arnold, 2002); Zara Steiner, *The Lights that Failed: European International History, 1919–1933* (Oxford University Press, 2005).
[26] In seizing Manchuria in 1931 Japan had initially sought a market for its industrial products, markets that were increasingly denied to it in the West.

be another's loss. Thus the industrial and trading game which, at least in theory, had allowed for increasing-sum outcomes had been transformed into a constant (or in relative terms) a zero-sum game among great powers. Conflict would increase accordingly. In each of these episodes, countries were stimulated (1) to act quickly; (2) to expand their territorial control; and (3) to advantage themselves on the basis of a game of constant-sum. Under the urgent pressures of the moment, they used deficient power to seek objectives which they could not expect to attain.[27]

Failures of peace: when history failed to turn

The 1780s and 1870s

The failures of war (based on excessive or inappropriate notions of power) raise the question of whether peace is ever possible. The balance of power does not uniformly secure it, and balances are often not formed.[28] Could transformations in power bring about a dynamic or even secular change in this situation? As Paul Schroeder shows, various attempts at peace have ruffled the placid surface of unremitting power competition, but – to this point – they have not endured. One period in which peace loomed, but did not break out, was the 1780s.[29] In that last decade before the French Revolution, change was in the air. The Industrial Revolution – the first stirrings of which Adam Smith failed to detect – was then proceeding in England. It happened at a time in which imperial expansion was reaching a dead end. Clive had previously succeeded in India, but the American colonies had revolted against the British starting in 1775. By 1783 they were independent of British rule. It appeared that other British acquisitions and dominions would go through the same process. After patient cultivation and a good deal of British investment, these colonies would declare independence and little could be done to stop them. The British thus began to question the imperial enterprise itself. And the Industrial Revolution offered an alternative method of gaining power – through intensive (industrial) expansion. The British were also worried about French and continental opposition to their imperial ventures. In France, Choiseul and then Vergennes spent vast amounts on the French fleet and their hopes had been vindicated in administering a colonial rebuff to Britain

---

[27] In this respect Frederick II was an exception; he did succeed in holding on to his conquests.
[28] See the differences between Paul Schroeder and Kenneth Waltz on this point.
[29] See Rock, *Why Peace Breaks Out.*

in the American theater. Having failed there, would the British take up the colonial quest once again? Would not internal expansion substitute for external gain?

A similar question was posed in the 1870s. For most of the nine-teenth century British economic expansion had neglected or gainsaid new imperial acquisitions. Its industry, however, required the stimula-tion of export-led growth. Further industrial expansion depended on trading with countries abroad. This raised no problem as long as tar-iffs were low or coming down, as they were after mid-century. During this period as well, and sparked by the Durham Report (1830), Britain began to ready her colonies for self-government. Disraeli mused in the 1850s that "colonies were a millstone 'round our necks." Other coun-tries also moved to lower tariffs, responding to British requests and incentives to sell in the British market. It was possible that European states might embrace a "trading" strategy as opposed to the old model of military expansion to get their power.

In both of these cases, however, the promise of peace was not ful-filled. The French Revolution in 1789 not only transformed French domestic politics, it also revolutionized military strategy. Now revolu-tionary and Napoleonic armies fighting for the nation would accept greater sacrifices and hardships to protect liberal institutions at home and to extend them abroad. Popular support of government and revo-lutionary nationalism provided a momentum to French armies that the continental aristocrats could not resist. One after another, French and Napoleonic armies toppled regimes in Italy, along the Rhine, in the Low Countries, Spain, and Switzerland. Prussia was nearly eclipsed as a great power when it was defeated by Napoleon in 1806. The French emperor occupied Vienna in 1809, always pressing for greater territor-ial concessions. In other words, military expansion took on a new lease on life and intensive (purely economic) expansion went into the dis-card. War and the acquisition of territory once again seemed to become profitable strategies.

In similar manner, peace and cooperation were undermined by developments in the 1870s and 1880s. Of course, new military tech-niques which Bismarck and Moltke had improvised made territor-ial expansion less expensive and more effective than it had recently been. Wars no longer involved the prospect of social revolution in the defeated countries. Thus, military (extensive) conflict could be hazarded once again. Wars did not go on for years, killing a whole generation of young men, but were settled decisively after the opening battles. At the same time, intensive expansion based on trade went into the doldrums. The tariffs of the late 1870s – enacted after the panic of 1873 – began to close continental markets to British produce. Russia, Germany, France, and the United States raised their duties. The increasing exclusion of British goods from continental markets posed the question of where now they would be sold. As both Eric Hobsbawm and Paul Kennedy point out, the choice was less-developed markets outside Europe – in Africa, Asia, and Latin America.[30] This was fine so long as these tributaries remained low-tariff enclaves. But what would happen if continental states – already with higher tariffs – expanded their empires overseas? Then Britain would be hampered or excluded from trade with much of the rest of the world. It was this perception[31] which brought a reluctant Great Britain back into the race for colonies. For a while Britain might stand back as France and others colonized Africa, but when others' empire meant tariffs, London could hold back no longer. By the 1890s Lord Rosebery, the British Foreign Secretary, was "pegging out claims for the future" in Africa and elsewhere. The imperial motive had returned with a vengeance.

This decisively changed the tone and substance of international politics. Those who respected and emulated Britain – as Kaiser Wilhelm II of Germany (nephew of Queen Victoria) certainly did – wanted to know what made Britain great. Was it her industrialization and economic growth – intensive factors – or was it her empire, based on extensive expansion? When the question was posed in the late 1890s the Kaiser came down in favor of empire and resolved to build a large German navy to acquire and protect a German empire. This, however, meant challenging the British navy and therefore threatening the security of the British Isles themselves. The Germans were not satisfied with intensive, merely industrial expansion, and the scene was thereby increasingly set for the First World War.

In each of these cases – where history failed to turn – short-term incentives supplanted what might have become long-term objectives. Intensive expansion was rejected for extensive expansion. Assumptions of constant-sum games replaced those of variable or (theoretically) increasing-sum. When it was determined that both territory and economics represented a finite sum, conflict could not be delayed for long.

---

[30] See Paul Kennedy, *The Rise and Fall of the Great Powers: Economic Change and Military Conflict* (New York: Random House, 1987); Eric Hobsbawm, *The Age of Empire: 1875–1914* (London: Weidenfield & Nicolson, 1987).

[31] Among many other sources, this result was stressed in William Langer's lectures on European history, Harvard University (1952–53).

The successes of peace: enduring periods of intensive maximization

1815–1848

Yet, the failures of peace did not obscure occasional, though temporary successes. After the Napoleonic Wars, the great powers set up a Concert of Europe in which the powers met to adjudicate differences and settle conflicts. They could do this for two reasons. First, the twenty-year period of war had virtually caused a social revolution in the body politic of Europe. Conservative regimes had been challenged and overthrown. The leagued aristocrats who settled matters at Vienna in 1815 were resolved that war should not occur again. They could then reoccupy their accustomed places of power without constant worry. Second, the industrial spirit was beginning to infect even continental states and the Industrial Revolution was moving east, first to Belgium and France, then to Prussia, the German states, and later Russia. The avoidance of war led economies to flourish. The leagued autocrats in the Concert could adopt a long-term perspective. The Concert mechanism also operated more quickly than the eighteenth-century Balance of Power. It could foresee and sometimes forestall conflicts, as it did over Belgium in 1830–31. The Concert was also animated by a conservative, legitimist ideology which led the autocrats, although not always France and Britain, to work together. By the revolutions of 1830 both Britain and France were resuming liberal colors. This made it increasingly difficult for them to cooperate with the conservatives of central and eastern Europe. But France and Britain were also eager to avoid a new war, certainly a new continental war. And the issues of the time surprisingly brought Russia and Britain together as the major guarantors of the Vienna settlement. Neither Britain nor France (under Louis Philippe) wanted to see a new French career of aggression founded on social revolution. Though Greece achieved its independence against the Ottomans in the late 1820s, Russia did not take advantage against Turkey. When Paris sponsored Egyptian Mehemet Ali's challenge to the Sultan, Britain and Russia were ready to rebuff the French in 1839–41. And in the 1830s both great powers made sure that Belgium's independence did not conduce to French power.

Thus there was an odd inconsistency in international politics which both limited France (as the aggressor of the Napoleonic Wars) and at the same time forged a link between France and the now more liberal Great Britain. After 1830 the "liberal two" more often worked together against the "conservative three," except where Turkey was concerned.[32] The Revolutions of 1848, however, completely overthrew the ideological consensus which had sustained the Concert. Conservatives had agreed to prevent war because it would also foment social revolution. Once two states decided that liberal and democratic institutions should be extended to others, they would no longer renounce military means under all circumstances. Equally, as a result of the 1848 revolutions, the conservatives recognized that their very existence was in danger. They would use every stratagem to reinsure their position even if it meant humming the strain of national unity and military conflict. Finally, new techniques of limited great-power war had been discovered. Countries could quickly defeat one another without social consequences. Austrian and Prussian conservatives could humble Denmark in 1864, a victory which helped them at home. Russia could lose the Crimean War (against Britain and France) in 1854–56 without becoming prey to revolution. Even Austria could be vanquished by Prussia in short weeks in 1866 without having to succumb to liberalism. Instead, the Austrian conservatives accepted nationalism and an equivalent position for Hungary in what then became the Dual Empire. Railways, the needle gun, and mobile artillery provided the punch for offensive, but successful war. Under the influence of Otto von Bismarck, the conservatives decided to use war and "Realpolitik" to bolster their position. The Concert of Europe should have prevented the Crimean and other wars but it failed once ideological solidarity had broken down. In one sense, the processes of social change in history – moving toward liberalism and democracy – were aligned against it.

By the 1860s the conservative regimes in Prussia, Austria, and Russia had jettisoned their long-term goals in favor of short-run ones. No longer could they rely purely on industrial expansion to improve the power of their states. Equally, as objectives switched from economic gain to territorial success, constant-sum struggles over real estate supplanted the more variable outcomes of economics.

1870–1890

This did not mean, however, that peace had been definitively undermined for all time to come. Once Russian, Austrian, and German conservatives had gained a new lease on life by either sponsoring or conceding to nationalism (1854–71), there could be a truncated peace.

---

[32] See, inter alia, Hajo Holborn, *The Political Collapse of Europe* (New York: Alfred A. Knopf, 1950).

This was made possible by Bismarck's coalitions which (though they were not universal) at least linked four major powers together: Russia, Britain, Germany, and Austria. Only France, the defeated power in the Franco-Prussian War of 1870–71, was left out. France could not be included because Bismarck had made the blunder of seizing Alsace-Lorraine after nationalism had rendered German rule there difficult if not impossible. France then became the unsatisfied power in Europe, and no colonial rewards from Berlin would ever fully reconcile it to the post-1871 order. The Bismarckian Concert,[33] however, was different from the prior Concert of Europe. Ideology had linked the previous authors of the Vienna settlement. The Bismarckian concert sought only peace, but it could not use ideology to promote it. France and Britain were becoming more liberal, but Austria and Russia were not. The unified Germany opted for universal suffrage in the Reichstag but still left the emperor and his ministers in control of the legislature. Thus, the barriers to war were practical, not ideological or military.

Bismarck did two crucial things to keep this refractory combination together. First, he brought in Russia even though there were crucial tensions between Austria (his main ally) and St. Petersburg. Second, he recruited Britain and did not make the mistake of pursuing a resolutely imperial policy. Germany got some colonial real estate almost by accident in 1884, but as long as Bismarck was Chancellor, he never sought to challenge Britain overseas. He absolutely refused to build a navy. He played both wings of his coalition against the other. He did not have to check Russia's aspirations in the east because Britain would do so. He would merely ratify the settlement reached through the efforts of others. Still, though his coalition was an inconsistent one, it was very effective, and it was more effective because it was inconsistent. Bismarck was never forced to line up on one side or the other. Thus the large multi-polar coalition which he formed did not split into Triple Alliance and Triple Entente. Had he continued in power, Bismarck would never have made Kaiser Wilhelm II's blunders after 1890.

During this period, long-term gain was always a possibility so long as it was sought intensively. Germany industrialized to compete with Britain, and its trade was critical to growth, but this did not make war inevitable. Britain also expanded intensively, but in the 1880–90s came back into the imperial quest. This stacked the odds against continuing German abstention from empire. When both countries shifted in favor of more real estate, short-term outcomes began to dominate long-term

---

[33] See Richard Rosecrance, *Action and Reaction in World Politics: International Systems in Perspective* (Boston: Little, Brown, 1963), chp. 5.

ones. And since territorial objectives had become crucial, the constant-sum game was reinstated with an imperial flourish.

The future

As we have seen, the tumblers twirling within the lock regulating peace have never been aligned over any long period, nor has the vault of inter-national comity been fully opened. This could change in the years immediately ahead, but there will still be differences of time horizon which could cause military conflict. The great advantage of the post-Cold War and post-9/11 system was that great powers as a group have generally resolved on intensive means of advancement.[34] Economic growth is to be the method of the future, accepted by Beijing and New Delhi as well as Europe, Japan, and the United States. Moscow is still concerned with its previous losses of territory, but entertains no realis-tic hope of territorial revision in its favor as previous Soviet component-states opt to join the European Union and NATO. The Baltics and Ukraine will become part of a larger Western Europe, and there is little that Russia can do about it. If this is true, a kind of Concert of Europe could be reconstituted among the great powers, with Russia as a lesser member.[35] The key change that has made this evolution possible is a shift in Beijing in favor of a "Japanese strategy" of advancement as com-pared to prior Soviet and Russian strategies. In one sense there are now two possibilities in world politics. One group of nations (at this point containing no great powers) favors the constant-sum game, extensive as opposed to intensive strategies and short-term outcomes. The second (containing all great powers with Russia as a lesser convert) endorses long-term strategies, intensive expansion, and variable-sum outcomes. Only certain terrorist hosts and nuclear-weapon "wannabees" fall into the first category. This bodes well for a long period in which peace among great powers will finally be unlocked. In addition, and in con-trast to the functioning of the Concert of Europe, the spread of lib-eralism will conduce not hinder the operation of a new Great Power Concert.

Such a Concert may not last forever. Intensive development does not solve one major problem in international relations – the spread of

---

[34] At least in respect of each other. The United States' attack on Afghanistan and Iraq (2001–03) shows that smaller and weaker states are not yet held to be inviolate. The United States paid a considerable cost for its "victory" in Iraq and still has not returned peace to Afghanistan.

[35] See Richard Rosecrance (ed.), *The New Great Power Coalition: Toward a World Concert of Nations* (Lanham, MD: Rowman and Littlefield Publishers, 2001).

nuclear weapons and other weapons of mass destruction to new and dissatisfied powers. As in the First World War, the malign ambitions of small but rising powers could disrupt relations among the great powers. Serbian ambitions offered the challenge in 1914, and the great powers reacted on opposite sides to Austria's threat of punishment. But by 1914 Germany had also begun to become a short-term maximizer. Serbia would never have been able to upset the solidarity of great-power relations had not Berlin been willing to accept a challenge. Today, Iran, North Korea, and possibly other states wish to acquire and hold their nuclear weapons. Most of the great powers seek to prevent this eventuality and the question is whether they will be divided over the means used. This issue has not been resolved and its outcome will depend upon re-establishing great power accord on such matters.

Conclusion

There are many reasons why states do not follow the mandates of power: domestic pressures, ideological preoccupations, normative or institutional restraints. Countries may find themselves in the "domain of gain" and take few risks, or they may reside in the "domain of loss" and become risk-acceptant. These and other reasons are examined in the chapters that follow. Here, however, I have tried to sketch possible and actual transformations in power that have brought changes in the practice of international politics. Perceptual differences have occasioned discontinuities in the understanding of diplomacy.[36] More important still, there have been concrete changes in maximization strategies. These changes have augured in favor of longer-term intensive strategies as compared to short-term extensive approaches. Since the 1970s, China and Japan are the first great powers to have relied almost wholly on intensive expansion. They are the first (along with the leagued states of Europe) to have elaborated (exclusively) trading strategies of advancement. This makes possible a great power coalition of nations which, like the Concert of Europe, can act to maintain the peace through diplomacy as much as force. This does not mean there are no threats to such a coalition or to its concerted action. Short-term maximizers striving to acquire nuclear weapons exist on the fringes of great power politics. They may yet win the support of one or more of the great powers as occurred on the eve of the First World War. Thus far, however, such a threat seems quite unlikely, if not entirely impossible.

---

[36] See Robert Jervis, *Perception and Misperception in International Politics* (Princeton University Press, 1976).

I have sought to show that states have perforce had to decide on whether to concentrate on building up military or economic power. The first is more threatening to other states than the second and causes more conflict. Before the Industrial Revolution, the first was the only option for states seeking to maintain or improve their security. Now, however, states have a choice, and the selection of economic power has diminished the amount of interstate violence. Military power may still be more useful in the short term, but economic development is the key to long-term influence. Leaders or states with a short-term horizon will concentrate on amassing military strength and territorial expansion; leaders with a longer-term view will focus on economic power.

Some might suggest that both long-term and short-term approaches are consistent with a single-minded pursuit of power. In this sense, leaders disagreeing on time preferences may still remain on their appropriate power lines. Yet, sometimes the choice they made sacrificed (at least short-term) power. When the United States opted for economic development in 1921, it overlooked looming threats to its short-term security in both Asia and Europe. When Frederick the Great expanded against Austria, he risked his long-term position. Alternatively, states neglected long-term advantages and sought to maximize illusory short-term strength. Germany in 1914 gave up long-term advantages in economic growth to try to change European boundaries in the short run. It failed and should rather have waited for its economic strength to mature. Sometimes, the "currency of power" changes, and in respect of the change, countries fail to maximize benefits or even to satisfice.[37] They are *ipso facto* thrown off their (reconstituted) power lines. This may happen when there is no change in physical strength, but a difference in technology and perception occurs on what constitutes power. In the longer term, the respective success of education systems may turn out to be the critical factor in national strength, but that has not yet fully been appreciated in theory and certainly not realized in practice.

---

[37] Herbert Simon's term means to aim for satisfactory outcomes, though they may be less than those maximally available.

3 Domestically driven deviations: internal regimes, leaders, and realism's power line

John M. Owen, IV

Can we predict accurately a state's behavior from its international power ranking? May we safely predict, with Thucydides' Athenians, that "the strong do what they can and the weak suffer what they must?" Not all structural realists answer in the affirmative. Waltz's[1] denial is the most prominent: his neorealism, he asserts, is a theory of international outcomes, not of foreign policy. It cannot predict when A will seek to ally with state B, but only when an A+B alliance will form. A systemic theory predicts systemic outcomes. Unit-level outcomes, such as alliance seeking, require unit-level explanations such as domestic politics or the traits of individual leaders.

Most structural realists find Waltz, in this one aspect, insufficiently ambitious. Elman,[2] Copeland,[3] Mearsheimer,[4] and others insist that international structure is strong enough to constrain, and hence explain, states' foreign policies as well. These scholars appear on firm ground: if a balance of power entails states' acting, intentionally or not, so as to form that balance, then it follows that a theory predicting that balance must predict that states will act so as to bring it about. Indeed, Waltz himself makes claims about individual states' policies as vindication for his theory; thus pressure from the international system caused the young Soviet Union to change from a revolutionary, disruptive power to a pragmatic one that aligned with Weimar Germany in 1922.[5]

All structural realists, then, agree that international structure socializes states into certain goals and behaviors, including acting as their place in the power hierarchy would dictate. Each state will hew to what the editors of this volume call its *power line*. The disagreement among realists seems to be over just how socialized states are, moment by

---

[1] See Waltz, *Theory of International Politics*.
[2] Colin Elman, "Horses for Courses: Why Not Realist Theories of Foreign Policy?" *Security Studies* 6 (1996), 7–53.
[3] Dale Copeland, *The Origins of Major War* (Ithaca: Cornell University Press, 2000).
[4] Mearsheimer, *The Tragedy of Great Power Politics*.
[5] Waltz, *Theory of International Politics*, pp. 127–28.

29

moment. For Waltz, unit-level variables may cause states to defy structure but structure will eventually chasten them. An arrogant France
will encounter foreign resistance and thereafter act more humbly; a
meek Germany will be exploited and thereafter assert itself more. For
Mearsheimer, structure's chastening is so severe in prospect that states
will be deterred from defying it. Anticipating the price they will pay
from deviance, France and Germany will both consistently hew to
their respective power lines. More precisely, Mearsheimer's offensive
realism predicts that *great powers*[6] will always act so as to maximize
material power. This is not a prediction of perpetual universal arms
races, for great powers will be prudent in seeking power. Thus both
Cold War superpowers continued to build their nuclear arsenals even
after the achievement of mutually assured destruction made an arms
race seem irrational to many. To his great credit, Mearsheimer also
acknowledges anomalies for offensive realism, such as Germany's decision not to crush France after the latter's ally Russia lost a war to Japan
in 1904–05.

So construed, realism is an exceedingly useful baseline theory. Its
simplicity gives it much potential theoretical power. But do real great
powers always hew to their power lines? Do they at least do so often
enough that complicating the theory is not worth the trouble? That
states sometimes "over-expand," or try to extend or maintain control
over foreign actors beyond their capabilities, is acknowledged even by
realists and is the subject of a large literature.[7] That states sometimes
overreact to foreign threats is if anything still more acknowledged;
indeed, for political scientists and historians, the default explanation
for a given war seems to be that one or both sides tragically exaggerated the menace posed by the other. Scholars less often acknowledge
that states sometimes "under-balance," or insufficiently oppose the
ambitions of other states, but Schweller[8] has explored this phenomenon as well.

Under what conditions, then, will great powers stray either above or
below their power lines? Several of the chapters in this volume – those

---

[6] Mearsheimer confines his claims to great powers, defined as states that "have sufficient military assets to put up a serious fight in an all-out conventional war against the
most powerful state in the world" (*The Tragedy of Great Power Politics*, 2003 edition,
p. 5).

[7] See Gilpin, *War and Change in World Politics*; Kennedy, *The Rise and Fall of the Great
Powers*; Jack L. Snyder, *Myths of Empire: Domestics Politics and International Ambition*
(Ithaca: Cornell University Press, 1991); Charles Kupchan, *The Vulnerability of Empire*
(Ithaca: Cornell University Press, 1994).

[8] Randall Schweller, *Unanswered Threats: Political Constraints on the Balance of Power*
(Princeton University Press, 2006).

on nineteenth-century Britain, on Japan and the United States in
the 1930s and 1940s, and on the end of the Cold War – argue that
domestic-political variables caused behavior anomalous for structural
realism. Others – those on Germany in the 1930s and the end of the
Cold War – stress individual leaders and their goals. In this chapter I
survey recent international relations (IR) literature for domestic mechanisms that might cause a state to be more ambitious or diffident than
structural realism would predict. These mechanisms relate to states'
preferences and their abilities to read and transmit information to other
states. A change of government (leadership) or of regime, or of the
degree of domestic coherence, may change a state's policies. Hitler's
policy was more aggressive than that of Gustav Stresemann or Kurt von
Schleicher; the Nazi dictatorship was more aggressive than the Weimar
Republic.

The abstract question

Suppose that at time t state A balances against state B; at $t+1$ state A
undergoes some sort of domestic change; and at $t+2$ state A reverses
course and bandwagons with B. Suppose that, throughout this period
t to $t+2$, the international distribution of military power remains constant, and thus so does A's power line. By definition, either at t A
is acting above its realist power line, or at $t+2$ A is acting below its
power line, or both. If the increments of time are small between $t+1$,
when the change of regime or government happened, and $t+2$, when
A changed policies, we have good reason to infer that the domestic
change in A accounts for A's change in behavior. In the following
sections I consider three types of domestic change that could cor-
respond to the change in A's actions: a change in domestic regime
or constitution; a change in who governs within a given regime; and
a change in the degree of national unity or coherence concerning
foreign policy. Each of these variables could implicate foreign policy
via a number of causal pathways. Among these, depending upon the
variable, are policy preferences, cognitive abilities, transparency, and
audience costs. In each section I discuss which of these pathways
could apply and how.

Domestic regime

One type of domestic change is an alteration of regime or basic political institutions. A democracy may become a fascist state; a communist
state, capitalist; a monarchy, a republic; a secular dictatorship, Islamist;

a federal state, centralized. In all of these, the change is in the constitution or fundamental structure of government, rather than simply
who rules. Siverson and Starr[9] have shown that states whose domestic
regimes change tend to change their alliance portfolios. Hagan[10] has
shown that domestic regime changes tend to be followed by changes in
voting patterns at the UN General Assembly. The vast literature on the
democratic or liberal peace implies that a non-democracy that becomes
a liberal democracy should become more accommodating of other liberal democracies, although its conflicts of interest with them would not
disappear. For some versions of the thesis, a liberal democracy is also
more accommodating of non-democracies; for other versions, less so.

Anecdotally, cases are not hard to find in which changes in domestic institutions have been followed hard by changes in foreign policy.
Identify a revolution, and the chances are good that you will find a
state that soon changed its external strategies and tactics. *Ancien régime*
France between 1714 and 1789 was a normal great power, fighting limited wars regularly, frequently in danger of bankruptcy because of those
wars, but avoiding general wars of the type that had chastened Louis
XIV (1701–14). But the First French Republic, inaugurated in 1792,
went on a rampage, and Europe was thrashed by more than two decades of general war. Either before or after 1792, France deviated from
its power line: either the France of Louis XV and XVI was too timid,
or Republican France was too ambitious, or both. Soviet Russia from
November 1917 reversed the war policy of Tsarist Russia, submitting to
a humiliating peace with Germany and betraying Russia's allies. Either
before or after November, Russia deviated from its power line. From
the 1953 overthrow of the Mossadeq government, monarchical Iran
was a close ally of the United States and had good relations with Israel.
The Islamic Republic of Iran, from its birth in early 1979, has been
overtly hostile to the United States, has worked to reduce US influence
in the Middle East, and has recently openly called for the destruction
of Israel.[11] In 1959, with the coming to power of Fidel Castro, Cuba
became less accommodating of (or subservient to) the United States

---

[9] Randolph M. Siverson and Harvey Starr, "Regime Change and the Restructuring of
Alliances," *American Journal of Political Science* 38 (1994), 145–61.

[10] Joe D. Hagan, "Domestic Political Regime Changes and Third World Voting
Realignments in the United Nations," *International Organization* 43 (1989), 505–41.

[11] See Stephen Walt, *Revolution and War* (Ithaca, NY: Cornell University Press, 1996)
for analyses of each of these cases. Walt argues that the cases still vindicate realism,
because the revolutions altered the balance of threat in the international system. As
several scholars have noted, however, Walt's notion of threat includes intentions as
well as material factors; unlike Mearsheimer and other structural realists, he also
allows that a state's domestic institutions may affect its military power.

and more accommodating of (or subservient to) the Soviet Union. The same is true of Nicaragua following the Sandinista Revolution of 1979. In the latter half of 1989 each of the Soviet satellites of Eastern Europe overthrew communist rule and ratified new democratic constitutions. Under these new regimes they became friendlier to the West and the Soviet-run Warsaw Pact dissolved in early 1991. Since then all of these have joined NATO, the US-led alliance that originally triggered the formation of the Warsaw Pact.

Some revolutions do not produce a sharp foreign policy change, at least in their early phases. France between 1789 and 1792 was at peace with its neighbors. Revolutionary Russia under Kerensky's democratic provisional government (March–November 1917) maintained the Tsarist alliance with the Western democracies against Germany. Still, it is clear that under some conditions a change in domestic constitution is followed closely by a change in external alignment. Small wonder, then, that in some times and places states have regularly spent dear resources trying to change or preserve the domestic regimes of foreign states. The liberal revolutions that periodically broke out in central and southern Europe in the decades following the 1815 defeat of Napoleon were typically followed by a sharp break with the absolute monarchies of Austria, Prussia, and Russia; hence those powers used force to overturn those revolutions and restore the balance of power. The 1848 revolutions in Italy produced republics that were hostile to Austria, traditionally hegemonic over the peninsula. Austrian troops invaded to overturn these revolutions, and the governments of Russia and Prussia approved, knowing that the balance of power in Europe was at stake. In 1944 and 1945 the United States and the Soviet Union imposed their regimes on the European states they occupied as a way to keep those states from joining the other's incipient bloc.[12] Soviet tanks reversed democratic reforms in Hungary in 1956 and Czechoslovakia in 1968, reforms tied up with those countries' moves away from the Warsaw Pact.

Who governs?

A full domestic regime change may not be necessary to effect a change in foreign policy. The change may be in the composition of government, in particular in its executive or legislative leadership. Within states that allow open dissent, elites usually disagree over at least some aspects of foreign policy. Some are hawks, some doves; some are economic

[12] John M. Owen, IV, "The Foreign Imposition of Domestic Institutions," *International Organization* 56 (2002), 375–409.

liberals, others favor autarky; some favor aligning with foreign state or coalition A, others with state or coalition B. Within liberal democracies, elections sometimes turn on sharp disagreements over external affairs, suggesting that voters expect foreign policy change under a new government. Authoritarian systems are more opaque and so foreigners can presume that they are virtually unitary actors. But typically elites in such systems can differ sharply over foreign policy. In the late 1940s Huang Hua and Zhou Enlai were more interested than Mao Zedong in seeking accord with the United States.[13]

The traditional realist rejoinder to this general observation is that once a dissenter takes office and gains both more information about the world and the responsibility to protect the national interest, he will alter his preferences and become essentially like the predecessors he criticized. Everyone is a critic until he becomes accountable; leaders are socialized into *raison d'état*. Kenneth Waltz reminds us that Henry Kissinger the scholar distinguished revolutionary from status quo states, but Kissinger the statesman "learned" that the United States must accommodate the communist Soviet Union.[14] In 1992 candidate Bill Clinton lambasted President G. H. W. Bush for "kowtowing" to China on human rights. Successors embark on policy pathways that deviate sharply from those of their predecessors, suggesting that someone – either they or their predecessors – was not following the nation's power line. Under Ronald Reagan in 1981, US policy quickly become more confrontational toward the Soviet Union and accommodating toward authoritarian anti-communist states than it had been under Jimmy Carter even in the latter's hawkish final year in office. Reagan increased military spending and support for anti-communist guerrillas in Afghanistan, Nicaragua, Angola, and elsewhere; initiated a missile defense program; used more militant rhetoric; and made it clear that he continued to regard Soviet–American arms control as detrimental to US interests. New leaders may also be more accommodating and "under-balance" rivals. Reagan began to reverse himself in 1985, when Mikhail Gorbachev replaced Konstantin Chernenko as General Secretary of the Soviet Communist Party. Gorbachev, who had long advocated deep reforms in Soviet domestic policies, quickly assumed a more conciliatory stance toward the United States. His rhetoric was more cooperative and he offered to accept an arms-control offer, the "Zero Option" in Europe that Reagan's more dovish critics had labeled

---

[13] Chen Jian, "The Myth of America's 'Lost Chance' in China," *Diplomatic History* 21 (1997), 77–86.

[14] Waltz, *Theory of International Politics*, pp. 62–64.

farcical. From 1980 through 1986, when Reagan and Gorbachev radically altered Soviet–American relations, the balance of nuclear power between the superpowers remained constant.

Here again, if variations in leadership were inconsequential to foreign policy, then governments would not need to pay much attention to who led other countries, at least as far as security was concerned. Foreign interventions to overthrow or preserve a leader would make less sense and be less common.[15] In fact, European history is scarred with international wars over monarchical succession. The Spanish of 1701–14 and Austrian of 1740–48 are most infamous, but the Franco-Prussian War of 1870–71 was triggered by a diplomatic row of the Spanish succession; and princes were perpetually conniving short of war to influence succession in foreign lands.[16] In modern history it is not difficult to think of American interventions to alter or preserve a target's leadership for the sake of that target's foreign policy. Less evident but as consequential are Washington's efforts to keep in power leaders judged more likely than the viable alternatives to uphold US interests. Since 1975 American aid to Egypt has exceeded $50 billion,[17] money that eases the domestic burdens of the friendly Mubarak regime. It is difficult to see how the House of Saud could remain in power absent its oil, intelligence, and military relations with the United States. In these countries and others, American administrations fear that the most viable alternatives are radical Islamists who would immediately find ways to hurt or at least blackmail the United States by means of terrorism, war, pursuit of WMDs, cutting oil production, or threatening Israel.

That point raises the relation of changes in government to changes in regime. Nearly always, a regime change entails a change in leadership. In 1791 France changed from an absolute to a constitutional monarchy and Louis XVI remained king, but power devolved from the royal court to the Assembly, and so in effect the leadership changed. Conversely, a change in leadership may be followed by a change in regime if the new leadership's vision for the country is so opposed to the status quo and creating new institutions would empower interests that share its vision. Thus have democratically elected leaders sometimes overthrown democracy, as Adolf Hitler did in Germany in 1933–34 and Vladimir Putin

---

[15] See Steven R. David, "Why the Third World Still Matters," *International Security* 17 (1989), 127–59.

[16] See Charles Lipson, *Reliable Partners: How Democracies Have Made a Separate Peace* (Princeton University Press, 2003), pp. 112–38.

[17] Charles Levinson, "$50 Billion Later, Taking Stock of US Aid to Egypt," *Christian Science Monitor* 96 (2004), 7.

and Hugo Chavez have been doing lately in Russia and Venezuela, respectively.

Regime and governmental changes, then, can lead to changes in foreign security policy, some of which appear to be changes in a state's fidelity to its power line. But how does this work? What processes connect cause to effect? The IR literature suggests several possibilities.

States' preferences

The most obvious pathway by which a regime or governmental change might lead to a policy change is via a change in the state's preferences. The question of what preferences are and how they are measured has occupied social science for decades. For economists, a consumer's preferences are captured in his utility function or preferred basket of goods. There has been much discussion in the IR literature of whether the things preferred are outcomes (the highest expected payoff from an interaction) or actions (to cooperate with state A in order to gain that payoff).[18] Moravcsik[19] has proposed that the core of liberal (i.e., non-realist) IR theory is the proposition that preferences over outcomes are generated within states rather than "externally," by their ranking in the international system. The trouble here is in distinguishing strategies from outcomes or means from ends: a state may want a given bargain to raise national income, but as a means to some other end such as conquest or security; or, conquest may be intended to raise national income. What at first appear ends may, upon scrutiny, look like means.

Perhaps the attempt to locate states' ultimate ends is doomed to endless regress or feedback loops. We can evade this quandary by simply noting that realism claims that a state's ends and means alike will be dictated by its relative power ranking. State A will prefer to balance against or bandwagon with B – whether as means or end – according to the distribution of military power among states in the international system. Liberal IR theory claims, by contrast, that A will prefer to balance or bandwagon depending in part upon A's domestic institutions or leadership.

But how do domestic regimes and leaders affect states' foreign policy preferences? Neo-Marxists generally claim that capitalist states promote capitalism abroad in order to enrich their own bourgeoisie (who control or disproportionately influence foreign policy). Capital abhors political borders in its quest for the highest rate of return on investment; thus

[18] Robert Powell, "Review: Anarchy in International Relations Theory: The Neorealist–Neoliberal Debate," *International Organization* 48 (1994), 313–44.

[19] Andrew Moravcsik, "Taking Preferences Seriously: A Liberal Theory of International Politics," *International Organization* 51 (1997), 513–53.

capitalists will push for a worldwide extension of capitalism and will seek to overthrow socialist regimes.[20] Covert US interventions in Iran in 1953, Guatemala in 1954, and Chile in 1973 are often cited as moments when the dependence of wealthy societies or capital on pliant client states was most clearly revealed. On this view, capitalist states are prone to act above their power lines via imperialism and eventual war.[21] Indeed, realists – at least those in the academy – tend to deplore these interventions.[22]

Snyder[23] argues that states with cartelized domestic politics will tend toward over-expansion. Over-expansion, or a state's acting above its power line, typically hurts many more actors within the state than it benefits – the beneficiaries are parochial interests such as armaments manufacturers and militaries – but each winner wins more than each loser loses. Hence winners are more motivated to push for over-expansion than losers are for a power-line policy. Enacting a rational policy is thus a domestic collective-action problem, analogous to achieving economic openness.[24] Parochial interests logroll among themselves and hijack foreign policy; they fool the nation as a whole with "myths of empire," stories about how over-expansion will redound to the general good. Such cartelized politics and the over-expansion that follows is more typical of democratizing states than of stable authoritarian or democratic states.[25] Similar arguments are offered by Lake[26] and Moore,[27] to the effect that authoritarian states are less constrained from rent-seeking, and hence imperialism and war, than democratic ones.

Others argue that states can be selective or discriminating regarding which states to over- and which to under-balance. One version is ideological: states with similar ideologies, and hence similar ideological opponents, have common interests.[28] The common interests derive

[20] See Andre Gunder Frank, *Capitalism and Underdevelopment in Latin America: Historical Studies of Chile and Brazil* (New York: Monthly Review Press, 1967); Fernando Henrique Cardoso and Faletto Enzo, *Dependency and Development in Latin America* (Berkeley: University of California Press, 1977).

[21] See Vladimir Ilyich Lenin, *Selected Works* (Moscow: Progress Publishers, 1963).

[22] Hans J. Morgenthau, "To Intervene or Not to Intervene," *Foreign Affairs* 45 (1967), 425–36.

[23] Snyder, *Myths of Empire*.

[24] See Mancur Olson, *The Rise and Decline of Nations: Economic Growth, Stagflation, and Social Rigidities* (New Haven: Yale University Press, 1982).

[25] See Edward Mansfield and Jack Snyder, *Electing to Fight: Why Emerging Democracies Go to War* (Cambridge, MA: MIT Press, 2005).

[26] David Lake, "Powerful Pacifists: Democratic States and War," *American Political Science Review* 86 (1992), 24–37.

[27] John Norton Moore, *Solving the War Puzzle: Beyond the Democratic Peace* (Chapel Hill: Carolina Academic Press, 2004).

[28] John M. Owen, "Transnational Liberalism and U.S. Primacy," *International Security* 26 (2001/02), 117–52. Also see Erik Gartzke, "Kant We All Just Get Along?" *American Journal of Political Science* 42 (1998), 1–27.

from the interdependence or demonstration effects of ideologies: if fascism or Islamism succeeds in one state, its adherents in other states are encouraged. Across countries, elites who share both a vision for the right ordering of society and a transnational ideological adversary prefer their states to have close relations; they also prefer distance from or confrontation with states of the competing ideology.[29] These preferences are especially strong when transnational ideological competition is high, that is, when several states are ideologically divided and teetering on the edge of a regime change. Thus, as mentioned above, between 1815 and 1849 the foreign alignments of smaller states in central and southern Europe depended heavily upon their domestic regimes: absolute monarchies aligned with Austria, Prussia, and Russia; liberal regimes with Great Britain. During the 1930s fascist states, notwithstanding competing ambitions and mistrust, became progressively closer and promoted their institutions abroad. In Europe just after the Second World War, liberal-democratic governments aligned with the United States, while communist parties (except for the Yugoslav) were subservient to the Soviet Union. In times of high ideological polarization, then, states will act below their power line vis-à-vis ideological confreres and above that line vis-à-vis ideological adversaries.[30]

Another version of the "discriminatory" hypothesis is specific to democracies. A large literature has developed in recent years claiming that democracies are more prone to keep their international commitments and are hence more attractive parties to international agreements. The tendency of liberal democracies to remain at peace with one another and in general to be more "reliable partners"[31] is not ideological, but rather driven by their various institutional constraints. The power of democratic legislatures can constrain executives to stick by international agreements.[32] Democracies' distinctive preferences, and the stability of those preferences, make their foreign commitments more robust; in particular, democratic alliances are more durable than non-democratic ones.[33] Russett and Oneal bring together various claims about liberal democracies into a "Kantian triangle," in which such states are more

[29] Mark L. Haas, *The Ideological Origins of Great Power Politics 1789–1989* (Ithaca: Cornell University Press, 2005).

[30] John M. Owen IV, *The Clash of Ideas in World Politics: Transnational Networks, States, and Regime Change 1510–2010* (Princeton University Press, 2010).

[31] Lipson, *Reliable Partners.*

[32] See Peter Cowhey, "Domestic Institutions and the Credibility of International Commitments: Japan and the United States," *International Organization* 47 (1993), 299–326; Lisa L. Martin, *Democratic Commitments* (Princeton University Press, 2000).

[33] See Kurt Taylor Gaubatz, "Democratic States and Commitment in International Relations," *International Organization* 50 (1996), 109–39.

likely to remain at peace with one another, become economically inter-dependent, and join and remain in international institutions. The three legs of the triangle are mutually reinforcing; democracies are in a vir-tuous cycle, and "under-balance" one another because they know they are better off doing so.[34]

Cognition and judgment

Holding preferences constant, some analysts argue that states' (or lead-ers') abilities to gather and process information and to judge the proper course of action vary. Realism assumes not perfect information but a rational investment in the gathering and processing of information.[35] Psychologists insist, however, that in various ways actual behavior departs from rationalism. Individual leaders may vary in their abilities to interpret information and how they judge what actions are indicated.[36] A new government might be too inexperienced to understand or exploit the state's information apparatus, or a new regime may have damaged or destroyed that apparatus in a revolution. It might be more concerned with internal than external security and invest more in the former. Its top leadership may have various biases and, owing to institutional fac-tors (e.g., arbitrary rather than constitutional rule), not hear opposing views. Stein[37] argues that misperceptions could alter outcomes when leaders' actions are contingent upon what they believe others' actions will be. Walt[38] argues that such misperceptions are especially likely fol-lowing revolutions. For instance, in 1792–93 the First French Republic declared war on Austria, Prussia, and Great Britain. France's leaders exaggerated foreign threats and acted more belligerently than was war-ranted; in the language of this volume, France in 1792–93 acted above its power line.

Leaders may vary according to how much risk they can tolerate. In the months before the 2003 Iraq War, some argued that Saddam Hussein was risk-seeking and hence unusually dangerous.[39] Prospect theory, which some regard as the chief challenge to rational-choice the-ory, holds as crucial whether leaders are operating in a domain of gains

---

[34] See Russett and Oneal, *Triangulating Peace*.
[35] See James D. Fearon, "Rationalist Explanations for War," *International Organization* 49 (1995), 379–414.
[36] See Robert Jervis, *Perception and Misperception in International Politics* (Princeton University Press, 1976).
[37] Arthur A. Stein, "When Misperception Matters," *World Politics* 34 (1984), 505–26.
[38] Walt, *Revolution and War*.
[39] Kenneth M. Pollack, *The Threatening Storm: The Case for Invading Iraq* (New York: Random House, 2002); on risk acceptance and war see Bruce Bueno de Mesquita, *The War Trap* (New Haven: Yale University Press, 1981).

or losses: if they are striving to retain something, they tend to accept more risk than if they are trying to gain something.[40] Thus a great deal rides on whether actors frame a situation as involving gain or loss. Prospect theorists lack a theory of framing, but one hypothesis is that different elites may frame the same event differently; one elite may see a situation as risking a loss, while another may see it as risking a gain.[41] Ronald Reagan may have been more willing than Jimmy Carter to take risks in confronting the Soviet Union because he operated in a domain of losses, being convinced the Soviets were bent on world domination and hence desiring to take from the United States; Carter, by contrast, framed the Soviet Union in more benign terms. Certainly the rhetoric of each politician suggested that this was the case: Carter scolded hawks for their "inordinate fear of the Soviet Union," while Reagan called the USSR an "evil empire." (Thus at least in some cases framing may point analysis back to ideology and preferences.)

Setting aside individual leaders, different domestic regimes may imply different national-security apparatuses, which in turn may implicate cognition and judgment. One historic justification of liberal democracy is that its more robust policy debates produce better decisions; liberals maintain that the fuller the debate, the more likely is the truth to be apprehended. A neglected passage of Kant's "Perpetual Peace" requires that rulers consult philosophers informally about war and peace.[42] John Stuart Mill's arguments for freedom of speech included the claim that it was for the public good.[43] Much recent IR literature supports these types of claim;[44] liberal democracies select wars that they are more likely to win. The inference is that non-democracies are more prone to deviate from their realist power lines. Regarding Ba'athist Iraq, Pollack argued that Saddam Hussein surrounded himself with sycophants afraid to contradict his optimistic predictions concerning defiance of the United States.[45] Thus Saddam exceeded his power line several times and provoked severe punishment: by invading

---

[40] Jack Levy, "Prospect Theory and International Relations: Theoretical Applications and Analytical Problems," *Political Psychology* 13 (1992), 283–310.

[41] Rose McDermott, "Prospect Theory in Political Science: Gains and Losses from the First Decade," *Political Psychology* 25 (2004), 289–312.

[42] From the Second Supplement in Kant, "Perpetual Peace": "Therefore, the state tacitly and secretly invites [philosophers] to give their opinions, that is, the state will let them publicly and freely talk about the general maxims of warfare and of the establishment of peace (for they will do that of themselves, provided they are not forbidden to do so)."

[43] John Stuart Mill, *On Liberty* (London: Duckworth, 1859).

[44] See Snyder, *Myths of Empire*; Dan Reiter and Allan C. Stam, *Democracies at War* (Princeton University Press, 2002).

[45] Pollack, *The Threatening Storm*, p. 254.

Iran in 1980, refusing to withdraw from Kuwait in late 1990, and barring weapons inspectors from unfettered access to suspected WMD sites in 2002 and 2003.

One link between regime type and cognitive ability could also be that different regimes tend to produce different types of leader. An absolute monarch, secure from constitutional accountability and encouraged to believe himself exceptional, may be more likely to place excessive confidence in his own capabilities. A duly elected prime minister may have had to convince others that he can listen to criticism, and so in office may tend to rely more on expert advice. Or societies themselves may vary in their capacity to learn what is in their interests and how to secure those interests. Cederman[46] argues that the democratic peace is best understood as a "macrohistorical learning process," in which liberal societies come over time to see the virtues of maintaining peace among themselves.[47]

Domestic cohesiveness

Even if we hold constant domestic regime and leadership, states' degree of national unity may vary. Sometimes a country is nearly united behind its government's foreign policy; sometimes it is evenly divided; sometimes the government finds itself domestically isolated. It stands to reason that, all else being equal, a state will follow a more consistent policy the more unified are government and society behind it. In a highly coercive state such as North Korea, this variable is irrelevant, as it is impossible to express or measure most dissent (apart from defection). For most states, however, dissent or questioning is permitted within limits.

The rule would apply most in constitutional democracies, where dissent against the government, if not the regime, is tolerated and allowed to spread. In a democracy, dissent can hamper a government from implementing its preferred foreign policy by a number of pathways. Directly, domestic divisions can lower the costs the state is willing or able to pay for a foreign policy. A national legislature with the power of the purse may prevent a government from confronting a rival as vigorously as it

---

[46] Lars-Erik Cederman, "Back to Kant: Reinterpreting the Democratic Peace as a Macrohistorical Learning Process," *American Political Science Review* 95 (2001), 15–31.

[47] Andrew Hurrell, "Kant and the Kantian Paradigm in International Relations," *Review of International Studies* 16 (1990), 183–205; Wade L. Huntley, "Kant's Third Image: Systematic Sources of the Liberal Peace," *International Studies Quarterly* 40 (1996), 45–76.

would like. Realists correctly point out that fear of appearing unpatriotic or cruel usually deters legislators, even in a war they oppose, from reducing funding to troops in harm's way. Yet, a government may be deterred by a dissenting legislature from raising funding as much as it would like. A compromising legislature is not a supine one. Thus during the Vietnam War Lyndon Johnson felt constrained not to extract too many resources from American society – by raising taxes or calling up the military reserve – owing to actual and potential opposition to the war.[48] But still he escalated the war.

Changes in the degree of national unity may also prod a government to become more hawkish than it would like. During the administration of Thomas Jefferson (1801–09), American public and elite opinion was divided as to how to respond to the Napoleonic Wars, and in particular whether the US merchant marine should carry goods from the Caribbean to the French-controlled continent of Europe. Republicans favored helping France (and hurting Britain), while most Federalists favored the opposite policies. The British seized US-carried cargoes, further polarizing Americans: Republicans blamed the British, while Federalists blamed the Republicans. In 1811 a number of young Republicans were elected to Congress who began a vigorous push for war with Britain. With Federalist strength fading, the War Hawk Congress got its war declaration in June, signed by President Madison.[49]

Or matters may work in the opposite way. Milner's theory of domestic politics and international relations posits that when the executive and legislative branches of government are from opposing parties, the prospect for international agreements is relatively dim; a state with divided government, then, may tend to act above its power line.[50] Many scholars have gone further and argued that domestically divided states are more prone to aggression and war. Diversionary theories of war like those of Rosecrance[51] build on the insights of sociologists like Lewis Coser that, in effect, balance-of-power theory operates at the domestic level: faced with an external threat, fellow citizens will set aside their differences and coalesce, at least as long as the external threat persists. Hence governments of divided societies have an incentive to magnify or create foreign threats. The government of A might confront B owing

---

[48] A. J. Langguth, *Our Vietnam: The War 1954–1975* (New York: Simon & Schuster, 2002), pp. 383–84.

[49] John Owen, *Liberal Peace, Liberal War: American Politics and International Security* (Ithaca: Cornell University Press, 1997).

[50] Helen Milner, *Interests, Institutions, and Information: Domestics Politics and International Relations* (Princeton University Press, 1997).

[51] Rosecrance, *Action and Reaction in World Politics*.

to its desire to unite A's society behind it. The Thatcher government certainly enjoyed a boost in popularity during and after the Falklands War against Argentina in 1982, and handily won re-election in 1983.[52] Whether a desire for re-election caused Thatcher to attack Argentine forces is another matter.

For centuries writers have argued that regime types differ according to how well they fight wars. Thucydides represents oligarchic Sparta as sluggish and reluctant to initiate war; democratic Athens he depicts as active and prone to conquer. Doyle[53] argues that Rousseau sees things in similar terms. Seeking a return to ancient republican virtue, Rousseau argues that republics fight harder than monarchies because the citizens have more at stake.[54] More recently, Reiter and Stam[55] concur with these long-dead writers: democratic armies, drawn from societies that value individual initiative, fight better than non-democratic ones. However, this finding must be interpreted in tandem with another, namely that democratic governments are more careful in choosing wars (see above); hence a selection effect taints the claim of democratic military effectiveness. These arguments do suggest a puzzle: why do countries – non-democratic ones – attack democracies? Why do the Hitlers and Tojos so egregiously misperceive the battlefield effectiveness of democracies? Why did Saddam Hussein twice underestimate how willing the United States was to attack Iraq? The answers might lie in the mechanisms outlined in the preceding section: perhaps authoritarian regimes tend to produce leaders who make bad decisions.

States may vary, too, according to how stable their governments or regimes are. The longer a government expects to remain in power, the more it will tend to take into account the long-term consequences of its policies. Leaders at risk will tend to pursue policies that shore up their power. Game theory generally holds that heavy discounting of the future tends to inhibit cooperation, as governments have less incentive to earn a cooperative reputation.[56] In security affairs, that could mean that a government with a short time horizon is tempted to overreach and even start a preemptive war, particularly when international insecurity calls

---

[52] See Brian Lai and Dan Reiter, "Democracy, Political Similarity, and International Alliances, 1816–1992," *Journal of Conflict Resolution* 44 (2005), 203–27.

[53] See Doyle, *Ways of War and Peace*.

[54] On the relation of state structures to state capacity more generally, see G. John Ikenberry, David A. Lake, and Michael Mastanduno (eds.), *The State and American Foreign Economic Policy* (Ithaca: Cornell University Press, 1989).

[55] Reiter and Stam, *Democracies at War*.

[56] See Kenneth A. Oye (ed.), *Cooperation under Anarchy* (Princeton University Press, 1986).

its future into doubt.[57] Yet, it is possible too that a future-discounting government may act below its power line, by for example appeasing a potential foreign patron to ward off its demise. Machiavelli reports that medieval Venice exploited this dynamic: when the Guelphs were in power in an Italian city, the Venetians would secretly nurture the Ghibellines so as to keep the Guelphs dependent upon Venetian aid.[58]

Foreigners' reactions to the state

Differences in a country's government or regime might also implicate how foreigners perceive and act toward that country. Foreigners might have more interests in common, or believe they do, with one type of regime or government than with another; overlapping preferences, all else being equal, should yield more cooperation or acting beneath power lines with one another. In the latter part of the nineteenth century, most American elites believed that republics (non-monarchies) had shared interests and indeed were on the same side of a long transnational struggle with monarchies; the prospects of republicanism in the United States turned on its successes elsewhere.[59] In early 1873 the administration of Ulysses S. Grant was on the verge of recognizing as belligerents Cuban rebels against Spanish rule; recognition would have placed the United States on a path toward intervention in Cuba and war against Spain. But a revolution in February toppled the Spanish monarchy and set up a republic. Sympathy for Spain rose sharply in Congress and the American press, and elites expected Madrid's young republican government to settle with the Cuban rebels and free the 500,000 slaves on the island. Notwithstanding a serious bilateral crisis over the Spanish execution of several Americans in Cuba, the two countries averted war.[60]

Or foreigners may simply find one type of regime or government more predictable than another and hence easier to deal with. Rationalist IR theory stresses that violent conflict is in the interests of no state, all else

---

[57] See Robert Axelrod and Robert Keohane, "Achieving Cooperation under Anarchy," in Oye (ed.), *Cooperation under Anarchy.*

[58] Machiavelli advises against this strategy, however, saying that in the event of war with a third state one faction will join that state in fighting you. Niccoló Machiavelli, *The Prince* (1532), trans. Harvey C. Mansfield Jr. (University of Chicago Press, 1985), chp. 20, pp. 83–87.

[59] And vice versa: see Abraham Lincoln's justification for the Emancipation Proclamation, namely to preserve the hope of freedom worldwide: "In *giving* freedom to the *slave*, we *assure* freedom to the *free* – honorable alike in what we give, and what we preserve. We shall nobly save, or meanly lose, the last best hope of earth." Lincoln, "Annual Message to Congress, Concluding Remarks" December 1, 1862), available at http://showcase.netins.net/web/creative/lincoln/speeches/congress.htm.

[60] Owen, *Liberal Peace, Liberal War.*

being equal. War is like a strike in industrial relations, a dead-weight loss on the way to a settlement that could have been reached beforehand. Hence war happens, even in an anarchical system, when states have insufficient information about one another's capabilities and intentions. Fearon[61] stresses how democracies have higher "audience costs" than non-democracies: democratic leaders will likely suffer greater punishments from domestic constituents for backing down during a foreign crisis. Knowing this to be so, foreign governments will be less likely to push democracies during a crisis for fear of provoking them into extreme policies. Schultz[62] emphasizes, by contrast, that liberal democracies are more transparent than other types of state; foreigners can better judge their capabilities and preferences and reach more efficient bargains with them. If democracy A is being confrontational toward B but dissent within A is significant, B knows it can push A harder; if A is domestically united, B knows it cannot. In both types of case, foreigners would be more likely to deviate from their own power line when dealing with non-democracies. Both of these mechanisms are consistent with recent tendencies for opaque states such as Ba'athist Iraq, totalitarian North Korea, and (to a lesser extent) Islamist Iran to encounter wide international counterbalancing, as other countries hedge against their uncertainty about these states' intentions and capabilities. Meanwhile, the vastly powerful but liberal-democratic United States has encountered far less counterbalancing than realists predicted in the 1990s.[63]

A government's time horizon may also affect how other governments treat it. The literature on international political economy stresses that markets forecast governments' monetary and fiscal policies in part based upon their time horizons; an unstable government is more likely to lower interest rates and run deficits, defecting from international agreements.[64] In security affairs, as mentioned above, a short time horizon might lead foreigners to hedge in their dealing with a government. Thus they might offer help in return for some sort of appeasement but also prepare for the government to act above its power line in order to extract short-

---

[61] See James D. Fearon, "Rationalist Explanations for War," *International Organization* 49 (1995), 379–414.

[62] See Kenneth A. Schultz, *Democracy and Coercive Diplomacy* (New York: Cambridge University Press, 2001).

[63] See G. John Ikenberry (ed.), *America Unrivaled: The Future of the Balance of Power* (Princeton University Press, 2002); T. V. Paul, James J. Wirtz, and Michael Fortmann (eds.), *Balance of Power: Theory and Practice in the 21st Century* (Stanford University Press, 2004).

[64] See Beth Simmons, *Who Adjusts? Domestics Sources of Foreign Economic Policy during the Interwar Years* (Princeton University Press, 1994); William Bernhard and David Leblang, *Democratic Processes and Financial Markets: Pricing Politics* (New York, Cambridge University Press, 2006).

term gains for itself. Western policies toward the Russian provisional government in the middle of 1917, between the March revolution and the Bolshevik *coup d'état* in November, seem to conform to this pattern. London and Washington not only worked with the Kerensky government but attempted to befriend the soviet (workers' council) that ran Petrograd, the capital; they also prepared for the worst.[65]

How would we know?

The question of anomalies for realism raises the more general one of how we would know if a state's foreign policy deviated from its power line. How do we identify a state's power line? Scholars sometimes resort to *ex post* inference, concluding from a successful outcome such as an averted war that state policies followed their power lines. But that begs the question. To falsify realism's claim, we would need to locate a state's power line *ex ante*. A fallback method would be to note that realism implies that states of the same rank in the same circumstances will act in the same fashion. Of course, in international relations our evidence is historical, not experimental, and neither ranking nor circumstances are ever precisely the same across time and space. But, following John Stuart Mill's method of difference, we can identify states of roughly similar power ranking that behave differently holding other variables constant.[66] And we can identify states whose domestic institutions remain constant and act similarly even when their power ranking changes and other variables do not (Mill's method of similarity). Several chapters in this volume carry out these sorts of comparative studies.

Sorting out which of the many mechanisms caused the change – preferences, cognitive abilities, audience costs, and the like – can likewise be difficult. Some of the mechanisms may coincide; a liberal-democratic regime may simultaneously constrain its executive from using force and be more transparent. Some may even be endogenous; compared to its predecessor a new government may simultaneously want a more confrontational foreign policy (have different preferences) and be prone to misinterpret the signals sent by foreign states as more hostile than intended (have lower cognitive abilities), with the preferences and cognitive misperceptions reinforcing one another. Sometimes it is easier to conclude that domestic institutions or leaders were consequential than to ascertain precisely how they produced those consequences.

---

[65] George F. Kennan, *Russia and the West under Lenin and Stalin* (Boston: Hutchinson Press, 1961).

[66] John Stuart Mill, *A System of Logic* (London: Longmans, Green, Reader, and Dyer, 1875).

Conclusion

We return, at the end, to the intra-realist debate over foreign policy theory. Structural realists may acknowledge that at least some of the claims in this chapter, and in the empirical ones that follow, are plausible. Sometimes great powers ignore or try to override the constraints of relative power. Can realism then fall back on the Waltzian position that individual states' foreign policies are outside the theory's scope after all? Perhaps so, but then the theory's utility deteriorates. Great powers, it seems, are sometimes able to sustain deviations from power lines for long periods – long enough to call into question the neorealist claim that international outcomes will regularly revert to a balance-of-power equilibrium. These long deviations are sustained by the enabling responses of other great powers. State A's over-balancing is often met with state B's under-balancing, which encourages A to continue its over-balancing, and so forth. Positive feedback seems to run through the international system.[67] The system eventually punished Nazi Germany for its imprudence, but not before being battered by the most destructive war in history, whose legacy continues to shape world politics. The Second World War itself was brought on by enabling or under-balancing by the other great powers; Hitler was (instrumentally) rational in September 1939 in thinking that Britain and France would acquiesce to the invasion of Poland.[68] Today the international system has yet to provoke a true counterbalance to America's vast military power. Doubtless an international balance of power will someday emerge, but thus far other powers have enabled the perpetuation of unipolarity. We have less and less reason to regard such a balance as the only stable equilibrium possible in international politics.[69]

If states reinforce one another's "irrational" acts, then it will not do to call the acts irrational; we would better say that states typically have a range of rational policies – a *power band*, rather than a power line – and that they are rational to test the width of that band. Or we might instead broaden our notion of what constitutes national power to include domestic properties of states. Perhaps, for example, liberal great powers are more likely to institutionalize their international relations and thereby prolong their power by making it more predictable and acceptable, at least to other liberal states.[70]

---

[67] Robert Jervis, *System Effects* (Princeton University Press, 1997).

[68] See A. J. P. Taylor, *The Origins of the Second World War* (London: Penguin, 1961).

[69] See Ikenberry (ed.), *America Unrivaled*.

[70] Bruce Russett and John Oneal, *Triangulating Peace: Democracy, Interdependence, and International Organizations* (New York: W. W. Norton, 2001); G. John Ikenberry, *After Victory: Institutions, Strategic Restraint, and the Rebuilding of Order after Major Wars* (Princeton University Press, 2001).

If states routinely defy realist logic, then why does that logic retain its hold over the study of international relations? Why does it continue to set the agenda in security studies if a majority of scholars say they are not realists? Why are liberals and constructivists defined, by themselves, as anti-realists? Why can we not collectively change the subject? Realism's staying power does not seem a function of its ability to predict state behavior or international outcomes. Too often realists beg the question, as suggested above; and when they do make predictions, such as that post-Cold War unipolarity will be ephemeral, they do not fare well. Realism's great virtue is, instead, its elegance. Like the gravity model of trade, it sets out an intuitively appealing baseline explanation for state behavior. Precisely owing to its empirical shortcomings, its elegance invites contradiction. If realism did not exist, we should have to invent it. Indeed, the collective "we" reinvent realism regularly, and then reinvent ways to gainsay it.

4   How international institutions affect outcomes

Robert O. Keohane and Lisa Martin

A generation ago, Imre Lakatos expounded a theory of scientific progress in the natural sciences.[1] Whether he meant his theory to apply to social science or not, it has proved to be a fruitful point of reference for students of international relations seeking to evaluate their own research programs and compare them with rival programs. Yet the Scottsdale Conference, where papers for this volume were discussed, clearly showed that Lakatos's framework does not provide a clear, operational framework for the analysis of research programs. As David Dessler convincingly argued, the "hard core" of Lakatos's research program cannot be defined, and we do not know what counts as a "novel fact." It is therefore relatively easy for research programs to avoid being labeled as degenerative. As Dessler also suggested, however, we can tell our stories in Lakatosian terms. Although Lakatos's criteria are ambiguous and his own formulations often contradictory, thinking about whether research programs are "progressive" remains, in our view, a useful way to help us evaluate their relative merits.

It is in this spirit that we engage in the current project. We are not scholars of the philosophy of science, and we are not particularly interested in arcane debates about what Lakatos "really meant" or what he "should have said." However, we find that his criteria for progressiveness provide sensible, if not unambiguous, criteria for the evaluation of scientific traditions.[2]

This chapter is reprinted from Elman, Colin, and Elman, Miriam Fendius, eds. foreword by Kenneth N. Waltz., *Progress in International Relations Theory: Appraising the Field*, pp. 71–108, © 2003 Massachusetts Institute of Technology, by permission of The MIT Press.

[1] Imre Lakatos, "Falsification and the Methodology of Scientific Research Programs," in Imre Lakatos and Alan Musgrave (eds.), *Criticism and the Growth of Knowledge* (Cambridge University Press, 1970).

[2] Robert O. Keohane, "Theory of World Politics: Structural Realism and Beyond," in Ada Finifter (ed.), *Political Science: The State of the Discipline* (Washington, DC: American Political Science Association, 1983), and in Robert O. Keohane (ed.), *Neorealism and Its Critics* (New York: Columbia University Press, 1986), p. 161.

For Lakatos, fruitful research programs must discover novel facts. Even if it is impossible to pin down what constitutes novelty, this criterion is crucial for us as social scientists to keep in mind, since so much work in our field merely relabels old observations with new terms. It may be difficult to ascertain, in international relations, whether a given fact generated by a theory is "novel," but it is easy to identify lots of facts generated by theory that are as old and worn as crumbling books. Like the philistine in the modern art museum, we know what we do not like – the recycling of geopolitical lore as theory – even though we may have trouble justifying our positive preferences.

At the end of the day, our theories and methods are only as good as the discoveries they help us to make. Generating novel facts requires specifying meaningful propositions that can be tested. For Lakatos, the process of discovering novel facts often occurs through the generation of anomalies. The key test of whether a research program is progressive is how it handles "the ocean of anomalies."[3] It cannot do so by violating its hard core, since this would render the program incoherent. If its practitioners simply try to "patch up" their program with an "arbitrary series of disconnected theories," their research program can properly be regarded as degenerate.[4]

In addition to the hard core, protected by the negative heuristic, research programs, for Lakatos, also contain "positive heuristics," which suggest to scientists what sorts of hypotheses to pursue. In a progressive research program, scientists pursue the positive heuristic of their program in such a way as to resolve anomalies. In the process of resolving anomalies, progressive research programs are those that discover new facts.

This chapter begins by describing the challenge that institutional theory has since the early 1980s posed to realism, particularly realism as systematized by Kenneth Waltz, and often referred to as "neorealism." We argue that institutional theory adopted almost all of the hard core of realism but that, by treating information as a variable, it was able both to account for extensive cooperation and to show how institutions were linked to such cooperation. The second part of this chapter addresses the challenges to institutional theory posed by realists in the 1980s. The result of these challenges, some of which were more productive than others, was to stimulate efforts at effecting various forms of synthesis between realism and institutionalism. Finally, we take up the most fundamental and difficult challenge posed to

---

[3] Lakatos, "Falsification and the Methodology of Scientific Research Programs," p. 135.
[4] Ibid., p. 175.

institutional theory: the claim that institutions are endogenous to state structure and therefore epiphenomenal. We suggest, using agency theory, that the endogeneity of institutions does not necessarily imply their irrelevance, but that institutional theory needs to deal forthrightly with the endogeneity problem if it is to continue to be progressive.

Institutional theory as a partial challenge to realism

Institutional theory proceeded roughly as a Lakatosian would suggest. It restated the core of the realist research program; identified and emphasized anomalies facing realism; proposed a new theory to resolve those anomalies; specified a key observational implication of its theory; and sought to test hypotheses based on that theoretical implication, searching for novel facts.

Institutionalists begin with a restatement of the explicit core assumptions of realism, which can be identified as follows: (1) states are the primary actors in world politics; (2) states behave as if they were rational, in the sense that they assess their strategic situations in light of their environments, and seek to maximize expected gains; (3) states pursue their interests (which prominently include survival), rather than behaving altruistically; (4) states operate in a world of "anarchy," without common government. Different realists claim to hold different assumptions, although the list of four above, including anarchy, is fairly conventional.[5] This list seems consistent with the argument, if not the explicit assumptions, of Kenneth Waltz in his classic book, *Theory of International Politics*.[6] Institutional theory fully shares the first

[5] See Joseph Grieco, "The Maastricht Treaty, Economic and Monetary Union, and the Neo-Realist Research Program," *Review of International Studies* 21 (1995), 27. Grieco lists "three assumptions," but one is that actors are "substantively and instrumentally rational," which we interpret as incorporating both assumption 2 and assumption 3, in our formulation. The editors of this volume add the assumption of self-help, which we regard as a derivation from the others, although some have questioned whether this derivation is logically sound.

[6] Kenneth N. Waltz, *Theory of International Politics* (Reading, MA: Addison-Wesley, 1979). Waltz's systematization of realism is often referred to as "neorealism," but to maintain simplicity of language, we refer throughout to realism, by which we mean the most explicit and systematic variants of that diverse school, in particular those developed by Waltz. Waltz denies that he assumes rationality or anarchy, claiming as he reaffirmed in the Scottsdale conference that he only assumes that "states want to survive." However, this statement contains the assumption that states are key actors, since if they were not actors, they could not "want" anything, even metaphorically, and if they were not key, his theory would presumably focus on the important actors. Furthermore, "want to survive" is a definition of their self-interest, and therefore implies self-interest. As one of us has argued elsewhere, for Waltz's theory to move from desires to actions, the rationality assumption seems essential, since evolutionary selection is not reliable in international relations. See Keohane, "Theory of World Politics." It therefore seems evident that Waltz makes the three assumptions that we

three of these assumptions. It also accepts the fourth assumption, that of anarchy, strictly defined as the absence of an external enforcer of agreements, although institutional theorists are careful to distinguish anarchy in this sense from chaos, and do not accept neorealist assertions that the fact of anarchy has far-reaching negative implications for cooperation.[7] Indeed, institutionalists have sought to show that there can be "cooperation under anarchy."[8] From a theoretical standpoint, one of the most striking features of institutional theory, in contrast to the "liberal" international relations theories with which it is often identified, is that it embraces so much of the hard core of realism.

On the basis of such assumptions as the four listed above, Waltz and his followers inferred that states would cooperate little except in response to the prospect of confronting dangerous concentrations of power, or alternatively in response to threat.[9] Institutional theory questions this inference.

Identifying anomalies in realism

Realism has been confronted with, in Lakatos's phrase, an "ocean of anomalies." Some of these anomalies derive from events that occurred before Waltz's influential 1979 formulation. For instance, Paul Schroeder has pointed out anomalies in Kenneth Waltz's argument about balancing, and John Vasquez has argued, using standards derived from Lakatos, that "the neotraditional research program on balancing has been degenerating," as a result of ad hoc attempts by realists to respond to such anomalies.[10] Other anomalies have appeared since 1979, either because important regularities seem to have been overlooked earlier, such as that democracies are disinclined to fight one another, or, because of new events such as the telecommunications revolution and the end of the Cold War, non-state actors and issue-networks are becoming more visible and apparently more consequential.[11]

ascribe both to institutional theory and to realism. Waltz is the scholar who has most popularized the notion of "anarchy," so we regard it as his business, not ours, if he decides that it is not so fundamental after all.

[7] Helen V. Milner, "The Assumption of Anarchy in International Relations Theory: A Critique," *Review of International Studies* 17 (1991), 67–85; Powell, "Review: Anarchy in International Relations Theory."

[8] Oye (ed.), *Cooperation under Anarchy*.

[9] Walt, *The Origins of Alliances*.

[10] Paul W. Schroeder, "Historical Reality versus Neorealist Theory," *International Security* 19 (1994), 108–48; John Vasquez, "The Realist Paradigm and Degenerative versus Progressive Research Programs: An Appraisal of Neotraditional Research on Waltz's Balancing Proposition," *American Political Science Review* 91 (1997), 910.

[11] Margaret E. Keck and Kathryn Sikkink, *Activists Beyond Borders: Advocacy Networks in International Politics* (Ithaca: Cornell University Press, 1998).

By themselves, these anomalies are not particularly disturbing from a Lakatosian perspective. Research programs confront anomalies and seek to resolve them. From the standpoint of institutional theory, however, one of these anomalies was telling: that international cooperation is extensive and highly institutionalized. Examples include the emergence of a highly rule-oriented trade regime under the General Agreement on Tariffs and Trade (GATT) and then the World Trade Organization (WTO); the significance in managing the global economy of the International Monetary Fund (IMF); the uneven but impressively institutionalized cooperation of the European Union (EU); the invention of a variety of regional and global environmental institutions; and even the robust institutionalization of security cooperation in NATO.[12] To the surprise of realist scholars, such institutionalization has not only continued after the disappearance of the Soviet threat, but has expanded, both in Europe and in the world political economy.[13]

The origins of modern institutional theory can be traced, following a classic Lakatosian pattern, to a disjunction between established realist theory and the stubborn, persistent fact of extensive, increasing, and highly institutionalized cooperation. Waltz predicted that states would be reluctant to engage in forms of cooperation that left them at risk of being taken advantage of by other states.[14] Because security is scarce in international politics, and the environment is highly uncertain, states are forced to behave in a highly risk-averse manner. Thus, realists argued against the likelihood of states engaging in extensive and persistent forms of cooperation. States might cooperate with one another, but only on a short-term, ad hoc basis. Because only these shallow forms of cooperation would arise, there was little need for international institutions in which to structure long-term patterns of

---

[12] Celeste Wallander and Robert Keohane, "Risk, Threat and Security Institutions," in Helga Haftendorn, Robert O. Keohane, and Celeste A. Wallander (eds.), *Imperfect Unions: Security Institutions over Time and Space* (Oxford University Press, 1999). Our examples, here and throughout the chapter, refer to both formal and informal institutions. Thus both formal organizations and informal sets of rules that make up some regimes or conventions are relevant to institutional theory; we see both as forms of institutions.

[13] John J. Mearsheimer, "Back to the Future: Instability in Europe after the Cold War," *International Security* 15 (1990), 5–56.

[14] Waltz, *Theory of International Politics*. George Downs and David Rocke in *Optimal Imperfection? Domestic Uncertainty and Institutions in International Relations* (Princeton University Press, 1995) refer to such cooperation as deep cooperation. They refer to forms of cooperation that involve sunk costs, implying that policies cannot be reversed without costs. If this is true, patterns of cooperation have a tendency to become locked in, and states can lose if others renege on cooperative arrangements. According to neorealist logic, this risk should prevent states from engaging in deep cooperation.

cooperation. Realism's predictions about cooperation and institutions were admirably clear: cooperation should be shallow and tenuous and institutions should be weak and have no observable impact on patterns of cooperation.

The very clarity of Waltz's argument made it difficult to evade the anomaly created by the fact of institutionalized cooperation. Keohane explicitly drew on Lakatosian ideas about research programs to note persistent discrepancies between neorealist predictions and actual state behavior.[15] In particular, he pointed out that states do, in fact, engage in persistent patterns of cooperation. In issues ranging from economic agreements to arms control and military alliances, states take steps that put themselves at risk of exploitation in the short term, in exchange for the promise of the longer-term benefits of cooperation. In addition, they have constructed institutions to sustain and enhance these patterns of cooperation. Keohane recognized that these institutions were not "strong," in the sense that many domestic institutions are understood to be strong: for example, they had little centralized enforcement power.[16] The puzzle prompted by this observation was: how could institutions facilitate cooperation among states that had conflicts of interest but nevertheless could benefit from cooperation?

Institutional theory

Institutional theory seeks to understand the anomalies facing realist theory by building on, but going beyond, some premises that it has in common with realism. Institutional theory seeks to understand the existence of international institutions, and how they operate. Institutions are defined as "persistent and connected sets of rules (formal and informal) that prescribe behavioral roles, constrain activity, and shape expectations."[17] They can take the form of formal intergovernmental or nongovernmental organizations, international regimes, and informal conventions. Following Douglass North, we conceive of organizations as actors or "players," and institutions as rules that define how the game is played.[18] Regimes are sets of rules and norms that may be formal or informal; conventions are informal understandings.

---

[15] Keohane, "Theory of World Politics."
[16] Below, we note that understandings of domestic institutions have substantially changed in recent years, so that the characterization of them as strong external enforcers of contracts and other agreements is no longer universally accepted.
[17] Robert O. Keohane, *International Institutions and State Power* (Boulder: Westview, 1989), p. 3.
[18] Douglass C. North, *Institutions, Institutional Change and Economic Performance* (New York: Cambridge University Press, 1990), pp. 4–5.

Early institutional theory sought to show that even given realist assumptions, international institutions should be seen as significant for the policies followed by states, and therefore for the realization of important values in world politics. Such authors as Robert Axelrod and Robert Keohane relied on analysis of mixed-motive games such as the Prisoners' Dilemma to identify factors that would support cooperation, and drew attention to the role of reciprocity and information in allowing states to reach the Pareto frontier of efficient international arrangements.[19] These formulations shared the traditional realist conceptualization of states as rational actors pursuing self-interest.

In comparison to the liberal idealism that preceded it, and the constructivism that has followed, institutional theory constituted an incremental modification of realism. Advocates of institutional theory embraced, rather than abandoned, the three core assumptions that it shared with realism; even disagreements over the anarchy assumption were not fundamental to institutional theory. The crucial assumption of realism altered by institutional theory was implicit rather than explicit. Changing this assumption, however, enabled institutional theorists to challenge the validity of the inferences about state behavior that realists had made on the basis of the shared assumptions.

The changed core assumption has to do with the informational environment of international relations. Realism assumes that information about the intentions of other states is pertinent, but of poor quality. States must therefore assume the worst, and thus behave in a defensive, wary manner.[20] More importantly, realists assume that states cannot systematically improve the information conditions in which they operate. This assumption dates back to classical realism, being a major part of the analysis of E. H. Carr, for example.[21] Scarce information, and the inability of states to do anything to improve the situation, forces states to adopt worst-case scenarios when choosing their strategies.

Institutional theory in contrast, explicitly treats information as a variable. Most important, it treats information as a variable that can be

---

[19] Robert Axelrod, *The Evolution of Cooperation* (New York: Basic Books, 1984); Robert O. Keohane, *After Hegemony: Cooperation and Discord in the World Political Economy* (Princeton University Press, 1984).

[20] Mearsheimer, "Back to the Future"; Waltz, *Theory of International Politics.* Charles Glaser, "Realists as Optimists: Cooperation as Self-Help," *International Security* 19 (1994), 50–90, has most directly examined this precept of realism, suggesting that under some conditions information is in fact not scarce, and that states can utilize signaling strategies to inform others of their intentions. He asserts that changing this assumption about information is consistent with realism.

[21] Edward Hallett Carr, *The Twenty Years' Crisis, 1919–1939* (New York: Harper & Row, 1939).

influenced by human action. Institutional theory agrees with realism that scarcity of information will impede the efforts of states to engage in cooperative activities with one another. However, since institutional theory assumes that information can be changed by human agency, it argues that states will take steps to improve the informational environment under these conditions, especially if scarcity of information is impeding the attainment of substantial mutual gains from cooperation. Institutional theory has focused on the role of institutions in improving the informational environment. They can do so in numerous ways, such as by providing information about the intentions and activities of others, by setting standards and identifying focal points, or by providing reliable causal information about the relationship between actions and outcomes. Institutional theory points out that states may be as concerned with providing information about themselves – hence bolstering their credibility and therefore the value of their commitments – as they are with acquiring information about others. States therefore construct institutions to improve both their information about others and their own credibility, to ameliorate the dilemmas and defensive stances otherwise dictated by realism's hardcore assumptions.

The shift from realism to institutional theory can be classified, in Lakatos's terms, either as an inter-program problemshift or an intra-program problemshift, depending on whether one views as central the assumption implicit in traditional realist theory that the information content of the system is a constant. We leave that debate to others; in view of the ambiguity of Lakatosian theory and of the scope for argument over realist–institutionalist differences, it is not very important to us to debate whether institutional theory began as a separate research program or merely an attempt to construct what one of the present authors once called "modified structural realism."[22] As we have emphasized, there is much in common between realism and institutional theory, particularly in its early years. Indeed, the closeness of the links between institutional theory and realism is indicated by the fact that institutional theory at the outset adopted realism's unitary actor assumption – although this decision was admittedly taken more for analytical convenience and rhetorical effect than out of deep conviction. It was a tactical decision, later reversed, rather than part of institutional theory's hard core.[23] As we argue below, this adoption of the unitary actor assumption had costs. Whether wise or not, institutional theory

[22] Keohane, "Theory of World Politics."
[23] Keohane and Nye discussed "the limits of systemic explanations" in Robert O. Keohane and Joseph S. Nye, *Power and Interdependence: World Politics in Transition* (Boston: Little, Brown, 1977/89), pp. 153–58.

shows that, for better or worse, it is a half-sibling of realism. Perhaps their closeness helps to explain the intensity of the disputes that have arisen between them.

Observable implications of institutional theory

Institutional theory's core assumption that variations in information could result from human agency generated an observational implication of its theory: states should devise strategies to construct international institutions that could provide information and reinforce credibility. The positive heuristic of the institutionalist research program, consisting of a "partially articulated set of suggestions or hints," in Lakatos's words, on how to change and develop the refutable aspects of the research program, was aimed at analyzing both institutional growth and state strategies to institute and maintain institutions.[24]

The logic of mixed-motive games combined with the scarcity of information led to specification of a heuristically novel fact: international institutions should engage more heavily in monitoring and information-sharing than in enforcement. In order for reciprocity to work efficiently to sustain cooperation, states required reliable information about other states' preferences and actions. Yet such information was hard to come by in international politics. The key original insight of institutional theory was that institutions could, through monitoring, provide such information. In particular, they could provide information about whether states were living up to their commitments. With this information timely in hand, states could devise strategies of decentralized enforcement that would allow cooperation to emerge as an equilibrium in a repeated game. The key proposition of institutional theory, therefore, was that international institutions should have substantial monitoring and information-sharing authority, while providing for decentralized enforcement by member states themselves.

Armed with their new theory, institutionalists explored a variety of issue-areas, observing what international institutions did. Investigating economic issues, such as those of the GATT and WTO, environmental regimes,[25] and security institutions,[26] they found ample support for the

---

[24] Lakatos, "Falsification and the Methodology of Scientific Research Programs," p. 135.
[25] Peter M. Haas, Robert O. Keohane, and Marc A. Levy (eds.), *Institutions for the Earth: Sources of Effective International Environmental Protection* (Cambridge, MA: MIT Press, 1993); Ronald Mitchell, *Intentional Oil Pollution at Sea: Environmental Pollution and Treaty Compliance* (Cambridge, MA: MIT Press, 1994).
[26] Haftendorn *et al.*, *Imperfect Unions*.

argument that institutions were significant participants in political processes, and that they provided information as the theory anticipated.

It is important to recognize, however, that the initial tests of institutionalist theory were weak and often methodologically flawed. Institutional researchers have tended to look for confirming evidence that institutions facilitated cooperation in the manner specified in the theory, rather than seeking to refute their theory. Understandably, they wanted to establish an "existence proof" for institutionalized cooperation, and to show how it happened by tracing causal mechanisms. Unfortunately, the result was selection bias in the empirical work on institutional theory, as researchers focused on those cases where it was easiest to make the claim that "institutions mattered." Because the incidence of institutions is not random – states create institutions when they expect them to be useful – looking for patterned variation in the relation between institutions and cooperation suffers from inferential problems.[27]

More generally, institutional researchers confront the problem of endogeneity, always a methodological challenge in a non-experimental science whose observations are not independent of one another. In principle, the investigator would like to discover how significant institutions are, controlling for structure. But it is hard to find enough comparable cases, across which institutional form varies but structure does not, to carry out standard statistical techniques.[28] The experimental alternative is also not available, unless one were to construct a simulation, which has its own validity problems.[29] Only with a very sophisticated simulation could one model the counterfactual world (without institutions) and the actual world (with them) with repeated runs to ascertain what differences the institutions make.

Hence institutional researchers have generally relied on hypothetical counterfactual analysis: imagining what patterns of cooperation and discord would have existed in the absence of institutions, or conversely, what impact a given set of hypothetical institutions might have had. But such imagined counterfactuals can always be challenged, and do not lend themselves to empirical testing.

---

[27] See Lisa L. Martin, *Coercive Cooperation: Explaining Multilateral Economic Sanctions* (Princeton University Press, 1992), for an attempt to identify such variation.

[28] For an outstanding attempt to do so, see Page Fortna, "A Peace that Lasts," Ph.D. thesis, Harvard University (1998).

[29] But see Lars-Erik Cederman, *Emergent Actors in World Politics: How States and Nations Develop and Dissolve* (Princeton University Press, 1997), for an interesting attempt to begin such modeling.

Another methodological difficulty in the existing institutionalist literature concerns inferences from observed outcomes about non-observable explanatory variables. This is a problem of endogeneity produced not by the real world but by faulty methods. For institutionalists, the growth of institutions is "explained" by the common interests of states in achieving joint gains through institutions. However, where institutions fail to become stronger, this can easily be taken, not as refutation of the theory, but as evidence of the strength of adverse interests. The key methodological problem here derives from the fact that interests are not directly observed. If interests are inferred from the value of the dependent variable – institutional growth – the test becomes meaningless. A real test of the theory requires *ex ante* rather than *ex post* specification of interests.

Both of these problems can be addressed by more rigorous tests: specifying interests *ex ante*, avoiding selection bias (preferably investigating many cases of a coherent class of events), and investigating difficult as well as easy cases, in an attempt to refute the theory rather than merely to confirm it. There is much room for improvement in the methods used to test institutional theory but the direction in which these methods should be taken seems clear.[30]

Institutional theory also, however, has a methodological strength that should not be overlooked – one that derives directly from the endogeneity of institutions to structures. Unless we explicitly consider the intervening role of endogenous institutions, we may be led into false inferences about the relation between structural variables and outcomes. For example, increased intensity of cooperation dilemmas may lead to the creation of stronger institutions and therefore more intense cooperation. If we only considered structural variables and outcomes, we would see an apparently perverse correlation: tougher cooperation problems would be associated with higher (or at least stable) levels of cooperation. We need to consider the role of institutions in order to make sense of observed patterns of behavior.[31]

---

[30] For a discussion of methods, many of which are appropriate to the evaluation of institutional theory, see Gary King, Robert O. Keohane, and Sidney Verba, *Designing Social Inquiry: Scientific Inference in Qualitative Research* (Princeton University Press, 1994). On counterfactuals, see Philip E. Tetlock and Aaron Belkin (eds.), *Counterfactual Thought Experiments in World Politics: Logical, Methodological and Psychological Perspectives* (Princeton: Princeton University Press, 1996).

[31] Recent work by Page Fortna does an impressive job of examining the effects of peace agreements. She finds that severe conflict between the parties, accompanied by expectations of continued animosities, often leads to more highly institutionalized agreements. Thus the correlation between institutionalization of peace agreements and the duration of subsequent peace may be negative, even if institutionalization itself has had positive effects. Fortna, "A Peace that Lasts."

Challenges to institutional theory

Until the 1990s, realists had two major responses to the challenge of institutionalist theory, which we characterize as "minimalization" and "denial." Often these criticisms were made by the same scholars. During the 1990s, the modal response, from self-described realists and others, has shifted toward synthesis: putting forward interpretations of events that are fundamentally consistent with institutionalist theory, while sometimes giving them different emphases, or different labels. The responses of the 1980s led to what we characterize as short-term challenges that are easily parried by institutional theory. The more synthetic arguments of the 1990s are, in our view, more important and more illuminating.

Realists in the 1980s sometimes viewed cooperation as a significant phenomenon in world politics, but minimized its significance, emphasizing that it takes place within the context of power realities, which fundamentally shape and limit it. In replying to Robert Keohane's criticisms in 1986, Kenneth Waltz crisply stated this view:

Some states sometimes want to work together to secure the benefits of cooperation. Cooperative projects in the present may lead to more cooperation in the future. But self-help systems do make the cooperation of parties difficult. As Gilpin puts it, "the traditional insights of realism ... help us to explain ... the ongoing retreat from an interdependent world."[32]

Joanne Gowa and Stephen Krasner made similar arguments, recognizing the insights of institutional theory but arguing that it failed to account adequately for the role of power. Gowa praised Robert Axelrod's book, *The Evolution of Cooperation*, for its insights into "the rationality of cooperation for mutual gain in the long run," but viewed his analysis as "more narrowly bounded than is apparent at first glance."[33] Krasner criticized the argument offered by Keohane in *After Hegemony* for de-emphasizing the role of power even while nominally recognizing its importance: "Neoliberal speculations about the positive consequences of greater information are fascinating ... But they obscure considerations of relative power capabilities, which draw attention to ... ultimately who wins and who loses."[34]

---

[32] Kenneth N. Waltz, "Reflections on *Theory of International Politics*: A Response to My Critics," in Keohane (ed.), *Neorealism and Its Critics*, p. 336; citing Robert G. Gilpin, "The Richness of the Tradition of Political Realism," in Keohane (ed.), *Neorealism and Its Critics*, pp. 301–21.

[33] Joanne Gowa, "Anarchy, Egoism and Third Images: *The Evolution of Cooperation* and International Relations," *International Organization* 40 (1986), 185; Axelrod, *The Evolution of Cooperation*.

[34] Stephen D. Krasner, "Global Communications and National Power: Life on the Pareto Frontier," *World Politics* 43 (1991), 366.

In effect, the minimization critique claimed that the insights of institutional theory could be accommodated within a somewhat broadened version of realism: that institutional theory did not violate realism's hard core. At the Scottsdale Conference, this also seemed to be Kenneth Waltz's position. More critical realist arguments attacked key assumptions of institutionalist theory. In 1986, Gowa quoted Waltz as arguing that insecure states, facing the possibility of cooperation for mutual gain, "must ask how the gain will be divided. They are compelled to ask not 'Will both of us gain?' but 'Who will gain more?'"[35] Joseph Grieco pushed this point further.[36] He noted that any cooperative arrangement would give rise to joint gains that could be divided in a multitude of ways among the cooperating parties. Division of these gains would be a matter of intense concern. In any setting, bargaining about the distribution of gains in order to increase one's absolute gain was to be expected.[37] But in the international arena, the dilemma went even deeper. Because inequalities in the distribution of gains could be transformed into increased inequality in power resources, and because the use of military force was always a possibility in International Relations, the deniers argued that states would never engage in cooperation that increased their absolute gains if it meant a relative loss.[38] Once again, the extremely risk-averse nature of states assumed by realism led to a prediction that cooperation would be shallow and infrequent. However, the causal logic that limited cooperation was now specified to be concern for relative gains and losses that could be transformed into a disadvantage during a military confrontation.[39]

In 1991, Robert Powell showed that concerns about relative advantages can be stated in standard absolute-gains terms. There is no need to include a separate term for relative gains that violates the core presumptions of rational-choice approaches. Powell showed that the importance of relative gains was conditional on the system creating "opportunities for one state to turn relative gains to its advantage and to the disadvantage of the other state," particularly through the use or threat of force.[40] The

---

[35] Gowa, "Anarchy, Egoism and Third Images," 177, quoting Waltz, *Theory of International Politics*, p. 105.

[36] Joseph Grieco, "Anarchy and the Limits of Cooperation: A Realist Critique of the Newest Liberal Institutionalism," *International Organization* 42 (1988), 485–507.

[37] Jack Knight, *Institutions and Social Conflict* (New York: Cambridge University Press, 1992).

[38] Grieco, "Anarchy and the Limits of Cooperation," 499.

[39] See John J. Mearsheimer, "The False Promise of International Institutions," *International Security* 19 (1994/95), 5–49.

[40] Robert Powell, "Absolute and Relative Gains in International Relations Theory," *American Political Science Review* (1991), 1303–20, reprinted in David Baldwin (ed.), *Neorealism and Neoliberalism: The Contemporary Debate* (New York: Columbia

critics who had raised the issue of relative gains were correct that such competition could impede cooperation, but they had over-generalized their argument. After Powell's clarification, the key question became the empirical one of identifying conditions under which one party could use asymmetrical gains to change the structure of the game to the disadvantage of its partner. Later work by George Downs and his colleagues pointed out that concerns about noncompliance could render cooperation shallow, relative to what would have been optimal in the absence of such concerns.[41]

The relative-gains debate gave rise to much unproductive argument and research; it did lead, though, to some clarification and development of institutional theory. Although institutional theory depends on common interests, one had never assumed that these interests must be equal or symmetrical.[42] The relative-gains debate forced institutional theorists to recognize explicitly that substantially unequal distribution of the benefits of cooperation could provide one partner with the wherewithal to fundamentally change the nature of the game, for example by starting a war. Insofar as this possibility exists, a model such as iterated Prisoner's Dilemma could be faulty. The probability that one partner could fundamentally reshape the nature of the situation must be incorporated into each state's utility function. However, as institutional theory emphasized, the probability that unequal gains would lead to a fundamental restructuring of the game varies; it is often low. Whether actors weigh others' gains positively or negatively is also a variable. Hence the extent to which concerns about others' gains might undermine cooperation must therefore also be treated as a variable – precisely as institutional theory had always prescribed.[43] Institutional theory also responded by noting that an important function of international institutions might be to mitigate relative-gains concerns by assuring a fairly equitable distribution of the gains from cooperation,

---

University Press, 1993), p. 1315. It has become very clear over the last decade that it would be a mistake to characterize security issues as necessarily more conflictual than economic ones. Empirically, security relationships between the United States and Japan, or the United States and Germany, have often been less conflictual than their economic relations. Based on institutional theory, we should expect more conflict in economic areas characterized by oligopolistic competition and first-mover advantages than in economic areas characterized by fragmented markets, and we should expect more conflict between potential adversaries than in security communities. For a fuller discussion, see Keohane, "Theory of World Politics."

[41] George W. Downs, David M. Rocke, and Peter N. Barsoom, "Is the Good News about Compliance Good News about Cooperation?" *International Organization* 50 (1996), 379–406.

[42] Keohane and Nye, *Power and Interdependence.*

[43] Keohane, *After Hegemony*, p. 123.

particularly where a highly asymmetrical distribution of gains could undermine support for existing institutions by changing the structure of the game. Thus, in spite of some dead ends and fruitless debates, the relative-gains conceptual challenge strengthened institutional theory. In Lakatosian terms, this strengthening occurred because institutional theory was able to respond effectively to the relative-gains challenge without altering its hard core.[44]

Some realists also presented an empirical challenge to institutional theory, based on predictions about the future of international institutions in Europe after the Cold War. John Mearsheimer quickly and boldly used Waltz's neorealist theory and Grieco's argument about relative gains to predict increased conflict and even war in Europe.[45] Mearsheimer's logic emphasized that states' concern with security in an anarchic world compelled them to put little confidence in international institutions. Post-World War II institutions rested on the power realities of the Cold War: US dominance of a Western alliance confronting a hostile Soviet bloc. Once these power realities were transformed with the end of the Cold War, intense patterns of conflict among European states would resume, he argued, increasing the chances of major crisis and war in Europe. NATO and the European Community would both be victims of these changes: "It is the Soviet threat that provides the glue that holds NATO together. Take away that offensive threat and the United States is likely to abandon the Continent, whereupon the defensive alliance it has headed for forty years may disintegrate."[46] With the departure of American forces, "relations among the European Community (EC) states will be fundamentally altered. Without a common Soviet threat and without the American night watchman, Western European states will begin viewing each other with greater fear and suspicion."[47]

Empirical evidence in the subsequent period did not support Mearsheimer's predictions. The European Union has become wider and deeper, and is in most respects stronger than ever, despite struggles associated with the inauguration of European Monetary Union (EMU) and with the "democratic deficit" implied by the weakness of the European Parliament compared to the Council of Ministers and the European Commission. Since international cooperation always arises from discord – and is never harmonious – institutionalists are not distracted by bargaining conflict, but focus on the institutional deepening

---

[44] The convergence that resulted from this debate supports the call of this volume's editors for tolerance as well as tenacity.

[45] Mearsheimer, "Back to the Future."

[46] Ibid., 52.   [47] Ibid., 47.

of the European Union during the 1990s.[48] The EMU itself transforms traditional state sovereignty and is entirely inconsistent with the realist vision of a collapsing European Union. NATO, while it experienced wrenching debates and a genuine crisis over intervention in the former Yugoslavia, played a decisive role in bringing the Bosnian war to an end in 1995.[49] In seeking to protect Albanian Kosovars, it extended its scope to offensive warfare, taking on new responsibilities and engaging in a high-risk transformation. Whether NATO's actions are wise or not, this institution is certainly a force to be reckoned with.

Thus, institutional theory has responded effectively to realism, with responses that are theoretically and empirically productive. Its response to the relative-gains attack has led to an increased focus on distributional impediments to cooperation, without requiring any changes in the hard core of institutional theory. The response to the empirical challenge did not require even modest changes in the focus of institutional theory. Instead, institutional theory's longstanding claim that established institutions should become especially valuable in the face of increased uncertainty has been borne out by events in Europe. The membership and operating procedures of European institutions have undergone important changes that allow them to respond more effectively to the new realities of European politics. These changes have taken place within the context of well-established, long-lived institutions, which have proven their worth in enhancing security and providing economic assurances in an increasingly uncertain environment. Thus, by the early 1990s, institutional theory had established itself as a respected "generic approach" to issues of international cooperation.[50] Its key insights about the functioning of international institutions concerned their role in providing information and their reliance on reciprocity as the mechanism for sustaining cooperation.

Attempts at synthesis

In the early 1990s, realism was unable to deny the reality of institutionalized cooperation, but had no theory to explain it. According to an old saying, "you can't beat something with nothing." On the whole, the prevailing response of realists, as represented, for instance, in the work

---

[48] See Andrew Moravcsik, *The Choice for Europe: Social Purpose and State Power from Messina to Maastricht* (Ithaca: Cornell University Press, 1998).
[49] Richard Holbrooke, *To End a War* (New York: Random House, 1998).
[50] Peter J. Katzenstein, Robert O. Keohane, and Stephen D. Krasner, "*International Organization* and the Study of World Politics," *International Organization* 52 (1998), 645–85.

of Stephen Krasner, has been increasingly to embrace institutionalist arguments while continuing to insist that distributional conflict and power should be emphasized. But there has been at least one valiant attempt, by Joseph Grieco, to construct a distinctively "realist theory" of cooperation.[51] Some of the most compelling critiques of institutional theory have come not from realism but from students of domestic politics, who have challenged the shared states-as-actors assumption of realism and institutional theory, and suggested the need for synthesis of a different sort.

As we have seen, Krasner criticized institutional theory for emphasizing attempts to reach the Pareto frontier, at the expense of analyzing distributional conflict along that frontier.[52] James Fearon has more recently argued that problems of distributional bargaining may prevent the formation of agreements, especially if the "shadow of the future" is long: if remote gains and losses loom large.[53] These are important points with which institutional theory must contend.

It is important to note, however, that institutional theory never denied the reality of distributional bargaining. Indeed, in *After Hegemony*, Keohane defined cooperation as mutual adjustment of interests, hence inherently conflictual: "cooperation is typically mixed with conflict and reflects partially successful efforts to overcome conflict, real or potential."[54] The original purpose of institutional theory was to show how, despite the fragmented political structure of international relations, and the pervasiveness of conflicts of interests and discord, cooperation can nevertheless, under some conditions, occur. However, the conflict of interests emphasized by institutional theory was that based on the fear that others would renege on cooperative arrangements, rather than on how to distribute the benefits of cooperation. Fear of reneging exists even among identical players; all are properly fearful of receiving the "sucker's payoff." The problem of distributing the benefits of cooperation, in contrast, is more pronounced when the interests of states are asymmetrical, for example when powerful states interact with weaker ones. In this instance, states will have strongly diverging preferences over the form of cooperation, creating a type of conflict of interest that was originally neglected by institutionalist theory. Over time, empirical and theoretical work has shown the importance of such asymmetries.

---

[51] Grieco, "Anarchy and the Limits of Cooperation."
[52] Krasner, "Global Communications and National Power."
[53] James D. Fearon, "Bargaining, Enforcement, and International Cooperation," *International Organization* 52 (1998), 269–305.
[54] Keohane, *After Hegemony*, p. 54.

Institutional theory's treatment of distributional conflict sheds light on its relationship to classic liberalism, as well as to realism. Often institutional theory is viewed as "liberal international relations theory," and liberalism is thought of as an optimistic creed that stresses harmony over conflict. Either of these propositions could be correct, but not both.

There is a form of liberalism – associated with writers such as James Madison, Adam Smith, and Immanuel Kant – that is individualistic and rationalistic without being optimistic about human nature or believing in harmony. Madison famously declared government to be "the greatest of all reflections on human nature."[55] Kant wrote of "the evil nature of man."[56] Smith counseled his readers that it is vain to expect help from the "benevolence" of others in society.[57] Anyone who regards these liberals as idealistic utopians has not read their work. All of these writers believed that some individuals are public-spirited, but that, as Madison said, "enlightened statesmen will not always be at the helm."[58] Institutional theory certainly falls within this tradition. It regards people as occasionally empathetic and public-spirited, but builds its theory on the assumption that, in general, while they are rational, they lack general benevolence, altruism, or idealism. Institutional theory has little in common with the optimistic liberal creed caricatured by E. H. Carr or Kenneth Waltz.[59] On the contrary, institutional theory assumes that cooperation derives from conflicts of objectives that are inherent in social life. "Harmony is apolitical.... Cooperation, by contrast, is highly political."[60]

Institutional theory recognizes distributional conflicts but, unlike realism, is not obsessed with them. It has been fairly criticized for not integrating distributional politics into its analysis: for taking such conflict for granted rather than developing theories about it. Issues of distribution were recognized as important, but remained outside the theory that generated hypotheses about institutions, which relied on the desire of participants to capture potential joint gains more than on

---

[55] James Madison, *The Federalist Nos. 10 and 51* (1787), in Jacob E. Cooke (ed.), *Alexander Hamilton, James Madison, and John Jay, The Federalist* (Middletown: Wesleyan University Press, 1961), p. 349.

[56] Immanuel Kant, "Eternal Peace" (1795), in Carl J. Friedrich (ed.), *The Philosophy of Kant* (New York: Modern Library, 1949), p. 442.

[57] Adam Smith, *The Wealth of Nations* (1776) (University of Chicago Press, 1976), p. 18.

[58] Madison, *The Federalist Nos. 10 and 51*, p. 60.

[59] Carr, *The Twenty Years' Crisis, 1919–1939*; Kenneth Waltz, *Man, the State and War* (New York: Columbia University Press, 1959).

[60] Keohane, *After Hegemony*, p. 53.

their struggle to capture larger shares of the reward. To develop progressively, institutional theory must do a better job of integrating distributional struggles "along the Pareto frontier" with efforts to move that frontier outward.

A realist theory of "binding"

In 1995, Joseph Grieco forthrightly confronted the anomalies facing realism, a theoretical framework to which he was committed.[61] Explicitly employing a Lakatosian framework, Grieco recognized that plans for EMU were anomalous for realism: "The decision by the EC countries to pursue the Maastricht path toward EMU conflicts with neo-realism's auxiliary hypothesis that states do not ascribe importance to institutions. It also conflicts with the neo-realist hypothesis that EC efforts at cooperation have been dependent upon U.S.–Soviet bipolarity."[62]

Grieco deserves great credit for identifying the anomaly that EMU posed for realism, and for trying to deal with it. Grieco's approach was to identify what he regarded as "auxiliary hypotheses" of realism about international institutions, and to propose their modification: "One is that states find it hard (but not impossible) to work together because of fears about cheating, dependency, and relative gains. Another is that international institutions are unable to dampen these state fears substantially, and therefore states do not ascribe much importance to them."[63]

Grieco's response was a "voice opportunities" thesis, which emphasized the desire of weaker states, under conditions of interdependence, to have a voice in decisions. This thesis "assumes that states favor institutionalized ties with a stronger partner as a way of allowing them to work for mutual gain and to avoid becoming a vassal of the partner."[64] In other words, weak states will use institutions to bind stronger states. In his article, Grieco briefly applied this theory, which he described as "derived from core realist assumptions," to the negotiations over EMU at Maastricht.

Grieco's honesty is commendable, but the irony of his analysis is equally notable. His "voice opportunities" thesis is institutionalist in all essentials. It incorporates the institutionalist stress on self-interest and mutual gain, and jettisons his earlier argument, which he attributed to realism, that "the fundamental goal of states in any relationship is to

---

[61] Grieco, "The Maastricht Treaty, Economic and Monetary Union, and the Neo-Realist Research Program."
[62] Ibid., 32. [63] Ibid., 27. [64] Ibid., 34.

prevent others from achieving advances in their relative capabilities."[65] The voice opportunities thesis is no more closely linked to core realist assumptions than is institutionalism: in fact, both arguments share the three key assumptions of realism stated above. To adherents of a research program, there is no support more welcome than that of former adversaries.[66]

Institutional theory and domestic politics

The most telling recent criticisms of institutional theory have attacked its weakest link: the unitary actor assumption, borrowed from realism. Institutional theory has all the limitations of any research program that takes actors and preferences as given. Scholars such as Andrew Moravcsik and Helen Milner have emphasized that the unitary actor assumption "leads to a neglect of the differences in internal preferences and political institutions within states."[67] Such an assumption also makes it difficult to think about how state institutions, such as legislative arrangements for monitoring international agreements, can be endogenous to patterns of delegation to international institutions. For example, variation in implementation of EU directives by states can be explained well only by taking into account variation in legislative arrangements, which are partly endogenous to the overall patterns of EU delegation.[68]

Institutional theory does help us explain state strategies, since those strategies are affected not only by fundamental preferences but by the constraints and opportunities in their environment, including those provided by international institutions. But institutional theory does not account for more fundamental preferences over outcomes: for instance, for compromising with neighbors who have different values and habits from one's own, or seeking instead to annihilate them or evict them from their homes.

---

[65] Grieco, "Anarchy and the Limits of Cooperation," 498.

[66] We also found it gratifying that Stephen Krasner emerged as a forceful, eloquent defender of institutionalist theory at the Scottsdale conference, especially emphasizing recent arguments to the effect that institutions may provide critical credibility for states.

[67] Helen V. Milner, "Rationalizing Politics: The Emerging Synthesis in International, American and Comparative Politics," *International Organization* 42 (1998), 772. See also Andrew Moravcsik, "A Liberal Theory of International Politics," *International Organization* 51 (1997), 513–53.

[68] Lisa L. Martin, *Democratic Commitments: Legislatures and International Cooperation* (Princeton University Press, 1999).

For IR theory to make really significant progress, it will need to go beyond institutional theory's analysis of institutional strategies to explain variations in state preferences. One way of doing so would be to develop theories with microfoundations: that is, theories that begin with individuals and groups and show how, on the basis of a coherent set of theoretical assumptions, varying preferences emerge.[69] Such theories would build on modern work on domestic institutions. Another approach would be to demonstrate how variations in the social construction of reality, as a result of ideas and identity, account for variations in preferences.[70]

In this broader understanding of international relations, institutional theory – and realism itself – will be important, since one needs an instrumental theory to get from preferences to policies. But they will not be sufficient, since preferences vary in important ways. Constructivists and liberals emphasizing domestic politics seek to "explicate variations in preferences, available strategies, and the nature of the players, across space and time," while rationalists try "to explain strategies, give preferences, information, and common knowledge. Neither project can be complete without the other."[71]

The endogeneity trap and the delegation escape

We have argued that institutional theory was able to turn the relative-gains challenge by realists into a confirmation rather than a refutation of institutional theory. Evidence of hard bargaining and disputes over the distribution of gains are in fact consistent with the conventional utilitarianism accepted by institutional theory, and do not require the additional (and confusing) assumption of concern for relative gains. Indeed, some of the observed activities of international institutions could be interpreted as designed to respond to the danger that asymmetrical bargaining outcomes could undermine states' support for institutions. Furthermore, the empirical predictions that Mearsheimer made in 1990, on the basis of his interpretation of neorealist theory, turned out to be much less consistent with emerging reality than institutionalist expectations.

---

[69] Moravcsik, "A Liberal Theory of International Politics"; Lisa L. Martin and Beth Simmons, "Theories and Empirical Studies of International Institutions," *International Organization* 52 (1998); Milner, "Rationalizing Politics"; Martin, *Democratic Commitments*.

[70] Alexander Wendt, *Social Theory of International Politics* (Cambridge University Press, 1999).

[71] Katzenstein *et al.*, "*International Organization* and the Study of World Politics," 682.

However, Mearsheimer raised a deeper theoretical and methodological challenge, although it was largely implicit in his argument. International institutions, he argued, "have minimal influence on state behavior," partly because "the most powerful states create and shape institutions."[72] State security interests, not institutions, account for the cooperation observed during the Cold War; hence, in Mearsheimer's view, international institutions are epiphenomenal.

Mearsheimer's logic drew directly on Waltz's theory and Grieco's application of it, emphasizing the weak nature of international institutions and the need for states to be obsessed with short-term security demands, hence with relative gains. Although he did not use this language, Mearsheimer suggested that international institutions are endogenous to state power and interests. The underlying claim was that international institutions are endogenous to international structure.

This charge is difficult for institutionalists to disprove, since it closely parallels the claims of institutionalist theory, and indeed may seem to follow directly from institutional theory's "hard core." Recall the five key assumptions of institutional theory, the first four of which are identical with neorealist assumptions: (1) states are the primary actors in world politics; (2) states behave as if they were rational utility-maximizers; (3) states pursue their interests (especially survival) rather than behaving altruistically; (4) no external enforcer of agreements exists; and (5) because they operate in an information-scarce environment, states have incentives to increase both their information about other states' actions, and their own credibility. These assumptions generate a "functional theory of international regimes": that these rational actors will devise institutions that meet their informational demands.[73] But at the limit, this functional theory of international institutions implies complete endogeneity: the theory is strongest when institutions are entirely explained by state interests and strategies.

This endogeneity, which constitutes such a strength from the standpoint of explaining institutions, seems to turn into a weakness in claiming that institutions have significant effects. Insofar as the theory of institutional origins and functions is accepted, the independent explanatory power of institutional theory seems to disappear. The structural factors accounting for institutions also seem to account for outcomes – which should therefore be seen not as effects of the institutions, but of these more fundamental factors.

---

[72] Mearsheimer, "The False Promise of International Institutions," 7, 13.
[73] Keohane, *After Hegemony*, chp. 6.

Institutional theory has not yet responded very well to this fundamental challenge. Institutional theory needs somehow to confront it in order to continue in a progressive direction. We suggest in this chapter a problemshift designed to resolve this problem, although we do not pursue this argument in detail. The problemshift that we propose makes agency theory central in international institutionalist theory, reconceptualizing the relationship between states and international institutions as one of delegation. We think that theories of agency, or delegation, may help provide an answer to the endogeneity conundrum. These theories allow us to take the endogeneity issue seriously, while integrating it in a productive manner into the research program. We characterize such a problemshift as "intra-program," since we retain the hard core of institutionalist theory as specified above.

Endogenous, yes; but epiphenomenal?

Institutional theory views international organizations as endogenous to state interests and strategies, but this does not mean that their organizational characteristics are irrelevant. Endogenous does not mean epiphenomenal. Thinking about institutions both in terms of organization theory and of agency theory highlights this important point.[74] We focus on organizations rather than on regimes and conventions, since organizations have the capacity to act, and organization theory can be used to analyze how their actions may diverge from the intentions of their founders. Regimes and conventions, being less formal than organizations, cannot rely as heavily on organizational dynamics to explain their persistence.

Three different sets of social science arguments help us to understand how international organizations that are created by, and beholden to, states can still exercise independent influence over events. The first argument concerns the multiple equilibria characteristic of non-zero-sum games; the second draws on organization theory; the third focuses on agency theory. We briefly indicate how each of these arguments may create space for significant action by international organizations.

The existence of multiple equilibria in game-theoretic solutions to virtually all interesting games opens up space for agency: structure, as game theory's folk theorem has taught us, is not determining, since rational players can, in equilibrium, pursue quite different

---

[74] Kenneth Abbott and Duncan Snidal have emphasized the role of international institutions as active organizations, although without using agency theory. Kenneth Abbott and Duncan Snidal, "Why States Use Formal International Organizations," *Journal of Conflict Resolution* 42 (1998), 3–32.

strategies.[75] Multiple equilibria are bad for game-theoretic solutions to problems of cooperation, but they are good for institutional theory. If game theory could pinpoint unique equilibria on the basis of structural theory, institutions could be seen simply as these equilibrium solutions.[76] They would not only be endogenous to structure, but epiphenomenal, since structure would be determining. But the existence of multiple equilibria means both that institutional characteristics cannot be predicted reliably from structure and that, once formed, institutions can have a major impact on which equilibria emerge. This impact derives from the tendency of institutions to persist over time, leading to the sort of path-dependence about which Douglass North has written so convincingly.[77] In delegation terms, the implication of multiple equilibria is that states could have an incentive to delegate authority to an agent, if they find: (a) that they cannot agree on a solution; and (b) that the agent will choose a solution that is superior for all of them to the status quo. This is a plausible way to interpret the willingness of states in Europe to agree to the extension of powers of the European Court of Justice.[78]

Organization theory points out that because institutions are costly to construct and change, and because those who design them are often risk-averse, we cannot expect institutions to change smoothly in response to changes in structural variables.[79] Like many domestic institutions, international institutions are designed at a particular time to solve a particular problem, but they can then persist and change, in a step-wise fashion rather than smoothly. Sunk costs and risk aversion help to account for the institutional inertia that is often observed. Gaps between the structure and the emerging functions of international institutions may help account for institutional failure. But when institutions remain stable in the face of changes in structural variables, we have an opportunity to observe the independent effect of institutions on

---

[75] The folk theorem shows that in games that are repeated over time, a large number of outcomes can be sustained as equilibria.

[76] Randall Calvert, "The Rational Choice Theory of Social Institutions: Cooperation, Coordination, and Communication," in Jeffrey S. Banks and Eric A. Hanushek (eds.), *Modern Political Economy: Old Topics, New Directions* (New York: Cambridge University Press, 1995), pp. 216–67.

[77] North, *Institutions, Institutional Change and Economic Performance*.

[78] Karen J. Alter, "Who are the 'Masters of the Treaty'? European Governments and the European Court of Justice," *International Organization* 52 (1998), 177–209; Geoffrey Garrett, R. Daniel Keleman, and Heiner Schulz, "The European Court of Justice, National Governments, and Legal Integration in the European Union," *International Organization* 52 (1998), 149–76; Walter Mattli and Anne-Marie Slaughter, "Revisiting the European Court of Justice," *International Organization* 52 (1998), 177–209.

[79] Keohane, *After Hegemony*, pp. 100–03.

state behavior. To take an obvious example, the structure of the United Nations Security Council, with the five victorious allies of World War II or their legal successors holding veto power, reflects the structural reality of 1945, and in some cases the aspirations, but it has had substantial effects on world politics well after that structural reality has been profoundly altered.

Another aspect of organizational stability is that legally binding actions by international organizations remain valid until they are reversed (unless a time limit has been set). Consider the UN economic sanctions established in 1990 against Iraq. These sanctions have remained in place despite widespread loss of support for them after the mid-1990s, as the humanitarian costs to the people of Iraq became obvious and as Saddam Hussein remained unswayed by them. They remained in place because of the so-called "reverse-veto procedure." Since the Security Council voted in favor of sanctions in 1990, the existing status quo throughout the 1990s was a sanctions regime. It would have required an affirmative vote of the Security Council to lift sanctions. Because the Security Council has five members with a permanent veto – most significantly the United States in this instance – one state can effectively maintain sanctions even after they have become unpopular. It would be extremely difficult to understand US policy toward Iraq, or the policies of many other states in the 1990s, without taking into account the specifics of Security Council voting rules. This case also illustrates the stability of institutions. If the United Nations were created anew today, it is highly unlikely that veto procedures, or the identity of the states with veto power, would look like the current Security Council procedures. Although the Security Council was certainly created by the great powers to serve their perceived interests, its organizational persistence means that this endogeneity of origins does not imply insignificance of effects.

Agency theory breaks the chain of endogeneity in another way. The initial assumption here is that international organizations are the agents of state interests. The powers and authority that such organizations acquire are the result of delegation of authority from their member states. Hence, the fundamental character of these organizations, when they are founded, can be explained by state interests. However, agency theory also recognizes explicitly that organizations are acting entities with leaders who have institutionally affected interests of their own – a fact that has often been obscured by the emphasis of institutional theory on structures of rules. Principals often find it useful to endow agents with discretion, and agents typically have superior information, at least about some issues, to that at the disposal of their principals. As a result, there is a potential for "agency slack" – for (admittedly endogenous) international organizations (historically and nominally creatures of states) to act independently, to some significant degree. Hence agency theory agrees with institutional theory's dual assertions: that organizations are endogenous, and that they have effects. Indeed, we think that agency theory can help to show how to transform endogeneity from a liability to an asset for institutional theory.

In institutional theory, as well as in agency theory more generally, agents take actions, which have real effects, within constraints set by their principals, whose support is essential for the agents to exist and to act. In the agency literature, outcomes are brought about jointly by principals and agents. Attention is not directed in agency theory to trying to determine which proportion of the outcomes is caused by each (as if they could be separated), but rather to analyzing the co-determination of outcomes by the rules (constraints and incentives) promulgated by the principals, and by the actions, within those constraints and incentives, taken by the agents. In effect, agency theory focuses on the processes (causal mechanisms) that generate outcomes, and seeks to understand how different conditions, by affecting those processes, affect outcomes. In this theory, endogenous organizations (the agents, coupled with the rules under which they operate) routinely have effects that cannot be reduced to the interests of the principals.

Agency theory thus allows us to direct attention away from the relatively intractable issue of ascertaining the effects of institutions, controlling for structure, toward a different set of questions: what are the conditions that affect the strategically interdependent actions of principals and agents, and therefore the outcomes (in terms of cooperation, institutional characteristics, or other dependent variables) that emerge from an agency relationship?

By turning our attention to theories of agency and delegation, we hope to make three progressive moves in the institutional theory research program. Methodologically, we hope to get around the endogeneity problem, by reframing the question of institutional effects. The issue is not "what are the effects of institutions, controlling for structure?" but rather, "what institutions emerge endogenously, and how do the resulting agency relationships affect outcomes in world politics?" This question helps to open two theoretical doors. First, it should enable us not to take institutions as given, reified entities, but instead help us to develop a theory of their development.[80] Second, using theories of

---

[80] See John Gerard Ruggie, "International Regimes, Transactions, and Change: Embedded Liberalism in the Postwar Economic Order," in Krasner (ed.), *International Regimes* (Ithaca, NY: Cornell University Press, 1983), pp. 195–231; Cederman, *Emergent Actors in World Politics*.

delegation should help us to reintegrate issues of distribution with functional theories that rely especially on the role of information in enabling independent actors to cooperate for joint gains.

The preceding paragraphs indicate why we think that the endogeneity of international institutions does not render institutional theory irrelevant. However, to avoid the endogeneity trap, we weaken the ability of structural factors to predict organizational behavior. Institutionalist theory thereby moves farther from its neorealist roots, putting more emphasis on agency, less on structure.

The argument of this section has revolved around a difficulty faced by institutional theory. Institutional theory's attempts to explain the origins and functioning of institutions have created an "endogeneity trap": it may seem that endogenous institutions cannot have the independent effects often attributed to them by institutionalists. For institutional theory to continue to be progressive, it must deal forthrightly with this problem. We have argued, on the basis of three different theoretical perspectives, that the endogeneity of international institutions to state power and interests does not render those institutions, and particularly international organizations, epiphenomenal. Multiple equilibria, organization theory, and agency theories all point to ways in which the characteristics of agents such as international organizations and the choices they make have important effects. We suggest a problemshift (in Lakatos's terms) toward viewing the relationship between states and international organizations as a problem of delegation. By so doing, we expect not only to help resolve the endogeneity anomaly, but also to generate some observable implications (in Lakatos's terms, hypotheses about "new facts") about the form of international organizations.

Conclusions: Institutions as endogenous and consequential

In Lakatosian terms, institutional theory shares much of its hard core with realism. However, institutional theory was inspired by the observation of serious anomalies in neorealist theory, and responded by changing one of the core assumptions of realism. Instead of treating information as a scarce commodity, whose provision is beyond the scope of intentional action, institutional theory treated information as a variable that could be influenced by the activities of states. This change in the hard core led to a change in the positive heuristic, directing researchers' attention to the attempts of states to improve their informational environment via the construction of international institutions.

Institutional theory has survived a number of attacks from skeptics, establishing itself at least initially as a progressive research program. The fact that it takes actors and preferences as given means that it should not be viewed as a comprehensive theory of world politics. Were it to take on such pretensions, it would be vulnerable to a powerful critique, both from theories emphasizing domestic politics and theories stressing the construction of interests and identities through human choice and human institutions. As compared to its initial rival, realism, institutional theory has empirically held up quite well, in helping us to understand how international institutions operate and the kinds of effects they exert. However, even within the limited range of its ambitions, experience over the last fifteen years reveals some serious methodological and theoretical shortcomings.

Methodologically, institutionalists have often been satisfied with "existence proofs" and weak tests of their information-oriented hypotheses about institutional action. They have found it difficult to distinguish the effects of institutions from the effects of underlying structure. More rigorous analysis that seeks to distinguish these effects is needed if institutionalist theory is to progress.

Three theoretical shortcomings of institutionalist theory are most evident. The first is that although distributional issues have been recognized from the beginning as important, they have not been adequately incorporated into institutionalist theory. This problem is not well specified by the formulation of "relative gains," but distributional issues lead to important problems of bargaining that shape the form and effects of international organizations. The second shortcoming is that institutional theory has until recently assumed that states are unitary actors. Important work is now being done to show that state preferences can be explained in ways that are consistent with, and that will enrich, institutional theory. Finally, there is the problem of endogeneity. Insofar as structures and functions explain the form and effects of international organizations, their own agency may seem to disappear – and institutionalist theory would seem to be easily folded into a more sophisticated version of structural realism. In this chapter we have relied on game theory, organization theory, and on theories of delegation to show that endogeneity – the fact that international institutions are created and maintained by states to suit their interests – does not reduce international organizations to inconsequentiality. There is space for agency: structures do not determine outcomes.

Our emphasis on organization theory and agency theory clearly refutes any suggestions that institutionalist theory assumes efficient adaptation of institutions to the circumstances of international politics. Such a claim would be inconsistent with a crucial argument of institutional theory: that the sunk costs involved in creating institutions, and the risks involved in discarding old institutions, create tendencies toward persistence of institutions even when circumstances change.[81] It would also be inconsistent with agency theory, which by no means assumes that agents' incentives will be perfectly aligned with those of principals, particularly when there are multiple principals. Taking sunk costs and agency incentives into account means that discrepancies between the "right" institution to solve a problem and the institution that is actually used may appear with some frequency: as circumstances change, institutions adapt in a "path-dependent" step-like manner, rather than smoothly. Recent institutional theory has, following work of Douglass North, clearly adopted the path-dependent rather than the functionalist-determinist position.[82] Structures, and the functions they are designed to perform, do not perfectly predict behavior, as our emphasis in this chapter on agency theory suggests.

Hence, an understanding of contemporary game theory, organization theory, and agency theory allows us to recognize the space between structure and the actions of international organizations. Actions are partially but not entirely endogenous to the power-interest structures in the neorealist sense, and to the institutional arrangements established by powerful states. Institutional design matters: institutions can be designed with built-in incentives for action consistent with designers' intentions, or they can be misdesigned. Rational anticipation ensures that there is likely to be some relationship between cooperation problems and the form of delegation, but organizational and agency problems make it likely that gaps will appear between problem and form.

In his most important argument, Imre Lakatos emphasized that progressive theories must not only patch up anomalies or apparent contradictions, but predict novel facts. Over the past fifteen years, institutional theory has predicted novel facts about the roles played by international institutions that have to some extent been corroborated. We hope that in the future its extension to politics and institutions within states will lead to further progressive explanation of important patterns of behavior in world politics.

---

[81] Keohane, *After Hegemony*, p. 102.
[82] Douglass C. North, *Structure and Change in Economic History* (New York: W. W. Norton & Company, 1981); North, *Institutions, Institutional Change and Economic Performance*.

5   Not even for the seventeenth and eighteenth
     centuries: power and order in the early
     modern era

Paul W. Schroeder

Political scientist Stanley Hoffmann once reportedly remarked that
Kenneth Waltz's structural realist or neorealist theory of international
relations[1] was a good theory for the seventeenth century. Whatever
else it might imply, as a factual statement the remark seemed accurate.
Neorealist theory, originally expounded by Waltz and now advanced in
various versions including the offensive realism of John Mearsheimer
discussed in this volume,[2] apparently fits European international politics in the early modern era especially well. The pattern of recurrent,
almost constant conflicts, crises, and wars in 1648–1789 seemed to
confirm a central neorealist principle: that interstate competition and
violent conflict derive from the systemic structure of international relations, in which various independent units in close contact and contin-
ual interaction with one another constantly compete for survival and
vital scarce resources. The system dynamics that neorealists see created by this structure also seem appropriate to this era as one in which
international anarchy, i.e., the absence of any recognized law-giver or
law-enforcing authority, compelled each unit to make its prime aim the
acquisition and exercise of power, especially military power, in order to
survive and be secure. The theory also seems to account for the principles and practices of amoral power politics that dominated the era, and
to explain its characteristic patterns of alliance and alignment: bids by
would-be hegemons and imperial powers to gain full security through
maximizing their power while weaker powers tried to survive either by
hiding from them, joining them, or coalescing and balancing against
them. In short, however it may apply to other periods in history, neorealist theory evidently fits the early modern era well.

   This chapter contends that while Hoffmann's remark is correct on
the surface about the early modern era (and also right in slyly implying
that neorealist theory does not work well for later centuries), at a deeper

[1] Waltz, *Theory of International Politics.*
[2] Mearsheimer, *The Tragedy of Great Power Politics.*

level the neorealist model, which Mearsheimer asserts in an especially uncompromising way,[3] is an unsatisfactory model for analyzing international politics even in the seventeenth and eighteenth centuries. This is a view that I have long held and occasionally expressed,[4] but here the argument will be somewhat different. My earlier contention was that whatever strengths neorealism might have for purposes of international relations theory, it would not do as a paradigm or heuristic tool for the international historian because its basic approach to international history was essentialist and unhistorical. That is, it failed to take seriously the nature of history as an account of the changes of things that change (Herbert Butterfield); it falsely rendered the central story of international history as cyclical in nature rather than directional, one of change, evolution, and development. It overlooked or downgraded the significance of major changes and developments in the basic structure, institutions, rules, and aims of international relations. It was therefore incapable of explaining how such changes were possible within the terms of structural realist theory, or of recognizing the vital differences these changes made in the actual practice of international politics and its outcomes. Hence theorists might use it and debate it if they wished, but historians should not rely on it to help solve their problems or conceive of their subject matter overall. In fact, the key historical insights come from seeing international politics as developmental in a dialectical fashion.

I still hold to this general critique and will return to some of these points later, but now believe that this critique does not go far enough, for several reasons. It invites the general reply that such criticism fails to understand the basic difference between theory and history and/or between social science and history, or how to use and do theory and social science, or what constitutes proof and disproof in them. It likewise prompts the response that neorealist theory is not intended to explain foreign policy or particular international actions and developments and their particular outcomes, much less solve questions of their historical interpretation and significance, but to establish the theoretical structure within which all such questions can be comprehended. How historians and other scholars deal with these and whether they find neorealist theory useful or not makes little difference so far as the theory is concerned. Realist political scientists may further argue that they are not ignoring or distorting historical

---

[3] Mearsheimer, *The Tragedy of Great Power Politics*, chps. 1–2.
[4] Paul W. Schroeder, "Historical Reality vs. Neo-Realist Theory," *International Security* 19 (1994), 108–48.

facts but simply stylizing and operationalizing them in ways that many historians find difficult and uncongenial, in pursuit of social scientific purposes and ends that make historians uncomfortable. Finally, given the notoriously undefined, virtually boundless and inexhaustible nature of the historical record, the multiplicity of cross-cutting and often irreconcilable narratives, viewpoints, and interpretations within it, and the unavoidable subjectivity and endless controversy that attend historiographical debate on every important issue in which historians engage, to argue simply on empirical grounds that neorealist theory unacceptably distorts history is to invite an interminable dispute over whose "facts," arguments, or interpretations are correct and decisive.

For these reasons, then, such an argument on historical evidence and inductive reasoning that neorealist theory distorts and denatures the history of international politics may be empirically sound, but has little chance of being determinative or convincing to the theory's adherents. What I propose to do here is to sketch out a somewhat different argument explaining why and how neorealist theory misunderstands the structure and therefore the history of international politics. The basic problem I see is not that neorealists (in this case Mearsheimer) do not know international history well enough or misuse and misinterpret it in the interest of their theory; even if that is true in some instances, it is not true of all, and represents at most a flaw capable of being corrected. It is that, however thorough their research and sophisticated their analysis of historical materials may be, the central neorealist concept of the structure of international politics and therefore neorealism's approach to international history are unsatisfactory because they are non-developmental and undialectical.

I mean by this that neorealist theory rests on linear, logico-deductive reasoning, almost syllogistic in form ("If A, then B and C, etc."). It starts from the assumption of anarchy and proceeds logically from this to structural responses and patterns of behavior. While it allows for considerable variation in behavior, tactics, and strategy in international politics at the unit level, depending on different individual and general historical circumstances, the basic patterns and possibilities of behavior remain fundamentally governed by the structural constraints and driving force of anarchy and the imperatives it imposes on actors as a condition of their survival in the resultant struggle for power. Mearsheimer is commendably forthright and uncompromising on this score, above all in his insistence that the system structure drives great powers to be eternally suspicious of other powers and therefore to try consistently to maximize their power.

Many scholars have criticized neorealism's insistence on the structural primacy of power politics – social constructivists by redefining anarchy and its imperatives;[5] liberal internationalists and idealists of various kinds urging the importance of other drives and motivations; institutionalists stressing the role of institutions, norms, rules, and practices; Marxists and others positing other, more fundamental societal structures governing international and domestic politics; historians insisting on historical contingency and on the importance of inductive reasoning based on rigorous research into the historical evidence, etc. But to all these objections, neorealists, including some moderate defensive ones, can reply that while other factors influence the course of international politics and certainly are important in understanding its history in detail, the fundamental dynamics of the system are still determined by structural anarchy – and like Mearsheimer point to the persistence of an ongoing struggle for power as evidence.

I contend that even if anarchy as earlier defined is recognized and accepted as structural in international politics (i.e., not fundamentally annulled or mitigated by developments within states or society), the response of units to this condition of anarchy is not, never has been, and never will be an essentially simple and straightforward struggle for power for purposes of survival and security, and cannot even for theoretical purposes be reduced to this. The response to anarchy instead is and always has been profoundly dialectical and developmental.

The same structure of anarchy that compels units that wish to survive and flourish in the international system to engage in a perennial struggle for power likewise drives them with equal force to engage in a perennial quest for order. The dialectic applies equally to suspicion and trust. The state of anarchy that impels states constantly to be on their guard against one another likewise compels them to try to devise various ways – rules, norms, practices, conventions, institutions – that enable them rationally and prudently to trust one another (i.e., to be able to rely on and make reliable calculations about one another, engage in common practices and performances with some measure of predictable response and reciprocity, and pursue some means of cooperation with one another). Without that minimal kind of trust, as someone has said, one could not even get out of bed in the morning, much less engage in international politics.[6] The two imperatives of power and order are

[5] See particularly Wendt, *Social Theory of International Politics*, and (with vastly greater attention to historical evidence), Richard Ned Lebow, *A Cultural Theory of International Relations* (Cambridge University Press, 2008).
[6] Geoffrey Hosking, "Trust and Distrust: A Suitable Theme for Historians?" *Transactions of the Royal Historical Society* 16 (2006), 95–116.

equally important and necessary; the two broad responses, springing from the same source, do not really represent different choices or alternatives in policy, but are so inextricably intertwined and interacting that it is almost impossible to separate them entirely in practice, and often difficult to distinguish whether a particular action or policy belongs more to the struggle for power or to the quest for order. Usually it partakes of both. Thus the logic suggested by the structure of anarchy may be linear, but the dynamics it engenders are profoundly dialectical, which makes the central task of understanding international politics, both theoretically and historically, one of tracing the actual, historical, dialectical interactions between the struggle for power and the quest for order that form its core.

This is not an attempt to develop a profound new insight, but rather to state an almost embarrassingly simple idea, so obvious that I may appear to be lecturing professors of literature on rudimentary rules of grammar. Yet the point seems to have been widely overlooked or, when recognized, brushed aside. Of course students of international relations of all kinds, theorists, social scientists, and historians alike, know about the search for order in international relations, and frequently analyze and discuss it. It is a favorite topic for members of the so-called English School, classical realists, and students of peace movements, international institutions, international law, economic integration and interdependence, rules and norms, and other themes. Structural realists, including Mearsheimer, do not deny that there has been a quest for order and may concede that it makes some difference in the history of international politics, but insist that it is not structural. In the long run and final analysis the struggle for power is decisive.[7] Even moderate, defensive realists tend to regard the quest for order as ancillary to the great power struggle for power, consisting of efforts to moderate it, cut its costs, limit and terminate particular wars, promote cooperation, and work toward greater peace and justice. Springing in good part from idealistic or humanitarian motives, these efforts fail to abolish or supplant the struggle for power, and when push comes to shove yield to the latter as the primary great power strategy for survival and prosperity.

My argument concerns not the relative importance or primacy of the two at any particular time, but their essential nature and relationship. It contends that the quest for order is the inseparable Siamese twin of the struggle for power, born of exactly the same dilemma and drive for security and survival, using many of the same devices, strategies, and

---

[7] Once again Mearsheimer makes this argument particularly forcefully (*The Tragedy of Great Power Politics*, pp. 29–54).

means, and seeking much the same ends. The thesis in a nutshell is that the structural anarchy of international politics (as earlier defined) simultaneously generates both a struggle for power and a quest for order; that both are constants, always present and interacting, dialectically related and inseparable. I further contend that while each can predominate at different times and over different periods, over the centuries the struggle for power has remained basically cyclical and unchanging, while the quest for order has constantly changed and developed, becoming more complex and growing stronger and more prominent. This suggests that the latter, however recessive and secondary it might once have been, could conceivably become over time the dominant partner in the dialectical relationship.

This chapter will have to indicate how this dialectic can be envisioned and why and how it works. This involves huge difficulties and obstacles, the first being limits of space. I must deal with an enormous topic, the international politics of the seventeenth and eighteenth centuries, involving many major components and subtopics, each complex and controversial, within the span of a fairly short chapter. A decent historical exposition of the case would require a book much longer than Mearsheimer's. What I will present here is therefore only a bare-boned prima facie case, full of lacunae, sweeping generalizations, apodictic assertions, and major omissions, undergirded with only a minimum of footnotes and references to the enormous historical literature. Think of it as no more than a state's attorney's opening argument to a grand jury on why he seeks an indictment.

A second difficulty lies in my limitations as an historian. My specialty in international history has been the late eighteenth, nineteenth, and early twentieth centuries. I have read fairly widely on earlier centuries but am not expert in them. My argument, insofar as it concerns details of fact and interpretation, is therefore provisional and subject to revision and correction.[8]

---

[8] This admission serves to answer a plausible objection that it is unfair for me to challenge Mearsheimer's theory on the basis of a period not examined in his book. The reverse is the case; looking at the early modern era favors his case in two respects. First, I know more about the modern era and would find it easier to challenge his thesis, thereby pointing out numerous exaggerations, distortions, omissions, and untenable factual assertions in his account of the modern era, and by showing how the two eras differ in character. For example, the heart of his argument, constantly repeated, is that the historical record proves that great powers are consistently driven to maximize their power. This generalization appears prima facie true for the early modern era, as I will show. It is highly dubious, however, for most of the nineteenth century. Even the great powers that Mearsheimer looks at (Britain, Russia, Bismarck's Germany) generally aimed to satisfice rather than maximize in terms of their power, and the great powers he does not examine (France, pre-Bismarckian Prussia, and in particular the

The third challenge is one I deliberately chose – the character of early modern European international politics. This was by all accounts a very chaotic, disorderly, war-prone era. The most obvious indicators of this are its major, prolonged systemic wars involving most or all the great powers and many smaller ones, usually fought to the point of exhaustion and far beyond the point of diminishing returns, ending often with peace treaties that brought not peace but only a truce before the next contest.[9] The era was also marked by the rise of princely absolutism,[10] professional standing armies,[11] and the fiscal-military state,[12] in which demands of war largely drove the bureaucratic and administrative expansion of royal authority and reforms served mainly to increase the state's extractive power. For most of the era a representational court culture prevailed, stressing the military glory and power of the monarch and making the conquest of territory a moral and political mandate.[13] Over

---

Habsburg Monarchy) usually aimed above all to maintain the general status quo even in times of crisis or war, seeking to expand their power, if at all, only within narrow limits for the purpose of maintaining the existing order.

[9] Merely listing the dates of the more important wars give some indication of the bellicism of the era: 1618–48 (not finally over until 1659); 1672–79; 1688–97; 1702–13 (in Western and Central Europe); 1700–21 (in Northern and Eastern Europe); 1733–35; 1740–48; 1756–63; 1768–74; 1775–83; and (the bridge to the modern era) 1787–1815. Of these, all but one (1733–35) were systemic wars in the sense of involving most or all of the major powers, and five can be termed world wars in the sense that the fighting and the stakes at issue extended far beyond Europe.

[10] On the controversy over the meaning, rise, and extent of princely absolutism, see Nicholas Henshall, *The Myth of Absolutism: Change and Continuity in Early European Monarchy* (London: Longmans, 1992); Ronald G. Asch and Heinz Duchhardt (eds.), *Der Absolutismus – Ein Mythos? Strukturwandel monarchischer Herrschaft* (Cologne: Böhlau, 1996). For discussion of the warlike disposition of princely states, see Johannes Kunisch, *Fürst, Gesellschaft, Krieg: Studien zur bellizistischen Disposition des absoluten Fürstenstaates* (Cologne: Böhlau, 1992).

[11] Fritz Redlich, *The German Military Enterpriser and His Work Force*, 2 vols. (Wiesbaden: F. Steiner, 1964–65); John Lynn, *Giant of the Grand Siècle: The French Army, 1610–1715* (Cambridge University Press, 1997); Jeremy Black (ed.), *The Origins of War in Early Modern Europe* (Edinburgh: Donald, 1987); Jeremy Black (ed.), *European Warfare 1453–1815* (New York: St. Martin's Press, 1999); David Parrott, *Richelieu's Army: War, Government, and Society in France, 1624–1642* (Cambridge University Press, 2001).

[12] John Brewer, *The Sinews of Power: War, Money and the English State, 1688–1783* (New York: Alfred A. Knopf, 1989); P. G. M. Dickson, *Finance and Government under Maria Theresa, 1740–1780*, 2 vols. (Oxford University Press, 1987); Jan Glete, *War and the State in Early Modern Europe: Spain, the Dutch Republic and Sweden as Fiscal-Military States, 1500–1660* (London: Routledge, 2002). An excellent summary and interpretation is Hamish Scott, "The Fiscal-Military State and International Rivalry during the Long Eighteenth Century," in Christopher Storrs (ed.), *The Fiscal-Military State in Eighteenth-Century Europe: Essays in honour of P. G. M. Dickson* (Aldershot: Ashgate Publishing, 2009), pp. 23–54.

[13] T. C. W. Blanning, *The Culture of Power and the Power of Culture: Old Regime Europe 1660–1789* (Oxford University Press, 2002); Hamish Scott and Brendan Simms (eds.),

its course, Machiavellian *raison d'état* gained the ascendancy in theory and practice over religious, moral, and legal scruple.[14] Divine right and dynastic succession served as the main principles for determining the legitimate possession of territory and authority and virtually guaranteed that conflicts and wars would arise over inheritance rights.[15] One could go on. If, therefore, one could plausibly show that even in this bellicist, disorderly era dominated by struggles for power, a quest for order and for more rationality and calculability in international relations was also at work, so intertwined with and inseparable from the struggle for power that neither can be correctly understood without the other, this would present a serious historical challenge to neorealist theory.[16]

Doing this even in the sketchy prima facie fashion promised, however, requires showing that the international system changed and developed in the early modern era in ways that can legitimately be termed systemic and structural. This means indicating how these changes were endogenous and purposive – i.e., that even though they were connected with and influenced by changed external circumstances and broader societal developments, they basically represented conscious efforts to make the practice of international politics more orderly, predictable, and subject to rational control. It requires further showing that these efforts were at least partly successful; and, finally, that they represented a collective response to the challenges and dangers of international politics created by systemic structural anarchy – a response just as natural and central as the struggle for power, and inseparably intertwined with the latter.

To repeat, this is a tall order that can be met here only in a preliminary, highly compressed and oversimplified way. If the chapter as a whole is like a state's attorney's opening argument, this part will resemble newspaper reports consisting solely of the headline and the opening paragraph. It will look at various aspects of the practice of international politics and describe briefly how these changed between 1648 and 1789

Cultures of Power in Europe during the Long Eighteenth Century (Cambridge University Press, 2007).

[14] Richard Tuck, *The Rights of War and Peace: Political Thought and the International Order from Grotius to Kant* (Oxford University Press, 1999); Robert Bireley, *The Counter-Reformation Prince: Anti-Machiavellianism or Catholic Statecraft in Early Modern Europe* (Chapel Hill: University of North Carolina Press, 1990).

[15] Johannes Kunisch, *Staatsverfassung und Mächtepolitik. Zur Genese von Staatenkonflikten im Zeitalter des Absolutismus* (Berlin: Duncker and Humblot, 1979).

[16] This claim and argument are not at all original; in advancing them, I acknowledge a debt to many European historians, especially in Germany, who have long researched and analyzed the early modern power–order dialectic. What I assert here may seem to them hardly more than a collection of truisms. For an overview of the huge literature, see Heinz Duchhardt (ed.), *Zwischenstaatliche Friedenswahrung im Mittelalter und früher Neuzeit* (Cologne: Böhlau, 1991).

and how this reflected a quest for order along with a struggle for power. The main aspects touched on include the role of religion; the rules, institutions, and practices of diplomacy; the constitution and recognition of legitimate state actors; the territorial scope, coherence, and stability of the system; the relations between greater and lesser powers and between state and non-state actors; the roles of trade and commerce, including overseas expansion and empire; the ideology and reigning ethos of the system; and finally the nature and conduct of war.

The change easiest to detect and most dramatic lies in the role of religion. The last half of the sixteenth and first half of the seventeenth centuries (conventionally, 1562–1648) were dominated by religious wars, both civil and international. There is much room for debate over how direct and primary a cause of war religious and confessional differences and hostility were, but no question of their importance as a leading factor. By the end of the eighteenth century the situation had decisively changed. The days when a state might go to war primarily or in large part to defend or spread its particular confession, punish heresy, unite Christendom, or defend it against non-Christian enemies was over.[17] It is tempting to ascribe this momentous change in international politics simply to changes in societal thought and attitudes over time – the exhaustion of religious passions, the growth of toleration, the acceptance of confessional differences, creeping secularization, attacks on the churches and traditional religion by Enlightenment philosophers and reforming statesmen, and the growth of national and state identity at the expense of religion. The reality is different and paradoxical. As scholars have shown, the eighteenth century was not only one of growing religious toleration, secularization, and critiques and attacks on the church, but also one of religious revival and renewed fervor.[18] In numerous important cases, national or ethnic identity became more closely united with religion and confession.[19] More important still for international politics, there could be no question in the seventeenth

---

[17] In symbolic indication of this, the Popes, who for centuries had called for crusades to liberate the Holy Land from the Ottoman Turks in hopes of reuniting Christendom under their authority and turning fratricidal European wars into holy wars, finally, with the outbreak of the Seven Years War in 1756, abandoned the appeal. Johannes Burckhardt, *Abschied vom Religionskrieg: Der Siebenjährige Krieg und die päpstliche Diplomatie* (Tübingen: Max Niemeyer, 1985).

[18] Derek Beales, *Enlightenment and Reform in Eighteenth-Century Europe* (London: I. B. Tauris, 2005); Tim Blanning, *The Pursuit of Glory. Europe 1648–1815* (London: Allan Lane, 2007), pp. 355–92.

[19] For example, in Britain – Linda Colley, *Britons: Forging the Nation, 1707–1837* (New Haven: Yale University Press, 1992); J. C. D. Clark, *English Society, 1660–1832: Religion, Ideology, and Politics during the Ancien Regime* (Cambridge University Press, 2000).

and eighteenth centuries of solving the problem of religion as a source of international conflict by separating religion and politics, church and state, or even by weakening the role and influence of the former, because the states and their rulers required religion and the church to establish and legitimate their authority and relied on them for indispensable help in state-building, social discipline, and social, economic, and cultural development.

In other words, religion ceased in the latter half of the eighteenth century to be a central cause of war and disorder not because it declined in importance and influence or was dethroned by other concerns or changed its nature, but because it became defused and de-fanged as a source of interstate conflict through a long, painful quest for order carried out in both domestic and international politics. Without going into any details, it normally involved the government's using and supporting established churches to undergird its authority, preserve public order, and generally promote what was called "the well-ordered police [i.e., civilized] state."[20] This could only be accomplished by working out difficult and painful compromises with church authorities over overlapping functions, jurisdictions, and rights and privileges, and on the international level trying to insure, through treaties, informal agreements, and, where necessary, armed force, that a government's own politico-religious authority and settlement would be respected by others, even while it simultaneously attempted to advance and protect the rights and interests of its co-religionists in other states. This effort quintessentially represented a political undertaking in search of order. The problem was particularly acute and complex in Germany (the Holy Roman Empire), the most confessionally divided part of Europe and the center of its worst religious wars in 1618–48. The main reason why Germany avoided more internecine war after 1648 and why the Holy Roman Empire itself, then apparently prostrate and dying, recovered, regained stability, and lasted until 1806 is that German politics on the domestic, imperial, and international levels were deliberately organized on the basis of confession, with numerous complex arrangements for preserving order and peace made on that basis.[21]

---

[20] Marc Raeff, *The Well-Ordered Police State: Social and Institutional Change through Law in the Germanies and Russia, 1600–1800* (New Haven: Yale University Press, 1983); Philip S. Gorski, *The Disciplinary Revolution: Calvinism and the Rise of the State in Early Modern Europe* (University of Chicago Press, 2003).

[21] For details, see (among many other works) Anton Schindling, *Die Anfänge des Immerwährenden Reichstags zu Regensburg: Ständevertretung und Staatskunst nach dem Westfälischen Frieden* (Mainz: P. von Zabern, 1991); Heinz Schilling, *Religion, Political Culture, and the Emergence of Early Modern Society: Essays in German and Dutch History* (Leiden: Brill, 1992); Heinz Duchhardt, *Balance of Power und Pentarchie 1700–1785*

The significance of this recognition, that religion became defused as a cause of war through a purposive quest for order inseparable from the ongoing struggle for power, is underlined by what happened when the fragile underpinnings of relative eighteenth-century religious peace were destroyed by the French Revolution and Napoleon. One major result was to revive wars undergirded by religion in a different form. By far the most savage and destructive fighting in the early years of the revolutionary wars occurred within France between revolutionary government forces fighting the Church and counterrevolutionary Catholic forces. All the most serious insurrections against French expansion and Napoleonic empire later, in Belgium, Rome, Calabria, Spain, the Tyrol, and even Egypt and Syria,[22] had a strong religious component. Religion joined with patriotism to stoke the resistance to Napoleonic conquest and exploitation in Prussia, Russia, Britain, and elsewhere. In other words, religion in the eighteenth century did not lose its power to mobilize people to fight. Instead the eighteenth-century international system developed ways to keep wars from being fought simply or chiefly over religion – products of a purposive quest for order – that proved reasonably effective until that system was overthrown.

In contrast to the role of religion, the story of changes in the arena of diplomatic rules, conventions, instruments, practices, and norms is fairly straightforward and can be summarized even more briefly. It is one of gradual if uneven evolution and development in the direction of greater order. The art of diplomacy and the craft of foreign policy were already highly developed in the early seventeenth century (witness the careers of Cardinals Richelieu and Mazarin, among many others), but the machinery and institutions of international relations even in advanced countries had, except for France, hardly developed much beyond those of the Italian city-states system of the fourteenth century. Permanent representation abroad was rare; most embassies served special purposes, often ceremonial; the position, functions, and immunity of representatives was unclear and insecure; questions of rank, precedence, and honor were extremely important, highly contested, and sometimes a direct threat to peace; and the professionalization and

---

(Paderborn: F. Schöningh, 1997); Heinz Duchhardt (ed.), *Rahmenbedingungen und Handlungs- Spielräume europäischer Aussenpolitik im Zeitalter Ludwigs XIV* (Berlin: Duncker and Humblot, 1991); Karl Otmar von Aretin, *Das Alte Reich, 1648–1806. Vol. 1: 1648–1684* (Stuttgart: Klett Cotta, 1993).

[22] On the role of Islamic religion and culture in frustrating Napoleon's Egyptian venture, see Juan Cole, *Napoleon's Egypt: Invading the Middle East* (New York: Palgrave Macmillan, 2007); for Spain's insurrection and War of Independence, see Charles Esdaile, *Fighting Napoleon: Guerillas, Bandits and Adventurers in Spain, 1808–1814* (New Haven: Yale University Press, 2004).

bureaucratization of permanent foreign services was largely unknown.[23] By the end of the eighteenth century the situation had greatly changed. Major powers now maintained permanent missions abroad, at least in the most important capitals, and standing foreign policy offices and apparatuses at home. The role and functions of diplomats had been clarified and their immunity was established in principle, if still some-times contested and violated in practice.[24] Some countries, notably France and the Habsburg Monarchy, had made major advances in the professional training of diplomats.

These advances clearly made the conduct of diplomacy and foreign policy more orderly. Two ways in which this shows up particularly well concern the nature and functions of alliances and the use of diplomatic instruments and institutions for peacekeeping and, in some cases, the enforcement of treaties and peace settlements. Seventeenth-century alliances were, as a rule, notoriously and incurably unstable. In great part this was due to the huge imbalances of power within the system, with so many small, weak actors riddled with internal divisions, and with France under Louis XIV (1661–1715) for most of the era so much richer and more powerful than any other unit. It owed something also to geographic incompleteness and lack of coordination in the system, so that events and developments in one sphere (e.g., the Baltic and north-ern or southeastern Europe and the eastern Mediterranean) strongly influenced those in the main theaters in the West but could not be effectively managed in coordination with them. (On this, more later.) But a good part of the problem also derived from the nature and pur-pose of seventeenth-century alliances. These were mostly temporary, ad hoc, intended for war or meeting some other emergency, and dis-tinctly predatory, and hence readily broken or abandoned when the immediate danger passed, or they ceased to pay off, or the obligations became vexatious or impossible to bear. Even so wealthy and powerful a monarch as Louis XIV, though he could bribe, pressure, and force states into alliance, could not keep them in it or form really durable combinations and partnerships, and this inability was only partly due to his own excessive ambitions and bellicosity.[25] There were serious

[23] Garret Mattingly, *Renaissance Diplomacy* (London: Jonathan Cape, 1955).
[24] Linda S. and Marsha L. Frey, *The History of Diplomatic Immunity*, 2 vols. (Columbus: Ohio State University Press, 1999).
[25] From the massive literature on Louis XIV's foreign policy, works I have found most helpful include Andrew Lossky, *Louis XIV and the French Monarchy* (New Brunswick: Rutgers University Press, 1994); John C. Rule (ed.), *Louis XIV and the Craft of Kingship* (Columbus: Ohio State University Press, 1970); Louis André, *Louis XIV et l'Europe* (Paris: Michel, 1950); Gaston Zeller, *Aspects de la politique française sous l'ancien régime* (Paris: PUF, 1964); Ragnhild Hatton and J. S. Bromley (eds.), *William*

attempts in the seventeenth century to form alliances and associations strictly for defense and collective security, but it can hardly be claimed that they proved effective and durable.[26]

The eighteenth century, however, beginning with the Peace of Utrecht that ended the War of the Spanish Succession in 1713, witnessed an evolutionary if not revolutionary change in the nature and function of alliances. Statesmen began to think in terms of natural and permanent connections and alliances between states, and systems of opposed and counterpoised alliances (Anglo-Dutch, Anglo-Austrian, Austro-Russian, Franco-Spanish, even Austro-French). Quite a few alliances lasted for decades; some, like the Austro-French one from 1757, even survived unsuccessful wars. It became possible seriously to use alliances for functions other than war and predation – to enforce, maintain, and even revise peace settlements (as did the Anglo-French entente from 1713 to 1731),[27] force compliance with treaties, construct positive security arrangements (e.g., the Dutch Barrier from 1709 on),[28] and work out informal arrangements for sharing or dividing influence in contested areas (Austria and France in Italy and Switzerland).[29]

Less obvious but worth mentioning are the increased currency and efficacy of international ideas and devices for order such as the European Concert and general congresses and conferences. The European Concert in the eighteenth century was certainly not the active instrument of international politics that it represented throughout the nineteenth century,[30] but the idea that the European family of states

---

III and Louis XIV: Essays by and for the Late Mark A. Thomson (Liverpool University Press, 1968); Lucien Bély, *Les relations internationales en Europe du 17ème et 18ème siècles [1610–1799]* (Paris: PUF, 1993); L. Bély, Jean Bérenger, and André Corvisier, *Guerre et paix dans l'Europe du XVIIe siècle* (Paris: SEDES, 1991); and Klaus Malettke, *Frankreich, Deutschland, und Europa im 17. und 18. Jahrhundert* (Marburg: Hitzeroth, 1994).

[26] For analyses of particular peacekeeping efforts and institutions in the seventeenth century, see Leopold Auer, "Konfliftverhütung und Sicherheit. Versuche zwischenstaatlicher Friedenswahrung in Europa zwischen den Friedensschlüssen von Oliva und Aachen 1660–1668," in Duchhardt (ed.), *Zwischenstaatliche Friedenswahrung*, pp. 153–83; Karl Otmar von Aretin, *Der Kurfürst von Mainz und die Kreisassoziationen 1648–1746* (Wiesbaden: F. Steiner, 1975).

[27] John H. Plumb, *Sir Robert Walpole*, 2 vols. (Boston: Houghton Mifflin, 1956–61); Paul Vaucher, *Robert Walpole et la politique de Fleury* (Paris: Plon-Nourrit, 1924); and, along with many works on the eighteenth century by Jeremy Black, his *Natural and Necessary Enemies: Anglo-French Relations in the Eighteenth Century* (London: Duckworth, 1986).

[28] Roderick Geikie, *The Dutch Barrier, 1705–1719* (Cambridge University Press, 1930).

[29] Guido Quazza, *Il problema Italiano de l'equilibrio Europeo, 1720–1738* (Turin: Deputazione subalpina di storia patria, 1965).

[30] One notes that Mearsheimer manages to analyze the structure and operation of the nineteenth-century system without ever mentioning the European Concert – a feat

formed a distinct community governed by common rules and norms of conduct and that the great powers shared the task and responsibility of preserving and supervising it was definitely alive and growing. While the Congresses at Cambrai and Soissons in the 1720s failed in their attempts to prevent wars and solve problems before they became critical, the very attempt represented a breakthrough with important implications for the future.[31]

True, these advances, if they made international politics somewhat more orderly and rational, did not necessarily make it more peaceful and moral or less competitive and conflictual. International peace (to say nothing of justice) is only a possible, not a necessary, aim and result of international order, though impossible without it. Statesmen in the eighteenth century continued to take the inevitability and necessity of war for granted, so that (to repeat) the early modern era's quest for order was indissolubly tied in with an ongoing struggle for power, and like it a response to anarchy and the imperatives of survival and security. This paradox and dialectic showed up in interesting ways. One historian argues that the Peace of Utrecht, which pacified most of Europe, reconciled Britain and France, temporarily ended the historic Bourbon–Habsburg rivalry, and confirmed the triumph of the principle and ideal of balance of power over that of "universal monarchy," also promoted an increase in espionage as a safer, more subterranean form of interstate competition and conflict.[32] The eighteenth century witnessed a considerable improvement in the volume and safety of international mail, due to improved services and communications and international postal conventions, and brought recognition of the sanctity of official diplomatic correspondence along with diplomatic immunity. It also saw major developments in black cabinet methods of intercepting mail so as to get round these obstacles to finding out what other regimes were up to. But these paradoxes are a natural consequence of the power–order dialectic, and confirm rather than negate an undeniable advance in order.

Besides the role of religion and the development of better instruments of diplomacy and statecraft, there were three other areas where

---

rather like explaining the course of post-1945 world politics without mentioning the United Nations Security Council.

[31] On the general themes of ideas, institutions, and practices of early modern international politics, the classic work remains Heinz Duchhardt, *Gleichgewicht der Kräfte, Convenance, Europäisches Konzert: Friedenskongresse und Friedensschlüsse vom Zeitalter Ludwigs XIV bis zum Wiener Kongress* (Darmstadt: Wissenschaftliche Buchgesellschaft, 1976); but see also Lucien Bély (ed.), *L'invention de la diplomatie. Moyen Age – Temps modernes* (Paris: PUF, 1998).

[32] Lucien Bély, *Espions et ambassadeurs au temps de Louis XIV* (Paris: Fayot, 1990).

a conscious quest for order and a resultant advance in order are evident. The first, most obvious and simple, is the triumph of the idea of balance of power over that of "universal monarchy" as the dominant regulative principle for international politics. This is the one area in which the decisive breakthrough, though long in coming, can be fairly precisely dated: 1688–1713, between the Glorious Revolution in England and the beginning of the Nine Years War (1688–97) and the Peace of Utrecht. In the sixteenth and early seventeenth centuries, at least five European powers, England, France, Spain, the Dutch Republic, and Sweden, made some kind of claim to "universal monarchy."[33] (A sixth, Muscovite Russia, could be added to the list.) As claims to actual possession of dominion or supremacy over the entire world, none of these, of course, made any sense. Even the greatest power, Habsburg Spain under Charles V (1516–55; simultaneously Holy Roman Emperor 1519–58), on whose empire the sun literally never set, found itself constantly at war, always in financial straits, and usually on the defensive, in particular in the Mediterranean.[34] China, India, and the Ottoman Empire were all more powerful and wealthier than any European state.

The various claims to universal monarchy should therefore be understood less as claims to actual hegemony in terms of power than as quasi-religious claims to leadership, preeminence, and legitimacy, remnants of the medieval hierarchical world view in which all power and authority emanated from God and was distributed hierarchically downward from emperor through kings, princes, and other divinely sanctioned orders as instruments for order. The Treaties of Westphalia, though recognizing the breakdown of this idea and establishing the idea of the sovereignty and coordinate status of individual territorial units, did not establish any new principle of order between these diverse polities. This was what the idea, also religiously inspired, of Louis XIV's France as the sun around which other European states would revolve as satellites was supposed to supply. Attacked as a bid for "universal monarchy," discredited by Louis's restless thirst for glory and conquest and his religious intolerance, and denounced as a threat to "the liberties of Europe" (i.e., the independence of its individual states), the idea of "universal monarchy" became essentially a propaganda slogan, a stick

---

[33] Johannes Burkhardt, *Der Dreissigjährige Krieg* (Frankfurt: Suhrkamp, 1992).
[34] James D. Tracy, *Emperor Charles V, Impresario of War: Campaign Strategy, International Finance, and Domestic Politics* (Cambridge University Press, 2002); Alfred Kohler, *Das Reich im Kampf um die Hegemonie in Europa 1521–1648* (Munich: R. Oldenbourg, 1990).

to beat France and Louis with, and ultimately yielded even in France to the guiding principle of "balance of power."[35]

As with the concept of state sovereignty supposedly enshrined in the Westphalian treaties and system since 1648, the idea of balance of power represented a regulative principle, moral ideal, and propaganda instrument more than a practical reality and working mechanism for international politics.[36] Balance-of-power slogans and supposed balancing techniques did not create stable balances of power, or prevent individual powers from bidding for actual hegemony in major areas (e.g., Britain's successful drive for control of all the world's sea lanes after 1783, or Russia's bid for supremacy in Eastern and Central Europe under Catherine the Great). Clearly aggressive and destructive policies could be defended on grounds of balance of power, and were so defended (e.g., the first partition of Poland in 1772, the Russo-Austrian plans for the reduction of Prussia in 1756, the Prussian seizure of Silesia in 1740). Nonetheless, the triumph of the balance-of-power idea represented part of the quest for order and helped promote greater order and system in international politics. It put a premium on more rational long-range calculation of possibilities; it at least encouraged more thought about systemic concerns such as maintaining the existence of all necessary actors; and it made it necessary to justify moves, even hegemonic and aggressive power-political ones, in terms of the European equilibrium, the stability of the system, and often peace.[37] No doubt much of this rhetoric fit La Rochefoucauld's definition of hypocrisy as the tribute vice pays to virtue, but it was worth something nonetheless.

More down to earth, but still more mixed and less obvious, was the advance in order connected with international trade, especially overseas and colonial trade. Here one has to grant that, for the most part, international trade in the seventeenth to eighteenth centuries remained in the general zone of disorder and uncontrolled competition and tended to foster war rather than to promote order and regulate competition so

---

[35] Franz Bosbach, *Monarchia universalis: ein politischer Leitbegriff der frühen Neuzeit* (Göttingen: Vandenhoeck and Ruprecht, 1988).

[36] Adam Watson, *Diplomacy: The Dialogue between States* (London: Methuen, 1982); Martin S. Anderson, *The Rise of Modern Diplomacy 1450–1919* (London: Longman, 1993).

[37] Perhaps the outstanding example of this is the thought and career of Prince Kaunitz, Austria's leading foreign policy statesman in the latter half of the century. Lothar Schilling, *Kaunitz und das Renversement des Alliances. Studien zur aussenpolitischen Konzeption Wenzel Antons von Kaunitz* (Berlin: Duncker and Humblot, 1994); Grete Klingenstein and Franz A. J. Szabo (eds.), *Staatskanzler Wenzel Anton von Kaunitz-Rietburg 1711–1794* (Graz: Andreas Schnider, 1996); Szabo, *Kaunitz and Enlightened Absolutism 1753–1780* (Cambridge University Press, 1994).

as to make wider cooperation and peace possible. The reigning economic ideology of the eighteenth century, despite the emergence of the theory of free trade in its latter half, remained one of beggar-my-neighbor state-centered mercantilism. The acquisition of territories for purposes, among others, of extracting their economic resources and controlling their commerce continued to be a prime object of power politics and war. One cannot point to any general decline in wars and crises arising over trade, colonies, and economic strong points and advantages in the eighteenth as opposed to the seventeenth century. Witness, for example, the importance both sides placed on controlling the trade of the Spanish empire in the War of the Spanish Succession;[38] the Anglo-Dutch campaign to suppress the Austrian-sponsored Ostend Company in the 1720s; the War of Jenkins' Ear in 1739 against Spain, a war promoted by a fairly narrow coterie of British merchants;[39] Frederick the Great's seizure of Silesia in 1740, in good part for its important economic resources; and the role competition for economic and commercial prizes played in the three Austrian–Prussian–Russian partitions of Poland in 1772–95. The competition for overseas trade, colonies, fisheries and fishing rights, and lucrative territories and strategic strong points during the eighteenth century presents a similar, even more glaring picture of power rivalry. In some respects, the sixteenth- to seventeenth-century dog-eat-dog struggles for domination in the Caribbean, North America, India, the southwest Pacific, and South America expanded and reached their climax in the latter eighteenth century, especially between Britain and France.[40]

Granting this, one still has to recognize that a search for order and the growth of order, if not peace and cooperation, made for major change in regard to international trade and commerce in the early modern era. There is a real difference between the chaotic conflicts

[38] Henry Kamen, *The War of Succession in Spain, 1700–1715* (London: Weidenfeld & Nicolson, 1969); Ragnhild Hatton, *Diplomatic Relations between Great Britain and the Dutch Republic 1714–1721* (London: East and West, 1950); Edward Gregg, *Queen Anne* (London: Routledge Kegan Paul, 1980).

[39] Jean O. McLachlan, *Trade and Peace with Old Spain, 1667–1750* (Cambridge University Press, 1940); Plumb, *Sir Robert Walpole*, fn. 26.

[40] Alan Frost, *The Global Reach of Empire: Britain's Maritime Expansion in the Indian and Pacific Oceans, 1764–1815* (Melbourne: Miegunyah Press, 2003); Vincent T. Harlow, *The Founding of the Second British Empire, 1763–1793*, 2 vols. (London: Longmans Green, 1952–64); P. J. Marshall, *The Making and Unmaking of Empires: Britain, India and America c. 1750–1783* (Oxford University Press, 2005). Two excellent recent works on the impact of the Seven Years' War in North America are Fred Anderson, *Crucible of War: The Seven Years' War and the Fate of Empire in British North America, 1754–1766* (New York: Alfred A. Knopf, 2000) and Colin G. Calloway, *The Scratch of a Pen: 1763 and the Transformation of North America* (Oxford University Press, 2006).

waged between Westerners over trade and empire in the Caribbean or in India and the southwest Pacific in the sixteenth to seventeenth centuries (when only loose connections linked the chartered companies and their metropolitan governments and involved little governmental supervision), and the situation in the mid eighteenth century when admiralty and prize courts were established. In the prior era, there were no viable distinctions between states of war and peace in the various theaters, and few practical distinctions could be drawn between piracy, smuggling, and legal trade. Later, the law of the sea was further developed, foundations were laid for effective governmental control over the activities of chartered companies and men on the spot,[41] and clearer lines of territorial demarcation were drawn. A similar case can be made that the purely aggressive-acquisitive trade wars of the seventeenth century, fought to destroy the competitor and seize his assets (the Anglo-Dutch wars of the mid seventeenth century, Louis XIV's Dutch War, the Northern Wars fought for the *dominium maris baltici*), differed markedly from the later wars fought in part for commercial advantage and control. The same sort of difference can be seen between the beggar-my-neighbor mercantilism of Cromwell or of Colbert under Louis XIV and the mercantilism of Pitt the Younger and Henry Dundas after 1784. The latter still enforced the British Navigation Acts and pursued British control of the seas and sea lanes more widely and aggressively than ever, but with the idea that once Britain was securely in charge of an expanding, freer world trade, others would also share and prosper in it.[42] To a considerable extent this actually happened. In the late eighteenth century, until the French revolutionary wars broke out, France and Spain, the chief targets of the British drive for world maritime domination, experienced important growth in their overseas commerce.[43] As for the United States, once the British colonies gained their independence,

[41] Kenneth R. Andrews, *Trade, Plunder and Settlement: Maritime Enterprise and the Genesis of the British Empire, 1480–1630* (Cambridge University Press, 1984); Holden Furber, *Rival Empires of Trade in the Orient, 1600–1800* (Minneapolis: University of Minnesota Press, 1976); Richard Pares, *Colonial Blockade and Neutral Rights 1739–1763* (Oxford: Clarendon Press, 1938); Pares, *War and Trade in the West Indies 1739–1763* (Oxford: Clarendon Press, 1936); Marcus B. Rediker, *Between the Devil and the Deep Blue Sea: Merchant Seamen, Pirates, and the Anglo-American Maritime World, 1700–1750* (Cambridge: Cambridge University Press, 1987).

[42] Frost, *Global Reach of Empire*, fn. 40.

[43] James D. Tracy (ed.), *The Rise of Merchant Empires: Long Distance Trade in the Early Modern World, 1350–1750* (Cambridge University Press, 1990), especially the chapters by Paul Butel, Carla Rahn Phillips, Herman van der Wee, and Larry Neal.

they notoriously shared in and profited from Britain's world naval and commercial empire.[44]

Finally, as earlier mentioned, one sees unmistakable evidence of a quest for order, this time closely connected with the desire for peace and law, in the revival and survival of the Holy Roman Empire. One need not perhaps go as far as its chief historian, K. O. von Aretin, does in describing the German Reich as a functioning and fairly effective if cumbersome entity for the governance of central Europe, representing order based on law and peace (a *Rechts-und Friedensordnung*) rather than power (*Machtordnung*).[45] What cannot be denied, however, is the achievement represented by its survival and continued functioning, and the contribution it made in providing some security for the empire's many diverse small units and in limiting or avoiding conflicts within it. The fact (emphasized by Aretin and others) that the Reich was undermined in the latter half of the eighteenth century by predatory European great-power politics, especially by Prussian–Austrian rivalry,[46] does not contradict his argument or the general notion of the power–order dialectic, but conforms to and reinforces both.

On the other hand, this dialectic does not embrace or explain everything important that happened in the evolution of the international system. Three major developments in the evolution of European states in the early modern era, briefly discussed above, directly and significantly affected the course of international politics. The first was the rise of the princely absolutist state enjoying greater power and reach over its subjects and various classes and elites than older feudal-constitutional elective monarchies. The second involved the development of the fiscal military state with its more efficient administrative-bureaucratic and fiscal-commercial machinery for developing and extracting resources for state purposes. Third was the partial supplanting of the sacral state, personally embodied in its monarch and seen by its subjects through the lens of a representational court culture, with an impersonal state of which the king was supposed to be the first servant and whose rulers and performance the general public, though excluded from power, could at least observe and discuss in a public sphere. Yet if these developments clearly changed the character of early modern politics, domestic and international, in crucial ways, these

---

[44] Charles R. Ritcheson, *Aftermath of Revolution: British Policy Toward the United States, 1783–1795* (Dallas: Southern Methodist University Press, 1969).

[45] Aretin's classic work is his *Heiliges Römisches Reich 1776–1806. Reichsverfassung und Staats-Souveranität*, 2 vols. (Wiesbaden: F. Steiner, 1967); but see also his *Das Reich, Friedensgarantie und europäisches Gleichgewicht 1648–1806* (Stuttgart: Klett Cotta, 1986).

[46] In addition to Aretin's works, see Tadeusz Cegielski, *Das Alte Reich und die Erste Teilung Polens 1768–1774* (Stuttgart: F. Steiner, 1988).

changes primarily affected the struggle for power. Their main results were to make states that successfully developed more rational, efficient means of taxation, public finance, and credit, bureaucratic administration, and centralized authority more effective at waging war and conducting foreign policy. Any impact they may have had in rendering international politics more orderly, rational, and predictable (e.g., by making units that were not unified states but composite monarchies or loose federations more capable of acting like rational unitary actors) were secondary and minor.

If these developments in state evolution changed and in certain respects heightened the struggle for power without much promoting the quest for order, one important advance in order emerged not as the result of a search for it, but simply out of power struggles and wars themselves. This was the geographical extension of the European system to include all of northern and eastern and much of southeastern Europe. As earlier mentioned, one of the major problems in trying to limit and end wars in the seventeenth and early eighteenth centuries was the system's geographical incoherence. There were two distinct centers of action, one western and southern (France, the British Isles, the Low Countries, Spain and Portugal, the Germanies, Italy, and the Habsburg Monarchy), the other northern (all the Baltic lands, the most important players being Sweden, Denmark, Poland, and Russia). Southeastern Europe remained mostly enemy territory, governed or dominated by the Ottoman Turks. Though international events and developments in these spheres constantly overlapped and impinged on each other, it was virtually impossible to bring all the important players into one system and coordinate the respective problems. This helps explain, for example, the failure of the British, Dutch, French, and various German governments' efforts to end the Great Northern War (1702–21) short of Russia's complete triumph.[47] By the later eighteenth century, this problem had essentially been solved. All the important players and areas, save the remaining Balkan portions of the Ottoman Empire (which did not belong to the European or Christian family of states), were part of one state system. This development, however, owed little to a conscious quest for order and a great deal to war – the fact that Prussia had forced its way into great-power status through successful aggression and defense of its territorial spoils against Austria in

---

[47] Walther Mediger, *Mecklenburg, Russland und England-Hannover 1706–1721*, 2 vols. (Hildesheim: Lax, 1967); Ragnhild M. Hatton, *George I, Elector and King* (Cambridge, MA: Harvard University Press, 1978); Hatton, *Great Britain and the Dutch Republic*, fn. 36; Michael Roberts, *The Swedish Imperial Experience, 1560–1718* (New York: Cambridge University Press, 1979).

1740–63, while Russia had done the same even more successfully at the expense of Sweden, Poland, and the Ottoman Empire.[48]

There were other areas in which the search for order appears largely absent or ineffective. The conduct of war was certainly rationalized and made more efficient and calculable in the eighteenth century by the decline in mercenary forces and the growth of professional standing armies and trained professional officer corps. Developments in weaponry and strategy and tactics and improvements in logistics and supply helped make war more humane to a degree, inflicting somewhat less disaster on civilian populations. Yet none of this really limited war, much less banned it. The older view that eighteenth-century wars were limited wars of position fought for restricted goals and concluded with compromise peace settlements is not really tenable. All the major wars were fought near or to the point of exhaustion of at least some of the major participants, and some conflicts like the War of the Spanish Succession or the Seven Years War caused great devastation and suffering over wide areas. Similarly, though the laws of war were advanced somewhat, general schemes for peace remained utopian. Diplomatic methods for third-party mediation of disputes and interventions to end war improved – witness the successful Russo-French intervention to terminate the Prusso-Austrian War of the Bavarian Succession in 1779 – but their use was limited and usually ineffective.

More important still were the structural causes of disorder and war in the early modern era not seriously addressed in the quest for order. A central one, arguably the most important of all, was that posed by dynastic succession. The fact that the legitimacy of a ruler's power and authority to rule his territories and occupy his throne depended on rules of dynastic succession – rules not merely complex and sometimes conflicting in themselves, but rendered worse by the tangled, often incestuous relationships among European ruling families – made almost every succession a potential cause for crisis and war, and gave every claimant, however implausible the claim, a pretext for raising a challenge and seeking compensation or provoking a war. Yet the eighteenth-century quest for order did almost nothing to meet or resolve this problem, probably because it was too difficult and the institution too central to the monarchical system to confront.[49] Another potent source of war, the danger of extra-European conflicts escalating and merging into

---

[48] H. M. Scott, *The Emergence of the Eastern Powers, 1756–1775* (Cambridge University Press, 2001).

[49] Kunisch, *Staatsverfassung und Mächtepolitik*, fn. 15; see also Kunisch (ed.), *Der dynastische Fürstenstaat. Zur Bedeutung von Sukzessions-Ordnungen für die Entstehung des frühmodernen Staates* (Berlin: Duncker and Humblot, 1982).

European ones, was not addressed, much less solved, in the eighteenth century. In the Seven Years War, the American Revolutionary War, and the earlier wars of the French Revolution the problem grew worse. Nor can one detect any particular effort in this supposed quest for order to address some of the war-generating problems that political scientists have identified and analyzed as more or less constant in international politics, e.g., entangling alliances, the security dilemma, the free-rider problem, and the overall difficulty of trying to survive through moderate policies in the environment of a predatory system.[50]

Taken all in all, these concessions might seem to make my case less than overwhelming. Neorealists like Mearsheimer will probably argue that it confirms their view after all. I show only, they may contend, that the practices of late eighteenth-century international politics differed in certain respects from those of the early seventeenth century, and that their evolution had made foreign policy somewhat more rational and subject to calculation. But the system for structural reasons was still dominated by struggles for power, and such advances in order and rationality as were tenuously and temporarily achieved regularly crumbled with the outbreak of war – precisely what happened to these alleged eighteenth-century advances in international order after 1792.

This reading of history, however, is unconvincing. Taken as a whole, it merely restates what was emphasized from the beginning: that the early modern era, including the whole eighteenth century, was a bellicist era, and that the modern international system, then in its gestation, infancy, and adolescence, was only beginning to cope with its inherent structural problems. It also illustrates and confirms other commonplace notions about international politics: that seeking order does not necessarily involve seeking peace, much less justice; that systems of order can be stable in the short term and repressive and unsustainable in the long term, thus becoming sources of disorder themselves; that an optimistic belief in the existence of an apparently stable system and order can tempt individual states to test its boundaries and violate its

---

[50] On this last point, the dangers of moderate policies in a *societas leonina*, see, for France in the reign of Louis XV, Orest Ranum, "Review Article: Louis XV and the Price of Pacific Inclination," *International History Review* 13 (1991), 331–38, and for France in the American Revolution, see Jonathan R. Dull, *The French Navy and American Independence, 1774–1787* (Princeton University Press, 1975); Jonathan R. Dull, "Vergennes, Rayneval and the Diplomacy of Trust," in Ronald Hoffman and Peter J. Albright (eds.), *Peace and the Peacemakers: The Treaty of 1783* (Charlottesville: University of Virginia Press, 1986), pp. 101–31; Orville T. Murphy, *Charles Gravier, Comte de Vergennes: French Diplomacy in the Age of Revolution* (Albany: State University of New York Press, 1982).

rules in the hope of getting away with illegal gains;[51] that the conviction that a vital element of order is being threatened or destroyed and must be restored can lead a state to choose war in order to save it;[52] and that major wars can and often do arise over what kind of international order should prevail.[53] In short, in the final analysis all this fits the picture of a dialectical relation between the struggle for power and the quest for order as inseparable twin responses to structural anarchy.

The historical record also illustrates a crucial difference between the two. At first glance the quest for power and order both appear cyclical. The quest for order in international politics regularly falls short of its goal and recurrently breaks down into major and systemic war. The ongoing struggle for power leads to periodic violent clashes between great powers and cycles of rise and fall. But again first appearances deceive. The struggle for power is genuinely cyclical; it goes nowhere in particular, merely repeating itself in the tragic pattern Mearsheimer discerns. The quest for order in international politics, however, is essentially linear and directional; it goes somewhere, advances even, sometimes especially, in war itself.

Evidence of this lies in what actually happened after the eighteenth-century international order was destroyed by the French revolutionary and Napoleonic wars. Many problems not faced or seen as insoluble in that old order were finally confronted squarely and, if not solved for all time, seriously and successfully addressed in 1815 and after. In the nineteenth-century system, dynastic connections and concerns remained important for sovereigns and governments and fairly often preoccupied European politics, but never were the real cause of a crisis,

---

[51] This kind of thinking, for example, lay behind Frederick II of Prussia's smash-and-grab seizure of Austrian Silesia in 1740.

[52] One sees this motive clearly in Austria's decisions for war in 1756, 1809, 1859, and 1914.

[53] Mearsheimer, driven by his exclusive emphasis on power, strategy, and geography, seems particularly blind to this point, which leads him to some astonishing factual assertions and interpretations. Two representative examples: he dismisses the French Revolution as playing any role in the origins of war in 1792, insisting that "Austria and Prussia provoked a war with France" for balance-of-power reasons, "ganging up on a weak and vulnerable France to gain power at its expense" (*The Tragedy of Great Power Politics*, p. 274). He similarly explains the German question in the 1860s as purely one of which great power, Austria or Prussia, "would absorb the Third Germany," and offers this explanation of the Danish–German conflict in 1863–64: "Prussia's first war under Bismarck (1864) was a straightforward case of two great powers, Austria and Prussia, ganging up to attack a minor power, Denmark." Their aim was to take the Duchies of Schleswig and Holstein away from Denmark" (p. 289). "It is not surprising that none of the European great powers balanced against Austria and Prussia in 1864," he further explains, "because the stakes were small." Historical assertions like this, scattered throughout the book, leave an historian familiar with the evidence shaking his head in amusement or dismay.

much less a war.[54] Europe was successfully fenced off from extra-European clashes and crises of imperialism as it was not and could not be in the eighteenth century. Not until 1898 with the Anglo-French Fashoda Crisis did any serious chance of a European war arise over a colonial issue. Alliances formed and used primarily for purposes of management and mutual restraint and expressly designed to maintain the territorial status quo became in the nineteenth century not merely possible, but the norm. The European Concert in the nineteenth century became an active, effective instrument not merely for preserving peace and legality, but in important ways also for promoting peaceful change (Belgium, Greece, the Ottoman Empire). The Vienna Settlement embodied serious collective security arrangements that worked for almost four decades. The German Confederation that succeeded the defunct Holy Roman Empire proved for decades a better, more useful law and peace order in Central Europe than its predecessor had been.[55] The smaller powers of Europe never enjoyed more genuine security from great-power threats and conquest, even if they lived under various forms of great-power hegemony. There were no more mercantilist wars. Freedom of the seas under British hegemony became a reality, international control of traffic on vital rivers and waterways a growing trend, and freer trade and commercial development a goal pursued even by authoritarian and protectionist governments. All this evidence of directional forward movement in the quest for order is ignored or trivialized by Mearsheimer, evidently because it fails to fit into his picture of international politics as a relentless struggle for power among great powers in which the quest for order could play no structural role.

Further objections from neorealists can readily be imagined, but rather than try to anticipate and answer them, let me speculate a bit on the general reactions international historians might have, were the bare-boned argument and purely prima facie case presented in this chapter fleshed out with the necessary research and exposition in a book. Quite a few would doubtless reject the main thesis; many historians are untheoretical, common-sense Machiavellians who assume that power politics always comes up trumps in international relations. I would anticipate other objections – disagreements on details of fact and interpretation,

---

[54] All the superficially plausible counter-examples – the disputes over choosing monarchs for new states like Greece, Belgium, Romania, Bulgaria, and Albania, or the Anglo-French tiff over the Spanish Marriages in 1845–46, or even the Hohenzollern candidature for the Spanish throne in 1870 – confirm rather than undermine this point.

[55] Mearsheimer predictably describes the Confederation as "an ineffectual political organization set up after Napoleon's defeat in 1815," that had no significance in the story of German unification (*The Tragedy of Great Power Politics*, p. 289).

critiques of various aspects of the general thesis and story line, and allegations of various methodological and historiographical sins, including an overschematization of history, reification, too little attention to contingency and chance, optimism, moralism, Whiggishness, teleological reasoning, determinism, Hegelianism, belief in historical progress, and who knows what else.

Only one thing, however, would surprise or greatly concern me: a general or widespread rejection by historians of the central thesis of this chapter, that the struggle for power and advantage endemic in international politics has historically been accompanied by and inextricably intertwined with a quest for order, that both constitute essential responses to the fundamental problem of structural anarchy, and that both sides of their interplay, whether one calls it dialectical or not, must be studied carefully in order to understand the course of international politics and the vast changes that have taken place over centuries in the international system. To that general proposition I would expect the most frequent response of historians to be one of casual assent: "Well, yes, of course – what else is new?" I would further be surprised if many of them failed to agree that a careful analysis of this dialectic was likely to throw more light on the structure and trajectory of international relations over time than still more iterations of social-scientific analyzing of balancing and bandwagoning or measurements of the relative stability of unipolar, bipolar, and multipolar systems. They might even conclude, with me, that such investigation could be more useful in indicating where international politics stands now and where it might be going.

6 Austria-Hungary and the coming of the First World War

Samuel R. Williamson, Jr.

From 1899 to 1912 the annual recruit intake for the armies of Austria-Hungary remained fixed at 136,000 men. If in 1890 Germany had 160,000 more troops than its Habsburg ally, by 1914 the difference had increased to 465,000.[1] Well might General Conrad von Hötzendorf, Chief of the Habsburg General Staff, object to participation in the Second Hague Peace Conference of 1907 with the curt observation: "the present condition of our army already has an appearance of the permanent limitation of armament."[2] The Danubian monarchy's failure to keep pace with its European rivals, as well as its allies, owed much to domestic political issues between Vienna and Budapest. But it also reflected a relatively passive approach to the monarchy's position in the European state system, a passivity that only the Second Moroccan Crisis (1911) and the Balkan Wars (1912–13) would totally disrupt. To be sure the government had nearly veered to war with Serbia (and possibly Russia) during the 1908–09 Bosnian Crisis, but once over there had only been a limited increase in Habsburg defense expenditures and no increase in manpower. If land forces and an aggressive foreign policy seeking power constitute central features of the "offensive realism" paradigm, then the Habsburg monarchy does not fit.

In keeping with John Mearsheimer's concept of "offensive realism," indeed of all "realists," the primary goal of the Austro-Hungarian monarchy before 1914 was to survive. It met the definition of a great power by its capacity as a state able to conduct war against its most powerful potential opponent, Russia, though not against a combination of enemies. After 1878 and its occupation of Bosnia-Herzegovina, rather than seek protection by aggressive expansionism in keeping with the theory of "offensive realism," the monarchy sought instead to preserve its

---

[1] Samuel R. Williamson, Jr., *Austria-Hungary and the Coming of the First World War* (New York: St Martin's, 1991), pp. 44–45; Mearsheimer, *The Tragedy of Great Power Politics*, pp. 187, 303.

[2] Quoted in Norman Stone, "Army and Society in the Habsburg Monarchy, 1900–1914," *Past and Present* 33 (1966), 107.

regional hegemon position in the Balkans by alliances, détentes, "band-wagoning," "buck-passing," "balancing," and caution. Handicapped at every point by its own internal political structure, Austria-Hungary did not have the choice to be more than an effective, cautious status quo power.[3]

Nor did the monarchy have the latent material and economic resources to allow for a competitive military build-up; it could not keep up with the Joneses, so to speak. The limited size of Habsburg military forces until 1912 and the modest increases of the next two years reflected a great power unwilling, indeed unable, because of domestic politics, to do more. A truly multinational empire, Austria-Hungary could only seek to survive as a state in any future conflict between Germany and Russia while simultaneously protecting its centuries' old role as the Balkan hegemon. For the monarchy, unlike any other great power, every foreign policy issue had some potential domestic consequence, whether it involved Serbs, Croats, Czechs, Italians, Poles, or Ruthenians. Thus, not surprisingly, Vienna's behavior before the fall of 1912 does not match the political power configuration that an "offensive realist" theory would predict. Unlike their propositions, in the Habsburg monarchy domestic and foreign policy issues (*Innen* and *Aussen*) were inseparable spheres, impossible to ignore and a conscious or latent consideration in all foreign policy decisions. To make matters worse, there was the sheer question of whether the Dual Monarchy of Austria-Hungary could survive the death of Emperor Franz Joseph and the accession of Archduke Franz Ferdinand, given his virulent views concerning Budapest. Almost certainly, the Hungarians would make a new attempt to achieve quasi-independence.

Then in late 1912, the First Balkan War rapidly altered the Habsburg's traditional hegemonic role in the Balkans. The rapid collapse of the Ottoman position and the sudden rise of an enlarged Serbia threatened Vienna's interests. In the subsequent tensions with Russia and Serbia, Austria-Hungary diligently maneuvered to protect its standing by preventing Serbia from accessing the Adriatic and by reinforcing its political and military ties with its German ally. In short, the Balkan wars and their aftermath challenged the "defensive realism" of Vienna; the issue of survival became more acute, not just militarily but psychologically as well. Yet the domestic political paralysis of Austria-Hungary continued, even as its international situation grew more parlous.

---

[3] Mearsheimer, *The Tragedy of Great Power Politics*, pp. 5, 17–22, 147, 162; also see Waltz, *Theory of International Politics*.

If one completed a balance sheet, or a power line, so to speak, for the monarchy in June 1914, the accounting would show a great power bent on preserving the status quo, seeking to survive, apprehensive about its hegemonic standing in the Balkans, uncertain about its relations with its three allies – Germany, Italy, and Romania – and possessing an army only slightly larger than that of twenty years before. In short, the ledger would barely resemble the one that the "offensive realism" approach would predict. The fact that the theory cannot explain this anomaly constitutes a major defect in the "offensive realism" approach.

But in July 1914 the theory suddenly seems appropriate. The monarchy's aggressive behavior in July 1914 would appear, paradoxically, to be a validation of many of the tenets of "offensive and defensive realism" as Vienna sought to ensure its survival by attacking Serbia, seemingly confident that the potential Russian hegemon would be checked by the actuality of the German hegemon. It is the explanation of this "apparent" paradox of Habsburg policy that this chapter examines.[4]

I

The years from the Congress of Vienna to the revolutions of 1848 had seen Prince Clemens von Metternich orchestrate a foreign policy that protected Habsburg interests.[5] Deftly shifting allegiances from partner to partner during these years, he fought – with a measure of success – to contain the forces of liberalism and nationalism within the Habsburg realm and in the larger German arena. In the Balkans, Ottoman power, though challenged, remained secure enough. And the Russian threat to Constantinople, though worrisome, remained contained, not least because of Britain's willingness to resist. For his part Metternich continued to convince even the Russians that the Near Eastern Question should be contained and controlled. The monarchy's role in Europe appeared essential. Indeed, Francis Palacky's famous dictum of 1848 had wide European support: "truly, if the Austrian empire had not existed for ages, it would be necessary, in the interest of Europe, in the

---

[4] On the general situation, see F. R. Bridge, *From Sadowa to Sarajevo: The Foreign Policy of Austria-Hungary, 1866–1914* (London: Routledge, 1972); F. R. Bridge, *The Habsburg Monarchy among the Great Powers, 1815–1918* (New York: Oxford University Press, 1990), pp. 1–48; Robin Okey, *The Habsburg Monarchy: From Enlightenment to Eclipse* (New York: Palgrave Macmillan, 2001); Günther Kronenbitter, *"Krieg im Frieden": Die Führung der k.u.k. Armee und die Grossmachtpolitik Österreichs-Ungarns 1906–1914* (Munich: Oldenbourg, 2003); and Williamson, *Austria-Hungary*.

[5] Paul Schroeder, *The Transformation of European Politics, 1763–1848* (Oxford University Press, 1994); Alan Sked, *Metternich and Austria: An Evaluation* (New York: Palgrave Macmillan, 2008); Bridge, *Habsburg Monarchy*, pp. 1–60.

interest of mankind itself, to create it with all speed" for "imagine if you will Austria divided into a number of republics and miniature republics. What a welcome basis for a Russian universal monarchy."[6] But then arrived the revolutions of 1848 and the collapse of Metternich's order. The arranged accession of the eighteen-year-old Franz Joseph to the Habsburg throne in December 1848 (though just in Vienna and only much later in Budapest) opened a new era in the monarchy's survival efforts.

For nineteen years, to 1867, the young ruler and a series of statesmen sought to rebuild and buttress Habsburg power, to preserve its holdings in Italy and Germany, and finally to salvage its future by the *Ausgleich* agreement in 1867 with the ever-troublesome Hungarians. In the process of seeking to survive, maintain, and then redeem its position, Vienna used all of the approaches of "realism": balancing, buckpassing, blood-letting, sometimes even appeasement. None worked, in part because Habsburg military force could not reinforce Vienna's diplomatic efforts, in part because Franz Joseph had no desire to risk the monarchy in a struggle to the end in Italy or Germany, and in part because domestic politics, the realists notwithstanding, intruded at every point. With the defeat at Sadowa, Franz Joseph had to renegotiate with the Magyars whom he had subdued in 1849 with Russian help. The 1867 agreement represented a strange, almost comical, effort to keep the dynasty intact.[7]

The new state had a central government under the monarch responsible for foreign policy, military and naval affairs, and finances of the so-called common monarchy. At the same time, however, the Austrian and Hungarian governments set their own financial contributions to the central regime, controlled the size of the common army, and in fact had their own armies as well, and the entire arrangement was subject to renegotiation every ten years. As one observer declared, the monarchy was always on notice and survival became the dynasty's number one agenda. Yet, closely linked to that, and part of the Austro-Hungarian approach, was the shared understanding in Vienna and Budapest that the monarchy would seek to retain its regional hegemon position in the Balkans after 1867. It is this key determination that henceforth

---

[6] The quotes are from Joachim Remak, "The Healthy Invalid: How Doomed the Habsburg Monarchy?" *Journal of Modern History* 61 (1969), 131–32.

[7] For a recent analysis of the *Ausgleich*, see part VI: "Die österreichisch-ungarische Monarchie as Staats- und Reichsproblem," in Helmut Rumpler and Peter Urbanitsch (eds.), *Die Habsburgermonarchie, 1848–1918*, vol. VII, *Verfassung und Parlamentarismus*, pt. 1, *Verfassungsrecht, Verfassungs-Wirklichkeit, Zentrale Repräsentativkrperschaften* (Vienna: Verlag der Österreichischen Akademie der Wissenschaften, 2000), pp. 1107–230.

shaped Habsburg policy, foreign and domestic, to the crucial days of July 1914.[8]

The first moves came in the 1870s when unrest among Balkan Christians under Ottoman rule provided a pretext for another Russo-Turkish confrontation. In this instance Vienna once more indulged in "buck-passing," but only after securing promises from Russia for gains in Bosnia-Herzegovina. London, assisted by German Chancellor Otto von Bismarck, curbed Russian–Bulgarian territorial gains made in the earlier Treaty of San Stefano at the Congress of Berlin in 1878. In the aftermath the Habsburgs gained administrative control of the two provinces, and no one doubted that eventually the two provinces would become a formal part of the Danubian state.[9]

The acquisition of Bosnia-Herzegovina demands further comment. First, the transfer of territory (even if provisional) represented, after the Treaty of Paris and the transfer of Alsace-Lorraine to Germany, the largest territorial gain (as compared to loss) by any European power between the Congress of Vienna and July 1914. Whether one defines this as a product of "offensive realism" or of successful "blackmail," the land gain and the population increase pushed the Habsburg holdings further than ever into the Balkans. With these gains came additional problems: pacification of the turbulent Slavs, creation of administrative arrangements, issues of public finance, and, of course, defensive arrangements to protect the gains. While Ottoman Turkey might retain titular sovereignty, Vienna and Budapest effectively controlled the provinces and acted accordingly.[10]

But a second consideration soon flowed from the gains: how to defend the territorial gains against internal unrest, against any potential Serbian appeal, and from the possibility that St. Petersburg might retract its concession to Vienna. For the next thirty years this challenge constituted a consistent problem for successive Habsburg foreign ministers. The responses reflected acute realism, occasional flexibility, and

---

[8] For exhaustive detail on the operation of Habsburg foreign policy, see Adam Wandruszka and Peter Urbanitsch (eds.), *Die Habsburgermonarchie, 1848–1918*, vol. VI, pt. 1, *Die Habsburgermonarchie im System des Internationalen Beziehungen* (Vienna: Verlag der Österreichischen Akademie der Wissenschaften, 1989).

[9] The older study by William L. Langer, *European Alliances and Alignments, 1871–1890* (New York: Alfred A. Knopf, 1931), pp. 59–169, remains very useful in understanding the complexity of the issues; Bridge, *Habsburg Monarchy*, pp. 104–49.

[10] On the Habsburg effort to subdue the new provinces, see Lászlo Bencze, *The Occupation of Bosnia and Herzegovina in 1878* (New York: Columbia University Press, 2005); Srecko M. Dzaja, *Bosnien-Herzegowina in der österreichisch-ungarischen Epoche (1878–1918): Die Intelligentsia zwischen Tradition und Ideologie* (Munich: Oldenbourg, 1994). Also see the comments in Robert J. Donia and John V. A. Fine, Jr., *Bosnia-Hercegovina: A Tradition Betrayed* (New York: Columbia University Press, 1994), pp. 75–119.

an unyielding commitment to defend the status quo. Moreover, some of Vienna's moves came quickly after the Congress of Berlin.

In 1879 Chancellor Otto von Bismarck and the soon-to-depart Habsburg foreign minister, Julius Andrássy, signed a secret alliance that sought to protect Vienna from the Russians and Berlin from the French. This peacetime alliance, unprecedented for the time, soon became the Triple Alliance with Italy's membership to follow in 1882. To buttress further the alignment, the Romanian king, German-born Carol, signed a secret protocol that made Romania a silent and highly secret partner in the alliance. Quite clearly, wary of Russia and afraid of its hegemon ambitions, Franz Joseph adopted a policy of "balancing" to protect both the dynasty and its newest territorial gains. Henceforth the German alliance, though not without frictions and disappointments, became the axiomatic bedrock of Vienna's international policy.[11]

But Franz Joseph and his ministers did not trust this approach alone. In the 1880s they participated with Britain and Italy in a pair of Mediterranean agreements that were designed to remind Russia (and reassure Constantinople) that further changes in the Balkans would be resisted. Vienna also worked to maintain its de facto control over successive Obrenović kings of Serbia, first Milan and then Alexander, through well-placed bribes. So long as Belgrade remained quiescent, the provinces of Bosnia-Herzegovina were fairly secure. Nor did the Habsburgs hesitate to work with the Russians directly. Through successive Bulgarian crises in the 1880s the two sides fenced, checkmated, and managed to cooperate enough to maintain an uneasy status quo in the Balkans.[12]

The decade of the 1890s, however, saw a series of changes in the international arena, changes that would eventually threaten the Habsburg enterprise in entirely new ways. The forced departure of Bismarck, who remained ever cautious about committing Berlin to a full defense of Austro-Hungarian interests in the Balkans, led to the Franco-Russian alliance of 1894. This new alignment fundamentally transformed Germany's strategic position, a change that General Alfred von Schlieffen immediately sought to counter. Luckily, however, for both Berlin and Vienna, Russia's attention shifted to the Far East and its expansionist ambitions there, where it remained until the disasters of 1904–05 at the hands of the Japanese. This halcyon respite gave Vienna

---

[11] The most recent studies are by Holger Afflerbach, *Der Dreibund: Europäische Grossmacht-und Allianzpolitik vor dem Ersten Weltkrieg* (Vienna: Böhlau, 2002), pp. 39–108, and Jürgen Angelow, *Kalkül und Prestige: Der Zweibund am Vorabend des Ersten Weltkrieges* (Cologne: Böhlau, 2000), pp. 25–117; and Langer, *European Alliances*, pp. 171–250.

[12] Bridge, *Habsburg Monarchy*, pp. 150–223; Langer, *European Alliances*, pp. 323–457.

a measure of added security at a fortuitous time, since the nationality quarrels within the monarchy reached new heights in Austria during the 1890s, and later between the dynasty and the Hungarians after
1903.[13]

Two other trends were equally troublesome. London became less
interested in the Mediterranean accords, concerned now with imperial
problems including Russia's threat to India and to the Far East. More
alarming still were the first repercussions from Kaiser Wilhelm II's
efforts to establish his personal rule over the apparatus of the German
government, to start a naval program certain to alarm London, and to
pursue a policy of *Weltpolitik* that soon rattled the other European chan-
celleries. Vienna's relationship with its ally suddenly acquired new risks,
risks that became apparent with the First Moroccan Crisis in 1905.[14]

Amid this kaleidoscope of changes, Vienna managed to secure a
détente with Russia over the Balkans. In 1897 the two rivals agreed to
a policy of the status quo, a policy that was extended in 1903 when Russia
was fully preoccupied with the Far East. In these instances, Vienna
had sought to "tether" St. Petersburg, that is, to create an arrangement
that fostered security through self-denial. It was an act of consummate
"defensive realism." Nor could it have come at a better moment, as the
political chaos within the Habsburg monarchy reached a crescendo in
1906 when Franz Joseph agreed to universal male suffrage in Austria
and threatened to do the same in Hungary unless the Magyars relented
in their demands about the common army. The internal tensions eased
somewhat but the international dangers now emerged with new intensity. The new threats came from all sides.[15]

The start of the Anglo-German naval race now had its impact. The
1904 *entente cordiale* between France and Britain soon became transformed, thanks to Germany's maladroit moves in Morocco in March
1905, into a quasi-alliance. The new entente only indirectly threatened
Austria-Hungary, but over time its corrosive impact became more

---

[13] For this and the next two paragraphs, see Bridge, *Habsburg Monarchy*, pp. 224–87;
Langer, *European Alliances*, pp. 459–509, and William L. Langer, *The Diplomacy of
Imperialism: 1890–1902*, 2nd edn., 2 vols. in 1 (New York: Alfred A. Knopf, 1956),
chps. 1, 2, 7, 20, 22, and 23; Afflerbach, *Der Dreibund*, pp. 365–591; Angelow, *Kalkül
und Prestige*, pp. 117–74.

[14] See John C. G. Röhl, *The Kaiser and His Court: Wilhelm II and the Government of
Germany*, trans. Terence F. Cole (Cambridge University Press, 1994) and *Wilhelm
II: Der Aufbau der persönlichen Monarchie, 1888–1900* (Munich: Beck, 2001) and
Wilhelm II. Der Weg in den Abgrund 1900–1914 (Munich: Beck, 2009).

[15] For an analysis of "tethering/tethering alliances," see the superb study by Patricia
A. Weitsman, *Dangerous Alliances: Proponents of Peace, Weapons of War* (Stanford
University Press, 2004); also Okey, *The Habsburg Monarchy*, pp. 283–360.

decisive as London increasingly viewed Vienna as simply an extension of Berlin.[16]

To the south, events in Serbia in 1903 now emerged with new gravity. The murder of the compliant King Alexander (and his mistress-turned-wife) in June 1903 brought the Karadjordević clan to power under King Peter. With his accession, a product of anti-Habsburg feeling among young Serbian army officers including Dragutin Dimitrijević (Apis of 1914 fame), Peter soon steered Belgrade away from the Habsburg orbit. In turn Vienna retaliated with a trade embargo on Serbian pork, the so-called "Pig War" which German traders carefully exploited to their own advantage. Eventually resolved in 1906, this episode provided a harbinger of more serious friction to come.[17]

But the biggest threat came from the wounded *soi-disant* hegemon, Russia. Confronted with a veritable revolution in January 1905, Tsar Nicholas II had grudgingly conceded a constitution and a Duma and then almost immediately set out to emasculate both. He appointed a new foreign minister, Alexander Isvolski, with a mandate to rebuild Russia's international reputation. For the new minister, that effort focused renewed attention on Russia's role in the Balkans and at the Straits of Constantinople. The full impact of these changes was not slow in coming.[18]

In Vienna in 1906, as the domestic tensions eased, there were a series of personnel changes whose importance became apparent gradually. First, Franz Joseph agreed to allow the Archduke Franz Ferdinand, his nephew and heir-apparent, to establish a military chancellery of his own at Belvedere Palace. Soon military and civilian leaders had to consider how the archduke would react to any given policy proposal, nor was the heir reluctant to offer his own opinions on a host of matters. An early indication of the shifting power arrangements came

---

[16]   On this, see Zara S. Steiner and Keith Neilson, *Britain and the Origins of the First World War*, 2nd edn. (London: Palgrave Macmillan, 2003); Samuel R. Williamson, Jr., *The Politics of Grand Strategy: Britain and France Prepare for War, 1904–1914* (Cambridge, MA: Harvard University Press, 1969).

[17]   David MacKenzie, *Apis, the Congenial Conspirator: The Life of Colonel Dragutin T. Dimitrijevic* (Boulder: East European Monographs, 1989); Samuel R. Williamson, Jr. and Russel Van Wyk, *July 1914: Soldiers, Statesmen, and the Coming of the Great War: A Brief Documentary History* (Boston: Bedford St. Martin's Press, 2003), pp. 15–42; John R. Lampe, *Yugoslavia as History: Twice There Was a Country* (Cambridge University Press, 1996), pp. 70–98.

[18]   On Russian foreign policy generally, see David MacLaren McDonald, *United Government and Foreign Policy in Russia, 1900–1914* (Cambridge, MA: Harvard University Press, 1992); on Isvolski, see the still-useful essay by G. P. Gooch, *Before the War: Studies in Diplomacy*, 2 vols. (London: Longmans, 1936–38), pp. 287–363. For the overall context, see William C. Fuller, *Civil–Military Conflict in Imperial Russia, 1881–1914* (Princeton University Press, 1985), pp. 129–263.

when the aged emperor agreed to appoint two men supported by Franz Ferdinand: Count Alois von Aehrenthal, the former ambassador to Russia, as the new foreign minister, and General Conrad as the new chief of the general staff. Within months the impact of these two upon Habsburg security policy became profound.[19]

Before examining the consequences of their efforts, and those of Count Berchtold who succeeded Aehrenthal in February 1912, a few comments about two of Mearsheimer's assumptions are necessary. "Offensive realism" gives, he notes, scant attention to either individuals or to domestic political issues. Few assertions are more likely to trouble historians than those two propositions, since historians believe that individuals make key decisions, rather than an anonymous "black box," and most historians would insist that domestic and foreign considerations cannot be easily separated, certainly when analyzing the war of 1914–18.[20] Let me be still more specific in the Habsburg case. Eleven different nationalities existed within the framework of Austria-Hungary. Almost every domestic political issue in either half of the monarchy involved profound trade-offs involving the nationalities. In addition, a series of ethnic groups had ties with states external to the dynasty: the Italians, the Romanians, the Serbs, the Poles, the Ruthenians, and more generally, the Slavs in Bohemia, in Bosnia, and in Croatia. And, ironically, there was the question of German-Austrians and their relationship to Germans in Germany. For Habsburg diplomats almost no foreign policy existed as a purely "foreign" issue – all had domestic consequences. Stated in this fashion, the traditional "realist" approach, however rationalized, that brushes aside domestic political considerations becomes *ipso facto* suspect.[21]

Almost equally questionable is the contention that individual decision-makers do not much matter. Even Mearsheimer's own analysis

---

[19] On the new role for Archduke Franz Ferdinand, see Samuel R. Williamson, Jr., "Influence, Power, and the Policy Process: The Case of Franz Ferdinand, 1906–1914," *Historical Journal* 17 (1974), 17–34; Kronenbitter, *"Krieg im Frieden,"* pp. 1–77; Bridge, *Habsburg Monarchy*, pp. 244–311; also see the chapter on Aehrenthal in Gooch, *Before the War*, vol. I, pp. 367–438.

[20] Mearsheimer, *The Tragedy of Great Power Politics*, pp. 10–11; Paul W. Schroeder, "History and International Relations Theory: Not Use or Abuse, but Fit or Misfit," *International Security* 22 (1997), 64–74; Jack S. Levy, "Too Important to Leave to the Other: History and Political Science in the Study of International Relations," *International Security* 22 (1997), 22–33.

[21] Adam Wandruszka and Peter Urbanitsch (eds.), *Die Völker des Reiches*, vol. III (2 pts) (Vienna: Verlag der Österreichischen Akademie der Wissenschaften, 1980); Williamson, *Austria-Hungary*, pp. 13–33. For an older, comprehensive study of the nationality/ethnic issues, see Robert A. Kann, *The Multinational Empire: Nationalism and National Reform in the Habsburg Monarchy*, 2 vols. (New York: Columbia University Press, 1950).

contradicts this position with his "great man" approach in discussing Napoleon, Hitler, and Stalin.[22] An analysis of their policies cannot be separated from them as individuals, yet elsewhere other heads of state, generals and admirals, and diplomats are readily subsumed under the rubric of "rational actor" and the "state." That approach, this chapter contends, simply will not explain Habsburg security policy, whether "defensive" or "offensive" in the last eight years before the Great War.

II

General Conrad inherited a proud but questionable military force. Friedrich Beck, his predecessor for twenty-five years and one of the few people ever called a "friend" by Franz Joseph, seldom pressed for larger expenditures, had only slowly organized the general staff, and was content to play catch-up with military technology.[23] The new commander wasted little time in challenging the old practices and strategic assumptions. An aggressive personality, the general exuded confidence, pressed for military increases, and warned of the monarchy's shortcomings. Convinced that states competed in a Darwinian world and either struggled and survived, or struggled and failed, he wanted the monarchy to compete. Indeed, in his first years as chief of staff he repeatedly urged war against his erstwhile ally Italy, not because he wanted to seize Italian territory but to influence perceptions about the monarchy's long-term prospects. Conrad would have easily accepted Mearsheimer's conceptualization of "offensive realism" and it was his steady refrain about the need to act that deeply influenced Vienna's decisions after Sarajevo in 1914. But in 1906–08 Conrad had to concentrate on revamping Habsburg war plans, advocating increased military expenditures, and making field maneuvers more realistic. His influence on foreign policy remained limited, at least until the fall of 1908. In the meantime, his senior diplomatic colleague, Aehrenthal, supplied the dynamic that eventually propelled the monarchy into its first war–peace crisis in four decades with the formal annexation of Bosnia-Herzegovina that fall.[24]

---

[22] Mearsheimer, *The Tragedy of Great Power Politics*, pp. 272–88, 305–22.

[23] On the Beck regime, see Scott W. Lackey, *The Rebirth of the Habsburg Army: Friedrich Beck and the Rise of the General Staff* (Westport: Greenwood Press, 1995). On the army generally, see the essays by Johann Christoph Allmayer-Beck, "Die bewaffnete Macht in Staat und Gesellschaft," and Walter Wagner, "Die k.(u.)k. Armee: Gliederung und Aufgabenstellung," in Adam Wandruszka and Peter Urbanitsch (eds.), *Die Habsburgermonarchie, 1848–1918*, vol. V (Vienna: Verlag der Österreichischen Akademie der Wissenschaften, 1987), pp. 1–141, 351–633.

[24] On Conrad, see Lawrence Sondhaus, *Franz Conrad von Hötzendorf: Architect of the Apocalypse* (Boston: Brill Academic Publishers, 2000), pp. 81–107; Manfried

The new foreign minister had served as ambassador to St. Petersburg from 1899 to 1906. Appreciative of Russian culture and well acquainted with all of the senior figures of the Russian government, Aehrenthal came to office with first-hand knowledge of the most likely hegemon challenger to Austria-Hungary. Furthermore, because he was a great Bohemian landowner, he also brought an acute, realistic understanding of many of the monarchy's persistent domestic issues, not least the struggle between Czechs and Germans for control of Bohemia. In short, the new minister brought excellent credentials to his job at the Ballhausplatz, home of the foreign ministry.[25]

Initially, Aehrenthal hoped to work with his new Russian counterpart, Isvolski, to continue a cautious policy in the Balkans. However, the Russian decision to settle a series of longstanding imperial issues with Britain in 1907 provided a painful reminder of the risks of an overly close association with Germany. Soon Aehrenthal realized that the new Triple Entente, though not yet called this, meant that Russia would resume its earlier assertiveness at the Straits, in the Balkans, and perhaps even in the monarchy's internal affairs as well. For his part, Aehrenthal wanted to remind Berlin that Vienna remained an independent power, capable of actions on its own.

The situation in Bosnia-Herzegovina gave Aehrenthal a chance to keep Russia connected, show some independence toward Berlin, and remind Europe that Austria-Hungary still mattered. To the credit of both foreign ministers, the first steps made by each in the Balkans appeared to suggest harmony. Aehrenthal pressed a long-dormant rail plan through Ottoman territory. News of the demands alerted Isvolski who in turn approached Vienna about a possible modus vivendi: the Habsburgs would support Russia's desire to open the long-closed Straits to Russian warships and Russia would accept conversion of Vienna's administrative control over the two provinces into a legal ratification. In early 1908 negotiations moved apace; Austria-Hungary would protect its position by negotiating a deal with the potential hegemon.[26]

Rauchensteiner, *Der Tod des Doppeladlers: Österreich-Ungarn und der Erste Weltkrieg* (Vienna: Verlag Styria, 1993), pp. 15–39; Kronenbitter, *"Krieg im Frieden,"* pp. 1–232.

[25] For a brief summary, see F. R. Bridge, "The Foreign Policy of the Monarchy," in Mark Cornwall (ed.), *The Last Years of Austria-Hungary: A Multi-National Experiment in Twentieth-Century Europe*, rev. edn. (University of Exeter Press, 2002), pp. 13–45. On the thorough interconnection of foreign and domestic issues in the monarchy, see the correspondence of Aehrenthal, skillfully edited by Solomon Wank, in *Aus dem Nachlass Aehrenthal: Briefe und Dokumente zur österreichische-ungarischen Innen- und Aussenpolitik 1885–1912*, 2 vols. (Graz: Wolfgang Neugebauer Verlag, 1994).

[26] On the 1908–09 crisis, see Bridge, *Habsburg Monarchy*, pp. 288–311; Kronenbitter, *"Krieg im Frieden,"* pp. 317–56; Williamson, *Austria-Hungary*, pp. 58–81.

Then the unexpected occurred. In Constantinople a revolution brought the so-called "Young Turks" to power with calls to modernize the Ottoman Empire. These mid-summer developments accelerated Aehrenthal's plans, since he feared the Turks would seek representation from Bosnia-Herzegovina for any new constitutional convention. He wanted no pretext for Turkish authority over the provinces.[27]

The resulting Bosnia crisis requires no detailed description.[28] The Habsburg minister invited his Russian counterpart, who had long scheduled a trip west, to stop at Buchlau (one of Count Berchtold's favorite estates) in September. There Aehrenthal and Isvolski agreed that Austria-Hungary would annex the two provinces, that Bulgaria would renounce any obligations to the Ottoman Empire, and that Vienna would support Russian claims at the Straits. A deal had been closed; the Austro-Russian détente continued.

Within days the entire scenario became a nightmare for the Russian foreign minister. Aehrenthal, anxious for a domestic political success and with the Delegations (the closest things to an imperial parliament) about to meet, decided to present Europe with the fait accompli of annexation. A nearly distraught Isvolski, then in Paris, had to hurry home to salvage his position, for contrary to his own expectations the Pan Slavic press denounced him and the tsar showed his displeasure. In an attempt to undo the mischief, St. Petersburg demanded an international conference, sought help from France, and complained bitterly of Aehrenthal's treachery. Serbia mobilized its military forces, prompting an expensive Habsburg rejoinder. Conrad, not surprisingly, demanded war with Serbia. Not until March 1909 did the crisis ease, complicated by a sharp German ultimatum to Russia to stop encouraging Serbia or face the consequences. St. Petersburg accepted the humiliation, while vowing not to let it happen again. Serbia, angry at Russia's failure, pledged revenge, or at least some Serbian officers clustered around the legendary Apis did so.

Aehrenthal had secured an apparent foreign policy triumph. Yet the triumph did not bring any surge of support for the dynasty in either Austria or Hungary. And the financial consequences of the partial mobilization disrupted the common budget, while delaying further modernization of Habsburg forces. In the years after 1909 Conrad

---

[27] On the "Young Turks," see M. Sükrü Hanioğlu, *A Brief History of the Ottoman Empire* (Princeton University Press, 2008), pp. 144–77, and M. Sükrü Hanioğlu, *The Young Turks in Opposition* (New York: Oxford University Press, 1995); Erik J. Zürcher, *Turkey: A Modern History*, 3rd edn. (London: I. B. Tauris, 2003), pp. 93–106.

[28] Bridge provides a succinct account in *Habsburg Monarchy*, pp. 268–96.

continually asserted that the monarchy should have gone to war against Serbia and, if necessary, against Russia.[29] He believed he had promises of German support and that Russia was still too weak to fight. If Mearsheimer can claim that Germany missed an opportunity, in "offensive realism" terms, to go to war in 1905, Conrad would make the same argument about 1909; a war might well have given the Habsburg hegemon in the Balkans a credible victory. But that risk neither Franz Joseph, nor Aehrenthal, nor the Archduke Franz Ferdinand, nor Berlin were prepared to take. Instead they accepted a more limited success, but one that carried very heavy consequences. These were not long in coming.

First, after a suitable interval, Isvolski became Russian ambassador to France and Serge Sazonov the new foreign minister. Behind the almost benign appearance of a banker, Sazonov brought a new confidence, a new assertiveness, and considerable deviousness to Russian policy. Vienna had acquired a dangerous, implacable foe whose role in accelerating the course to war in July 1914 remains much under-appreciated. However judged, after 1909 the chances for an Austro-Russian détente over the Balkans had essentially disappeared. Their relationship had acquired an increasingly zero-sum dimension, though it took time for this character to be grasped in Vienna or Budapest.[30]

A second consequence also had a negative long-term impact. The unnecessarily harsh German ultimatum to St. Petersburg reinforced belief in the British Foreign Office that Vienna had became a virtual satellite of Germany. Although London appreciated that the two allies could differ, Sir Edward Grey treated them as a pair and became convinced that in any major crisis Berlin could control Austria-Hungary. In that sense he took a "buck-passing" approach to the problems of the Balkans.

The British assessment did not, moreover, change during the Second Moroccan Crisis. Despite Vienna's almost complete indifference to the further German provocation of the Anglo-French entente, London still viewed them as a linked pair.[31]

---

[29] Kronenbitter, "Krieg im Frieden," pp. 339–67; Williamson, Austria-Hungary, pp. 70–74; Sondhaus, Conrad, pp. 96–99; Bridge, From Sadowa to Sarajevo, pp. 300–38.

[30] Gooch's essay on Sazonov remains useful, Before the War, vol. II, pp. 289–370; for a broader view, see Ronald P. Bobroff, Late Imperial Russia and the Turkish Straits: Roads to Glory (New York: I. B. Tauris, 2006).

[31] On the British attitude, see F. R. Bridge, "Relations with Austria-Hungary and the Balkan States, 1905–1908," in F. H. Hinsley (ed.), British Foreign Policy under Sir Edward Grey (Cambridge University Press, 1977), pp. 165–77; also D. W. Sweet, "The Bosnian Crisis," in Hinsley (ed.), British Foreign Policy under Sir Edward Grey, pp. 178–92.

From Vienna's point of view the negative impact of Agadir was almost immediate and very dangerous. With the two alliance/entente structures preoccupied, Italy had peremptorily moved to seize Tripoli (Libya) from the Ottomans. The Italian military machine displayed no great prowess, but the entire expedition meant that the Ottoman leaders were exposed in Macedonia and Albania, their last bastions in the Balkans. Although a dying Aehrenthal realized the dangers that a distracted Constantinople faced, Sazonov and his colleagues were more effective in taking advantage of the situation. In a series of "offensive realism" moves, the Russians by late spring 1912 had helped to create a Balkan League of Serbia, Bulgaria, and Greece (and later Montenegro) that had a single goal: push Turkey from Europe. The final stages on the road to the First World War were about to begin.[32]

In Vienna a new set of leaders now confronted a rapidly changing international situation. In November 1911 an exasperated Franz Joseph removed Conrad as chief of staff. The aggressive general had urged anew an attack on Italy while it fought in Tripoli. The emperor/king finally told him that peace, not war, was his policy. While Conrad remained on active duty, General Blasius Schemua became the new army commander.[33] Count Leopold Berchtold joined the general in the top leadership, replacing the dying Aehrenthal as foreign minister. Berchtold was an aristocrat of such background that he could sit in the upper house of either Austria or Hungary (he chose the latter). The new minister had just completed a tour as ambassador to Russia. Like his predecessor, he knew the Russian leadership well, or thought he did. Considered by many contemporaries a dilettante and light-weight, Berchtold managed, against heavy odds, to salvage an effective defensive position during the Balkan Wars and would become, in July 1914, one of the key drivers in Vienna's decision for war. But that was in the future.[34]

During his first six months in office Berchtold learned of the existence of the secret Balkan League and grasped its dangers for Austria-Hungary. He managed, along with war minister General Moritz von Auffenberg and General Schemua, to convince the Hungarian leadership to increase the recruit contingent from 136,000 to 181,000, in

[32] Barbara Jelavich, *Russia's Balkan Entanglements, 1806–1914* (Cambridge University Press, 1991), pp. 197–264.

[33] Kronenbitter, *"Krieg im Frieden,"* pp. 71, 297–99; Gunther E. Rothenberg, *The Army of Francis Joseph* (West Lafayette: Purdue University Press, 1976), pp. 163–66.

[34] On Berchtold, see the work by Hugo Hantsch, *Leopold Graf Berchtold: Grandseigneur und Staatsman*, 2 vols. (Graz: Styria, 1963); the chapter by Gooch, "Berchtold," in *Before the War*, vol. II, pp. 373–447; Bridge, *Habsburg Monarchy*, pp. 312–44; Williamson and Van Wyk, *July 1914*, pp. 43–72.

part because all could reference the Italian attack on Libya as well as the woeful disparity of numbers between the monarchy's armed forces and those of Italy and Russia. Nor could anyone ignore the surge in German military expenditures after Agadir.[35] Meanwhile, in the background were reliable reports of increased Franco-Russian cooperation, a cooperation that threatened their German ally and created strategic problems for the monarchy. Amid this confusion, Berchtold in September attempted, too late to be successful, to convince the other European powers to intervene with the Ottomans about conditions in Macedonia and thus thwart the Balkan League. Surprisingly, even Sazonov showed some interest. But events moved too quickly.

On October 8 Montenegro declared war on Constantinople and the other League members quickly joined. Almost immediately Berchtold and the Habsburg leadership confronted a volatile international situation. Along the common border with Russia came reports that the Russian troops, normally scheduled for release at the end of their service period and estimated at 220,000 men, would remain on active duty, a step clearly intended to signal to Vienna to stay out of the Balkan fighting. And, to the surprise of all, the Balkan allies rapidly defeated the Turkish forces, so much so that any Austrian hope that Turkey could prevent Serbian gains proved illusory. In these circumstances Serbia gained new territory, threatened to gain access to the Adriatic through Albania, and suddenly became a significant strategic threat to be confronted.[36]

The Habsburg response, in a classic "defensive realism" exercise, had multiple approaches. By November Berchtold and Franz Joseph could no longer resist the military demands for partial mobilization, both along the Russian border and in Bosnia-Herzegovina. Undertaken piecemeal, these actions caused panic in Galicia, alarm in St. Petersburg, and a huge financial drain on the monarchy. Before they ended, in the summer of 1913, the military measures had cost the equivalent of an entire year's military budget and completely disrupted a Habsburg economy showing signs of genuine growth.[37]

Over time the military measures, with the real prospect of war, prompted the emperor to bring Conrad back as chief of staff, a step

---

[35] Rothenberg, *Army of Francis Joseph*, pp. 165–66; Kronenbitter, *"Krieg im Frieden,"* pp. 172–78; and on the German efforts, David Stevenson, *Armaments and the Coming of War: Europe, 1904–1914* (Oxford University Press, 1996), pp. 180–243.

[36] Stevenson, *Armaments and the Coming of War*, pp. 243–71; Kronenbitter, *"Krieg im Frieden,"* pp. 369–413; Williamson, *Austria-Hungary*, pp. 121–48; and the still-valuable E. C. Helmreich, *The Diplomacy of the Balkan Wars, 1912–1913* (Cambridge, MA: Harvard University Press, 1938).

[37] Williamson, *Austria-Hungary*, pp. 156–60.

that assured new demands for military action regardless of the consequences. The military situation, moreover, brought high-level talks with Berlin, exchanges that eventually saw the Germans caution their ally about a winter war. In March 1913 new negotiations eased the prospect of an Austro-Russian clash.[38]

But the entire episode revealed the new willingness of St. Petersburg to engage in a policy of assertive diplomacy. These steps, coupled with the sudden surge in Russian rearmament and military expansion, prompted new concern in Vienna and downright apprehension in Berlin. By the spring of 1914 both General Helmuth von Moltke, chief of the German General Staff, and Conrad could talk of a preventive war. For the two allies, the Russians represented the expansionist, dangerous hegemon.

If the Habsburg military measures were expensive, they nevertheless gave effective credibility to Berchtold's efforts. In early December 1912 he had managed to convince the great powers to recognize, ironically on the principle of nationality, the creation of a new Albanian state, a move that blocked Serbia's access to the Adriatic. He also backed Grey's convocation of an ambassadors' conference in London that sought to bring peace to the Balkans. In their mediation efforts the great powers were helped by the illness among the troops of the Balkan armies, a sudden revival of Turkish military fortunes, and the sheer strain of war on the Balkan governments. The talks in London put an end to major fighting, while leaving a series of dangerous border and boundary disputes about the size of Albania jeopardizing the peace.

Berchtold's diplomatic gains enabled him, with the strong support of Franz Joseph, to resist Conrad's pleas in December 1912 for war with Serbia. Once more the aged monarch opted for caution, a caution that winter weather and an ambivalent Germany reinforced. In this prudence the ruler got additional support from his nephew. While Franz Ferdinand flirted with support for a military confrontation in early December, he reversed course and never thereafter altered it. He became a force for peace and restraint.[39]

The archduke's cautious position merits further comment. With a virtual shadow government ready to take power, with a clear (and

---

[38] On the Austro-Russian tensions, almost entirely ignored by historians, see Samuel R. Williamson, Jr., "Military Dimensions of Habsburg–Romanov Relations during the Era of the Balkan Wars," in Bela K. Kiraly and Dimitri Djordevic (eds.), *East Central European Society and the Balkan Wars* (New York: East European Monographs, 1987), pp. 317–37. Also see Richard C. Hall, *The Balkan Wars, 1912–1913: Prelude to the First World War* (London: Routledge, 2000).

[39] Sondhaus, *Conrad*, pp. 119–24.

reciprocated) hostility to the Magyars, and with mounting domestic tensions in the monarchy, the very question of the monarchy's survival became a topic for discussion. While a strong supporter of the development of the Habsburg navy, the archduke never lost sight of the crucial importance of the army.[40] If the public discussions about the monarchy's future were sober and pragmatic, the private ones were sometimes alarmist and pessimistic. Yet the principle of Habsburg dynastic power, with its 1,000-year history, and the continuation of the German alliance kept Austria-Hungary among the great powers. If state survival ranks high on the objectives of either "defensive realism" or "offensive realism," that objective was always paramount for the leadership of the Habsburg state. The next eighteen months brought the survival issue increasingly to the fore.

The year 1913 saw Vienna on the verge of war twice more, once with Montenegro in May over the shape of Albania's borders and in October with Serbia over the same issue. In each instance a forceful Habsburg stance had resolved the crisis, a lesson not lost on the policy-makers in Vienna. For its part, the Russians had offered only limited support for its two Slavic client states in the Balkans. The Russians, like the Habsburgs, were not especially happy with the outcome of the two Balkan wars, in their case because the victorious powers showed little deference to St. Petersburg.[41]

On the other hand, Sazonov soon exploited the changing Balkan scene to his advantage. Magyar treatment of the three million Romanians living in Transylvania had never been easy. Efforts to ameliorate the situation faltered on the shoals of Magyar politics. Even István Tisza, now returned as Hungarian prime minister, could not agree to concessions there. In this context the Romanian leaders, miffed over this issue and their own modest gains from the Second Balkan War, found Sazonov's new attention increasingly attractive. This attention had a single goal: pull Bucharest away from its secret ties to the Triple Alliance. By early 1914 Berchtold clearly grasped that the Russian ploys were becoming increasingly effective; indeed, in June 1914 Sazonov, on a state visit to Romania, actually stepped over the border into Transylvania, a step that could only be labeled as provocative.

---

[40] On the archduke, see the essays in Robert A. Kann, *Erzherzog Franz Ferdinand Studien* (Vienna: Oldenbourg, 1976); on the naval build-up, see Milan N. Vego, *Austro-Hungarian Naval Policy, 1904–14* (London: Routledge, 1996), and Lawrence Sondhaus, *The Naval Policy of Austria-Hungary, 1867–1918: Navalism, Industrial Development, and the Politics of Dualism* (West Lafayette: Purdue University Press, 1994).

[41] Bridge, *Habsburg Monarchy*, pp. 319–28; Williamson, *Austria-Hungary*, pp. 135–63.

Nor did Berchtold's alliance problems end with Romania. Tensions with Italy, always close to the surface, flared in 1913 and 1914, as the simmering issue of irredentism erupted anew. A series of offensive Habsburg measures in Trieste and the rejection of a proposal to create an Italian faculty at the University of Innsbruck inflamed the situation. But the Italian politicians also found anti-Habsburg sentiments played well, creating a temptation they did not resist. The two powers struggled as well over which would have the most significant influence in the newly created Albania. Even face to face sessions in Abazzia in April 1914 between Berchtold and Foreign Minister Antonino San Giuliano failed to resolve the tension.[42]

Relations with Berlin were more cordial. Kaiser Wilhelm showered attention on Franz Ferdinand and visited Vienna on his many travels. But the German ruler disliked Vienna's mounting irritation with Romania and dismissed the dangers posed by Serbia to Habsburg interests, whether in Bosnia-Herzegovina or in Austria-Hungary proper. In fact, the German monarch refused to appreciate how deeply the Habsburgs worried about Serbia. Still, he remained loyal to the dynasty and expressed confidence for the monarchy's future, even as his own diplomats privately worried about what would happen on the death of Franz Joseph.[43]

Change on the external canvas was matched by two important domestic changes for Berchtold. The appointment of Tisza as the Hungarian prime minister completely altered the dynamics of decision-making among the top eight leaders. Unlike his predecessor, Tisza had strong views about foreign policy and no hesitancy in presenting them. Indeed, after a conversation with Kaiser Wilhelm in 1914, the German ruler declared him the most interesting man in the monarchy, a statement that made Franz Ferdinand most unhappy. To ensure that he would be heard (and to keep a pulse on the situation at the court in Vienna), Tisza asked István Burián, the former common minister for Bosnia-Herzegovina, to represent him in an office within five minutes of Berchtold's. For his part Tisza wanted to shore up the German alliance but he also expressed a willingness to discuss matters of common interest with the Russians. His flexibility on this issue might have offered the monarchy a chance to ease tensions with St. Petersburg, though the gambit soon came to nothing in early 1914, not least because

---

[42] Afflerbach, *Der Dreibund*, pp. 788–812; Angelow, *Kalkül und Prestige*, pp. 424–65.

[43] For a detailed analysis of Austro-German relations, see Jiri Koralka, "Deutschland und Die Habsburgermonarchie 1948–1918," in Adam Wandruszka and Peter Urbanitsch (eds.), *Die Habsburgermonarchie, 1848–1918*, vol. VI, pt. 2, *Die Habsburgermonarchie im System des Internationalen Beziehungen* (Vienna: Verlag der Österreichischen Akademie der Wissenschaften, 1993), pp. 113–38.

the Russians appeared to support some Slavic groups within Austria-Hungary who resorted to terror and to internal subversion.[44]

The other domestic development centered on the increasing paralysis of the Austrian government. Karl Stürgkh, the prime minister since 1911, had no interest in parliamentary government. After all, he could use the emergency Paragraph 14 to govern in the absence of the Reichsrat. The continued Czech–German frictions in Bohemia were also played out in the Reichsrat, leading him finally to prorogue the body in March 1914, a step that caused further tremors about the monarchy's long-term ability to address the problem of nationalities.[45]

In the late spring of 1914 a series of events occurred that would define the July crisis. First came the decision by Franz Ferdinand to proceed with the long-scheduled trip to Bosnia for army maneuvers despite the emperor's recent serious illness. Then came the decision of Gavrilo Princip and others, aided and abetted by Apis and the Black Hand in Belgrade, to use the occasion of the visit for an attempt at assassination. In this Serbian maelstrom a new, bitter clash between military and civilian officials meant that the prime minister, Nikola Pašić, could not, once he learned of the plot, stop it, nor, once it succeeded, allow Austria-Hungary to investigate the conspiracy within Serbia.

Finally, in mid-June Berchtold concluded that Habsburg foreign policy had to regroup, to seek a new departure. The German alliance remained the key but the isolation of Serbia now became the chief operational goal. This would be done, with or without Romania's help, and it might require Bulgarian assistance. But Berchtold and his senior colleagues had concluded, in perfect keeping with the tenets of "defensive realism," that the South Slav message championed by Serbia had to be rebuffed, firmly and definitively. If this meant a clash of wills with Russia, so be it.[46]

---

[44] Williamson, *Austria-Hungary*, pp. 143–89; also John Leslie, "The Antecedents of Austria-Hungary's War Aims: Policies and Policy-Makers in Vienna and Budapest before and during 1914," in Elisabeth Springer and Leopold Kammerhold (eds.), *Archiv und Forschung: Das Haus-, Hof- und Staatsarchiv in seiner Bedeutung für die Geschichte Österreichs und Europas* (Vienna: Verlag für Geschichte und Politik, 1993), pp. 323–40.

[45] See Lothar Höbelt, "'Well-tempered Discontent': Austrian Domestic Politics," in *The Last Days of Austria-Hungary*, pp. 47–74; Catherine Albrecht, "The Bohemian Question," in *The Last Days of Austria-Hungary*, pp. 75–96; John Boyer, *Culture and Political Crisis in Vienna: Christian Socialism in Power, 1897–1918* (University of Chicago Press, 1995), pp. 164–368.

[46] For a summary, see Williamson, *Austria-Hungary*, pp. 184–89; Mark Cornwall, "Serbia," in Keith Wilson (ed.), *Decisions for War 1914* (New York: Routledge, 1995), pp. 55–96.

III

As the Habsburg monarchy faced the July crisis, how did its foreign and security policies measure against the propositions of Mearsheimer's "offensive realism"? Operating in a dangerous multipolar situation that was by definition anarchic, Austria-Hungary had sufficient military power to defend itself against another great power (Germany excepted) if there was just a unilateral clash. On the other hand, by 1914 the emerging Russia hegemon called this Habsburg ability severely into question. And, however defined, if the monarchy confronted two powers, even if was one was minor (Serbia), the chances for victory were greatly reduced. Survival had always been the first consideration of dynastic policy since 1815; a century later the chances of survival either internationally or domestically seemed less reassuring than at any time since the 1870s.[47]

To this point the monarchy's behavior and Mearsheimer's assumptions match. But he takes the argument a step further, insisting the international system has no room for status quo powers and that states – after calculation – always seek to expand their hegemonial position. In their calculations military power, especially land military power, represents the *sine qua non* of power, a point that successive generations of Habsburg statesmen seem to have missed as they remained content with their statistically inferior position.

Taken more broadly, how does the Habsburg experience match off with the Mearsheimer model, for the years from 1900 to June 1914? There are, to be sure, points of congruence. The 1908 decision to annex Bosnia-Herzegovina, whose administration after 1878 could have been called "offensive realist," reflected an assertive stance not merely content with survival or the status quo. Yet the 1908 Young Turk revolt did threaten the status quo, so Aehrenthal's haste even at the risk of a major crisis could be seen as "defensive," not "offensive." So too could the Habsburg reaction to Sazonov's increasingly bold moves after 1911 – the Balkan League, de facto partial mobilization during the First Balkan War, the wooing of Bucharest, the upsurge in Russian

---

[47] For a recent analysis of how the German and Habsburg generals viewed the security situation on the eve of war, see Günther Kronenbitter, "The German and Austro-Hungarian General Staffs and Their Reflections on an 'Impossible' War," in Holger Afflerbach and David Stevenson (eds.), *An Improbable War? The Outbreak of World War I and European Political Culture Before 1914* (New York: Berghahn Books, 2008), pp. 149–58; also see Annika Mombauer, *Helmuth von Moltke and the Origins of the First World War* (Cambridge University Press, 2001), pp. 164–81.

military manpower – be viewed as defensive, survival approaches, not expansionist or excessively risky.

The relationship with Berlin with its touches of monarchical solidarity and German assurances constitutes both a balancing act to offset Russia and a bandwagoning/tethering approach to keep St. Petersburg and Berlin from ever becoming too close. To be sure, the Anglo-German naval race aided the Habsburg effort, for it made Berlin increasingly rely on Vienna, just as the naval race made France more necessary than ever for London. In that sense realism – whether defensive or offensive – as a theoretical approach describes how external factors drive foreign policy. Yet in this assessment "defensive realism" far more often provides an adequate, persuasive analytical framework to understand the actions of Vienna and Budapest. On that scale, Waltz, not Mearsheimer, appears to have the edge.[48]

But a historian of the Austro-Hungarian monarchy should not let the analysis rest there. To an extent unusual, but not unknown (the contemporary United States being one example), foreign policy is not solely a function of a state reacting to external events. Domestic politics and internal power alignments, constitutional structures and their differences, and, in a multinational setting, relationships among ethnic groups within and without the state, simply cannot be ignored. No explication of Habsburg policy after 1859 toward Italy can ignore the question of Italian irredentism. An alliance with the Italian government might obscure the fact on occasion, but the issue of unredeemed Italians within Austria always played a part in Habsburg diplomacy toward Italy. The same, of course, was equally true of the Romanians under Magyar control and policy toward Romania. The Poles, as usual, presented an even more interesting case, divided as they were between Germany, Russia, and Austria. Few calculations of Habsburg policy could ignore the Russian willingness to stir and meddle in Galicia. And then there were the Slavs, those in Bohemia and Slovakia and those in Bosnia-Herzegovina and Croatia. The often seething nationalism, the siren calls of Pan Slavism, and the Serb–Russian connection ensured that Russia's policies toward the Balkans intimately impacted upon Vienna's policy choices. In that fashion, "realism" with its black-box approach remains inadequate to describe or account for the foreign policy of a state like Austria-Hungary, which may explain its almost total absence in theoretical approaches to international relations. But enough

---

[48] On this issue, see Paul Schroeder, "Historical Reality vs. Neo-realist Theory," *International Security* 19 (1994), 108–12, 147–48. Also see Robert Jervis, *System Effects: Complexity in Political and Social Life* (Princeton University Press, 1997), pp. 108–24.

said for criticism at this point. We now turn to see how either theory works in the world of Vienna and Budapest in the month of July 1914.

IV

The deaths of Franz Ferdinand and his wife Sophie on Sunday, June 28, 1914, in Sarajevo set in motion the events that brought about the First World War. Without those deaths, 1914 would almost certainly have passed as another peaceful year. But Sarajevo and the Habsburg reaction to it altered everything; and by the end of July a European, then a world war had come.[49]

This chapter does not need to recount every stage of the Danubian government's decision process. Some key points do, however, require emphasis. First, the decision for a preventive military attack came from the Habsburg, not the German, decision-makers. By July 3 all of the Habsburg leadership, save Tisza, believed Serbia must be punished. The German response to Vienna's request for support, the infamous "blank check," gave Berchtold the confidence to move ahead. But the decision for war was Habsburg; the German support ensured that it would happen, even if some in Berlin doubted their ally would actually take action. To be sure, Berlin's almost cavalier approach to their decision guarantees it a rightful place of condemnation, even as many historians now credit both Berlin and Vienna with key decisions of the crisis.

With German support secured, Berchtold worked to convince Tisza that only war would solve the Serbian threat. This did not come easily, for the Magyar leader feared war and wanted to negotiate instead. To overcome this resistance Berchtold and Burián exploited Tisza's fears that a Belgrade left unchecked might soon turn its attention to agitation among the Romanians under Magyar rule. Thus the Serb threat had potential domestic consequences for Tisza. Nor could he, or the others in Vienna, ignore reports from Bosnia that suggested domestic unrest would continue there (and even might spread) unless Belgrade's

---

[49] The best analysis of July 1914 is now Hew Strachan, *The Outbreak of the First World War* (Oxford University Press, 2004); also see Williamson, *Austria-Hungary*, pp. 190–216; Kronenbitter, *"Krieg im Frieden,"* pp. 455–519; Rauchensteiner, *Der Tod des Doppeladlers*, pp. 67–85. These analyses do not, it should be noted, agree with that of Copeland, *The Origins of Major War*, with its excessive focus on Germany as the sole prime mover in 1914; the same is also true of Keir A. Lieber, "The New History and World War I and What It Means for International Relations Theory," *International Security* 32 (2007), 155–91. A more balanced perspective can be found in Stephen Van Evera, *Causes of War: Power and the Roots of Conflict* (Ithaca: Cornell University Press, 1999), pp. 193–239.

support for the South Slav movement were checked once and for all. Previous promises by Serbia to curb these efforts appeared worthless. These considerations were not trivial and lend strong support to the argument that internal, domestic pressures helped to propel Vienna forward.[50]

On the other hand, Tisza exacted a stiff price. While Conrad might talk of partitioning Serbia or reducing it to a vassal state and while Alexander Hoyos had also discussed these possibilities in Berlin on July 5 as part of his mission, Tisza would have none of it. His *quid pro quo*, negotiated in detail, remained unambivalent: the monarchy would take no substantive territory from Serbia. He wanted no additional Slavs in the monarchy, period. And on July 19 his fellow ministers finally agreed to this condition, even as Conrad after the meeting dismissed the pledge of restraint.[51] Nevertheless, the Habsburg monarchy went to war to punish Serbia, to bring about regime change, and to remind the world that it was a great power. But the leaders, save possibly Conrad, saw this action as necessary for the monarchy's status as a great power, taken to ensure survival, not necessarily for expansion. It was "defensive," not "offensive" realism that united the leaders in Vienna and Budapest.

In their deliberations the leaders, who had already faced four war–peace crises in the previous eighteen months, minimized the threat of the Russian hegemon. Even though St. Petersburg could not be ignored, the Habsburg decision-makers believed that open German support, plus the aura of monarchical solidarity, would keep the war local and Russia out. That proved to be the most significant miscalculation of the crisis, for Sazonov (almost certainly in agreement with the French whose leaders had just visited the Russian capital) escalated the Russian responses from the moment news of the ultimatum reached St. Petersburg on July 24.

New evidence shows the Russian military ordering troop measures in the late afternoon of July 24, before any other power, save Serbia,

[50] Leslie, "The Antecedents of Austria-Hungary's War Aims," pp. 341–47; Samuel R. Williamson, Jr., "Aggressive and Defensive Aims of Political Elites? Austro-Hungarian Policy in 1914," in Afflerbach and Stevenson (eds.), *An Improbable War*, pp. 61–74. Rudolf Jerabek, *Potiorek: General im Schatten von Sarajevo* (Graz: Styria, 1991), pp. 82–96.

[51] An abbreviated English version of the two meetings, with commentary, is found in Luigi Albertini, *The Origins of the War of 1914*, 3 vols. (London: Oxford University Press, 1952–57), vol. II, pp. 164–78, 254–58; after the meeting on July 19, Conrad told General Alexander Krobatin, the war minister: "We will see; before the Balkan wars the powers also talked of the status quo; after the war no one concerned himself with it." See Franz Conrad von Hötzendorf, *Aus Meiner Dienstzeit, 1906–1918*, vol. IV (Vienna: Rikola, 1923), p. 92.

had taken any substantial military steps. The actions of that day were followed by further measures the next day that amounted to partial mobilization. Unlike in 1912–13, the Russian steps were not limited just to the Habsburg frontiers but also went into operation along the borders with Germany. Not surprisingly, by July 26 reports from German agents began to reach Berlin that alarmed the military authorities. In turn the German political leaders, led by Chancellor Theobald von Bethmann Hollweg, gradually began to think anew about their decision to back Vienna, a reconsideration that Kaiser Wilhelm's return to Berlin strengthened. The idea of a "Halt in Belgrade" had appeal, even as Bethmann delayed in pressuring Vienna to slow down. Amid this confusion, Berchtold decided to forestall any German change of heart by getting Franz Joseph to declare war on Serbia on July 28.[52]

The war declaration, followed by an exchange of gunfire causing casualties near Belgrade that same night, essentially doomed any remaining chance for peace. But not for the reason advanced by Mearsheimer (drawing on Copeland) that Germany thwarted efforts to resolve the crisis, but rather that Russia took further military steps that left Berlin – under its war plans – no freedom. The tsar agreed, then rescinded orders for general mobilization on July 29, then the next day he accepted Sazonov's and the military arguments that action was necessary, not least to help the French who wanted early Russian pressure to deflect or impede the German attack in the west. With Russia's general mobilization, the Germans could wait no longer even though Wilhelm II momentarily stopped some of the western troop movements in the evening of July 31 when it appeared that Britain might stay out. That hope proved illusory and the German attack plans moved ahead. The German invasion of Belgium provided the catalyst for British intervention, though such involvement would probably have occurred even had the Germans been more cautious about the neutral state. By August 4 war had come to Europe with the European allies, save Italy, now at war. All proclaimed it a defensive war, necessitated by the actions of others; all soon came to have grandiose ambitions for what the war might bring. But those ambitions, later historians notwithstanding, were muted in the crucial July–August discussions.[53]

Did war come because of Germany's desire to be a hegemon or were the causes more prosaic and thus more complicated? That consideration deserves attention at the end of this discussion. The commentary

---

[52] Samuel R. Williamson, Jr. and Ernest R. May, "An Identity of Opinion: Historians and July 1914," *Journal of Modern History* 79 (2007), 347–50.

[53] Strachan, *The Outbreak of the First World War*, pp. 102–27; Stevenson, *Armaments and the Coming of the War*, pp. 379–88.

to this point shows that a single-factor analysis – Germany seeking hegemonic status – is inadequate to explain 1914. The unfolding crises had many other players and the Germans were not the only drivers in July. And even German behavior, though irresponsible and sloppy and dangerous and unhelpful, had a defensive character to it. The death of the archduke was not an insignificant event, nor was Serbia innocent of involvement. The maintenance and credibility of the Habsburg monarchy was in Germany's interest and, Berlin hoped, in the interest of Europe as well. The delays in Vienna in presenting the ultimatum, the Franco-Russian resolve to back Serbia, the unilateral Russian actions to adopt its own policy of militant diplomacy but this time along the German frontier as well: all contributed to the escalation of the crisis. To be sure a German *volte-face* would have slowed the momentum to war but so too would have an Austrian or a French or a Russian delay. So "offensive realism" offers little secure footing as an explanation for July 1914.

Conrad, of course, represented the "offensive realist" in action, but that action – of an individual in a system that minimizes the individual – should not be exaggerated. Alone of the Habsburg leadership (and with intense personal reasons as well), he wanted the monarchy to expand, he wanted war, and he saw all of it in black-and-white terms.[54] But offsetting those strident demands was the base point of his argument: he wanted the monarchy to survive, not just action for action's sake – though he often sounded like that. Survival represented a key consideration, yet he advocated risks in 1914 that put survival clearly into question. Conrad put it bluntly to a newspaperman after Sarajevo: "In the years 1908–9 it would have been a game in which we could see all the cards … in 1912–13 it would have been a game with some chances of success … now it is a sheer gamble (*'ein va banque-Spiel'*)."[55]

One final set of comments. If one wanted to construct a more useful paradigm for understanding international relations, a new kind of realism, it would contain the following points. First, it would recognize the anarchic nature of international politics. But it would then put survival of the state or the regime or the government as the second feature. And it would stress the impact of the government's history, culture, organizational structure, religion, and leadership with recognition that individual leaders do make a difference. Then it would address the various means that states use to survive, including merely upholding

---

[54] On Conrad's desire for war and victory so he could marry Gina von Reininghaus, see Sondhaus, *Conrad*, pp. 108–38.

[55] Quoted in Albertini, *The Origins of the War of 1914*, vol. II, p. 122.

the status quo (as in the case of Sweden) or expansionism (Russia in the nineteenth century) or war (Hitler), along with the tactics of balancing, buck-passing, bandwagoning, and even appeasement. And at each point the interaction of domestic and international considerations would be analyzed. Theoretical approaches to international relations are useful exercises and are to be encouraged, but a few verifiable, consistent factors and sheer historical realism about the actual situation are imperative for their credibility. Otherwise, we have theories that misstate and mislead; history is replete with the results of such ideas actually put into action.

7 British decisions for peace and war 1938–1939: the rise and fall of realism

Zara Steiner

For many years, the dominant approach to the study of international relations has been that of structural realism. Because this theory has such a long pedigree, there is a great divergence of views among those who call themselves or are called "realists" or "neorealists." In order to give shape to this chapter, I have arbitrarily selected what I consider to be the main features of the realist case, knowing that many variants of the model exist. Realists begin with the assumption that states live in an anarchical international environment where there is no authority above that of the state. As a result, great powers, usually the focus of realist theorists, must rely on "self-help" to survive. They seek to maximize their power as against other states, though occasionally they will try to achieve absolute power without regard to the other players in the system. States which try to increase their power necessarily make other states feel more insecure and they will respond by adopting strategies to enhance their chances of survival. Structural realists or defensive realists, following Kenneth Waltz, argue that when great powers act aggressively, their would-be victims try to balance against the aggressor and check its threat to their survival. The anarchical conditions of the international life encourage states to behave defensively so that they can protect themselves and try to maintain their power positions. Some structural realists argue that since military power usually favors the defense (the offence–defense balance), it will be a major risk to take offensive military action. Great powers are more inclined, therefore, to behave defensively in order to ensure their safety. Offensive realists, with John Mearsheimer as their major advocate, on the contrary, argue that since states are always trying to maximize their power, they are disposed to think offensively even when their motive may be simply to survive. They, of course, think carefully about the balance of power and the reaction of other states before taking offensive action but, nonetheless, will try to use their offensive capabilities to acquire more power. Realists of both schools view states as unitary, rational units and are more interested in the behavior of the "black boxes" or "billiard balls" than what goes on within them. They concentrate on the systemic determinants of state behavior and, for the most part, pay less attention to internal variables, i.e., the roles played by individuals, domestic political considerations, ideas, ideology, and non-security goals. Maintaining the balance of power takes precedence over the pursuit of all other national goals. There is considerable disagreement about the definition of power and how it can be measured but realists of all persuasions accept that military power and the requisite wealth and population to raise and project military force are central to the power equation. There are various ways that states increase their power or respond to would-be aggressors. At one extreme, they can go to war or threaten to go to war in order to shift the balance in their favor. To stop aggression, they may go to war, build up their armaments in order to threaten war, seek alliances (balancing) to block the bid for power, or shift the burden of resistance to another country or group of countries (buck-passing). Almost all realists adopt a systemic approach to the analysis of state behavior; some will incorporate elements of decision-making, deterrence, and behavioral theories in their models but these will be of secondary interest.

In the pages that follow, I would like to suggest that neither the "defensive" nor the "offensive" realist interpretation of great-power behavior is adequate to explain British strategy in 1938–39. In particular, I will argue that the domestic determinants of foreign policy were as important as the external environment and that political and moral factors were more critical than the economic and military determinants of policy-making.[1] I will suggest, moreover, that even estimates of economic and military strength can be influenced by perceptions that are based on non-material factors. The realities of an impending war may lead to the adoption of new frames of reference that alter state behavior.

From the outset, one must accept that states are not, in reality, rational, unitary actors and that this is merely a short-hand that theoreticians adopt. Second, and this reservation would be perfectly acceptable to most model-builders, decision-makers or states often act out of ignorance and misperceive or misjudge the power equation. There is no doubt, for instance, that both British and French intelligence and their respective governments exaggerated German war readiness whether in

---

[1] Reference should be made to Richard Rosecrance and Zara Steiner, "British Grand Strategy and the Origins of World War II: Domestic versus Economic Determinants of Policy," in Richard Rosecrance and Arthur A. Stein (eds.), *The Domestic Bases of Grand Strategy* (Ithaca: Cornell University Press, 1993), pp. 124–53, for further examination of some of these points.

terms of equipped armies or front-line aircraft in 1938 or 1939. States are often the victims of mirror imaging. As we shall point out, intelligence analysts were more aware of German weaknesses than the sheer counting of numbers of men, bombers, and fighters would suggest but, nevertheless, the Allied sense of military inferiority was a major factor in British and French decision-making at Munich and led to a distorted view of the balance of power in 1938. It is possible, too, that despite the correct analysis of the power situation, the wrong conclusions can be drawn. Knowing that the German economy was in difficulties in the spring and summer of 1939, some in London continued to hope, as they had earlier, that Germany's raw-material weaknesses and lack of foreign exchange would act as constraints on German aggression once Hitler was convinced that Britain and France would go to war if he attacked Poland. It can be argued, however, that it was, in fact, Germany's dubious economic future that led Hitler to gamble on war rather than to wait until his military machine was ready as his generals wanted. Hitler's response to Germany's production difficulties was to invade Poland despite the warnings that Britain and France would honor their alliance with Warsaw. In this case, offensive behavior was mainly, though not exclusively, domestically determined.[2]

The example of Godesberg

There is little evidence that Chamberlain's decision to find a settlement of the Czech crisis by giving Hitler most of what he wanted was primarily a way of winning time for rearmament. Chamberlain had rejected the advice of those who wanted faster rearmament so that negotiations could be conducted from strength. On December 12, 1937, the cabinet decided not to give the funds needed to build up an enlarged expeditionary army (field force) that would go to the continent to fight alongside France. This decision was not revoked until February 1939 and then mainly in order to reassure the French. Even after Munich when the rearmament effort was intensified, the prime minister dragged his feet, anxious that rearmament should not make the task of reaching an accommodation with Hitler more difficult. Fundamental to his thinking was the intention to avoid war which he thought would be catastrophic for Europe, for Britain, and for the domestic equilibrium that the Conservative party had established at home. The experience of the Great War was a searing experience for him; the costs had been

---

[2] See Adam Tooze, *The Wages of Destruction: The Making and Breaking of the Nazi Economy* (London: Allen Lane, 2006), pp. 312–16.

horrendous, with over a million casualties, and the basic issues were not settled. Behind Chamberlain's policy of limited liability and deterrence was the prime minister's determination to avoid British involvement in another European war and his hope to avoid such a war through compromise and conciliation with those threatening the peace. The prime minister's views, shared, if for different reasons, by the majority of the cabinet, provide the key to an understanding of the British attitude in the autumn of 1938.[3]

On what grounds did the British choose appeasement over war or alliances or buck-passing in September 1938? The background to the Munich Crisis has been examined in considerable detail, so only a few generalizations are necessary here. Whether valid or not, there is no doubt that the differentials in military power gave weight to the prime minister's decision to give way to Hitler's demands, but strategic issues were not the determining factor. The defense estimates in the spring and summer of 1938 drew attention to the disparity between the size of the two air forces and the number of planes being produced in Britain and Germany.[4] Though the air staff knew that the Germans could not reach Britain using the North Sea route unless they violated the neutrality of the Low Countries or moved their bombers to northeast Germany – and neither was probable in 1938 – the government continued, in September, to stress the dangers of German bombing and the inadequacies of Britain's defenses. In part, their arguments were being used to force the government to speed up the completion of the radar chain and to build up Fighter Command. The chiefs of staff never warned the cabinet of a knock-out blow; the possibility had been dismissed. Yet the prime minister articulated what many were thinking when he envisioned the destruction of thousands of homes by bombing as he flew back to London after his second fateful visit to Hitler. He told his colleagues, "he had felt that we were in no position to justify waging a war today."[5] In a private paper, General Ismay, the secretary of the CID, while admitting that if Germany conquered Czechoslovakia, its

---

[3] R. A. C. Parker, *Chamberlain and Appeasement* (Basingstoke: Palgrave Macmillan, 1993), chps. 7 and 8. John Charmley argues that Chamberlain wanted, as he always had, an Anglo-German entente but agrees that the prime minister's first purpose was to avert the war that he believed was only a few days away. John Charmley, *Chamberlain and the Lost Peace* (London: Ivan R. Dee, 1989), pp. 105 and 108.

[4] Wesley Wark, *The Ultimate Enemy: British Intelligence and Nazi Germany 1933–1939* (London: I. B. Tauris, 1985), p. 69. For an updated account of comparative figures, see Zara Steiner, *The Triumph of the Dark: European International Relations* (Oxford University Press, 2006).

[5] Cab 23/95 quoted in Uri Bialer, *The Shadow of the Bomber: The Fear of Air Attack and British Politics, 1932–1939* (Royal Historical Society: London, 1980), p. 157.

prestige and war potential would be increased, stressed the weakness of Britain's defenses as the reason for avoiding war:

If we were to go to war with Germany tomorrow, the greatest danger to which we would be exposed, and equally Germany's only chance of obtaining a quick decision, would lie in the possibility of a knock out blow from the air ... it would be better to fight her in say six to twelve months than to accept the present challenge.[6]

We now know, of course, that neither Germany nor Britain could have launched a strategic bombing campaign against the other in 1938 (or in 1939) and that on September 22, 1938, the head of a special Luftwaffe staff looking at the problem of an air attack on Britain had concluded that a "decisive war against England appears to be ruled out with the means now available."[7] In September 1938, French intelligence reported that most German planes were deployed for action against Czechoslovakia and not against France. The fear of a "knock-out blow" was based on a misperception of German air strategy. The worst-case scenario lacked reality. The fear of bombing may have buttressed the prime minister's case, but it only strengthened his determination to avoid war not just in the autumn of 1938 but at any time in the future.

Similarly, though British military intelligence correctly estimated that in July 1938 the German regular army would consist of forty-six divisions, it exaggerated the number of first-line reserves and the number of motorized and armored divisions that Germany could put in the field. The Germans had an army of forty-eight active-duty divisions, of which less than one-quarter consisted of motorized or mechanized divisions.[8] Neither information about the thin German covertures of the western frontier (work on the West Wall had just begun and the French had a five-to-one superiority in troops on the border) nor an estimate of the numbers of divisions that the French and Czechs could put in the field led to any reconsideration of the assumption that Germany could launch an attack with impunity.[9] The military never considered (though some ministers asked for such an appreciation) how far the German absorption of Czechoslovakia would adversely affect France's position (something recognized by Daladier) and alter the future European balance of power. In their pre-Munich strategic assessments, the chiefs of staff reported only that nothing could be done to prevent Germany from

[6] PRO/Cab 51/544, Note by General Ismay, September 20, 1939.
[7] Quoted in Wark, *The Ultimate Enemy*, p. 68.
[8] Williamson Murray, *The Change in the European Balance of Power, 1938–1939* (Princeton University Press, 1984), pp. 218–19.
[9] Ibid., pp. 239–42; Wark, *The Ultimate Enemy*, pp. 108–09.

defeating Czechoslovakia and from launching air attacks on Britain. No assessment of the present or future military balance was offered.[10] The main purpose was to avoid a war and not to estimate the costs of abandoning Czechoslovakia.

With regard to the navy, Britain could claim a large margin of superiority over Germany; the naval chiefs were still concentrating on building a two-ocean fleet that could contain Japan and Germany. The Anglo-German naval agreement of 1935 assured Britain of its quantitative and qualitative superiority over Germany. There was no comparison between the two powers in the number and tonnage of ships of all classes. At this time, the Germans had only a small submarine fleet that could not threaten Britain's sea lanes. The navy was confident that the Germans would stick to the terms of the naval agreement and had every reason to avoid war until its own future building programs could be fulfilled.

The British were aware of the economic difficulties faced by the Reich in 1938. They might not have known of the full extent of the problems created by Hitler's decision after the May crisis to prepare for war by October 1938. The seizure of Austrian gold and foreign exchange, while easing the foreign-exchange situation, proved insufficient for the needs of a country embarked on a major rearmament campaign. The raw-material situation in the summer of 1938 was extremely serious and the shortage of workers, both skilled and unskilled, was felt by each of the German services. All those Germans who opposed war in 1938, and they were a very disparate group, agreed that given the state of Germany's armaments and its economic position, the country could not risk a major war with Britain and France, particularly if those countries were backed by the United States. The Reich's finance minister, Schwerin von Krosigk, prepared a memorandum for Hitler on September 1, 1938, asking that war be postponed. He warned that "[t]he fact that England is not ready for war militarily, does not prevent England formenting it." Britain held two trump cards, he claimed, the soon-expected participation of the Americans in the war and Britain's knowledge of Germany's financial and economic weakness. Krosigk predicted that the Allies would not "run against the West Wall but would let Germany's economic weakness take effect until we, after early military successes, become weaker and weaker and finally will lose our military advantage due to deliveries of armament and airplanes by the

---

[10] Talbot C. Imlay, *Facing the Second World War: Strategy, Politics and Economics in Britain and France, 1938–1940* (Oxford University Press, 2003), p. 80.

US."[11] Hitler dismissed Krosigk's warnings; after Munich, he raised his armament demands. While Germany's financial and economic difficulties were reported to the Foreign Office by members of the British embassy in Berlin and were noted by the Industrial Intelligence Centre (IIC), they had more to do with Germany's capacity to engage in a long war than to mount a war against Czechoslovakia. At the time, they did not lead to any modification of the worst-case scenario should there be war with Germany. The IIC, overly impressed by the capacities of a totalitarian regime to mobilize its society for war, argued that the Germans were well advanced in their preparations for a total war, if not yet ready. While noting Germany's raw-material, labor, and financial difficulties, the intelligence services conveyed an exaggerated impression of Germany's military strength, above all its powerful army built with such astonishing speed and its capacity to mobilize the economy for an all-out war. Coupled with the knowledge of Britain's unpreparedness, the IIC assessment confirmed the highly pessimistic reading of the European military balance of power.

The strategic arguments did not shape Chamberlain's policies. He reached his decisions in September before the reports of the chiefs of staff were received. He never asked his advisers to consider the possibility of a British effort at deterrence nor was he interested in the effects of the loss of Czechoslovakia. The more positive chief of staff appraisal presented on the eve of his flight to Germany had no effect on his determination to reach a compromise with Hitler at Czechoslovakia's expense. At most, one can argue that the prime minister was acting defensively; on the assumption that Britain had only limited interests in Eastern Europe and that he did not want Britain to be forced to intervene in support of France in any Franco-German war. Plan Z, Chamberlain's personal proposal for settling matters directly with Hitler, was not based on military or economic intelligence, though information that the Führer was in a volatile state may have strengthened the prime minister's resolve. The pessimism of his military advisers only reinforced Chamberlain's determination to negotiate with Hitler and made it easier for him to convince his cabinet colleagues that his policies were right, but it was not the reason why he went to Germany. He believed he could convince Hitler not to go to war, but instead to effect change by peaceful means, and that he could get the Führer to agree to a general European peace settlement.

There was a moment when Chamberlain returned from Godesberg, with all the determinants of power exactly the same, that the majority

---

[11] Quoted in Tooze, *The Wages of Destruction*, p. 272.

of the cabinet was prepared to reject Hitler's terms even at the cost of war. The prime minister was telling the truth when he warned Hitler that public opinion in Britain had hardened. There had been a groundswell against further concessions. At Godesberg, Chamberlain informed Hitler that support for his policies had been changed into charges that he was selling out the Czechs and giving way to dictators. He was booed as he left for his second trip to Germany. Fearful that Chamberlain had not fully grasped the extent of the public opposition to his policies, Halifax sent him a telegram reporting on the change in public feeling and insisting that it was now up to Hitler to make concessions.[12] The sources are diverse and difficult to assess but public demonstrations, newspaper comment and letters to the editors (*The Times* was an exception in publishing an equal number of letters on both sides of the argument), ministerial correspondence, and personal contacts provide ample evidence that the public felt that Britain should stand by Czechoslovakia. Chamberlain not only raised the point with Hitler but referred to the state of public feeling in the full cabinet meeting on September 24. It would be wrong to assume that the sharper public tone was responsible for the cabinet turn against Chamberlain but it was a factor in its decision. Even dominion opinion shifted against conciliation, with South Africa the only real standout. Chamberlain felt that he had to move in accordance with the cabinet particularly after Halifax joined his opponents. He could not accept the Godesberg terms but he did not relinquish his intention to continue negotiations with Hitler if given the opportunity. On September 26, he agreed that parliament should be summoned to meet two days later. The cabinet also decided that reservists should be called up in order to mobilize the fleet and man the anti-aircraft defenses. On September 28, the fleet was fully mobilized and the news publicized. It was fortunate for Chamberlain's purposes that this was a short crisis and that parliament only returned on the 28th.

We enter the world of counterfactual history to ask what would have happened if Hitler had not stepped back. For, though in hindsight it appears that he had gotten almost all that he wanted without a war, at the time Hitler believed he had been cheated of his conflict and had been wrongly convinced by his advisers and by Mussolini to accept what Chamberlain offered. In a sense, Chamberlain's policy succeeded.

---

[12] For the best discussion of British opinion at the time of Munich, see Sarah Wilkinson, "Perception of Public Opinion: British Foreign Policy Decisions about Nazi Germany, 1933–1938," unpublished Ph.D. thesis, University of Oxford (2000). For a different view with regard to the Halifax telegram, see Andrew Roberts, *"The Holy Fox": A Biography of Lord Halifax* (London: Weidenfeld & Nicolson, 1991), p. 114.

Hitler stepped back from war but, of course, at the price of getting almost everything he wanted and at high price for the future of Czechoslovakia. The cabinet revolt after Godesberg had little to do with the realities of power; nothing had changed in systemic terms but a revised perception of Hitler's behavior, reinforced by perceptions of public feeling, altered the balance in the cabinet. The importance and power of the prime minister was starkly demonstrated throughout the crisis, though after Godesberg the cabinet tried to check Chamberlain's independent actions. The role of the main actors was crucial. Mearsheimer is wrong when he claims that it does not matter who heads the government. The prime minister was able to regain the diplomatic initiative at home and kept it, temporarily and not without challenge, until the start of the new year. The feeling of relief at the time of Munich that there was not to be war made Chamberlain a popular hero. The vote for the Munich Agreement in the Commons was overwhelming, though newspaper comment on Churchill's speech of censure was widespread and positive. The Godesberg revolt, usually accorded no more than a line in realist accounts, deserves deeper analysis.

The decision for war

Having accepted the Munich Agreement which vastly improved Hitler's strategic position in Europe and weakened France, why did Britain go to war in September 1939? Had the measures of power moved decisively in Britain's direction? Had either balancing or buck-passing improved Britain's position? The evidence suggests the contrary. The existing balance of power in terms of comparative military strength had moved against Britain and France. The West Wall had been considerably strengthened and the number of German troops that could be assigned to withstand an Allied attack while moving into Poland had been greatly increased. Germany was in a stronger military position in 1939 than in September 1938. It had sufficient modern planes to back up its armies in any offensive against Poland and still enjoyed a margin of air superiority over its enemies. The British had considerably strengthened their defensive positions but still could offer the French only limited help. After Munich the Chamberlain government had announced a plan to increase the number of fighters in the Royal Air Force (RAF) by 50 percent but, in fact, had only added a third year to contracts for these fighters. The French were warned that a substantial proportion of Fighter Command would have to be kept back for the defense of the United Kingdom. Nor was there any question of an Allied offensive campaign against Germany. The RAF could not mount a strategic bombing campaign, having neither the planes, the trained crews, nor the technical equipment to take such an action. The idea of a massive retaliation campaign was temporarily abandoned. Neither could the British back a French offensive against Germany (never planned in any case), for an expanded British Expeditionary Force (BEF) was still on the drawing board. In September 1939, the British were able to provide only four inadequately trained and equipped divisions as the BEF. The problems of preparing regular units for service on the continent, only decided in February 1939, were compounded with the declaration of conscription which put an additional burden on the army high command. Yet in September, Britain took the decision to go to war against its better-armed adversary.

There were some reasons for the greater confidence in Britain's war preparedness both among the military and in the public at large. In defensive terms, the British were better off in 1939 than in 1938. Unknown to the public, the radar chain was almost complete and covered much of the south and east coasts. Whereas in September 1938, only five of the eighteen radar stations had been built, and Britain had only 100 Hurricane and two Spitfires in operation, by September 1939 the radar screen was in place, a communication system between ground and air forces had been established, and both Hurricanes and Spitfires were coming off the assembly lines. Britain's Air Raid Precaution (ARP) measures that were already in operation would reach a high degree of readiness within the year.[13] In October 1938, Britain's first-line fighters were mostly obsolete biplanes; by September 1939, not only had the number increased, from six to twenty-six squadrons, but most of the new planes were fast, single-seat monoplane fighters. There was far less fear of a knock-out blow (an imaginary nightmare in 1938), though admittedly three-and-a-half million people (over a million scheduled for evacuation) left London in early September after war was declared.[14] It was expected that Britain and France would soon match the German air force and surpass its production of planes. There was, however, no provision for their two air forces to work together and neither government intended to begin bombing for fear of German retaliation. In one of the last prewar comparisons of strength made by British air intelligence, it was estimated that Germany had 4,210 first-line aircraft as

---

[13] Wark, *The Ultimate Enemy*, p. 214. Figures are from the chief of staff's amendments to its Joint Planning subcommittee's last prewar strategic survey completed on January 18, 1939.

[14] David Reynolds, *Britannia Overruled: British Policy and World Power in the Twentieth Century* (London: Longman, 1991), p. 140.

against 1,998 for the RAF, and 1,750 German long-range bombers as against 832 for the RAF.[15]

Any change in the ratio of land forces was still in the future. A war scare in early 1939 raised the specter of a French retreat into isolation and the army chiefs, backed by their naval counterparts, insisted on an expansion of the BEF and the opening of staff talks with the French. With Chamberlain, the Treasury, and the RAF in opposition, the decision was taken in February to start the talks and to expand the BEF to nineteen divisions (six regular and thirteen territorial). In May, the figure was raised to thirty-two divisions. This was not preparation for a continental commitment on the scale of World War I but it represented a distinct change in British grand strategy. Much was made of France's defensive capacities and the possible extension of its frontier defenses to the sea. The charge was later made that Britain would fight to the last Frenchman. The two post-Munich papers prepared by the IIC and the War Office and circulated in January and July 1939, despite striking a note of greater optimism, called attention to the significant increases in the strength of the German army. Apart from some elements of exaggeration, particularly with regard to tank strength and German reserves, the estimates were not far out of line. The British anticipated that the Germans could field a wartime army of between 121 and 130 divisions in 1939; the figure in September was 106.

The naval balance was still heavily in the Allies' favor. The Germans only possessed two battle cruisers that were combat ready. Those two ships, the pocket battleships (glorified heavy cruisers), and the heavy cruisers barely constituted a threat to the British and French navies. The German U-boats represented a latent threat but in September 1939, only twenty-six were ready for war. In strategic terms, this imbalance, as Williamson Murray has pointed out, meant that in the short term the Western Powers could inflict significant damage on the German economy by a blockade, at least until Russian supplies began to flow into Germany. It was only as war was actually on the horizon that the navy was forced to adjust to the collapse of the Anglo-German naval agreement. The naval chiefs succumbed to some false alarms, including a submarine panic in March–April. It was accepted that the navy would not have the time to fulfill its plans for a two-power fleet and the maintenance of its global supremacy but would instead have to prepare for an immediate war. There were no plans for offensive

---

[15] Figures are all from Wark, *The Ultimate Enemy*, pp. 73 and 214. The German figures are not correct but the important point is what the British believed to be true rather than what was true.

operations (the proposals for knocking Italy out of the war at its onset had been abandoned) and the current position with regard to the Fleet Air Arm, antisubmarine warships, and convoy escorts was still far from satisfactory. But though the navy was not at maximum readiness for a war against Germany, it clearly enjoyed a considerable margin of superiority.[16]

The figures presented by the intelligence service left no doubt of the margin of German air and land superiority, but the last prewar strategic appreciation of February 1939 and reports from the intelligence services in the months that followed were more optimistic than the worst-case scenarios of 1938. The February strategic appreciation focused on a German–Italian war against Britain and France in Western Europe, the North Sea, and the Mediterranean and paid very little attention to Germany's eastern and southeastern flanks or to the Soviet Union. The more negative assessment of Germany's prospects had its roots in the temporary February lull which the military authorities attributed mainly to Hitler's domestic difficulties and to Allied rearmament. Far greater importance was now given to Germany's acute shortages of raw materials and foreign exchange and the reported stresses and strains in the German economy. Having formerly attributed a high degree of efficiency to the German rearmament process, it was now reported that the German economy had only limited room for future expansion. Taxes would have to be raised in an already highly taxed country and this would affect civilian morale. The German economy, it was reported, would run into supply difficulties, between twelve and eighteen months after the outbreak of war. The anticipated civilian backlash and the shortages of raw materials gave new importance to the efficacy of the British blockade weapon. Even the resources of southeastern Europe and those of Germany's possible allies would be insufficient for a German victory in the long war that the British intended to fight. An economic blockade would pull Hitler down as Germany already had used up her hidden resources. "Everything she has is in the shop window," army intelligence reported, "and that is not really at all a satisfactory basis on which to commence a war."[17] Service intelligence reports underlined Britain's existing advantages in terms of air defense, latent economic strength, and popular morale. It is true that the IIC, anxious to curb what it thought was the exaggerated optimism of the military intelligence services, was cautious about making

---

[16] Joseph A. Maiolo, *The Royal Navy and Nazi Germany, 1933–39* (Basingstoke: Palgrave Macmillan, 1998), p.189.
[17] Quoted in Wark, *The Ultimate Enemy*, p. 226.

predictions about the future. Yet its head argued that given the lack of raw materials, Germany was far from ready for a total war and would be forced to "stake everything on a quicker victory than has ever been known in history before in similar circumstances."[18] Particularly in the spring and early summer of 1939, when considerable hope was placed in the creation of a Grand Alliance that would include Britain, France, Poland, and Turkey, with the USSR, if not an ally, at least maintaining a pro-Allied neutrality, the IIC reported that the encirclement of Germany by hostile states with their frontiers closed to trade would make the British blockade more effective and create "critical shortages of everything."[19] Even the announcement of the Molotov–Ribbentrop Pact did not shatter such illusions as the IIC put the best gloss possible on what Russia would actually give Germany while admitting (in an appendix to its report) that the former could become a major supplier of essential items, including food and oil, to the Reich.

The intelligence reports on Germany's financial and economic difficulties were accurate. Hitler was repeatedly warned by his military advisers in the spring and summer of 1939 that the current military schedules could not be met and that Germany was in no position to challenge the productive capacity of the Allies, particularly, as was expected, when the British Empire and the Americans would come to their assistance. Already during the winter and spring of 1939, Germany faced new financial and economic difficulties arising out of its balance-of-payments problems. In the face of Reichsbank warnings of the risk of inflation, Hitler replaced Schacht with the far less able but more pliable Walter Funk and abolished all formal limitations on the expansion of the money supply. If the internal checks to rearmament could be removed, the loss of foreign exchange posed more intractable problems. Germany had to increase its exports to pay for essential imports, even if there had to be cuts in the allocation of raw materials to the service industries. This is the explanation of Hitler's unusually long discussion of economic policy in his well-known address to the Reichstag of January 30, 1939, when he told his audience that Germany had no option but to "export or die."[20] The Wehrmacht was particularly hard hit by the cuts in steel allocations and after March 1939, ammunition production collapsed. As war with Poland approached, the army's armaments

---

[18] Ibid., p. 181.
[19] Ibid., p. 183.
[20] This discussion depends on the material found in Adam Tooze's *The Wages of Destruction: The Making and Breaking of the Nazi Economy* (New York: Viking Press, 2007). For Hitler's speech, see Max Domarus (ed.), *Hitler: Speeches and Proclamations, 1932–1945* (Mundelein, IL: Bolchazy-Carducci Publishers, 1997), pp. 1047–67.

program "was grinding to a virtual standstill."[21] Luftwaffe production schedules were also slowed; the Luftwaffe got only 45 percent of the Reich's aluminum supplies in 1939, though Germany was the world's largest producer. Lutz Budrass, writing on the Luftwaffe, has shown that only twenty-eight Ju 88s (the most advanced German bomber that would have the range and capacity to be an effective strategic bomber) were produced before war began. The first mass-produced Ju 88 was ready only in September 1939 and the Luftwaffe chiefs anticipated a peak of production of 172 planes as late as mid-1940.[22] The navy remained unaffected by problems of resource allocation but its programs would take some years to implement. Dockyards had to be built and skilled labor found before the building program could begin. The Wehrmacht's chief economist, Major General Thomas, told members of the German Foreign Ministry that in an all-out arms race with the "democracies," time was not on Germany's side. If the Americans contributed to the Allied war effort, the gap would be huge. Hitler was fully aware of the situation and was kept informed, at his own request, of the existing and future shortages of available weapons and ammunition. He may well have anticipated American support for the Allies. It has been argued that it was because he knew the German window of opportunity was a short one that he went to war in the summer of 1939 and demanded an immediate offensive in the west after the conquest of Poland.[23]

It must be said that even after Prague and the giving of guarantees to Poland, Romania, and Greece, the British took few positive steps to cut Germany's sources of raw materials. The dangers of the German economic penetration of southeastern Europe were finally recognized and both the British and French became more active in the region, but with only limited results. In part, the British were unable to take full advantage of the situation because of concerns about their own finances (their reserves, along with those of the French, were still greater than those of Germany) and their own armament needs. They had to adopt an order of priorities that suited not only their national but their imperial requirements.

More could have been done if the Treasury and Board of Trade had adopted a more liberal attitude toward loans and trade. What was accomplished was too little and too late. The British, moreover,

---

[21] Tooze, *The Wages of Destruction*, pp. 302–5.
[22] Lutz Budrass, *Flugzeugindustrie Und Luftrustung in Deutschland 1918–1945* (Dusseldorf: Droste, 1998), p. 572.
[23] See Tooze, *The Wages of Destruction* and the discussion in Murray, *The Change in the European Balance of Power*, pp. 332–33.

continued to trade with the Germans in the spring of 1939. This trade was as economically important to Britain as it was to Germany, and was not only tolerated but even encouraged. There were, too, some lingering, if diminishing, hopes that an economic arrangement might relieve the pressure on Berlin and strengthen the hand of the moderates even after Schacht had vanished from the scene.

The reports of the intelligence services qualified the exaggerated picture of the enemy's military capabilities and its prospects for the future. The abandonment of the pre-Munich worst-case scenario had as much to do with the realization that war was probable as with a more accurate appraisal of German rearmament and the weaknesses in its armed services. Though the accelerated pace of British rearmament contributed to the more positive mood, the change in the frame of reference was critical. With war in sight, the services stressed the weaknesses in the German position to give point to the long-war strategy with which Britain hoped to win the war. It was the only strategy available. An accurate appraisal of the financial and economic situations of Britain and Germany in the summer of 1939 might have suggested that neither country could engage in a long war. Yet both countries went to war despite warnings that neither could sustain such a conflict. Already in 1938, there were worries whether "our own [Britain's] economic and political system will stand (1) more rearmament and (2) a slump as well as Germany."[24] In 1939, Chamberlain feared that increased rearmament might "break the country's back." In the British case, the chief challenge to the long-war strategy came from the Treasury.[25] The mounting defense expenditure resulted in sharp declines in Britain's gold and foreign currency reserves and in the value of the pound. Between March 31 and August 22 gold and foreign currency reserves fell by over one quarter. In August, the losses became catastrophic. Yet the country was dependent on imports for food and rearmament; some historians have estimated that some 25 to 30 percent of the materials needed for rearmament had to be imported. Because of the American neutrality acts and Britain's failure to repay its World War I war debts (the Johnson Act), Britain could not borrow from the United States as it had during the first years of the 1914–18 war. It could not devalue the pound as the Americans, who failed to appreciate the financial difficulties Britain

---

[24] Quotation from William Strang of the Foreign Office in George Peden, "A Matter of Timing: The Economic Background to British Foreign Policy, 1938–1939," *History* 69 (1984), 22.

[25] See the discussion in Imlay, *Facing the Second World War*, pp. 103–04 and in Rosecrance and Steiner, "British Grand Strategy and the Origins of World War II," pp. 135–38.

faced, would meet any depreciation with a competitive devaluation of the dollar. In the spring of 1939, Treasury officials had already warned a CID subcommittee that the current financial situation was far worse than in 1914. In July, the Treasury noted that British reserves would barely last three years and might run out sooner, given the current rate of rearmament. According to Sir John Simon, the Chancellor of the Exchequer, the continuing gold losses would directly affect Britain's "staying power in a war."[26] Some ministers like Lord Halifax believed that if the war lasted, "the attitude of the United States would be sufficiently favorable to us to enable us to win the war."[27] At best, this would happen only at some future and indeterminate date and depended on circumstances over which the British had little or no control. It was an "unspoken assumption" without any basis in the immediate reality. Whatever their hopes for the future, few thought it wise to count on assistance from Washington. No one assumed that the Germans would face a major financial–economic crisis before the blockade could become effective. It was essential, therefore, that Britain should be in a position to sustain the blockade in order to win the war of attrition. The Treasury was denying that this was possible; its warnings were ignored because its advice was unacceptable – it would mean that Britain could not afford to resist Germany.[28] A country that could not go to war was no longer a great power.

There appeared no alternative to preparing for a war which the defense chiefs hoped could be postponed until 1940 but which Britain could win only because of its superior staying power. The government might have decided to use all the country's resources in an effort to win the short war, but given that no strategic bombing campaign was possible and that there was no BEF for any joint Anglo-French offensive, it is difficult to see how this would have been possible. Some officers had their doubts about the long-war strategy.[29] Like the French, if somewhat later, senior British naval officers considered a series of "hard blows" against Italy at the outset of war. Knocking Italy out would free

---

[26] Quoted in Imlay, *Facing the Second World War*, p. 104. R. A. C. Parker, "The Pound Sterling, the American Treasury and British Preparations for War, 1938–1939," *English Historical Review* 387 (1983), 261–79, still remains the important source. See also George Peden, *The Treasury and British Public Policy, 1906–1959* (Oxford University Press, 2000), pp. 245–313; Paul Kennedy, *Strategy and Diplomacy, 1870–1945* (London: Fontana, 1983), pp. 89–106.

[27] R. A. C. Parker, "Economics, Rearmament and Foreign Policy: The United Kingdom before 1939 – A Preliminary Study," *Journal of Contemporary History* 10 (1975), 645.

[28] Imlay, *Facing the Second World War*, p. 104.

[29] See the extended discussion of these critiques both in Britain and France in ibid., pp. 48–50, 100–05; Reynolds M. Salerno, *Vital Crossroads: The Mediterranean Origins of the Second World War, 1935–1940* (Ithaca: Cornell University Press, 2002), chp. 4.

capital ships for other theaters of war, above all in the Far East. By the summer, however, the chiefs of staff decided that a knock-out blow was beyond Britain's means. They argued, too, that Italian belligerence might be a liability for Germany, forcing the Germans to divert their forces to help the Italians in the Mediterranean.[30] Some military men, too, were uneasy about waiting until the balance of power shifted decisively in the British and French direction before taking action. This was, as they argued, a shot in the dark without any actual time limit in mind. Unfortunately, none could propose an acceptable offensive strategy. Britain went to war prepared to defend in the short run and assume the offensive in the long run. It remained wedded to the long-war strategy despite the Treasury warnings that this was not a financially sustainable option. In fact, the financial crunch came in March 1941, even earlier than the Cassandras predicted.

Realists argue that nations will improve their position by balancing or buck-passing. The British tried both. In February 1939, after a war scare and repeated warnings that France would settle with Germany unless assured of an alliance, the British decided to open staff talks with France and expand the BEF. Chamberlain played down the significance of these decisions but Britain, though not planning an army of 1914–18 proportions, had changed direction and revised its strategy. The three-staged staff talks, which began at the end of March and continued at intervals during the summer, confirmed the British commitment to a continental strategy. It was clear, however, that the French could expect only limited assistance from Britain in the air or on land. It was the French who pushed for the pooling of resources – military, economic, industrial, and financial – with limited success. As the stronger power, the British were reluctant to commit themselves to joint overseas supply and purchase proposals. No systematic attempt was made to study the lessons of inter-allied organization in the First World War. It was only a month before war began that a memorandum circulated that summarized the 1914–18 inter-allied economic organization and warned that the establishment of a central coordinating committee was necessary.[31] At the outbreak of war, seven French missions were in direct contact with the British but there was no single authority in Britain coordinating

---

[30] The historical debate continues. See Murray, *The Change in the European Balance of Power*, pp. 314–21; Reynolds M. Salerno, "The French Navy and the Appeasement of Italy, 1938–1940," *English Historical Review* 445 (1997), 66–104. Imlay, *Facing the Second World War*, pp. 48–50.

[31] Margaret Gowing, "Anglo-French Economic Collaboration up to the Outbreak of the Second World War," in *Les Relations franco-britanniques de 1935 a 1939* (Paris, 1975), pp. 179–88. Maiolo, *The Royal Navy and Nazi Germany, 1933–39*, p. 180.

these activities. The main focus of British planning was on the safety of the home islands. It was only in the second stage of a long war that Britain would use its naval, financial, and economic resources to secure Germany's defeat. Given its dependence on France in the first instance, it is surprising that the chiefs of staff did not probe too closely into the state of the French army but accepted General Gamelin's assurances that any initial German attack could be contained.

Two other attempts were made at balancing or buck-passing with little success. Chamberlain had realized the importance of conciliating the Americans. And the Anglo-American trade agreement, more favorable to the United States than to Britain, was finally signed in October 1938. The prime minister backed the agreement because he "reckoned it would help to educate American opinion to act more and more with us and because I felt it would frighten the totalitarians."[32] Events in the summer of 1939 confirmed the prime minister's fears that the Americans were unreliable. In the Far East – though naval talks, begun in 1938, were revived in mid-June 1939 – during the Tiensin crisis, the Americans refused to act together with the British, though they gave independent support. Britain, having considered retaliatory action, was forced to retreat. In July 1939, the Roosevelt administration, responding to congressional pressure but without consulting London, gave the six months' statutory warning that the US–Japan trade treaty would not be renewed when it lapsed in January, but it was the Nazi–Soviet Pact and not American economic action that relieved the pressure on London in the Far East.

The European situation appeared even less promising. Roosevelt's attempt to repeal the arms embargo in the summer of 1939 was defeated in both the House and Senate. It remained in place though the "cash-and-carry" provisions of the Neutrality Act lapsed. The congressional refusal was a blow and Chamberlain was indignant. "I have not been disappointed," he claimed, "for I never expected any better behavior from these pig-headed and self-righteous nobodies."[33] British confidence in President Roosevelt was shaken and the usual Foreign Office clichés about American words without actions resurfaced. While many believed, or at least hoped, that at some point American assistance would be forthcoming, no one could rely on this future possibility.

---

[32] David Reynolds, *The Creation of the Anglo-American Alliance 1937–41: A Study in Competitive Cooperation* (Chapel Hill: University of North Carolina Press, 1981), p. 18.
[33] Ibid., p. 57.

There was one other possibility for "buck-passing." The giving of guarantees to Poland, Romania, and Greece represented a second fundamental change in British policy. Although there were some indications before Prague that Britain was beginning to interest itself in Eastern Europe, above all in Romania and Yugoslavia, in order to check German economic expansion, the guarantees, much disliked by the service departments and without any military back-up, represented a new stage in Britain's continental orientation. She was now engaged in Eastern as well as Western Europe. Prodded by the public and fueled by his own anger over Hitler's march into Prague, Chamberlain was prepared to construct a "peace front" of states threatened by German aggression. It was a policy of deterrence based on a concept of collective security without any military teeth. The prime minister tried to narrow the commitment to Poland but Britain was pledged to underwrite its security in peacetime and had yielded to the Poles the right to take independent action. In Chamberlain's view, this was still a limited commitment but again it marked a sharp deviation from past policy. The only way to give teeth to the Polish guarantee was to include the Soviet Union. From the start, the prime minister opposed any close association with Moscow and he never abandoned his objections to an alliance. He not only distrusted the Soviets but he wanted to avoid dividing Europe into contending ideological blocs that would make the appeasement of Germany impossible and lead to war. The French were the first to recognize the necessity of including the Soviet Union; after considering abandoning their obligations in Eastern Europe and then reversing this decision, France required an Eastern Front and only the Russians could make it functional. British parliamentary and public support for an alliance as well as cabinet pressure forced Chamberlain to act. By May, he was isolated in the cabinet in his opposition to opening talks. The chiefs of staff, who changed their position, and the Foreign Office were in agreement that only a two-front war could increase the strain on Germany's resources and reduce the period of her resistance. There were fears, too, that without an alliance, Russia would turn to Germany. This would be a disaster for Poland and a serious, if not a grievous blow to the Allies. On May 24, it was agreed to open talks with the Soviets. Despite continued public and political backing, the government did not make the negotiations their top priority. As the Russians continually raised the price of their participation in an alliance, Halifax blew hot and cold, particularly since Poland and the Baltic states were strongly opposed to the Soviet guarantee that Molotov demanded. Repeated concessions were made, often at Poland's expense, but once Hitler decided to negotiate with Stalin, the Allies could not match the German offers. On July 15, Chamberlain commented:

I am glad to say that Halifax is at least getting fed up with Molotov ... If we do get an agreement ... I am afraid I shall not regard it as a triumph. I put as little value on Russian military capacity as I believe the Germans do ... I would like to have taken a much longer time with them all through, but I could not have carried my colleagues with me.[34]

The cabinet was told three days later that, "If the negotiations should, after all, fail, the Foreign Secretary said that this would not cause him very great anxiety, since he felt that, whatever formal agreement was signed, the Soviet Government would probably take such action as best suited them if war broke out."[35] This was an entirely reasonable assumption but, in terms of realist theory, hardly explains British hesitancy. Neither Chamberlain nor Halifax were convinced that an alliance with the Soviet Union would deter Hitler; both hoped that the very prospect of Allied resistance would be enough to stop him. The announcement of the Nazi–Soviet Pact failed to have the impact on the Chamberlain government that Hitler anticipated, though the French were devastated. There was no disagreement in the cabinet that the Polish alliance would have to be honored.[36] Whatever the final maneuverings during the last days of peace, a German march into Poland would mean war. The Polish guarantee presented a clearer case than Belgium in July 1914. Honor was engaged but so was the confirmation of the growing sense among all sectors of the country that Hitler had to be stopped by war.

Almost every assessment of capabilities suggests that Britain should not have gone to war in the summer of 1939. Neither France nor Britain had made any preparations to assist Poland, which was in a worse military situation than Czechoslovakia. Except in the Far East, Britain's diplomatic situation had not improved. In retrospect, the permanent under-secretary, Alexander Cadogan, noted: "We lived on bluff for the last ten years of the peace, and we have been living on a larger degree of bluff in other parts of the world, i.e., in the Far East, for nearly half a century."[37] Yet when its 'bluff' was called, Britain went to war. In the

---

[34] Chamberlain Papers, NC 18/1/1107, Chamberlain to Hilda, July 15, 1939.
[35] Cab 23/100 (1939) quoted in Rosecrance and Steiner, "British Grand Strategy and the Origins of World War II," p. 145, fn. 58.
[36] Lothar Kettenacker, "Grossbritannein; Kriegserklärung als Ehrensache," paper delivered at conference in Dresden, sponsored by the German Historical Institute, London (March 31–April 3, 2005). The paper, in an English version 'Great Britain: Declaring War as a Matter of Honour', will appear in Lothar Kettenacker and Torsten Riotte (eds.), *War and Society in Western Europe* to be published in 2010.
[37] TNA, FO371/25208/W11399, Comment by Cadogan on a memorandum by Orme Sargent of 28/10/1940. I owe this reference to Lothar Kettenacker.

last resort, the decision was taken because the political elite and the public at large had decided that "Hitler's Germany was incorrigibly and irrevocably determined on the conquest of Europe by force and had at any costs to be stopped."[38] This hardening of opinion was due, in the first instance, to Hitler's behavior; Kristallnacht, which shook both the politicians and the public, the false rumors of a German attack on the West which mainly affected the political and military leaders, and the march into Prague intensified both official and public hostility toward Germany. Prague proved a catalyst in the moves toward a continental commitment. At the time of Munich, Chamberlain could argue that Hitler's aims were limited and restricted to enforcing the principles of self-determination. By the spring of 1939, even Chamberlain had lost confidence in any deal with Hitler but still hoped that the German people might repudiate their irrational leader. The long war of nerves that began with Hitler's demands for Danzig and lasted into August convinced the public that war was probable, though many hoped it could be postponed or averted. At no time during these months, although there were moments of misplaced optimism, was there any sign from Hitler that he sought a peaceful settlement in Europe or an understanding with Britain except on unacceptable terms.

The changes in official and public mood intersected. As the government increased its preparations for war, the public increasingly accepted its probability and welcomed measures that might have been rejected in 1938. Labour's opposition to conscription was surprisingly muted. Mounting hostility to Nazi Germany took precedence over existing doubts about government controls over industrial manpower. With regard to bringing Churchill into the cabinet, a clear warning to Hitler and the Soviets, public opinion ran ahead of the prime minister. This sea change in sentiment, what A. J. P. Taylor called an "underground explosion," can be seen in the increasing ministerial opposition to Chamberlain's policies and the latter's awareness of his political isolation. Opinion polls and the summer by-elections showed continued support for the prime minister but they showed, too, massive backing for war preparations. In an ill-natured debate on August 2 over the adjournment of the House of Commons until October 3 which an angry prime minister made a question of confidence, Chamberlain won an easy victory but Churchill's support outside of the Commons broadened and increased.

In the final crisis, public feeling as siphoned through parliament, when it was finally recalled, narrowed the freedom of the prime minister

[38] Donald Cameron Watt, *How War Came: The Immediate Origins of the Second World War, 1938–1939* (London: Pantheon, 1989), p. 387.

and cabinet and made the sending of an ultimatum to Germany the only option available. The official response to the Nazi–Soviet Pact was different from what Hitler intended; a letter dispatched to Hitler made it clear that Britain intended to stand by Poland. Nevertheless, the last days of August saw a flurry of diplomatic activity, particularly after Hitler called back his troops already posed for an assault. Hitler tried to separate Britain from Poland while the British tried to get Hitler to substitute negotiation for military action. Chamberlain and some members of the cabinet believed that Hitler was weakening and having second thoughts. During the last week of August, Hitler attempted to bully, bribe (including the offer of an alliance), and trick the British into abandoning the Polish alliance. At the same time, Göring's envoy, the innocent and loquacious Swedish businessman, Burger Dahlerus, shuttled between Berlin and London, bringing offers from Hitler of a pact, an alliance, and a Polish settlement. The British stood firm but recommended direct negotiations between Poland and Germany with any agreement guaranteed by the other powers. Hitler accepted the terms while ordering on the same day, August 28, that the attack on Poland should begin on September 1. Over the weekend, August 25–27, the government and Foreign Office worked to salvage something from Hitler's offers and sent him a carefully balanced reply to the alliance offer. Halifax thought, as did his officials, that Hitler was in difficulty, and that if he could be brought to the negotiating table, he "could be beat."

The diplomatic charade continued mainly because of Hitler's continued attempts to disassociate Britain from Poland but also because the British (and French) leaders were prepared to explore any possibility, however slight, to preserve the peace. The British misperceptions of their opponent had much to do with the final exchanges. Chamberlain's basic misunderstanding of Hitler's nature and Halifax's excessive rationalism and detachment were critical to the misunderstanding both of Hitler's position and the feeling in Britain. Neither man could understand how anyone in his right mind (and there was always the possibility that Hitler was mad) would actually want war. Nor could Halifax appreciate the emotional wave unleashed by the government's seeming irresolution that led to a would-be parliamentary revolt and a cabinet sit-down strike. As late as August 30, ministers, officials, and the City still thought that Hitler would see reason. On August 31, Halifax believed that Hitler might retreat (he was a "beaten fox") and German–Polish talks could begin. The head of the Secret Intelligence Service told the Foreign Office that a military revolt in Berlin was not out of the question. Cadogan thought it would be enough to "stand firm." While there was no possibility of a deal with the Swedish envoy, Dahlerus' efforts, which continued until minutes before the British ultimatum ran out, created a false impression of Hitler's willingness to negotiate.

Hitler assumed that the British would stand down. They had not fought for Czechoslovakia, why should they fight for Poland, particularly when he offered to guarantee the British Empire? The British leaders thought that Hitler would retreat; he could gain the substance of his demands without going to war. They believed that they had made it clear that Britain would fight if German troops moved into Poland. Each side thought that the other would act "rationally" within the terms of their own assumptions. The German attack began at 4:45 a.m. on September 1 with the bombing of Polish armament dumps on the island of Westerplatte. News of the attacks and the bombing of Polish cities were soon confirmed. Yet the British ultimatum was not sent until September 2 and the Anglo-German war did not begin until 11 a.m. on September 3. What happened between those two days had nothing to do with the weighing of the possibilities of victory or defeat. On the morning of September 1, the cabinet dithered; some ministers were reluctant to include a time limit in the note sent to Hitler demanding the recall of his troops. Parliament was summoned for the evening and Chamberlain made a dignified statement that won the sympathy of the House of Commons. Churchill was asked to join the cabinet but no public announcement was made. On September 2, rumors circulated that Chamberlain and Halifax were planning some form of Munich. The facts were that the French were dragging their feet and wanted a forty-eight-hour ultimatum to mobilize and evacuate their cities without German action. Daladier's speech to parliament, referring to peace eleven times and to war only three times was an indication of his careful handling of the chamber. He was so unsure of his political backing that he did not ask for a declaration of war but only funds to enable France to face the obligations of the international situation.

The scene was very different in Britain. When on September 2, the prime minister and foreign secretary agreed to wait until noon or even midnight on the next day (Sunday, September 3) for Hitler's reply to Britain's warning, all the other ministers insisted that war should begin at midnight. A statement would be made to parliament at 6 p.m. The House was adjourned until 7:45 with everyone expecting Chamberlain to say that war would soon begin. Instead, he spoke of waiting for Hitler's reply; delayed, perhaps, because of the Italian proposal for a conference. There was fury in the Commons and when the deputy leader of the opposition, Arthur Greenwood, rose to speak for "the working classes of England," the ultra-right-wing Tory, Leo Amery, shouted, "Speak for England." As they left the House, Greenwood told the prime minister that unless there was an ultimatum to Germany before 11 a.m. tomorrow, "no one on earth could hold the House of Commons."[39] Halifax found the whole parliamentary performance "disgusting" and never forgave those cabinet ministers who thought he and the prime minister were planning another Munich. Assembling in Sir John Simon's room, over a dozen ministers insisted that Simon, one of the most loyal of Chamberlain's supporters, write to the prime minister demanding the expiry of the ultimatum by noon the next day. The rebels went to see the prime minister, still at the House, and insisted that if France could not agree to the noon ultimatum, Britain should go to war alone. Still not content, they reassembled in Simon's room and refused to leave until assured that the ultimatum would be sent. Last attempts were made to move the French, to no avail. The cabinet met just before midnight; the ultimatum would be presented at 9 p.m. and expire at 11 the next morning.

It is perfectly true that neither Chamberlain nor Halifax were prepared to abandon the Polish alliance and that the last delays were due to the French. Nonetheless, until the very last minute, they did everything possible to avoid war and might have pursued the conference idea if it had materialized. Public feeling made further delay impossible. Almost to the end, decision-making was concentrated in the hands of the prime minister and foreign secretary, though the cabinet had to be consulted. At the end, the mood in parliament and the action of the cabinet was decisive.

Most people did not question Britain's ultimate victory. Politicians and officials were less certain. Chamberlain made his position clear when he told his sisters that there could be no peace until Hitler disappeared and his system collapsed: "But what I hope for is not a military victory – I very much doubt the feasibility of that – but a collapse of the German home front."[40] Chamberlain, unlike his advisers, did not expect a German offensive but feared a "specious appeal" from Hitler. He was open to any genuine peace offers, if there were a coup against Hitler. His confidence increased as the Germans failed to mount an offensive. He wrote Roosevelt in October 1939:

My own belief is that we shall win, not by a complete and spectacular victory, which is unlikely under modern conditions but by convincing the Germans that they cannot win. Once they have arrived at that conclusion, I do not believe they can stand our relentless pressure, for they have not started this war with the enthusiasm or the confidence of 1914.[41]

---

[39] Ibid., p. 580.
[40] Quoted in Reynolds, *Britannia Overruled*, p. 140.
[41] Quoted in Reynolds, *The Creation of the Anglo-American Alliance*, p. 76.

Many shared his view that the German economy and morale were fragile and that time was on the Allies' side. The warnings of the Treasury were discounted; the reports from the intelligence services encouraged faith in the long-war strategy. Alexander Cadogan was more forthright and less optimistic when he wrote in his diary on September 6: "We shall fight to the last and may win – but I confess I don't see how."[42] There were few references to American assistance in September. The Treasury imposed tight exchange controls and restricted what could be bought from the Americans to essentials. Little was expected in the way of loans or other signs of generosity even when the arms embargo was repealed.

If there were doubts and fears in the ruling elites, there was also a shared relief that the long period of waiting and indecisiveness was over. The general feeling in the electorate, as far as can be judged, was that Britain had no choice but to go to war. It was a great power with a navy second to none and with a vast empire. Some had felt guilty about the selling-out of Czechoslovakia. Britain as a great power could not face another Munich. With right on their side, few believed in anything but eventual victory. It was in a mood of resignation but also with relief that Britain went to war. The absence of a bombing campaign in September encouraged faith in the government and in eventual victory. Churchill's presence in the cabinet was reassuring but there was no critique of Chamberlain.

British grand strategy had become divorced from all the normal calculations of costs and benefits in the last months of peace. The country went to war when many of its leaders believed that it could not achieve a military victory. The reports of the intelligence services were for the most part accurate, though their analyses were far better at judging capabilities than intentions. At the same time, Britain's leaders sometimes ignored service advice and relied on their "instincts" in interpreting Hitler's behavior. They were misled by their own world views and assumptions just as Hitler was misled by his. John Ferris has rightly claimed that the British elite treated "their outlook and behavior as universal norms, which they were not."[43] Neither Chamberlain nor Halifax could understand a statesman like Hitler, while their own behavior confused the Führer who had his own mistaken stereotyped

[42] Dilks (ed.), *The Diaries of Sir Alexander Cadogan, O.M.*, p.

[43] John Ferris, "Intelligence," in Robert Boyce and Joseph A. Maiolo (eds.), *The Origins of World War Two: The Debate Continues* (Basingstoke: Palgrave Macmillan, 2003), p. 312. This discussion is based on Ferris's important essay, which I read in an extended, earlier version.

image of the British leaders. In September, each expected the other to compromise, neither anticipated war against each other in August 1939. Misconceptions were not the result of rational analysis but derived from mutual incomprehensions arising from skewered images and conflicting ideologies. We are in a very different world than that projected by either the offensive or defensive realists. On the grounds of power, a war between Germany and Britain could have been predicted. Germany would have to defend its claims to hegemony by using force; Britain would have to defend its existing power position by a resorting to war. Other options were foreclosed. Yet the war that broke out in September 1939 arose from false assumptions made by leaders on both sides. To explain the immediate origins of the war requires a different level of analysis than that offered by the realists.

8 Realism and risk in 1938: German foreign policy and the Munich Crisis

Niall Ferguson

I

It is no coincidence that realism in its classical form was a child of the Second World War. In Hans Morgenthau's formulation, realist theory assumes that states act as individuals ("Germany attacked Poland"), that they have clear interests, and that they expand their power when and where they can in ways that have their roots in "human nature."[1] International relations, in short, are conducted between rational actors with (as an economist would say) relatively simple utility functions. According to Kenneth Waltz, states seek to ensure their own survival in a more or less anarchic world, either by increasing their own internal strength or by "external balancing," in other words, forging alliances with other states. Cooperation between states can never be universal because a combination of states is only meaningful when it is directed against another state or a combination of states.[2] At all times, the national security of the individual state must be paramount. A more radical theory ("offensive realism") is that great powers always aim at more than mere survival; they seek hegemony, making conflicts between great powers inevitable.[3] Peace can be based only on a balance of power in which each would-be hegemon's acquisitive impulses are checked by other states' individual or combined capacities for retaliation.

The uniting theme of this volume is that foreign policy is more commonly the product of competing individuals and interest groups acting within a complex institutional framework and, as a result, strategy is not always commensurate with available means and room for maneuver. As the editors observe in their introduction, "History abounds in instances in which people in one government find actions of another regime hard to understand in light of their understanding of power

---

[1] Hans J. Morgenthau and Kenneth W. Thompson, *Politics among Nations: The Struggle for Power and Peace*, 6th edn. (New York: Alfred A. Knopf, 1985).
[2] Waltz, *Theory of International Politics*.
[3] Mearsheimer, *The Tragedy of Great Power Politics*, esp. p. 21.

relationships ... Some of the most important events in world history have occurred as a result of nations over-exercising or under-using their power." Few cases illustrate the point better, it might be thought, than the mutual misunderstandings that propelled Germany and Britain toward war in 1939. Repeatedly after he became German Chancellor in 1933, Adolf Hitler "over-exercised" Germany's power. By contrast, British leaders "under-used" theirs, with disastrous consequences. Though its antecedents can be traced back as far as Thucydides, realism was developed as a doctrine of international relations precisely in order to prevent such a huge error from being repeated. Though not uncritical of "extreme" realists (the "heirs of Machiavelli"), E. H. Carr directed most of his fire in his seminal *Twenty Years' Crisis* at the "utopian" tradition in Anglo-American liberalism and particularly on the institutions bequeathed to Europe by President Woodrow Wilson – not only the League of Nations, but the new states erected in Central and Eastern Europe on the principle of national self-determination.[4] Liberal utopians like Arnold Toynbee and Norman Angell might pin their hopes of perpetual peace on the perfectibility of mankind, but it was "profitless to imagine a hypothetical world in which men no longer organise themselves in groups for purposes of conflict ... As has often been observed, the international community cannot be organised against Mars."[5] The realist alternative, in Carr's view, was to accept that "Power is a necessary ingredient of every political order. Historically, every approach in the past to a world society has been the product of the ascendancy of a single Power."[6] That did not necessarily make war inevitable. But "peaceful change" required "an adjustment to the changed relations of power; and since the party which is able to bring most power to bear normally emerges successful from operations of peaceful change, we shall do our best to make ourselves as powerful as we can."[7]

It is easy to forget, however, that this very insight had made Carr a strong proponent of appeasement, which he defined as peaceful adjustment to Germany's postwar revival through "removals of long recognized injustices of the Versailles Treaty."[8] The first edition of *The Twenty Years' Crisis* even lauded the Munich Agreement as having corresponded "both to a change in the European equilibrium of forces and to accepted canons of international morality" – a passage conspicuously

---

[4] Edward Hallett Carr, *The Twenty Years' Crisis, 1919–1939: An Introduction to the Study of International Relations* (London: Palgrave Macmillan, 1946).
[5] Ibid., p. 231.   [6] Ibid., p. 232.
[7] Ibid.   [8] Ibid., p. 222.

absent from later editions.[9] Only when it finally became clear to Carr that Hitler could not be appeased (in around July 1939), did he switch to arguing for an alliance with the Soviet Union. For the British government to give a guarantee to Poland without an assurance of Russian support struck him as "the final recipe for disaster."[10] Ironically, this had been grasped a great deal earlier by the liberal leader writers of *The Economist*, one of whom (Toynbee) was among the principal targets of Carr's broadside against utopianism.[11]

Carr's belated volte-face on appeasement should have made readers more skeptical than they generally have been about the value of his theory. The other founding fathers of realism, by contrast, were highly critical of appeasement. For Reinhold Niebuhr, sheer pusillanimity had led the Western powers to sacrifice Czechoslovakia at Munich, whereas this was clearly one of those "moments in history when the covert threat of force which underlies all political contention must be brought out into the open."[12] Significantly, this was written six weeks before Hitler had revealed his true colors by carving up the rump Czechoslovakia. Hans Morgenthau had been hostile to appeasement even before Munich. As he put it in a speech in June 1938, "The retention of the decencies and amenities of civilized life involves, nay demands, a struggle in which we all ... must participate." He was even more forthright in his diary shortly after Chamberlain's first encounter with Hitler at Berchtesgaden: "If we don't stop Hitler now he is going right on down through the Black Sea – then what? ... The fate of Europe for the next one hundred years is settled."[13] Chamberlain's motives might have been noble, Morgenthau later argued in *Politics among Nations*, but "his policies helped to make the Second World War inevitable."[14] Carr had applauded Munich because he had mistaken Hitler's true "imperialistic designs" for a desire merely to adjust the European status quo. He had also overlooked "the contingencies inherent in political prediction" – in other words, had based his endorsement of appeasement on wishful

---

[9] Jonathan Haslam, *The Vices of Integrity: E. H. Carr, 1892–1982* (London: Verso, 1999), p. 73.

[10] Michael Cox, "An Autobiography," in Cox (ed.), *E. H. Carr: A Critical Appraisal* (Basingstoke: Palgrave Macmillan, 2000), p. xix.

[11] See, for example, "The Shadow of the Sword," *Economist*, March 19, 1938, p. 609; "Hope from Despair," *Economist*, September 17, 1938, p. 529; and "Vain Sacrifice," *Economist*, September 24, 1938, p. 577; "Eleventh-hour Reprieve," *Economist*, October 1, 1938, p. 3.

[12] Reinhold Niebuhr, "Must Democracy Use Force, II: Peace and the Liberal Illusion," *The Nation* (January 28, 1939), pp. 117–19.

[13] Barbara Rearden Farnham, *Roosevelt and the Munich Crisis: A Study of Political Decision-Making* (Princeton University Press, 2000), p. 100.

[14] Morgenthau and Thompson (eds.), *Politics among Nations*, p. 6.

thinking, rather than contemplating the worst-case scenario that Hitler was simply unappeasable and hell-bent on war.[15]

An important implication of Morgenthau's analysis was that Hitler himself was, for a time at least, a realist. His intention, according to Morgenthau, was always to pursue "a policy of imperialism, of continental, if not world, dimension," but he cleverly disguised this until March 1939, hitting "by a stroke of propagandistic genius ... upon the principle of national self-determination in order to disguise and justify his policies of territorial expansion."[16] This was the opposite mistake to the one made by Germany's leaders before 1914, who had in fact wanted no more than adjustments to the status quo, but had talked and acted as if they had much grander imperialistic ambitions.[17] Henry Kissinger's account of German policy in *Diplomacy* echoes this point: "Hitler was most successful when the world perceived him as pursuing normal, limited objectives. All his great foreign policy triumphs ... were based on his victims' assumption that his aim was to reconcile the Versailles system with its purported principles."[18] To be sure, we know now that Hitler was a megalomaniac with genocidal intentions, haunted by his own sense of impending mortality and obsessed with expunging the humiliation of Germany's collapse in 1918 by waging another war – one in which Germany would either triumph or fight to a *Götterdämmerung*-like finish. But:

the West's obsession with Hitler's motives was ... misguided ... The tenets of the balance of power should have made it clear that a large and strong Germany bordered on the east by small and weak states was a dangerous threat. *Realpolitik* teaches that ... Germany's relations with its neighbours would be determined by their relative power ... Once Germany attained a given level of armaments, Hitler's real intentions would become irrelevant.[19]

John Mearsheimer goes further, arguing that even Hitler's conscious motives were in large measure realistic: "Straightforward power calculations were central to Hitler's thinking about international politics ... Hitler ... thought and behaved like German leaders before him,"[20] with the difference that he had learned from their mistakes:

Hitler did indeed learn from World War I. He concluded that Germany had to avoid fighting on two fronts at the same time, and that it needed a way to win

[15] Ibid., pp. 22, 68, 77.
[16] Ibid., pp. 79, 111.
[17] Ibid., p. 113.
[18] Henry Kissinger, *Diplomacy* (New York: Simon & Schuster, 1994), p. 289.
[19] Ibid., p. 294.
[20] Mearsheimer, *The Tragedy of Great Power Politics*, p. 182.

quick and decisive military victories. He actually realized these goals in the early years of World War II ... Hitler's diplomacy was carefully calculated to keep his adversaries from forming a balancing coalition against Germany, so that the Wehrmacht could defeat them one at a time ... There is little doubt that Hitler acted skillfully.[21]

Even the "critical mistake" of invading the Soviet Union was "a wrong decision, not an irrational one."[22] Indeed, Dale Copeland suggests that it may even have been the right decision from the vantage point of offensive realism, given the fact of "Germany's marked inferiority in potential power versus Russia." Long before 1941, it was clear to Hitler that Germany had to take military action against the Soviet Union before Stalin's industrialization program was complete, after which the odds against German success would be hopeless. He took a similar calculated risk, in other words, to the one made by Chancellor Theobald von Bethmann-Hollweg in 1914.[23] Given the parlous condition of the Red Army in 1941, it was far from inevitable that the German invasion would end in catastrophic defeat.

Perhaps the most brilliant version of the realist case was made by A. J. P. Taylor nearly forty-five years ago in *The Origins of the Second World War*.[24] According to Taylor, "The cause of the war was ... as much the blunders of others as the wickedness of the dictators ... Far from being premeditated, [it] was a mistake."[25] The British said they wanted to uphold the authority of the League of Nations and the rights of small and weak nations; but when push came to shove in Manchuria, Abyssinia, and Czechoslovakia, imperial self-interest trumped collective security. They fretted about arms limitation, as though an equality of military capability would suffice to avoid war; but while a military balance might secure the British Isles, it offered no effective security for either Britain's continental allies or her Asian possessions. With withering irony, Taylor called Munich a "triumph for British policy [and] ... for all that was best and most enlightened in British life."[26] In reality, war with Germany was averted at the price of an unfulfillable guarantee to the rump Czechoslovakia. If handing the Sudetenland to Hitler in 1938 had been the right decision, why then did the British not hand him Danzig – to which he had in any case a stronger claim – in 1939? The answer was that by then they had given their militarily worthless guarantee to the Poles. Having done so, they failed to grasp what

[21] Ibid., p. 217.   [22] Ibid., p. 219.
[23] Copeland, *The Origins of Major War*, pp. 118–45.
[24] Taylor, *The Origins of the Second World War*.
[25] Ibid., pp. 136, 269.   [26] Ibid., p. 235.

Churchill saw at once; that without a "grand alliance" with the Soviet Union, Britain and France might find themselves facing Germany alone. By contrast with the bungling Western statesmen, Hitler was a realist, whose foreign policy was essentially the same as "that of his predecessors, of the professional diplomats at the foreign ministry, and indeed of virtually all Germans."[27]

The editors of this volume, however, argue that "Germany and Japan ... initiated conflicts they could not possibly win ... In both instances, the international power balance did not facilitate their ideologically driven quests for territorial gain ... [They] moved well beyond their economic and military limits." One of the editors has previously posed the question why Hitler proceeded with the invasion of Poland in September 1939 after it had become clear, against his expectations, that Britain and France would honor their commitments to Poland if he did so. At the very least, Rosecrance argues, a rational Hitler would have been deterred from subsequently attacking France and Britain by the relatively even balance of forces on the Western Front and the well-known advantages enjoyed by defenders against attackers.[28] The answer to the question offered by Dominic Johnson is that by 1939 Hitler had succumbed to "positive illusions" about Germany's relative strength which his military advisers had been able to hold in check a year before.[29] At some point after Munich, in other words, Hitler ceased to be realist.

What both the realists and their critics have in common is a tendency to understate what Kissinger once called "the problem of conjecture" – in his view, "perhaps the deepest problem ... in foreign policy":

Each political leader has the choice between making the assessment which requires the least effort or making an assessment which requires more effort. If he makes the assessment that requires least effort, then as time goes on it may turn out that he was wrong and then he will have to pay a heavy price. If he acts on the basis of a guess, he will never be able to prove that his effort was necessary, but he may save himself a great deal of grief later on ... If he acts early, he cannot know whether it was necessary. If he waits, he may be lucky or he may be unlucky. It is a terrible dilemma.[30]

---

[27] Ibid., p. 97.

[28] Alan Alexandroff and Richard Rosecrance, "Deterrence in 1939," *World Politics* 29 (1977), 404–24.

[29] Dominic D. P. Johnson, *Overconfidence and War: The Havoc and Glory of Positive Illusions* (Cambridge, MA: Harvard University Press, 2004), pp. 94–97, 99f., 102–07.

[30] Henry Kissinger, "Decision Making in a Nuclear World," Henry Kissinger Papers, Library of Congress, pp. 4–6.

By underestimating a nascent threat, the line of least resistance may prove costly in the end. But the bolder course of preemption or early military retaliation may go unrewarded precisely because it prevents that threat from ever being realized. The critical point is that all such decision-making takes place under uncertainty. Even approximate probabilities can be assigned to only a few possible scenarios; most are simply unknowable or, to put it differently, lie in the "fat tails" of a distribution which is anything but normal.[31] Moreover, even the most dogmatic realist cannot free himself from the many cognitive biases that we know afflict the human mind. Psychological experiments show that we all too readily fall into such cognitive traps as the fallacy of conjunction, confirmation bias, contamination effects, the affect heuristic, scope neglect, overconfidence in calibration, and bystander apathy.[32] Hitler confessed on more than one occasion to being a gambler. When the date for the invasion of Poland was definitively set for September 1, despite the news that Britain would not stand aside, Hermann Göring warned him that he should not play *va banque* (go for broke). "All my life I have played *va banque*," was Hitler's reply. He was, to put it mildly, anything but risk averse. Moreover, just as Kahnemann and Tversky's "prospect theory" predicts, Hitler gambled more recklessly when he began to lose.[33] The "hardcore" realist assumption that a rival state's actions can be predicted on the basis of its interests and capabilities clearly cannot therefore be sustained, even when we are absolutely sure that a realist is in charge of policy. As is evident from Carr and Morgenthau's diametrically different views of appeasement, realist policy-makers need to know what kind of realists they confront on the other side: status quo adjusters or imperialists thirsting after world domination. Motives do matter.

II

What, then, was Hitler gambling to win? This is not a difficult question to answer because Hitler answered it repeatedly. He was not content, like Stresemann or Brüning, merely to dismantle the Versailles Treaty – a task that the Depression had half-done for him even before he became

---

[31] See, for example, Ian Bremmer and Preston Keat, *The Fat Tail: The Power of Political Knowledge for Strategic Investing* (Oxford University Press, 2009).

[32] Eliezer Yudkowsky, "Cognitive Biases Potentially Affecting Judgment of Global Risks," in Martin J. Rees, Nick Bostrom, and Milan Ćirković (eds.), *Global Catastrophic Risks* (Oxford University Press, 2008), pp. 91–119.

[33] Daniel Kahneman and Amos Tversky, "Prospect Theory: An Analysis of Decision under Risk," *Econometrica* 47 (1979), 263–91.

Chancellor. Nor was his ambition to restore Germany to her position in 1914. It is not even correct, as the German historian Fritz Fischer suggested, that Hitler's aims were similar to those of Germany's leaders during the First World War, namely to carve out an Eastern European sphere of influence at the expense of Russia. Hitler's goal was different. Simply stated, it was to enlarge the German Reich so that it embraced as far as possible the entire German *Volk* and in the process to annihilate what he saw as the principal threats to its existence, namely the Jews and Soviet Communism (which to Hitler were one and the same). Like Japan's proponents of territorial expansion, he sought "living space" in the belief that Germany required more territory because of her over-endowment with people and her under-endowment with strategic raw materials. The German case was not quite the same, however, because there were already large numbers of Germans living in much of the space that Hitler coveted. When Hitler pressed for self-determination on behalf of ethnic Germans who were not living under German rule – first in the Saarland, then in the Rhineland, Austria, the Sudetenland, and Danzig – he was not making a succession of quite modest demands, as British statesmen (not to mention E. H. Carr) were inclined to assume. He was making a single very large demand which implied territorial claims extending far beyond the River Vistula. Hitler wanted not merely a Greater Germany; he wanted the Greatest Possible Germany. Given the very wide geographical distribution of Germans in East Central Europe, that implied a German empire stretching from the Rhine as far as the Volga. Nor was that the limit of Hitler's ambitions. For the creation of this maximal Germany was intended to be the basis for a German world empire that would be, at the very least, a match for the British Empire.[34]

Was this an irrational ambition? Not necessarily, given the conditions of the 1930s. In a world without free trade, empires offered all kinds of advantages to those who had them. It was undoubtedly advantageous to Britain to be at the center of a vast sterling bloc with a common currency and common tariff. And what would Stalin's Soviet Union have been if it had been confined within the historic frontiers of Muscovy, without the vast territories and resources of the Caucasus, Siberia, and Central Asia? The importance of empire became especially obvious to the self-styled "have not" powers when they adopted rearmament as a tool of economic recovery. For rearmament in the 1930s – if one wished to possess the most up-to-date weaponry – demanded copious supplies

---

[34] See most recently Mark Mazower, *Hitler's Empire: Nazi Rule in Occupied Europe* (London: Allen Lane, 2008).

of a variety of vital raw materials. Neither Italy, Germany, nor Japan had these commodities within their own borders other than in trivial quantities. By contrast, the lion's share of the world's accessible supplies lay within the borders of one of four rival powers: the British Empire, the French Empire, the Soviet Union, and the United States. Thus, no country could aspire to military parity with these powers without substantial imports of commodities whose supply they all but monopolized. For three reasons, it was not possible for the "have nots" to rely on free trade to acquire them. First, free trade had been significantly reduced by the mid-1930s. Second, Italy, Germany, and Japan lacked adequate international reserves to pay for the imports they required. Third, even if their central banks' reserves had been overflowing with gold, there was a risk that imports might be interdicted by rival powers before rearmament was complete. There was therefore a compelling logic behind territorial expansion, as Hitler made clear in his memorandum of August–September 1936, which outlined a new Four Year Plan for the German economy.

This important document, drafted by Hitler himself, began by restating his long-run goal of a confrontation with "Bolshevism, the essence and goal of which is the elimination and the displacement of the hitherto leading social classes of humanity by Jewry, spread throughout the world." Strikingly, Hitler singled out as a particular cause for concern the fact that "Marxism – through its victory in Russia – has established one of the greatest empires as a base of operations for its future moves." The existence of the Soviet Union, he argued, had enabled a dramatic growth in the military resources available to "Bolshevism." Because of the decadence of the Western democracies and the relative weakness of most European dictatorships, who needed all their military resources merely to remain in power, only three countries could "be regarded as being firm against Bolshevism": Germany, Italy, and Japan. The paramount objective of the German government must therefore be "developing the German Army, within the shortest period, to be the first army in the world in respect to training, mobilization of units [and] equipment." Yet Hitler then went on to enumerate the difficulties of achieving this within Germany's existing borders. First, an "overpopulated" Germany could not feed itself because "the yield of our agricultural production can no longer be substantially increased." Second, it was "impossible for us to produce artificially certain raw materials which we do not have in Germany, or to find other substitutes for them." Hitler specifically mentioned oil, rubber, copper, lead, and iron ore. Hence, "[t]he final solution lies in an extension of our living space, and/ or the sources of the raw materials and food supplies of our nation. It is the task of the political leadership to solve this question one day in the future."

Yet Germany was not yet in a military position to win "living space" through conquest. Rearmament would therefore only be possible through a combination of increased production of domestically available materials (e.g., low-grade German iron ore), further restriction of non-essential imports (e.g., coffee and tea), and substitution of essential imports with synthetic alternatives (e.g., *ersatz* fuel, rubber, and fats).

Hitler's memorandum was primarily an emphatic repudiation of the earlier "New Plan" favored by Hjalmar Schacht, which had aimed at replenishing Germany's depleted hard-currency reserves through a complex system of export subsidies, import restrictions, and bilateral trade agreements. Hitler dismissed brusquely Schacht's arguments for a slower pace of rearmament and a strategy of stockpiling raw materials and hard currency. The memorandum was also an explicit threat to German industry that state control would be stepped up if the private sector failed to meet the targets set by the government. However, the most important point in the entire report was the timetable it established. Hitler's two conclusions could not have been more explicit:

1. The German armed forces must be ready for combat within four years.
2. The German economy must be fit for war within four years.[35]

Historians have long debated whether this should be treated as evidence of a concrete Nazi plan for war. Of course it should. By decisively sanctioning an acceleration in the pace of rearmament and overriding Schacht's warnings of another balance-of-payments crisis, Hitler's Four Year Plan memorandum significantly increased the likelihood that Germany would be at war by 1940. In the words of Major General Friedrich Fromm of the Army's Central Administrative Office: "Shortly after completion of the rearmament phase, the Wehrmacht must be employed, otherwise there must be a reduction in demands or in the level of war readiness."[36] The interesting thing to note is that, by aiming for war in late 1940, Hitler was being relatively realistic about how long his proposed strategy of autarky could be sustained. By 1940 at the latest, in other words, Germany would need to have begun acquiring new living space.

---

[35] Wilhelm Treue, "Hitlers Denkschrift zum Vierjahresplan 1936," *Vierteljahreshefte für Zeitgeschichte* 3 (1955), 184–210.
[36] Tooze, *The Wages of Destruction*, chp. 7.

The concept of *Lebensraum* had been originated in the late 1890s by Friedrich Ratzel, Professor of Geography at Leipzig, and developed by the Orientalist and geopolitical theorist Karl Haushofer, whose pupil Rudolf Hess may have introduced the term to Hitler in the early 1920s. We can see now that the argument was based on an excessively pessimistic view of economic development. Since 1945 gains in both agricultural and industrial productivity have allowed "haves" and "have nots" alike to sustain even larger populations than they had in 1939. By the end of the twentieth century, Italy's population density was 17 percent higher than sixty years before, Britain's 28 percent higher, France's 42 percent higher, Germany's 64 per cent higher, and Japan's 84 percent higher. As a result of decolonization, all these countries had been "have nots" (in the interwar sense) for most of the intervening years, yet their economies had grown significantly faster than in the periods when some or all of them had been "haves." Clearly, "living space" was not as indispensable for prosperity as Haushofer and his disciples believed. In the context of the 1930s, however, the argument had a powerful appeal – and particularly in Germany, Italy, and Japan. In the late 1930s Germany had the fourth-highest population density of the world's major economies (363 inhabitants per square mile), after the United Kingdom (487), Japan (469), and Italy (418).[37] Under the Treaty of Versailles, however, Germany had been deprived of her relatively few colonies, whereas Britain had added to her already vast imperium, as had France. If, as Hitler had learned from Haushofer, "living space" was essential for a densely populated country with limited domestic sources of food and raw materials, then Germany, Japan, and Italy all needed it. Another way of looking at the problem was to relate available arable land to the population employed in agriculture. By this measure, Canada was ten times better endowed than Germany and the United States six times better. Even Germany's European neighbors had more "farming space": the average Danish farmer had 229 percent more land than the average German, the average British farmer 182 percent more, and the average French farmer 34 percent more. To be sure, farmers in Poland, Italy, Romania, and Bulgaria were worse off; but further east, in the Soviet Union, there was 50 percent more arable land per agricultural worker.[38]

Living space had a secondary meaning, however, which was less frequently articulated but in practice much more important. This was the need that any serious military power had for access to strategic raw

---

[37] Figures from *The Statesman's Yearbook* (London: Palgrave, 1939).
[38] Tooze, *The Wages of Destruction*, table 4.

materials. Here changes in military technology had radically altered the global balance of power – arguably even more so than post-1918 border changes. Military power was no longer a matter of "blood and iron," or even coal and iron, as it had been in Bismarck's day. Just as important were oil and rubber. The production of these commodities was dominated by the United States, the British Empire, and the Soviet Union, or countries under their direct or indirect influence. American oilfields alone accounted for just under 70 percent of global crude petroleum production; the world's next-largest producer was Venezuela (12 percent). The Middle Eastern oilfields did not yet occupy the dominant position they enjoy today: between them, Iran, Iraq, Saudi Arabia, and the smaller Gulf states accounted for less than 7 percent of total world production in 1940. The critical point was that oil production in all these countries was in the hands of British or American firms, principally Anglo-Persian, Royal Dutch/Shell, and the successors to Standard Oil. Nor was modern warfare solely a matter of internal combustion engines and rubber tires. Modern planes, tanks, and ships – to say nothing of guns, shells, bullets, and the machinery needed to make all these things – required a host of sophisticated forms of steel, which could be manufactured only with the admixture of more or less rare metals. Here too the situation of the Western powers and the Soviet Union was dominant, if not monopolistic. Taken together, the British Empire, the French Empire, the United States, and the Soviet Union accounted for virtually all of the world's output of cobalt, manganese, molybdenum, nickel, and vanadium, around three-quarters of all chromium and titanium, and half of all tungsten. The former German colony of South-West Africa, now securely in British hands, was practically the only source of vanadium. The Soviet Union, followed distantly by India, accounted for nearly all manganese production. Nickel was virtually a Canadian monopoly; molybdenum an American one.[39]

The case that Germany, Italy, and Japan lacked living space was therefore far from weak. Germany had abundant domestic supplies of coal and the biggest iron and steel industry in Europe, but before the 1930s needed to import all its rubber and oil. A direct consequence of Hitler's Four Year Plan memorandum was therefore a huge investment in new technologies capable of producing synthetic oil, rubber, and fibers using domestic materials such as coal, as well as the creation at Salzgitter of a vast new state-owned factory designed to manufacture steel from low-quality German iron ore. Yet by the time Hitler addressed

---

[39] "Munition Metals," *Economist*, October 1, 1938, pp. 25ff.

his senior military leaders on November 5, 1937 – a meeting summarized by Colonel Count Friedrich Hossbach – it had become apparent that this enormously expensive mobilization of internal resources could not possibly deliver the level of rearmament the service chiefs regarded as necessary before 1943–45. Autarky was not a sustainable solution. It was for this reason that Hitler turned his attention to the possibility that "living space," and the resources that came with it, might be acquired sooner rather than later, and *without* the immediate need for a full-scale war with the Western powers or the Soviet Union. As recorded by Hossbach, Hitler sketched out three "scenarios":

1. A German bid for *Lebensraum* in Europe, implying war with "the rest of the world" by 1943–45 at the latest, after which date "only a change for the worse, from our point of view, could be expected."
2. An immediate attack on Czechoslovakia in the event of a major French domestic crisis.
3. An attack on Austria and Czechoslovakia in the event of an Anglo-French–Italian war in the Mediterranean, which he believed could happen "as early as 1938." [40]

The critical point, Hitler argued, was that – despite being Germany's "hate-inspired antagonists" – Britain and France might not necessarily act in concert in the event of a German "lightning strike" against Czechoslovakia:

Actually, the Fuehrer believed that almost certainly Britain, and probably France as well, had already tacitly written off the Czechs and were reconciled to the fact that this question could be cleared up in due course by Germany. Difficulties connected with the Empire, and the prospect of being once more entangled in a protracted European war, were decisive considerations for Britain against participation in a war against Germany. Britain's attitude would certainly not be without influence on that of France. An attack by France without British support, and with the prospect of the offensive being brought to a standstill on our western fortifications, was hardly probable. Nor was a French march through Belgium and Holland without British support to be expected … It would of course be necessary to maintain a strong defense on our western frontier during the prosecution of our attack on the Czechs and Austria. And in this connection it had to be remembered that the defense measures of the Czechs were growing in strength from year to year … The incorporation of these two States with Germany meant, from the politico-military point of view, a substantial advantage. [41]

---

[40] For the text of the famous memorandum, see http://avalon.law.yale.edu/imt/hossbach.asp.

[41] Ibid.

This, too, was not prima facie an unreasonable proposition. Italy had acquired new living space in Abyssinia without having to fight a wider war. Japan too seemed well on her way out of the ignominious category of "have nots," fighting only China to secure control over Manchuria. Germany was the laggard of the three powers that banded together in November 1936 to form the Rome–Berlin Axis and the Anti-Comintern Pact. To be sure, not all of those present at the meeting described by Hossbach – notably the Minister for War, Field-Marshal Werner von Blomberg and the Commander-in-Chief of the Army, Werner von Fritsch – were persuaded by Hitler's arguments, particularly about the risks of French intervention.[42] But it was surely not wholly fantastic to imagine Germany making territorial acquisitions in Central Europe without precipitating a premature confrontation with the Western powers. Constrained by imperial overstretch, economic anxieties, and domestic political war weariness, the British looked less than eager to fight to preserve the integrity of Austria, Czechoslovakia, or Poland.[43] And the French were unlikely to act without British support.

III

Was Hitler therefore, as the documents quoted above seem to indicate, the quintessential offensive realist? The best way to answer this question is to examine closely his conduct during the crisis that he himself precipitated over Czechoslovakia in September 1938. It is important to bear in mind that, by this time, Hitler was merely using the alleged grievances of the Sudeten Germans as the pretext for a war which he intended would wipe Czechoslovakia off the map.[44] He repeatedly threatened to take military action against the Czechs, even when his demands were being met. Each time, the British government had the option to call his bluff. Unfortunately, Chamberlain and his advisers failed to appreciate the weakness of Hitler's position. Had they realized how hollow Hitler's threats were, and how vulnerable he was making himself, they could quite easily have inflicted a heavy diplomatic setback on him, and quite possibly a military and domestic setback too. Their fatal error was to believe, in the words of the Foreign Secretary, Lord

---

[42] Gerhard Weinberg, *The Foreign Policy of Hitler's Germany: Starting World War II, 1937–1939* (University of Chicago Press, 1980), p. 39.

[43] For a full discussion of the British side of the story see Niall Ferguson, *The War of the World: History's Age of Hatred* (London: Allen Lane, 2006), chps. 9 and 10.

[44] Richard J. Overy, "Germany and the Munich Crisis: A Mutilated Victory?" in Igor Lukes and Erik Goldstein (eds.), *The Munich Crisis, 1938: Prelude to World War II* (London: Routledge, 1999), p. 194.

Halifax, that firmness with Hitler would only "drive him to greater violence or greater menaces" – a wholly incorrect inference from the May
war scare, when the Czechs had mobilized in the mistaken belief that
Hitler was about to attack.[45] Likewise, when Duff Cooper proposed
"semi-mobilization" of the Royal Navy, Chamberlain dismissed the
idea as "a policy of pin-pricking which ... was only likely to irritate"
Hitler.[46] Instead, Chamberlain pressurized the Czech government into
granting autonomy to the Sudeten Germans.[47]

Reports now reached London that Hitler was planning unilaterally
to send in German troops. Here was another chance for Britain to call
Hitler's bluff. Indeed, on September 9, Chamberlain was prevailed upon
by his inner cabinet to send an explicit warning to Berlin that, if France
intervened, "the sequence of events must result in a general conflict
from which Great Britain could not stand aside."[48] But Chamberlain,
with the encouragement of Halifax and Henderson, decided at the last
minute that the telegram should not be handed to the German Foreign
Minister, Joachim von Ribbentrop. Halifax's rationale for this was,
as he put it to the cabinet, that "Any serious prospect of getting Herr
Hitler back to a sane outlook would probably be irretrievably destroyed
by any action on our part ... involving him in a public humiliation."[49]
As far as Halifax was concerned, Czechoslovakia was already as good
as finished. Rather than approve naval mobilization, as Cooper urged,[50]
Chamberlain's inner circle backed his ill-judged "Z Plan" – a personal
visit to Germany to make a "face to face" appeal to Hitler's vanity.[51]
What the Z Plan meant in practice was that Hitler would be offered a
plebiscite in the Sudetenland, at which the inhabitants could be expected
to vote for another *Anschluss*. The rump Czechoslovakia might then be
given some kind of guarantee.

As is well known, the first meeting between Chamberlain and Hitler
was held on September 15 at the latter's mountain retreat, the Berghof,

---

[45] See, for example, Halifax to Newton, August 31, 1938, in E. L. Woodward and Rohan
Butler (eds.), *Documents on British Foreign Policy, 1919–1939*, 3rd Series [henceforth
DBFP], vol. I, (London: His Majesty's Stationery Office, 1949), pp. 195f. Sir Nevile
Henderson, *Failure of a Mission, Berlin 1937–1939* (London: G. P. Putnam's, 1940),
pp. 146f.

[46] John Julius Norwich (ed.), *Duff Cooper Diaries, 1915–1951* (London: Weidenfeld &
Nicolson, 2005), p. 256.

[47] Runciman to Halifax, September 5, 1938, in *DBFP*, vol. II, pp. 248f.

[48] Halifax to Kirkpatrick, September 9, 1939, in *DBFP*, vol. II, pp. 277f.

[49] Ian Goodhope Colvin, *The Chamberlain Cabinet: How the Meetings in 10 Downing
Street, 1937–1939 Led to the Second World War, Told for the First Time from the Cabinet
Papers* (London: Taplinger Publishing Company, 1971), pp. 147–51.

[50] Norwich (ed.), *The Duff Cooper Diaries*, p. 259.

[51] Colvin, *Chamberlain Cabinet*, p. 153.

just outside Berchtesgaden. Hitler made it clear he would settle for nothing less than the immediate cession of the Sudetenland to Germany, without a plebiscite. "The thing has got to be settled at once," he declared. "I am determined to settle it. I do not care whether there is a world war or not. I have determined to settle it and to settle it soon and I am prepared to risk a world war rather than allow this to drag on."[52] This, again, was a bluff. However, persuading himself that Hitler's objectives were nevertheless "strictly limited" to "self-determination" for the Sudetenland, Chamberlain did not dissent and returned to London. After much deliberation, and objections from Cooper and the other so-called "war-boys" who were growing restive with appeasement, the cabinet acquiesced, provided that a plebiscite would be held before the "transfer."[53] When the French premier Édouard Daladier came to London, he expressed understandable indignation, but to no avail. All that remained to be done was to bully the Czechs into capitulating.[54]

Chamberlain set off for Germany again – this time bound for Bad Godesberg – with what he hoped was the solution. He met Hitler on September 22. The meeting was a fiasco. Claiming that he now had to take into account Polish and Hungarian claims with respect to their minorities in Czechoslovakia, Hitler rejected the idea of a plebiscite out of hand.[55] In desperation, Chamberlain offered to drop the plebiscite if only territory with a population that was over 50 percent German were handed over at once; the rest could be referred to a commission, as had happened with disputed territory after 1918. Alleging continued violations of the Sudeten Germans' rights, Hitler insisted on immediate cession of the territory, to be followed by German military occupation. Indeed, if no agreement were reached, he threatened to send German troops into the Sudetenland on September 28, just six days later. To reinforce this crude ultimatum, more German troops were moved to the Czech border, bringing the total number of divisions there to thirty-one.[56] Chamberlain blustered, saying that British public opinion would not tolerate a military occupation; Hitler replied that German opinion

---

[52] Parker, *Chamberlain and Appeasement*, p. 163.
[53] Colvin, *Chamberlain Cabinet*, pp. 156ff. See also Richard Lamb, *The Drift to War, 1922–1939* (London: W. H. Allen, 1989), p. 245.
[54] Masaryk to Halifax, September 18, 1938, in *DBFP*, vol. II, p. 400; Newton to Halifax, September 19, 1939, in *DBFP*, pp. 406f., 411f., 414f., 416f.; Phipps to Halifax, September 20, 1939, in *DBFP*, p. 422; Halifax to Newton, September 21, 1938, in *DBFP*, pp. 437f.; Newton to Halifax, September 21, 1938, in *DBFP*, pp. 447, 449f.
[55] Ivone Kirkpatrick, *The Inner Circle: The Memoirs of Ivone Kirkpatrick* (London: Palgrave Macmillan, 1959), p. 115; Henderson, *Failure of a Mission*, p. 153.
[56] Phipps to Halifax, September 21, 1938, September 22, 1938; Halifax to Newton, September 22, 1938, in *DBFP*, vol. II, pp. 451, 456, 461.

would stand for nothing less. Chamberlain complained that Hitler was presenting him with a *Diktat*; Hitler solemnly replied that, if he read the text of the German demands carefully, he would see that it was in fact a "memorandum." Flummoxed, Chamberlain agreed to communicate this memorandum to the Czechs. Hitler responded by agreeing to postpone the date of his threatened occupation by three days, a quite empty "concession."[57] The prime minister returned to London and put on a brave face, his analysis of the situation mystifyingly unaltered.

Again Britain had the chance to call Hitler's bluff. Predictably, Duff Cooper now pressed for "full mobilization," echoed by the other "war-boys" (Winterton, Stanley, de la Warr, and Elliot). Leslie Hore-Belisha also declared himself in favor of mobilizing the army.[58] Halifax too – hitherto so loyal to Chamberlain – jibbed: Hitler was "dictating terms, just as though he had won a war." So did Lord Hailsham, another erstwhile supporter.[59] With the news that the French as well as the Czech government had rejected the German demands, and the appearance of Daladier to confirm France's readiness to fight if necessary, Chamberlain had no alternative but finally to take a firmer line.[60] Now he proposed sending his confidant Horace Wilson to Germany to present Hitler with a choice: to refer the dispute to a joint German, Czech, and British Commission or face war with Britain too if France should enter on the side of the Czechs.[61]

For a fleeting moment it seemed as if Hitler had overplayed his hand. The Czechs were readying for war. The French sent a telegram to London asking the British to "(a) mobilize simultaneously with them: (b) introduce conscription: [and] (c) 'pool' economic and financial resources," requests repeated when General Maurice Gamelin, Chief of the French General Staff, visited London on September 26.[62] Chamberlain phoned Wilson, now in Germany, and informed him that the French had "definitely stated their intention of supporting Czechoslovakia by offensive measures if [the] latter is attacked. This would bring us in: and it

---

[57] Kirkpatrick, *Inner Circle*, pp. 120f; Lamb, *Drift to War*, pp. 248ff.

[58] Norwich (ed.), *The Duff Cooper Diaries*, p. 264; Duff Cooper, *Old Men Forget* (New York: Carroll & Graf), pp. 234ff.

[59] Colvin, *Chamberlain Cabinet*, p. 164; Lamb, *Drift to War*, pp. 151ff.; Parker, *Chamberlain and Appeasement*, pp. 170ff. Cf. Halifax to Chamberlain, September 23, 1938, in *DBFP*, vol. II, pp. 483f., 490.

[60] Gerhard L. Weinberg, "The French Role in the Least Unpleasant Solution," in Maya Latynski (eds.), *Reappraising the Munich Pact: Continental Perspectives* (Washington, DC: Woodrow Wilson Center Press, 1992), pp. 30f.

[61] Parker, *Chamberlain and Appeasement*, pp. 173ff; Lamb, *Drift to War*, p. 254.

[62] Brian Bond (ed.), *Chief of Staff: The Diaries of Lieutenant-General Sir Henry Pownall, Vol. I: 1933–1940* (London: L. Cooper, 1972), p. 163; Weinberg, "French Role," p. 35.

should be made plain to Chancellor [Hitler] that this is [the] inevitable alternative to a peaceful solution."[63] Although the prime minister still refused to heed Churchill's advice to link Russia to the Anglo-French threat, Halifax issued a press statement that, in the event of a German attack on Czechoslovakia, "France will be bound to come to her assistance and Great Britain and Russia will certainly stand by France."[64] On September 27, Chamberlain reluctantly agreed to mobilize the fleet, a decision Duff Cooper was able to make known to the press.[65] In London gas masks were issued and trenches dug in the parks; the fantasy that war would mean instantaneous German air raids on the capital continued to exert its fascination.[66] Even in the Berlin embassy "there was general satisfaction that the die had been cast."[67]

Yet, unbeknown to his colleagues, Chamberlain had diluted his instructions to Wilson by sending a message via the German embassy that Hitler should not consider the rejection of his demands as the last word.[68] Instead of warning Hitler of Britain's intention to support France and Czechoslovakia in the event of a war, Wilson allowed himself to be intimidated by Hitler's fury at Czech intransigence. Within a few days, Hitler declared, "I shall have Czechoslovakia where I want her." To Wilson's consternation, "He got up to walk out and it was only with difficulty he was prepared to listen to any more and then only with insane interruptions."[69] This was precisely the kind of theatrics at which Hitler excelled. To increase the pressure on Chamberlain's feeble emissary, Hitler brusquely brought forward the deadline for acceptance of his demands to 2 p.m. on September 28, just two days later.[70] Wilson went even weaker at the knees after hearing Hitler rant and rave at the Berlin Sportpalast in Berlin, and recommended not relaying Chamberlain's warning at all. He was overruled and did as he was asked on the 27th, but "more in sorrow than in anger."[71] Hitler was unmoved: "If France and England strike, let them do so," he retorted.

---

[63] Halifax to Henderson, September 26, 1938, in *DBFP*, vol. II, p. 550.
[64] R. A. C. Parker, *Churchill and Appeasement* (London: Palgrave Macmillan, 2000), pp. 180ff.
[65] Norwich (ed.), *The Duff Cooper Diaries*, p. 269.
[66] Parker, *Chamberlain and Appeasement*, p. 178.
[67] Kirkpatrick, *The Inner Circle*, p. 126.
[68] Lamb, *Drift to War*, p. 253.
[69] Henderson to Halifax, September 26, 1938, in *DBFP*, vol. II, pp. 552f. See also Kirkpatrick, *The Inner Circle*, p. 123.
[70] Henderson to Halifax, September 27, 1938, in *DBFP*, vol. II, p. 574f; Weinberg, "French Role," p. 32.
[71] Parker, *Chamberlain and Appeasement*, p. 176; Norwich (ed.), *The Duff Cooper Diaries*, p. 268.

"It is a matter of complete indifference to me. I am prepared for every eventuality."[72]

This was Hitler's last bluff. On the evening of September 27 he sent a note to Chamberlain effectively dropping his earlier threat to use military force by 2 p.m. the next day. In this note Hitler agreed that German troops would not move beyond the territory the Czechs had already agreed to cede; that there would be a plebiscite; and offered to make Germany a party to any international guarantee of Czechoslovakia's future integrity. Evidently, Wilson's warning ("more in sorrow than in anger") had been more effective than it had appeared at the time.[73] Having so frequently sought to accelerate the crisis, Hitler now eagerly accepted Mussolini's suggestion (prompted by Chamberlain) of a twenty-four-hour suspension of mobilization.[74] And he hastily sent a message to London inviting Chamberlain to attend a four-power conference in Munich.[75]

The crucial point is that Germany was simply not ready for a European war in 1938. Her defenses in the West were still incomplete; in the words of General Alfred Jodl, Chief of the National Defense Section in the German High Command (OKW), there were only "five fighting divisions and seven reserve divisions on the western fortifications, which were nothing but a large construction site to hold out against one hundred French divisions." No senior German military officer dissented from this view.[76] Nor could Germany count on Stalin's repudiating the Soviet commitment (made in 1935) to defend Czechoslovakia; Red Army units in the military districts of Kiev and Byelorussia were in fact brought to a state of readiness during the Czech crisis.[77] It was not inconceivable that the Romanian government would have granted them passage to the Czech frontier.[78] Moreover, the Soviet Foreign Secretary Maxim Litvinov repeatedly stated that the Soviets would honor their commitments to Czechoslovakia if the French did so too, or would at least refer the matter to the League of Nations.[79] Indeed,

---

[72] Henderson, *Failure of a Mission*, p. 160; Kirkpatrick, *The Inner Circle*, p. 125; Lamb, *Drift to War*, p. 256.

[73] Dilks (ed.), *The Diaries of Sir Alexander Cadogan*, pp. 106–09.

[74] Henderson, *Failure of a Mission*, pp. 163ff.

[75] Dilks (ed.), *The Diaries of Sir Alexander Cadogan*, p. 109.

[76] Lamb, *Drift to War*, p. 239.

[77] P. M. H. Bell, *The Origins of the Second World War in Europe*, 2nd edn. (London: Longman, 1997), p. 266.

[78] De la Warr to Halifax, September 15, 1938, in *DBFP*, vol. II, p. 354f.; Lamb, *Drift to War*, pp. 263f.

[79] See, for example, Chilston to Halifax, September 4, 1938; Newton to Halifax, September 6, 1938, in *DBFP*, vol. II, pp. 229ff., 255f.; Scott Newton, *Profits of*

on September 24, Litvinov explicitly told the British delegation to the League of Nations that, if the Germans invaded Czechoslovakia, the "Czechoslovak-Soviet Pact would come into force" and proposed a conference between Britain, France, and the Soviet Union to "show the Germans that we mean business."[80] As Hitler admitted to Jodl, he could not "attack Czechoslovakia out of a clear sky ... or else I would get on my neck the whole world. I would have to wage war against England [and] against France, which I could not wage."[81]

Because of the danger of British and French intervention, only a part of the Wehrmacht's seventy-five divisions – the British military attaché in Paris estimated just twenty-four – could have been deployed in an attack on Czechoslovakia.[82] Nor were the Czechs to be dismissed lightly; the British military attaché fully expected their thirty-five well-equipped divisions to "put up a really protracted resistance" against an attacker who would have enjoyed neither decisive numerical superiority nor the element of surprise.[83] In 1939 German reserve officers confessed to a British journalist that the Czech defenses had been "impressive and impregnable to our arms. We could have gone round them, perhaps, but not reduced them." Hitler himself later admitted that he had been "greatly disturbed" when he discovered the "formidable" levels of Czech military preparedness. "We had run a serious danger."[84] "Operation Green" – the planned pincer movement by the 2nd and 10th Armies – might have ended in disaster had it been launched.[85] As General Sir Henry Pownall put it, with classic understatement, even if the Germans had left only nine divisions along the Siegfried Line in the

---

Peace: The Political Economy of Anglo-German Appeasement (Oxford University Press, 1996), p. 81f.

[80] Phipps to Halifax, September 23, 1939; Geneva delegation to Halifax, September 23, 1938, in *DBFP*, vol. II, pp. 489, 497f.

[81] Overy, "Germany and the Munich Crisis," pp. 204, 207–10.

[82] D. C. Watt, "British Intelligence and the Coming of the Second World War in Europe," in Ernest R. May (ed.), *Knowing One's Enemies: Intelligence Assessment before the Two World Wars* (Princeton University Press, 1984), p. 253; Lamb, *Drift to War*, p. 251; Newton to Halifax, September 27, 1938, in *DBFP*, vol. II, p. 567. See also Williamson Murray, "The War of 1938: Chamberlain Fails to Sway Hitler at Munich," in Robert Crowley (ed.), *More What If? Eminent Historians Imagine What Might Have Been* (London: Pan Books, 2003), pp. 261f.

[83] Newton to Halifax, September 6, 1938, in *DBFP*, vol. II, pp. 257ff.; Phipps to Halifax, September 28, 1938, in *DBFP*, vol. II, pp. 609f.

[84] Ian Colvin, *Vansittart in Office: An Historical Survey of the Origins of the Second World War Based on the Papers of Sir Robert Vansittart* (London: V. Gollancz, 1965), p. 274. John W. Wheeler-Bennett, *The Nemesis of Power: The German Army in Politics, 1918–1945* (London: Palgrave Macmillan, 1953), p. 419.

[85] Murray, "War of 1938," pp. 263f.

West and five to defend East Prussia against the Red Army, what Hitler was contemplating was "certainly a bit risky."[86]

German naval preparations were also woefully behindhand. In all there were just seven destroyers, three "pocket" battleships, and seven submarines available.[87] Moreover, the Germans could count on no effective support from abroad. Poland might possibly have come in on the German side for a share of the Czech carcass, though she might equally well have jumped the other way. The same could be said of Hungary. Mussolini might conceivably have sided with Hitler. But none of these countries posed a significant threat to the Western powers. On the contrary, it would have been very easy for the British and French to inflict heavy losses on the Italian Mediterranean fleet.[88] As for Japan, it is highly unlikely that her government would have chosen this moment to pick a fight with the Western empires, given the difficulties they were encountering in China and the growing preoccupation of her generals with the Soviet threat from the north.

Finally, Germany's much-vaunted capacity to bomb London was largely a figment of British imaginations – the result of a grave failure of intelligence gathering and interpretation.[89] In fact, the Germans preferred to see bombers in a tactical role, supporting ground forces (hence the small dive-bombers like the Stuka and Junkers Ju 87 developed in the mid-1930s and "tested" in the Spanish Civil War); their investment in bombers capable of cross-Channel operations was far smaller than the British feared, and when they did launch the Battle of Britain they initially targeted airfields and other military targets, not urban centers.[90] There was no plan whatever to bomb Britain in the event of a war in 1938, despite Göring's brazen threat to Henderson that the Luftwaffe would leave "little of London left standing" in the event of a war.[91] As General Helmuth Felmy, commander of the 2nd Air Fleet, admitted in late September 1938, "given the means at his disposal a war of destruction against England seemed to be excluded."[92] British preparations for possible German attacks were thus pointless.[93]

German military unreadiness had important political implications within the Third Reich. No one was more aware of Germany's

---

[86] Bond (ed.), *Chief of Staff*, p. 160.
[87] Murray, "War of 1938," p. 265.
[88] Ibid., pp. 268ff.
[89] Watt, "British Intelligence," pp. 258f.
[90] Ibid., pp. 259f.
[91] Henderson, *Failure of a Mission*, p. 152.
[92] Murray, "War of 1938," p. 267.
[93] J. R. Colville, *Man of Valour: The Life of Field-Marshal the Viscount Gort* (London: Collins, 1972), p. 112.

military weaknesses than Ludwig Beck, the Chief of the General Staff since 1935. Beck was convinced from the moment the idea was first bruited that Hitler was playing with fire in contemplating an attack on Czechoslovakia. In his view, Hitler's strategy of building up the diplomatic tension and then presenting the great powers with a fait accompli was fraught with danger.[94] Such a move might well lead to a general European war that Germany could not hope to win. Unlike others who had ventured to doubt Hitler's wisdom as a strategist, Beck survived the purge of January 1938.[95] Hitler had certainly strengthened his control over the German military by replacing Blomberg with himself as Commander-in-Chief and Keitel as his adlatus, and putting the supine Walther von Brauchitsch into Fritsch's former post. Beck's resignation in late August therefore removed what was probably the biggest political threat to Hitler's position. But it did not end the possibility of military opposition to Hitler. Beck urged his successor, General Franz Halder, to involve himself in the coup against Hitler that was now being seriously discussed by General Hans Oster, Deputy Chief of the *Abwehr*, and Hans Gisevius, an official in the Interior Ministry. Halder later claimed that he, Beck, retired General Erwin von Witzleben, and others had conspired to overthrow Hitler, but that Chamberlain's decision to fly to Germany had deprived them of their opportunity.[96]

To be sure, the anti-Hitler elements within the German military and civilian elites were diverse and disorganized.[97] We have no way of knowing if a coup might have succeeded had Hitler suffered a major diplomatic reverse over Czechoslovakia. Yet the absolute refusal of the British authorities to heed the signals that reached them, even from such impeccable sources as Ernst von Weizsäcker, State Secretary in the German Foreign Office, was to say the least strange.[98] After Munich, the chances of a regime change in Berlin faded swiftly. The misnamed "Opposition" did not abandon their attempts to establish dialogue with

---

[94] Nicholas Reynolds, *Treason Was No Crime: Ludwig Beck, Chief of the German General Staff* (London: Kimber, 1976), pp. 148, 151.

[95] Peter Hoffman, "Ludwig Beck: Loyalty and Resistance," *Central European History* 14 (1981), 339; Gerhard Weinberg, "The German Generals and the Outbreak of War, 1938–1939," in Adrian Preston (ed.), *General Staffs and Diplomacy before the Second World War* (London: Croom Helm, 1978), pp. 29–31.

[96] Lamb, *Drift to War*, pp. 266ff.

[97] Peter Hoffman, *The History of the German Resistance, 1933–1945*, 3rd edn. (London: Blackwell Publishing, 1977), p. 63. See also Gerhard Ritter, *The German Resistance: Carl Goerdeler's Struggle against Tyranny* (London: Praeger, 1958), p. 93.

[98] See, for example, Warner to Halifax, September 5, 1938, in *DBFP*, vol. II, pp. 242f.; Hoffman, *German Resistance*, pp. 63–67. For a different view see Wheeler-Bennett, *Nemesis of Power*, pp. 414f. See also Dilks (ed.), *The Diaries of Sir Alexander Cadogan*, pp. 94f. Beck himself sent Ewald von Kleist-Schmenzin to London as his emissary.

London. Carl Goerdeler, the former Price Commissioner and Mayor of Leipzig, visited England at Christmas 1938. Six months later Adam von Trott zu Solz, a well-connected former Rhodes Scholar, met with both Chamberlain and Halifax.[99] Other visitors included Lieutenant-Colonel Count Gerhard von Schwerin, who urged that Churchill be brought into the government.[100] But the moment had passed. Nor should we overlook a further dimension to German weakness at that time. As Hitler was disgusted to discover, the German people – the *Volk* whose living space he was striving to enlarge – had little appetite for war. The British were well aware of this. Junior officials at the Berlin embassy reported that "public opinion" was "much alarmed at German military measures"; there was "a general fear that an attack on Czechoslovakia may lead to a European war which Germany would be likely to lose."[101] Henderson himself noted that "not a single individual in the streets applauded" when a mechanized division paraded through Berlin on September 27.[102] "War would rid Germany of Hitler," Henderson remarked on October 6, in a rare moment of perspicacity. "As it is, by keeping the peace, we have saved Hitler and his regime."[103]

The tragedy of 1938 is that the British and French governments so completely misread the balance of power at the very moment it tipped most strongly in their favor. Cadogan was convinced: "We *must* not precipitate a conflict now – we shall be smashed." The Chiefs of Staff shared this view.[104] "Chamberlain is of course right," General Edmund Ironside, head of the Eastern Command, wrote in his diary: "We have not the means of defending ourselves ... We cannot expose ourselves now to a German attack. We simply commit suicide if we do."[105] Gamelin was equally in awe of the Germans. Like the British, the French were convinced that the Germans had the capacity to bomb to reduce their cities "to ruins."[106] One of his senior staff officers envisaged such rapid mobilization in Germany that fifty divisions would quickly be available for deployment against France.[107] The result – incredibly – was

[99] Peter Hoffman, "The Question of Western Allied Co-operation with German Anti-Nazi Conspiracy, 1938–1944," *Historical Journal* 34 (1991), 443ff.

[100] Parker, *Churchill and Appeasement*, p. 231.

[101] Ogilvie-Forbes to Halifax, September 11, 1938, in *DBFP*, vol. II, p. 289. See also Kirkpatrick, *Inner Circle*, pp. 111f.

[102] Henderson, *Failure of a Mission*, p. 161.

[103] Colvin, *Vansittart in Office*, p. 273.

[104] David Dilks, "'The Unnecessary War'? Military Advice and Foreign Policy in Great Britain, 1931–1939," in Preston (ed.), *General Staffs and Diplomacy*, pp. 103, 123.

[105] Michael Howard, *The Continental Commitment: The Dilemma of British Defence Policy in the Era of Two World Wars* (London: Maurice Temple Smith Ltd., 1972), p. 122.

[106] Phipps to Halifax, September 22, 1938, in *DBFP*, vol. II, pp. 473f.

[107] Ibid., pp. 609f.

that no Anglo-French military talks were held at any point during the Sudetenland crisis; the most the Chiefs of Staff were willing to contemplate was the dispatch of just two ill-equipped Field Force divisions to France in the event of war.[108] Generals are often criticized for planning to fight the last war instead of the next one. In 1938 British generals did not even plan to fight the last war. If they had, things might have turned out very differently. For it was the Germans, not the British and French, who risked being "smashed" in 1938. All the British had to do was to commit unequivocally to a joint Anglo-French defense of Czechoslovakia. Rather than flying back and forth like a supplicant, Chamberlain should have sat tight in London, declining to take calls from Germany. We cannot, of course, say for sure what would have happened.[109] But the chances of a German humiliation would not have been negligible.

Time was of the essence. As Sir Robert Vansittart put it, Britain's policy was one of "cunction" (delay) to gain time for rearmament. The Chiefs of Staff argued, on the basis of the Royal Air Force's fears of a German knock-out blow, that "from the military point of view the balance of advantage is definitely in favour of postponement ... we are in bad condition to wage even a defensive war at the present time."[110] It was certainly true that Fighter Command had been woefully neglected up until this point and much more had to be done to make British air defenses ready.[111] The British army too could only become stronger after Munich.[112] But time is relative. Its passage no doubt did allow the British to bolster their defenses. But it simultaneously allowed Hitler to increase his offensive capability too. It is true that German rearmament had to be reined in toward the end of 1938. It is also true that the Germans became convinced that time would be against them if they delayed war much after 1939.[113] But, on balance, time was more on Germany's side than on Britain's in the year after September 1938. The German army grew significantly more than the British or French armies combined between 1938 and 1939. In naval terms, it is true, Germany stood still while the British and French added substantially to their fleets. But in the air, which contemporaries tended to see as

---

[108] Brian Bond, *British Military Policy between the Two World Wars* (Oxford University Press, 1980), pp. 280f.

[109] For some speculations, see Murray, "War of 1938"; R. H. Haigh and D. S. Morris, *Munich 1938: The Peace of Delusion* (Sheffield Hallam University, 1998), pp. 51ff.

[110] Howard, *Continental Commitment*, p. 123.

[111] Haigh and Morris, *Munich 1938*, pp. 49f.

[112] Colville, *Man of Valour*, pp. 115ff.; Bond (ed.), *Chief of Staff*, p. 122.

[113] Tooze, *The Wages of Destruction*, chp. 9.

decisive, the rivals were, at best, neck and neck. German additions to first-line Luftwaffe strength somewhat exceeded British additions to the RAF reserves. In combination, the British and French had more first-line aircraft than the Germans in 1939, but the difference had been larger in 1938 (589 compared with 94). Another way of demonstrating this is to compare figures for military aircraft production in 1939. Germany built 8,295, Britain 7,940, and France 3,163. The Soviet Union out-built all three with 10,565 new aircraft.[114] But in 1938 the Western powers could consider the Soviets as potential allies. By 1939 Stalin was Hitler's ally.

What was more, Hitler gained immediately from Munich. With Czechoslovakia emasculated, Germany's eastern frontier was significantly less vulnerable.[115] In occupying the Sudetenland, the Germans acquired at a stroke 1.5 million rifles, 750 aircraft, 600 tanks, and 2,000 field guns, all of which were to prove useful in the years to come.[116] Indeed, more than one in ten of the tanks used by the Germans in their western offensive of 1940 were Czech-built.[117] The industrial resources of western Bohemia further strengthened Germany's war machine, just as the *Anschluss* had significantly added to Germany's supplies of labor, hard currency, and steel. As Churchill put it, the belief that "security can be obtained by throwing a small state to the wolves" was "a fatal delusion": "The war potential of Germany will increase in a short time more rapidly than it will be possible for France and Great Britain to complete the measures necessary for their defence."[118] "Buying time" at Munich in fact meant widening, not narrowing, the gap that Britain and France desperately needed to close.[119] To put it another way: it would prove much harder to fight Germany in 1939 than it would have proved to fight Germany in 1938.

IV

It was not just in military terms that Germany was weak in 1938. Of equal importance was her acute economic vulnerability. As we have seen, Schacht's New Plan had been abandoned two years before because his system of bilateral trade agreements could not deliver the amounts

[114] Richard Overy, *The Air War, 1939–1945* (London: Europa Publications Ltd., 1980), p. 21.
[115] Howard, *Continental Commitment*, pp. 124f; Bond (ed.), *Chief of Staff*, p. 164.
[116] Lamb, *Drift to War*, pp. 262f.
[117] Haigh and Morris, *Munich 1938*, pp. 80f.
[118] Ibid., p. 60.
[119] Sidney Aster, "'Guilty Men': The Case for Neville Chamberlain," in Patrick Finney (ed.), *The Origins of the Second World War* (London: Arnold, 1997), pp. 69ff.

of raw materials needed for the rapid rearmament Hitler wanted.[120] But the Four Year Plan could not possibly have improved matters much by 1938. Domestic iron-ore production had certainly been boosted, but the increment since 1936 was just over a million tons, little more than a tenth of imports in 1938. No more than 11,000 tons of synthetic rubber had been produced, around 12 percent of imports.[121] The rationale of annexing Austria and Czechoslovakia – as Hitler had made clear in November 1937 – was precisely to address the shortages of raw materials that were continuing to hamper German rearmament.[122] Had war come in 1938, the journalist Ian Colvin had it on good authority that Germany had only sufficient stocks of gasoline for three months.[123] In addition, the German economy was by now suffering from acute labor shortages. The irony was that German problems were in large measure a consequence of the upsurge in arms spending that had been set in train by the Four Year Plan.[124] Göring himself had to admit that the German economy was now working at full stretch. By October, German economic experts were in agreement that a war would have been "catastrophe."

As Colvin's testimony suggests, Germany's economic problems were no secret. Indeed, their financial symptoms were highly visible. Schacht's resignation as Economics Minister – which he submitted in August 1937, though it was not accepted until November – was widely seen as a blow to the regime's fiscal credibility, although he stayed on as Reichsbank President.[125] Aside from his objections to the Four Year Plan, Schacht had two concerns: the mounting inflationary pressure as more and more of the costs of rearmament were met by printing money, and the looming exhaustion of Germany's hard-currency reserves. These problems did not go away. German exports were a fifth lower than the year before. In July 1938 Germany had to give in when Britain insisted on a revision of the Anglo-German Payments Agreement and continued payment of interest due on the Dawes and Young bonds, issued to help finance reparations.[126] The anti-appeasing commercial attaché in the British embassy in Berlin had a point when he argued

---

[120] Newton, *Profits of Peace*, pp. 55–57.
[121] Tooze, *The Wages of Destruction*, table 6.
[122] Overy, "Germany and the Munich Crisis," pp. 194–200.
[123] Colvin, *Vansittart in Office*, p. 273.
[124] Tooze, *The Wages of Destruction*, chp. 8.
[125] Ronald M. Smelser, "Nazi Dynamics, German Foreign Policy and Appeasement," in Wolfgang J. Mommsen and Lothar Kettenacker (eds.), *The Fascist Challenge and the Policy of Appeasement* (London: Allen & Unwin, 1983), pp. 38f.
[126] C. A. MacDonald, "Economic Appeasement and the German 'Moderates', 1937–1939: An Introductory Essay," *Past and Present* 56 (1972), 115ff.

for canceling the Anglo-German Payments Agreement. By further reducing Germany's access to hard currency, that would have struck at the German economy's Achilles heel.[127] Small wonder the German stock market slumped by 13 percent between April and August 1938. The German Finance Minister Schwerin von Krosigk warned that Germany was on the brink of an inflationary crisis. In a devastating Reichsbank memorandum, dated October 3, 1938, Schacht said the same. Hitler might brush aside these arguments, urging Göring to step up the already frenetic pace of rearmament. But by now the goals had entered the realm of fantasy: an air force with more than 20,000 planes by 1942; a navy with nearly 800 vessels by 1948. Even if there had been enough steel for such feats of engineering, there would not have been enough fuel for half the bombers to fly or half the battleships to sail. The Reichsbank was now manifestly struggling to finance the government's mounting deficits by selling bonds to the public; its hard-currency reserves were exhausted. When Schacht and his colleagues repeated their warnings of inflation Hitler fired them, but he could no longer ignore the need to "export or die."[128]

British officials worried a great deal about their own shortages of labor and hard currency. But in both respects the German position was far worse. Did contemporaries not realize this? One way of seeing the Munich Crisis afresh is to view it from the vantage point of investors in the City of London. It is sometimes claimed that the Munich Agreement lifted the London stock market. Little evidence can be found to support this.[129] The market was in any case depressed by the recession of 1937. To make matters worse, there were substantial outflows of gold, amounting to £150 million, between the beginning of April and the end of September 1938. It is significant that Munich did nothing to arrest these outflows: another £150 million left the country in the months after the conference. From February 1938 until March 1939, in the face of widening current-account deficits, sterling slipped steadily downward against the dollar. The Chancellor of the Exchequer attributed these outflows to

the view [that] continues to be persistently held abroad that war is coming and that this country may not be ready for it, and lying behind that anxiety is, of course, the further anxiety created by the obvious worsening of our financial

---

[127] Ibid., p. 121.
[128] Tooze, *The Wages of Destruction*, chp. 9.
[129] For more details see Niall Ferguson, "Earning from History? Financial Markets and the Approach of World Wars," *Brookings Papers on Economic Activity* 1 (2008), 431–77.

position, by the heavy increase in the adverse balance of trade, and by the growth of armament expenditure.[130]

On this basis, the Treasury was able to make its usual argument that rearmament could not be accelerated any further. But it could equally well have been argued that Britain might as well fight sooner rather than later, when her reserves might be still further depleted. By July 1939, Britain's gold reserves were down to £500 million; in addition the Bank had around £200 million in disposable foreign securities. The drain on British reserves by this stage was running at £20 million a month.[131] As Oliver Stanley put it: "The point would ultimately come when we should be unable to carry on a long war."[132] This is the key. What it means is that Britain would have been better off financially, as well as militarily, if there had been a war in 1938. Not only would war have come sooner, it would almost certainly have been shorter, given the weaknesses of the German position described above. This gives the lie to the old claim that appeasement bought Britain precious time.[133] For Britain, time was at a discount.

V

On close inspection, then, Hitler was anything but a realist, offensive or otherwise, in the decisive month of September 1938. He was a very reckless gambler. He was also a very lucky one, at least in the short term. For if Chamberlain had earnestly called Hitler's bluff over Czechoslovakia rather than repeatedly making concessions to him, Germany's position would have been far more exposed than it was in 1939. By going to war with Germany later rather than sooner, Chamberlain might have unwittingly saved the Third Reich. He certainly improved Hitler's chances of winning the war. In effect, Hitler the gambler presented Britain with an option as to the timing of the Second World War. Unfortunately, Chamberlain – at one time the hero of the pioneer realist E. H. Carr – chose the wrong year because he failed to grasp the disadvantages to Britain and the advantages to Germany of further "cunction." In that sense, Churchill was half right: the war of 1939 was indeed an "unnecessary war." But what had been necessary to stop it was a war in 1938 – a war which the un-realist running Germany was reckless enough to risk.

[130] Parker, "Economics, Rearmament and Foreign Policy," 643.
[131] Newton, *Profits of Peace*, pp. 114–18.
[132] Parker, "Economics, Rearmament and Foreign Policy," 644.
[133] See, for example, Peden, "A Matter of Timing," 25f.

Subsequent events, it is scarcely necessary to add, revealed only more starkly Hitler's lack of realism. Historians continue to debate how unrealistic it was of Hitler to order the invasion of the Soviet Union. His preeminent biographer has no doubt that the decision was an almost suicidal mistake based more on Hitler's ideological biases than on any rational assessment of the risks involved.[134] Yet the logic of *Lebensraum* had always pointed in the direction of such a move. Moreover, there were three good reasons for attacking the Soviets sooner rather than later. The Red Army's poor performance in Poland and subsequently in Finland exposed how enfeebled the Soviet officer corps had been by Stalin's purges. The Red Army, Hitler and his military advisers agreed, would be easy meat for the Wehrmacht's tried-and-tested blitzkrieg tactics. Second, Hitler had failed to win the Battle of Britain. However, it was not unreasonable to hope that British morale would be dealt a death-blow if the Soviet Union could now be put to the German sword. Finally, Stalin was doing better out of the Nazi–Soviet Pact than Hitler had intended. Despite leaving nearly all the fighting to the Germans, the Soviets ended up with a slightly larger share of the Polish population. In June 1940 they also proceeded to acquire the Baltic states. In violation of the secret protocols of the Ribbentrop–Molotov Pact, Stalin also unilaterally demanded that Romania cede to him Bessarabia and northern Bukovina, which included some of Romania's most productive agricultural land. When the Soviets made it clear that they intended to extend a "security guarantee" to Bulgaria, Hitler discerned fresh evidence that Stalin intended to preempt him in the Balkans. Indeed, Hitler's attack on Stalin seemed such an obvious next move for Germany that it was anticipated by nearly all informed observers apart from Stalin himself. Once again, Hitler acknowledged that he was gambling. Yet the odds were not as overwhelmingly against him *ex ante* as they now seem with the benefit of hindsight. This was not like the Japanese attack on Pearl Harbor – which clearly was an act of strategic desperation with a patently low probability of success. What clearly *was* irrational was for Hitler to make the occupation of Eastern Europe so relentlessly brutal in character that the potential for any kind of legitimate anti-Soviet empire was frittered away.[135] Irrational, too, was Hitler's comically ill-informed view of the United States as an adversary. "I don't see much

---

[134] See most recently Ian Kershaw, *Fateful Choices: Ten Decisions that Changed the World* (London: Penguin Books Ltd., 2007).
[135] Ferguson, *War of the World*, chp. 13.

future for the Americans," declared the *Stammtisch* sage in 1942, in one of his dinner-table monologues:

> In my view, it's a decayed country. And they have their racial problem, and the problem of social inequalities. Those were what caused the downfall of Rome, and yet Rome was a solid edifice that stood for something ... The German Reich has 270 opera houses – a standard of cultural existence of which they over there have no conception. They have clothes, food, cars and a badly constructed house – but with a refrigerator! This sort of thing does not impress us.[136]

By the time he spoke those words, Hitler had managed to embroil Germany in a war against the British Empire, the Soviet Union, and the United States. Extensive though his conquests had been between 1938 and 1941, they had not given the Nazi empire and its economically much inferior confederates sufficient resources to stand a serious chance of success in such a conflict. The strategic odds, as is now well known, were overwhelmingly against the Axis powers from 1942 onwards. The tragedy nevertheless remains that such a global conflagration was ever necessary to curtail Hitler's ambitions. Though the odds were less overwhelmingly against Germany in the summer of 1938 than they were four years later, they were still sufficiently skewed that a Churchillian policy of confrontation rather than appeasement would have stood a good chance of success. Of all the decision-makers who made the Second World War happen, Chamberlain was nearly as unrealistic as Hitler.

---

[136] H. R. Trevor-Roper (ed.), *Hitler's Table Talk, 1941–44: His Private Conversations*, trans. Norman Cameron and R. H. Stevens, 2nd edn. (London: Weidenfeld & Nicolson, 1973), January 7, 1942; August 1, 1942.

9 Domestic politics, interservice impasse, and Japan's decisions for war

Michael Barnhart

If the quintessential test for a state is to have its managers identify perfectly with it and with perfect rationality identify its interests, few states have been universally well-served. The fault is hardly with those managers. The interests of the state are seldom self-evident and nearly always subject to debate. Even in absolute monarchies or dictatorships, the sovereign's advisers offer competing policies.

Imperial Japan legally was such an absolute monarchy, with its emperor granted nearly unlimited power, in theory. More, the leaders of Japan's Meiji Restoration had a near tabula rasa on which to design a new state, one that would benefit from their intense study of the West and its institutions. Keenly aware of the West's threat, these leaders – inspired, dedicated, and intelligent all – deliberately set out to build a rational state capable of dealing with that threat.[1] They failed spectacularly.

In reality, Japan was not an absolute monarchy. It was a virtually headless state from 1868 to 1945. For its first forty-five years, a measure of consensus was provided by the commitment of its founding generation to the avoidance of sharp internal disputes. Japan could ill-afford these, menaced by the West as it was. But the construction of that consensus required the construction of a governing apparatus that, ironically, acted to make consensus impossible once the founding generation passed away. In its place arose a structure of autonomous and highly competitive ministries – bureaucracies – that created professional and powerful allegiances to themselves. In consequence, the last thirty years of Imperial Japan were wracked by chronically severe, sometimes crippling, ultimately self-destructive bureaucratic rivalries. By far the most severe, crippling, and destructive rivalry arose between the Imperial Army and Imperial Navy. Their officers came to see each other as implacable enemies who, alas, could never be truly vanquished. This enemy, the army for the navy and vice versa, with a radically different

---

[1] And domestic threats to their new state's legitimacy, not under study here.

assessment of the foreign threat and the policies needed to address that threat, would always be with them.

This ultimately suicidal rivalry could have been mitigated by any number of factors. A central locus of sovereign authority, whether the emperor or the prime minister, would have been one answer. The ability of other power centers to impose their will, or at least influence the military services, might have saved Japan from the disaster of 1945. Least plausible but still possible, the reestablishment of a foreign-policy consensus among all concerned elites, or at least the leaders of the army and navy, could have avoided catastrophe. None of these occurred. Given the way in which Meiji Japan created itself, none was ever very likely.

The foundation of interservice rivalry was laid in the Meiji Constitution itself. That document decreed that, while the emperor was sovereign over all matters of foreign and defense policy for Japan, he would be counseled by the army and navy which were his sole and sovereign instruments in protecting his realm. Unhappily for all concerned, the constitution did not specify procedures to govern policy decisions if the army and navy disagreed.

At first no difficulties arose on this point because Japan had no navy. The earlier national regime of the Tokugawa shogunate had maintained a modest coastal patrol, as Japan's relations with Korea and China hardly required anything more. But the two domains – Chōshū and Satsuma – which had furnished the initiative and leaders of the Meiji Restoration, had experienced Western naval power first-hand and were well aware of the usefulness of naval power. After Chōshū effectively captured control of the new Imperial Army, many Satsuma leaders saw the creation of a navy as fulfilling the doubly desirable objectives of restraining Chōshū influence in the new government while neutralizing the Western naval threat. Frustrated for nearly twenty years by the need to contain domestic discontent and occasional rebellion (the most famous, of 1877, arising out of Satsuma itself) and Japan's stark fiscal inability to construct a modern, hence quite expensive, fleet, naval leaders finally came into their own in the 1890s.

The Imperial Japanese Navy was ultimately created upon the interconnected foundations of doctrine and politics. Dynamic naval leaders like Yamamoto Gonnohyōe studied then preached the ideas of American Alfred Thayer Mahan. The secret to British (and increasingly American) global dominance was a powerful navy based upon a core of heavy battleships capable of defeating an enemy's battle fleet and imposing control over the seas. Of course, a strong Japanese battle fleet required a powerful Imperial Navy.

It also required rather powerful funding. For a Japanese economy dwarfed by Britain and America, the effort would be Herculean, not only in terms of securing the funds and establishing the necessary industrial base in time,[2] but also in winning the consent of Japan's elites to making the effort in the first place. Yamamoto and his colleagues succeeded by assiduously courting the new political party leaders in the equally new Diet – to the alarm and disgust of the leaders of the Imperial Army.[3]

The army was the backbone of the new Meiji state. It suppressed internal dissent and rebellion. It furnished the clearest example to every Japanese of direct service to the divine emperor. Not least, its leaders, such as Yamagata Aritomo, saw themselves as the wisest guarantors of Japan's sovereignty in a hostile world. They were deeply suspicious of the new political party leaders, whom they saw as civilian parvenus mainly interested in further enriching themselves without regard to the safety of the nation. Instead of forming alliances with these politicians, Yamagata's first instincts were to wall them off from any role in national security policy-making. His methods were straightforward. Partymen were to be denied the prime ministership and, above all else, the army (and navy) portfolios. Indeed, wherever possible the Ministries – not just Army and Navy but Foreign, Finance, Justice, and, another Yamagata favorite, Home – would be staffed from starting functionary through vice-minister strictly through an examination and internal promotion system. In the case of the army and navy, of course, this aim was eminently possible: only graduates of the service academies would become officers and only those passing through the services' staff colleges would become senior ones.

Yamagata succeeded in denying the politicians access to army personnel or policy, but he still needed a budget year after year. The army would eventually resolve this dilemma with a series of reluctant compromises with the party leaders, but not before it saw the navy threaten to surpass it in spending. Part of the navy's success was in its basic strategy of accommodation, indeed alliance, with the partymen. But admirals also knew the value of direct public-relations efforts to the electorate, and the navy's impressive performance in the Sino-Japanese

---

[2] The earliest ships of the Imperial Navy were purchased abroad, often from British yards, almost until the First World War.

[3] For doctrine, see Sadao Asada, *From Mahan to Pearl Harbor: American Strategic Theory and the Rise of the Imperial Japanese Navy* (Annapolis: Naval Institute Press, 2006); for politics, J. Charles Schencking, "Bureaucratic Politics, Military Budgets, and Japan's Southern Advance: The Imperial Navy's Seizure of German Micronesia in the First World War," *War in History* 5 (1998), 308–26.

War of 1894–95 and Russo-Japanese War ten years later dramatically enhanced its prestige among the public and the party leaders alike.

Still, during these years major interservice clashes were avoided through the intermediary influence of the personal ties of the Meiji founders. These "senior statesmen," or *genrō*, had disagreements to be sure, particularly over the role of (and their role in) political parties. But these disputes never became crippling because the *genrō* never allowed them to become so lest the Meiji state itself fail. But the *genrō* could not live forever, and neither could the emperor.

The death of Emperor Meiji in 1912 and the "Taishō Crisis" of that same year saw the first manifestation of unfettered army–navy disagreements that would plague Imperial Japan till its end. But it was only the first. Japan's reaction to the outbreak of the First World War, its response to the Bolshevik Revolution, and the challenges to the Pacific of the Allied victory in Europe all contributed to critical tensions between army and navy leading to catastrophic impasse by the 1930s.

The Taishō Crisis began as a purely budgetary one. The party government submitted a budget featuring sharp retrenchment in all categories save one: naval spending. The army, already disappointed with the government's refusal to send reinforcements to Manchuria in the wake of the Chinese revolution a year earlier, withdrew its minister from the cabinet and refused to name a replacement, forcing the entire body to resign. The new prime minister was more to the army's liking, but the old government refused to cooperate with him, a recipe for impasse that the old meant to resolve by calling for elections. The elections almost certainly would have vindicated the old government, so the army (and new prime minister) secured a rescript from the emperor calling for no elections. When the Diet refused to obey, constitutional crisis loomed. It was resolved only through the prime minister's resignation. His successor was none other than Yamamoto.[4]

Interservice rivalry also determined Japan's entry into the First World War. Under the terms of the Anglo-Japanese Alliance, Japan – that is, the Imperial Navy – was delighted to intervene to commence patrols against German shipping and to seize German islands throughout the Pacific. But, to the consternation of the British (and horror of the Chinese), Japan also invaded Germany's leased territory in China's Shantung peninsula. This was the Imperial Army's price of acquiescence. Sino-Japanese relations took a further turn for the worse after Japanese forces occupied the entire peninsula, not just the leasehold,

---

[4] Yamamoto's victory would prove short-lived. Within months a scandal over naval contracting would compel his resignation as a gleeful army attacked him openly.

and Japan insisted on far-reaching concessions from the new Chinese government, the so-called Twenty-One Demands that stirred even American ire.

These steps angered China, Britain, and the United States, but they kept the Imperial Army satisfied and so avoided another domestic crisis. Much the same logic was on display when the Russian regime fell in 1917. The army insisted on intervention in Siberia to forestall Bolshevik control there in order to safeguard Japanese interests in Manchuria and Korea. In fact, these actually were army interests in Manchuria, Korea, and most recently Shantung. By 1917 Japan's governor of Korea invariably was a general. The South Manchurian Railway, Japan's administrative organ for Manchuria, was increasingly staffed and dominated by army (or ex-army) officers. In marked contrast to every earlier intervention, the army had refused to cede control of Shantung to any civilian authority. The same would be the case in Siberia, as the army dispatched forces far larger than the Tokyo government had indicated to foreign powers.

The army's justification for its increasingly unilateral actions was, in essence, constitutional. The Meiji Constitution vested the right of supreme command (the right to determine Japan's defense policies) in the emperor, through His army and navy. This right was absolute and beyond civilians' ability to question.

This reading was hardly lost on leaders in the Imperial Navy. But they faced a more complicated path to command unilateralism. Victory in the First World War had spurred a naval race among the victors. But Japan had scant hope of catching Britain, let alone a furiously building America, in any such race even if the Imperial Navy had unfettered access to the entire defense budget, something an army with growing continental interests was hardly likely to permit. Yet not to race held awful prospects, particularly to a navy that knew only a Mahanian tradition. And political success: during the First World War the Imperial Navy had persuaded the Diet to fund a mammoth "Eight-eight" (for eight battleships and eight battlecruisers) building program.

By all logic, the Imperial Navy ought to have expanded its "Eight-eight" program and engaged in a protracted naval race with the Americans. The navy had the foreign threat as justification and the domestic base in the Diet to support just such an effort. The army surely would have objected, but it had been confronted successfully during the Taishō Crisis and there was every indication it could be bested again.

But the navy did not even make the attempt. Instead, it accepted a comprehensive limit on battleship construction that, even more remarkably, accorded it an inferior position to Britain and the United States. Why?

The opportunity for naval restraint arose from American political dynamics that led Washington to propose naval limitation talks.[5] Japan's acceptance of a treaty in 1922 limiting it to 60 percent of the battleship tonnage of Britain or the United States, however, was made possible only by the policy determination and political skill of senior admiral Katō Tomasaburō. Katō realized that Japan could not match America in a building competition. He hoped that the army's adventures in Siberia, and especially China, would not so poison relations with Washington that any agreement would be impossible.

In the short term, Katō's hopes were correct. But the resulting Washington Treaty System contained the seeds of its own destruction. The army, for example, was willing to tolerate the status quo in China so long as it guaranteed Japan's (meaning the army's) rights in Manchuria and northern China and so long as a weak and divided China posed no threat to the army's preparations for war against the Soviet Union. However, the recovery of Soviet power and, even more alarmingly, the rise of a potentially unified China convinced the rising, new generation of army leaders that radical action against China and much stronger preparations against the Soviet Union were necessary by the end of the 1920s.

Within the navy, opposition arose much more quickly. Younger officers – who stood the most to lose professionally from a smaller battle-fleet – were appalled that Katō would not even attempt to compete with the Americans. For them, the Washington system was a humiliation to be eradicated as rapidly as possible. Katō's argument that Japan could not compete was irrelevant. Even before the Washington agreements were signed, these officers plotted the removal of so-called "treaty faction" admirals. By the early 1930s, they had succeeded.

This visceral rejection of the Washington naval treaties by a new generation of admirals guaranteed that the Imperial Navy of the 1930s would not follow the meek realism of the prior decade. Likewise, the rise of Soviet power and a Chinese threat convinced army leaders that their interpretation of the menace to Japan's interests was the correct one even as its "young officers" seethed over budgetary reductions the army had suffered in the 1920s. By 1931 those young officers resolved to overthrow the remaining façade of Chinese sovereignty in Manchuria

---

[5] See Thomas H. Buckley, *The United States and the Washington Conference, 1921–1922* (Knoxville: University of Tennessee Press, 1970); Roger Dingman, *Power in the Pacific: The Origins of Naval Arms Limitation, 1914–1922* (University of Chicago Press, 1976).

even if doing so provoked a crisis with both the Soviet Union and the West.

Historians have long known that the initiative behind the occupation of Manchuria belonged to majors and colonels stationed there. But the fact remains that their superiors in Tokyo made no substantive attempt to stop them and, in the face of that tacit approval, Japanese civilian and naval authorities were helpless despite their reservations over the step. Indeed, many younger civilian officials openly approved of the occupation and favored a thorough renovation of Japan's polity along fascist lines. They, along with their counterparts in the army, were not interested in, or at least not concerned about, Japan's rapidly worsening relations with China, the Soviet Union, Great Britain, and the United States.

In this sense it indeed is fair to assert that Japan's path to Pearl Harbor, and its destruction that followed, was a straight one from 1931. To be sure, there were tactical differences of opinion within the army. Should the Chinese Nationalists be neutralized after Manchuria was secured, or should first priority go to preparations northward against the Soviets? Should the army pause and consolidate Manchuria economically and push major efforts to build heavy industry in Japan to prepare for a protracted, "total" war against the West in a decade or so? The army elected to pursue all of these objectives simultaneously.

And that was just the army. The navy, which ought to have been acutely aware of how every new battleship built made it more dependent upon Western, especially American, sources of oil, abrogated all naval limitation agreements by the end of 1934 and commenced colossal building projects shortly after. This at a time when the army's adventures in China strained Japan's relations with the West badly. Had a sort of collective insanity infected Japan's leaders?

The answer is that there were no leaders of Japan through these years. There were leaders of the army and navy. There was a prime minister, often drawn from army or navy senior officers after 1932 (and a wave of assassinations or assassination attempts upon civilian politicians). There was the emperor. But no one had the authority to impose a unified direction, or indeed direction of any kind, to Japan's defense policy. The flaw was not in the leaders, but in the polity.

Decisions were made in such a polity in a combination of direct initiatives (what might be termed policy by fait accompli) and excruciating compromise. The Manchurian occupation stands as a fine case of the former. But it was swiftly followed by the multiple assassinations from 1932 through 1936. Young officers either intimidated senior political leaders or murdered them. The favored targets were finance and prime ministers who attempted to restrain military spending, which accelerated markedly after 1930. Internal army debates were sometimes settled in this way, too. Nagata Tetsuzan, head of the "total war" officer clique, was murdered in his office in 1935 by a colleague convinced that a policy of patience played into Chinese and Soviet hands. While senior officers did not participate in these crimes directly, they easily blocked meaningful prosecution of the plotters by denying the authority of non-military courts to try such cases.

Senior officers themselves were fully capable of independent action. The decision to send heavy reinforcements into China after fighting broke out between Japanese and Chinese forces around the Marco Polo Bridge outside Beijing in July 1937 is a case in point. Technical authority concerning troop movements was lodged with the head of the Army General Staff's Operations Division – not the chief of staff, nor the army minister, certainly not the prime minister or cabinet. That head, Ishiwara Kanji, believed that adventures against either China or the Soviet Union would sap Japan's resources while making it further dependent upon the West, which he regarded as Japan's true antagonist. Ishiwara therefore opposed reinforcement and urged a quick, local settlement of the dispute. But subordinates in the Operations Division's China Section – strong proponents of escalation to bring the Chinese into line once and for all – kept up a steady flow of calls for reinforcement, combining these with (sometimes willfully) incorrect intelligence that large Chinese forces were being rushed into the area. Ishiwara gave in.

Once he did, further escalation was inevitable. Reinforcements required a higher headquarters organization than had existed for Japanese forces around Beijing and that headquarters required a senior general as commander. Matsui Iwane, the choice, quickly expanded the fighting beyond Beijing. After the Chinese Nationalists engaged Japanese forces at Shanghai, Matsui decided upon an offensive up the Yangtze valley into Nanjing. It was taken, with heavy civilian casualties and a major international incident, by year's end. Ishiwara resisted these escalations. He avoided Nagata's fate, but was shunted off into a newly created staff office that ended his career.

Far from limiting its involvement in China, the Imperial Army expanded operations in central and southern China in an attempt to force the Nationalists to the peace table. As the strain on army forces, in fact the Japanese economy itself, mounted, one might have expected care to avoid confrontations with the Soviet Union and the West. The opposite happened. Some senior officers, such as Ishiwara or retired

Ugaki Kazushige, clearly understood the dangers of expansion. But they either were shunted into meaningless positions or denied access to meaningful ones. Ugaki, for example, became foreign minister briefly in 1938 (his appointment itself testimony to how little influence in Foreign Ministry had) to actively pursue negotiations with China. These went nowhere in the face of army field commanders certain that the best way to peace was through conquest.

While Ugaki was attempting restraint, those same field commanders initiated skirmishes with Soviet forces along the Manchurian border. The first, at Changkufeng in 1938, was merely a battlefield punishment for Japanese forces. The second, a year later at Nomonhan, was a full-fledged disaster that could have turned catastrophe but for Soviet restraint due to the unsettled conditions in Europe.

The Imperial Navy pushed for additional operations in southern China, specifically the capture of Hainan Island and Kwangtung province. The navy was partly sincere in pointing out that occupying these areas would complicate Western efforts to supply aid to China. But it had a larger agenda as well. The war in China was overwhelmingly the army's war. Even by early 1938 that war threatened the completion of existing naval expansion programs and jeopardized the start of any new ones. The navy needed a mission to justify its continued hold on resource and funding allocations. The "Southward Advance" promised to provide that mission.

The Southward Advance was not invented in the 1930s, but it was perfect for the navy's purposes then. Japan's destiny lay seaward: to control the islands of the west Pacific, including the oil-rich East Indies, and adjoining land such as Indochina. Oil was a strong attraction, made stronger by growing American hostility toward Tokyo as the China war dragged on. But the key benefit, for the navy, of the Southward Advance was that it would require a strong navy. No reduction of shipbuilding, no diversion of steel to the army's operations in China, could be allowed to jeopardize the potential realization of the Southward Advance.

This advance, or rather its advocacy, was also well timed to influence another army project: the opening of discussions with Nazi Germany for an alliance. The army intended the Soviet Union as the sole target of such an alliance and was determined to get one, even if that meant bringing down the cabinet by withdrawing the army minister from it. But while a new prime minister (and cabinet) could be selected easily enough, the navy's consent was indispensable since the navy, of course, could ruin cabinets too. The navy was willing to consider an alliance with Germany, but only if the United States was a target as well and the occupation of Hainan finally undertaken.[6] Hainan was occupied but the alliance not signed: Germany elected to neutralize Soviet opposition to German plans in Europe directly through the Nazi–Soviet Pact of August 1939.

The outbreak of war between Germany and the West in September initially alarmed Japanese leaders in Tokyo. Besides the failure to ally with Germany or otherwise address the Soviet threat, Japan also confronted a worsening shortage of resources and equipment necessary to continue the war against China. Britain, now at war with Germany, was hardly a reliable source of these any longer and the United States, though technically neutral, would be far more likely to supply Britain's war rather than Japan's.

Imperial Army generals in China, however, had a different perspective. The Chinese would find Western aid harder to come by. Accordingly, the army broadly expanded offensive operations in China, called for increasingly severe austerity measures for civilians in Japan, and resisted any suggestions for accommodation with the West.

This stance seemed vindicated by Germany's astonishing victories of the spring of 1940 over the Netherlands, Belgium, and France. Army planners immediately proposed the occupation of the Dutch East Indies – a southward advance. The navy strongly objected. On the surface, this objection seems puzzling. The Southward Advance was the navy's own idea, specifically designed to ensure a strong naval role and concomitant funding. But the army's version of that advance stipulated a lightning strike into the East Indies only. For this, the Imperial Navy would be little more than a ferry service. Naval leaders also objected that the plan was unrealistic. Great Britain, still in the fight against Germany and with significant possessions around the East Indies, would not stand idly by. But when the army grudgingly agreed that the attack could target British colonies in the southwestern Pacific too, the navy played its trump. The Americans would not remain aloof either. They would certainly come to the aid of the Dutch and British. In short, any advance to the south had to be the navy's Southward Advance, meaning war against the Netherlands, Britain, and the United States. Given the Americans' colossal naval construction program started immediately after the fall of France, Japan should rein in its operations in China and devote the freed resources to naval building programs.

---

[6] Exactly what obligations were at stake in the alliance was problematic and consumed months of negotiations with Germany and between the army and navy. In essence, Germany wanted Japan to go to war against the Soviet Union once Germany did. The navy would not sanction such an assurance.

The Imperial Navy had no intelligence that in fact the Americans would rush to Britain's aid.[7] It was enough that the army, which had virtually no assessment capabilities regarding the West, could not disprove the navy's assertion of "Anglo-American indivisibility" and that the risks of assuming such divisibility were too high to allow the army's version of the advance to proceed. More fundamentally, it was enough that the navy simply vetoed that version, as Imperial Japan lacked any mechanism for resolving such an interservice impasse.

That impasse was resolved, but only through painful negotiations between the army and navy. The army could occupy the northern half of French Indochina, useful to cut off Western supply routes to China and as preparation for possible moves on British or Dutch colonies. The army could revive alliance discussions with Germany, so long as America remained a target. There would be no attack on the East Indies, but Japan would open negotiations with Dutch authorities to obtain access to oil resources there (and Japan's delegation would be chosen by the navy, not the army). And the navy would receive very substantial increases in its budgetary and steel allocations for the coming fiscal year, some of those increases coming directly from the army's quota.

This interservice impasse reappeared in the spring of 1941, but with the services exchanging positions. Now the navy favored a swift advance to the south and the army resisted one. This startling dual volte-face is explained by a piece of intelligence that both army and navy did have by that time: the impending German attack on the Soviet Union. While the alliance with Germany (signed in September 1940) did not demand a military response (courtesy of the Imperial Navy's continued veto to such a requirement), the army was eager to prepare one. Such preparations required no southward advance in 1941, but rather a northward one. For the navy, the possibility of war with the Soviet Union was thoroughly alarming. It would be an all-army affair that would doom the Southward Advance and, more importantly, all the budgetary and resource concessions the navy had won. Worse, time was against the navy. The American Pacific Fleet alone would dwarf it by early 1943 given the scale of American naval building already undertaken. The Southward Advance – against Dutch, British, and Americans – not only had to begin, it had to begin quickly.

---

[7] This assertion has the classic difficulty of proving a negative. However, decades of work in the naval archives by Japanese scholars and numerous published recollections of Japanese naval leaders have yet to turn up any indication that the Imperial Navy knew what American President Franklin Roosevelt would do, much less whether the American Congress would allow him to do it.

The impasse of 1941, like that of 1940, was resolved through protracted and painful negotiation between Japan's co-sovereigns. The army won the navy's consent to prepare for war against the Soviet Union by reinforcing Manchuria. The navy won the army's consent to prepare for war against the West by occupying the southern half of French Indochina. How matters might have evolved once both preparations were complete is speculative, because a new round of interservice negotiations was compelled in July and August by the American freeze of Japanese assets (and resulting cutoff of American oil shipments to Japan) as a result of the Indochinese occupation.

The American freeze was a shock to army and navy leaders alike. Both had calculated that Washington would avoid confrontation with Japan as it moved to assist Britain in Europe. Both had assumed that the alliance with Germany would instill further caution in the Americans. Both were wrong. But it was the army that had to pay the higher price. Faced with the prospect of rapidly declining oil reserves, it had no choice but to agree to a swift execution of the Southward Advance on the navy's terms. Planning for an attack on the Soviet Union was scrapped, at least for 1941. Yet the army hedged its bets. Even after acrimonious negotiations with the navy forced it to agree to simultaneous attacks on Dutch, British, and American possessions in the southwest Pacific, it offered an absolute minimal number of army forces to accomplish these rather far-reaching objectives. Even then, it secured the navy's agreement that no additional troops would be forthcoming and that those committed to the Southward Advance would be returned (mainly to China and Manchuria) as rapidly as possible.

The Imperial Navy saw the American asset freeze as a decidedly mixed blessing. On the one hand, it compelled the army to adopt the navy's position on the key issue of the scope (and timing) of the Southward Advance. There would also be scant objection to still further increased warship construction. On the other hand, the navy now finally had to confront Admiral Katō's logic of twenty years earlier: confrontation with the Americans was unwise because Japan simply had no way to match them in naval capacity. It seems clear that all but the most rabid naval leaders understood this fact perfectly well in 1941. But what was the alternative? In the autumn of 1941, as the navy began to sidle away from the prospect of war by supporting fresh negotiations with the United States and securing the services of retired admiral Nomura Kichisaburō to lead them, the army bitterly accused the navy of accepting increased budgets – indeed weakening the army's war capacities in doing so – without having the determination to ever use its warships.

Nomura's negotiations in Washington failed. The chief stumbling block, as historians have long recognized, was Japan's position in China. To put it another way, that block was the army's refusal to surrender that position.[8] War came in December 1941 with attacks on British, Dutch, and American possessions in the southwest Pacific – and Hawaii.

The Pearl Harbor attack represents one more case of army–navy discord in Imperial Japan. The navy, since even before Katō's time, had been aware that the American fleet was likely to outsize it. In Mahanian terms this was doubly unwelcome, since, as any Mahanian knew, a naval war had to end in a single, climactic battle where the largest number of guns would prevail. For decades the Imperial Navy had planned, and built, for such a battle. The formula was simple: seize or besiege the American Philippines; use long-range submarines and aircraft based on Japan's mid-Pacific islands to weaken the American battle fleet as it rushed eastward to the rescue; and ambush that battle fleet in the western Pacific, using extraordinarily long-ranged torpedoes and the monstrously large guns of the *Yamato*-class battleships to pound the Americans as they attempted to close the range, and obliterate their fleet once they finally did.[9]

This battle plan underpinned the Southward Advance. But some officers, particularly Admiral Yamamoto Isoroku, believed that the Americans might not follow the script. In early 1941, he proposed moving the climactic battle, in essence, to Hawaii, with a surprise strike on the Americans by carrier-borne aircraft.

Yamamoto's plan was not only a gambler's throw of the dice, risking all on avoiding detection. It also would disrupt the carefully negotiated agreement between the army and navy for carrying out the Southward Advance. Since Yamamoto demanded, upon threat of resignation, that all six of Japan's fleet carriers be used against Hawaii, none of them would be available to provide air support for operations in the southwest Pacific. Since such support was imperative, the army would have to offer additional air assets of its own. The army did so, but not without securing additional promises that these assets, like most of its ground forces, would be provided only on a temporary basis.[10]

---

[8] As is also well known, the army, suspicious that Nomura and the navy would weasel out of war at the army's expense, sent one of its officers to Washington to monitor Nomura directly.

[9] Stephen E. Pelz, *Race to Pearl Harbor: The Failure of the Second London Naval Conference and the Onset of World War II* (Cambridge, MA: Harvard University Press, 1974); Edward S. Miller, *War Plan Orange: The U.S. Strategy to Defeat Japan, 1897–1945* (Annapolis: Naval Institute Press, 2007); Asada, *From Mahan to Pearl Harbor*.

[10] Michael Barnhart, "Planning the Pearl Harbor Attack," *Aerospace Historian* 29 (1982).

The Hawaiian attack and Southward Advance were great successes. But both were undertaken on a basis that nearly ensured Japan's ultimate defeat. In the spring of 1942, the navy would ask the army to provide troop support for either an invasion of Australia or operations against British India. The army refused, citing the interservice agreement of 1941, ensuring that an opportunity to place heavy pressure on the British government was missed. Indeed, the army was unresponsive throughout the Pacific War. It was late to recognize the threat of the American counteroffensive in the Solomon Islands in late 1942 (in part because the navy did not divulge its catastrophic losses at Midway). It refused to commit major reinforcements to the Pacific islands throughout 1943. It effectively abandoned the Philippines in 1944 even as the navy was banking on a major showdown there to deal the American invaders crippling losses at Leyte. The Imperial Navy was crippled instead.

That, at least, ended the co-sovereignty of Japan's two armed services, since only one remained by late 1944. Unhappily for the Japanese people, the Imperial Army was determined to survive the war. To this end, it devised the admirably direct strategy of binding itself to the people so directly and so closely that the Americans would have to obliterate Japan in order to end the Imperial Army. The *kamikaze* air and sea squadrons and the training of children to use bamboo spears to attack the Americans were only the most macabre manifestations of this strategy. It ought to have worked, but it had one unavoidable vulnerability. As the army's representatives pointed out at every command or cabinet conference, they fought to preserve the Meiji polity: the emperorship. This line of argument was unassailable, especially given the Americans' refusal to offer any assurances concerning the emperorship. But it also gave the emperor himself real policy leverage for the first time. Convinced that the army's umbilical strategy would in fact doom the Japanese people as well as itself, particularly after Soviet intervention closed off any hope of a negotiated solution, Emperor Hirohito declared that he was willing to sacrifice himself to save his people. The army had no answer for this (save to argue that Hirohito was deranged or at least unsettled and needed to be taken into army custody or perhaps even compelled to abdicate – options the army actively considered in August 1945 but in the end declined to pursue) and the rest, as they say, is history.

The implications of Japan's story for contemporary debates over the nature of the behavior of great powers are alarming. Japan certainly was offensively minded or, to put it more accurately both the Imperial Army and Navy were. But Japan, in the broadest sense, was senseless to its international environment and engaged in offensive action with risks far outweighing potential benefits. It did so because its internal structure mattered, mattered critically. Its domestic politics, in particular its interservice dynamics, were malign in the extreme. The Imperial Army and Navy may well have pursued their own institutional interests coherently and rationally, but the result was unreal and disastrous for the Japanese people and, ultimately, both services. The fault was not in the international system, but in the Meiji polity itself.

A "realist" Imperial Japan?

History grants the magic wand of hindsight. It is an instrument historians are loath to use, as it invariably distorts their ability to understand the world their subjects saw. Yet temptation remains, if only to speculate: if we could travel in time back to 1941, or even earlier, with news clips from our world in hand, and show them to the leaders of Imperial Japan – show them the absolute catastrophe that awaited their country by 1945 – would they have done anything differently?

This is, in essence, what realism requires us to do, and why many historians have trouble with it. But even if we grant realism's premises, would Imperial Japan's policy-makers have acted differently once we stepped out of our time machine?

It is hard to believe that they would have. The Imperial Navy in particular faced an excruciating dilemma: fight the West or admit it was useless as a tool of Japan's security. Even Yamamoto Isoroku, a man fully aware of the risks being undertaken, embraced war before humiliation. If we take the navy out of the equation (as our magic wand becomes bigger), it may have been in retrospect that Imperial Japan would have been better served by a 1941 attack upon the Soviet Union, as indeed most elements in the Imperial Army preferred. Doing so, however, would have required the sufferance of the United States or, more particularly, the continued flow of American oil. This was simply not in the cards, as the Imperial Navy repeatedly and correctly argued.

If we take the Imperial Army out of the picture as well, then Japan enjoys the possibility of rapprochement with the West – exactly the course pursued after 1945. There were some Japanese leaders who favored such a course in the interwar period. But they were never remotely in a position to contest the control of the military's conception of Japanese security. It is, in fact, impossible to conceive of any force powerful enough to contest that control short of one capable of imposing terms of virtually unconditional surrender upon Japan. If our time travelers encountered those few leaders favoring rapprochement, how many of those leaders would have agreed to pay the price Japan did for ridding itself of the military's control of security affairs? And, if the answer to this question is "none," where are we left in our consideration of realism as a meaningful tool for judging how nations should behave?

10   Military audacity: Mao Zedong, Liu Shaoqi, and China's adventure in Korea

Andrew B. Kennedy

In the study of international relations, it is popular to imagine leaders as constrained by the distribution of material power. If military balances and alliance patterns do not dictate foreign policy, they can still pose powerful incentives that leaders ignore at their peril. For this reason, leaders often give way before stronger rivals, or at least defer military conflict with them as they build up their own strength. Nonetheless, some leaders are much less deferential when the balance of power is not in their favor. Rulers from Alexander the Great to Ho Chi Minh have fought for remarkably audacious goals, even when their forces were out-numbered or outgunned. In fact, states have launched wars against significantly stronger adversaries at least eleven times since World War II alone.[1] In short, while leaders often avoid conflict with more powerful states, the exceptions to this rule are too numerous and noteworthy to ignore.

Why do leaders vary in their willingness to attack the forces of stronger opponents? Or to use a term employed in this volume, why are some leaders more willing to punch above the "power line" of their state? It is tempting to focus on individual tolerances for risk as an explanation. Typically, risk-taking refers to the selection of choices that offer a wider array of potential outcomes: "risky" options promise relatively great rewards if successful but relatively great costs if they fail.[2] Defined in this way, attacking a stronger state seems like a fairly risky option, other things being equal. If successful, such military action could eliminate important threats, allow for national expansion, and enhance the

---

[1] T. V. Paul notes ten such cases between 1945 and 1993. See T. V. Paul, *Asymmetric Conflicts: War Initiation by Weaker Powers* (Cambridge University Press, 1994), pp. 3–4. Since 1993, Pakistan's attack on India in the Kargil War of 1999 represents another case.

[2] Rose McDermott, *Risk-Taking in International Politics: Prospect Theory in American Foreign Policy* (Ann Arbor: University of Michigan Press, 1998), p. 40; Jeffrey W. Taliaferro, *Balancing Risks: Great Power Intervention in the Periphery* (Ithaca: Cornell University Press, 2004), p. 26.

state's prestige. If unsuccessful, however, such attacks could lead to a particularly punishing defeat and possibly the destruction of one's state. Leaders who are relatively risk-tolerant, whether for situational or dispositional reasons, would thus seem the most likely ones to launch such attacks.

Nonetheless, the risk-tolerance approach is unsatisfying in a crucial respect: it fails to explain why a leader would believe that his state can prevail over a more powerful adversary. After all, even the most risk-acceptant individuals take risks not as ends in themselves but because they perceive some chance to make great gains by doing so. They are not heedless, but hopeful. For a risk-acceptant leader to attack a stronger opponent, therefore, he must believe that victory is somehow possible. Yet without further explanation, it remains unclear why a leader would harbor such hope.

Previous studies of asymmetric conflict are helpful in this regard. These suggest that a variety of contextual considerations can convince leaders that victory is possible against a stronger rival. Leaders may have limited aims that they hope to achieve quickly, or they may expect support from powerful allies.[3] In some cases, their states may even enjoy local superiority at the site of the conflict.[4] Alternatively, leaders may discount a certain foe's superior power since they see it as lacking resolve or "culturally inferior."[5]

This chapter offers a different type of explanation. Without denying the importance of contextual considerations, it argues that the beliefs that leaders have about their own state are also crucially important. In particular, it focuses on convictions that leaders hold concerning the martial prowess of their own armed forces. As explained below, a high level of confidence in this regard can inspire leaders to initiate conflict with stronger opponents, even when the disparity in power is considerable. In a sense, this approach builds on T. V. Paul's insight that "military or civilian groups that value the use of force" may be more likely to challenge more powerful rivals.[6] The focus here, however, is not militaristic regimes, but the mindsets of specific individuals, which after all can vary widely within the same government.

---

[3] Paul, *Asymmetric Conflicts*, pp. 15–37.
[4] T. V. Paul, "Why has the India–Pakistan Rivalry Been so Enduring? Power Asymmetry and an Intractable Conflict," *Security Studies* 15 (2006), 606–07.
[5] Michael P. Fischerkeller, "David versus Goliath: The Influence of Cultural Judgments on Strategic Preference," unpublished Ph.D. dissertation, Ohio State University (1997).
[6] Paul, *Asymmetric Conflicts*, p. 33.

To explore how a strong sense of martial prowess can affect foreign-policy choices, this chapter focuses on the decision-making of Mao Zedong in particular. As one of the most important military thinkers of the twentieth century, Mao is certainly worth studying in this regard. At the same time, Mao's martial confidence was far from universally shared by his colleagues. As discussed below, Liu Shaoqi, Mao's heir-apparent for much of his time in power, had a significantly weaker sense of martial prowess than did Mao. Liu thus offers a useful contrast to Mao at the highest level of the Chinese state, one that can help us ascertain the relative importance of Mao's individual views. While one might also compare Mao with Zhou Enlai, this comparison is less illuminating since Zhou was less willing to differ with Mao and since Zhou's views were probably more similar to those of Mao in any case.[7]

Given the constraints of space, this chapter will focus on China's decision to intervene in the Korean War in October 1950. There are several reasons to focus on this decision in particular. First, as perhaps the single most important military decision that the People's Republic of China (PRC) has made since 1949, the intervention in Korea has intrinsic historical importance. In addition, since China chose to confront the most powerful state in the system, as well as some of its allies, it represents a case in which China sought to rise above its own power line, as discussed below. Lastly, the debates that took place within the PRC's leadership prior to intervention are relatively well-documented, so there is considerable historical evidence that may be scrutinized.

Most extant studies of China's intervention in Korea have sought to discern what Mao believed was at stake for his country in the conflict. In general, these have stressed either his security concerns or his ideological agenda.[8] With a few exceptions, the equally important question of why Mao believed that China could succeed in Korea has received

---

[7] Unlike Liu, Zhou's military experience prior to taking power was extensive. See *Zhou Enlai Junshi Huodong Jishi, 1918–1975* [A Record of Zhou Enlai's Military Activities, 1918–1975] (Beijing: Central Documents Press, 2000).

[8] Allen Whiting's pioneering study initially emphasized China's security concerns. See Allen Whiting, *China Crosses the Yalu: The Decision to Enter the Korean War* (New York: Macmillan, 1960). In contrast, Chen Jian has stressed Mao's revolutionary ideology. See Chen Jian, *China's Road to the Korean War: The Making of the Sino-American Confrontation* (New York: Columbia University Press, 1994). Subsequently, Tom Christensen has renewed the emphasis on security concerns. See Thomas J. Christensen, *Useful Adversaries: Grand Strategy, Domestic Mobilization, and Sino-American Conflict, 1947–1958* (Princeton University Press, 1996), pp. 149–76; Thomas J. Christensen, "Windows and War: Trend Analysis and Beijing's Use of Force," in Alastair Iain Johnston and Robert Ross (eds.), *New Directions in the Study of China's Foreign Policy* (Stanford University Press, 2006), pp. 54–58.

much less scrutiny.[9] This is an important gap in the literature, since it was the feasibility of standing up to the United States that generated the most debate within the Chinese leadership prior to intervention. This chapter thus focuses on this question in particular.

The remainder of this chapter proceeds as follows. The first section defines the term "martial prowess" and explains how perceptions of such prowess should shape foreign policy. The second section then compares the different senses of martial prowess that Mao and Liu Shaoqi developed during the Chinese revolution. The third section assesses the role that Mao's martial confidence played in China's decision to intervene in Korea, contrasting his stance with that adopted by Liu in particular. The conclusion considers the broader implications of this case study and suggests additional cases that could be explored in future research.

Perceptions of martial prowess and foreign policy

The notion that military forces vary in terms of martial prowess may be as old as warfare itself. Sun Zi's *Art of War* repeatedly extols those "skilled" at military conflict, while ancient Sparta was famous for its dedication to martial excellence. Nonetheless, the concept remains vaguely defined, so it is important to make clear how the term will be used here. In this chapter, martial prowess refers to the ability to overcome material disadvantages on the battlefield through a combination of skill and will.

Let us first take the question of skill. In general, military commanders seek to prevail by pitting strength against weakness. In land warfare, commanders typically engage in "differential concentration" – massing superior forces at a particular point in order to overwhelm the adversary at that location.[10] Local successes achieved in this way can then be replicated elsewhere, weakening the adversary gradually, or they may be exploited to break through the enemy's lines, leading to more dramatic successes. Weaker states – whether they are deficient in troops, weaponry, transport systems, or all of these – can still attempt such concentrations, but their task is more difficult given their

---

[9] One prominent exception is Zhang Shuguang, *Mao's Military Romanticism: China and the Korean War, 1950–1953* (Lawrence: University Press of Kansas, 1995). Zhang's intriguing study begins by exploring Mao's "military romanticism," but it then departs from this focus to become a more comprehensive account of China's approach to the war.

[10] Stephen D. Biddle, *Military Power: Explaining Victory and Defeat in Modern Battle* (Princeton University Press, 2004), p. 41.

resource limitations. As Clausewitz noted, "the forces available must be employed with *such skill* [emphasis added] that even in the absence of absolute superiority, relative superiority is achieved at the decisive point."[11] In short, the ability to generate local superiority at the right place and the right time is important for all militaries, but it is a particularly tough challenge for those facing a more powerful state or coalition. So why would a leader believe that his forces were particularly skilled in this regard?

I offer three possible answers to this question. First, a leader may believe that his military excels at integrating its different parts into a cohesive entity.[12] Integration increases combat power not through technology but through organization that facilitates concerted action by different military units. It thus allows militaries to generate greater force with fewer numbers. Second, a leader may perceive his military as exceptionally flexible and responsive to new information.[13] By allowing militaries to exploit opportunities as they appear, superior flexibility once again facilitates the task of achieving local superiority. Third, a leader may believe that his military is particularly proficient at concealing itself and misleading the adversary – denial and deception. As other scholars have noted, these practices have obvious appeal to weaker combatants.[14] Denial makes one harder to attack, while deception can cause the opponent to become more vulnerable, creating opportunities for surprise attacks on weaker points.

There are thus several reasons why a leader might believe that his military excels at generating local superiority despite material disadvantages. To possess a strong sense of martial prowess, a leader need not perceive his military as exceptional in all of these regards – the above list may not even exhaust all of the possibilities. Instead, the question is whether a leader believes that his military can consistently generate local superiority by relying on some capability (or combination of capabilities) that it possesses.

[11] Carl Von Clausewitz, *On War*, trans. Michael Howard and Peter Paret (Princeton University Press, 1976), p. 196.

[12] For a comparable conception of integration, see Allan R. Millett *et al.*, "The Effectiveness of Military Organizations," in Allan R. Millett and Williamson Murray (eds.), *Military Effectiveness* (Boston: Allen & Unwin, 1988), pp. 13–14. For a somewhat broader conception, see Risa Brooks, "Introduction," in Risa Brooks and Elizabeth Stanley (eds.), *Creating Military Power: The Sources of Military Effectiveness* (Stanford University Press, 2007), pp. 10–11.

[13] Again, for a similar conception of flexibility, see Millett *et al.*, "The Effectiveness of Military Organizations," p. 15. For a broader conception, see Brooks, "Introduction," pp. 11–12.

[14] Rod Thornton, *Asymmetric Warfare: Threat and Response in the Twenty-First Century* (Cambridge: Polity Press, 2007), pp. 66–68.

While skill is vital in combat, will is no less important. Accordingly, leaders must also see their troops as highly motivated in order to possess a high level of martial confidence. While difficult to define precisely, Van Creveld defines this key attribute of martial excellence as: "discipline and cohesion, morale and initiative, courage and toughness, the readiness to fight and the willingness, if necessary, to die."[15] While such willpower can obviously fluctuate, it is often viewed as an enduring attribute of particular military forces. The Athenian statesman Pericles, for example, famously celebrated the valor with which his fellow citizens regularly fought for their city, "gain(ing) easy victories over men defending their homes."[16] More recently, scholars have explored the sources of consistently superior troop commitment in militaries ranging from the Nazi *Wehrmacht* to the British Indian Army.[17]

The volitional aspect of martial prowess is important for all militaries, but it is particularly crucial for those that confront stronger adversaries. In particular, weaker states face the danger that their troops will be intimidated by the adversary's superiority. For a leader to be confident in such a situation, he must believe that his soldiers will persevere despite the disadvantages that they face. Once again, there is more than one reason why leaders might be confident in this regard. They may see their troops as particularly cohesive at the unit level, an attribute that scholars have linked to superior combat performance.[18] Alternatively, they may perceive broader beliefs among the rank and file about the worthiness of the national cause and the honor of dying for it.[19]

To sum up the discussion thus far, I argue that leaders hold beliefs about the martial prowess of their armed forces, beliefs which reflect both the skill and will that they attribute to their military. As such, perceptions of martial prowess are not the same as perceptions of "military power," defined as the quantity and technological sophistication of the resources that the state can wield in armed conflict. Instead,

[15] Martin L. Van Creveld, *Fighting Power: German and U.S. Army Performance, 1939–1945* (Westport: Greenwood Press, 1982), p. 3.

[16] Thucydides, *The Peloponnesian War*, trans. Walter Blanco (New York: W. W. Norton, 1998), p. 73.

[17] Omer Bartov, *Hitler's Army: Soldiers, Nazis, and War in the Third Reich* (Oxford University Press, 1991); Morris Janowitz and Edward Shils, "Cohesion and Disintegration in the Wehrmacht," in Edward Shils (ed.), *Center and Periphery* (University of Chicago Press, 1975); Stephen Peter Rosen, *Societies and Military Power: India and Its Armies* (Ithaca: Cornell University Press, 1996); Van Creveld, *Fighting Power*.

[18] Janowitz and Shils, "Cohesion and Disintegration in the Wehrmacht."

[19] Bartov, *Hitler's Army*. See also Dan Reiter, "Nationalism and Military Effectiveness: Post-Meiji Japan," in Brooks and Stanley (eds.), *Creating Military Power*, pp. 27–54.

martial prowess refers to qualities that could allow a state to overcome shortcomings in military power.[20] Nor is martial prowess as broad a concept as "military effectiveness," since this latter term often includes the ability of the military to procure high-tech weaponry.[21] Instead, martial prowess concerns what a military can do with the resources it already has.

Of course, leaders who possess high levels of martial confidence may or may not be justified in their beliefs. Nonetheless, it is the leader's beliefs that are of interest here, and not the state's actual proficiency at warfare, since my goal is to explain leaders' policy preferences rather than military outcomes. In particular, I seek to explain why leaders vary in their willingness to initiate military conflict with stronger opponents.[22] Presumably, leaders with high levels of martial confidence will be more likely to authorize such operations. In particular, perceptions of martial prowess should shape leaders' preferences in this regard by influencing the kinds of outcomes that they anticipate as they contemplate such attacks. Confident in the skill and will of their military, leaders with strong senses of martial prowess should be more optimistic in the face of material disadvantages, so they should see best-case outcomes as more attainable than their less confident counterparts do. By the same token, leaders with high levels of martial confidence should see worst-case outcomes as less likely, compared with those who lack their confidence. Lastly, if a given leader's sense of martial prowess is limited to a particular form of warfare, we should naturally expect that such effects will be limited to that particular domain.

Assessing the martial confidence of Mao and Liu

If a given leader possesses a "strong" sense of martial prowess, such confidence will presumably be evident in his speeches and writings. But which texts are most relevant and what should we look for in them? To answer the first question, the most useful texts are likely to be

---

[20] To be sure, if skill and will are imagined as enduring attributes that states can possess, they might simply be considered ingredients of "military power," broadly defined. Recent analyses of this problem have rejected this solution, however, since endlessly broadening the definition of "power" to include every factor that can influence victory or defeat ultimately leads to circular explanations of military outcomes. See Mearsheimer, *The Tragedy of Great Power Politics*, pp. 57–60.

[21] Brooks, "Introduction," pp. 1–26; Millett *et al.*, "The Effectiveness of Military Organizations," pp. 1–30.

[22] By "military conflict," I am not referring to small-scale border clashes and the like, but larger operations approved by the political leadership. By "stronger opponents," I mean opposing states or coalitions that possess greater overall military and economic resources.

private or confidential documents that address questions of military conflict. Private texts should be more likely to reveal genuinely held beliefs, since public ones might praise the martial competence of one's military simply to boost morale or appease nationalistic constituencies. In addition, it is important to start with texts that pre-date the decision one wishes to explain. These earlier texts can reveal whether a given leader possesses a pre-existing sense of martial prowess that could have informed the decision(s) in question. If so, we can then scrutinize more contemporaneous documents from the policy-making process to see if this martial confidence influenced actual military decisions.

To answer the second question, I assess perceptions of martial prowess in terms of three criteria. First, to qualify as having a "strong" sense of martial prowess, it should be clear that the leader in question has devoted significant attention to military matters in the past. This would seem to be a minimum requirement. Second, the leader must express confidence about his state's ability to defeat more powerful adversaries. It is important to be specific here: is the leader confident across all forms of combat, or is his sense of prowess focused on one mode of fighting in particular? The answer to this question has obvious implications for the kind of military boldness we should expect from a given leader. Third, one must ask *why* the leader believes his state can prevail over stronger opponents. Confidence rooted only in disdain for a particular enemy's competence or resolve is unlikely to be portable. In contrast, confidence that reflects a strong belief in the skill and will of one's own military would seem relevant regardless of the adversary.

Using these criteria, how did Mao and Liu compare when they took power in 1949? Since space here is limited, and since I have explored this question at length elsewhere, what follows is a necessarily brief exposition of Mao and Liu's different senses of martial prowess.[23]

To begin, it is no secret that Mao wrote prolifically about military conflict during the Chinese revolution.[24] In contrast, Liu's writings tended to focus more on party affairs and political questions. When Liu did write about military matters, it was with much less detail than Mao. In one essay, Liu shied away from discussing specific aspects of

---

[23] Andrew Bingham Kennedy, "Can the Weak Defeat the Strong? Mao's Evolving Approach to Asymmetric Warfare in Yan'an," *The China Quarterly* 196 (2008), 1–16. See also Andrew Bingham Kennedy, "Dreams Undeferred: Mao, Nehru, and the Strategic Choices of Rising Powers," unpublished Ph.D. dissertation, Harvard University (2007), pp. 56–85, 96–105.

[24] See *Mao Zedong Junshi Wenji* [Mao Zedong's Collected Military Writings] (Beijing: Military Sciences Press, 1993), vols. I–V.

strategy and tactics, saying that "[t]here have been many books written on the subject ... I am not going into details here."[25] As discussed
below, Mao's much greater attention to military matters accords with
the different roles he and Liu played in the revolution.

Broadly speaking, Mao's revolutionary writings make clear that he
developed a strong confidence in his forces' ability to outfight more
powerful adversaries, a finding that resonates with the work of other
scholars who have touted his "military romanticism."[26] Mao's martial
confidence, however, did not emerge fully formed at the outset of the
revolution. In fact, there were times in the 1930s when Mao was more
conservative in his military outlook than many of his colleagues. This
was true in 1932, when Mao's emphasis on guerrilla tactics against
the Nationalists, or Guomindang (GMD), was denounced as "vulgar
conservatism."[27] It was also true after war broke out with Japan in 1937,
when Mao warned his colleagues against confronting the Japanese
forces too aggressively. Only after World War II, as the CCP fended off
the much stronger GMD's offensives, did Mao's sense of martial prowess reach its zenith.[28]

Mao's growing confidence toward the end of the revolution reflected
much more than disdain for the Nationalists. Flush with victory, he
had come to see his forces, now renamed the People's Liberation Army
(PLA), as an extraordinary fighting force, one that was both highly
skilled and well-motivated. In terms of skill, Mao had become quite
confident in his forces' ability to produce local advantages against superior opponents through unconventional forms of land warfare. These
included not only guerrilla warfare but also what he called "mobile"
warfare, which resembled guerrilla warfare in its emphasis on mobility
and surprise but involved greater concentrations of troops ranging over
larger territories and wielding greater firepower. Mao made his confidence in this regard clear in a report to the party's central committee
in late 1947: "Although we are inferior as a whole (in terms of numbers), we are absolutely superior *in every part and every specific campaign*
[emphasis added], and this ensures our victory in the campaign."[29]

[25] "Various Questions Concerning Fundamental Policies in Anti-Japanese Guerrilla
Warfare," October 16, 1937, in *Collected Works of Liu Shao-ch'i* (Hong Kong: Union
Research Institute, 1968), vol. I, p. 28.

[26] Stuart R. Schram, *The Thought of Mao Tse-Tung* (Cambridge University Press, 1989),
p. 55; Zhang, *Mao's Military Romanticism*.

[27] *Zhonggong Zhongyang Wenjian Xuanji* [Selected Documents of the CCP Central
Committee] (Beijing: Central Party School Press, 1991), vol. VIII, p. 201.

[28] For more on this point, see Kennedy, "Can the Weak Defeat the Strong?" 10–15.

[29] "Muqian Xingshi he Women de Renwu [The Present Situation and Our Tasks],"
December 25, 1947, in *Mao Zedong Ji* [Collected Writings of Mao Zedong] (Hong
Kong: Modern Historical Materials Supply Press, 1975), vol. X, pp. 101–02.

In Mao's view, such consistent success reflected "the tempering of the People's Liberation Army (PLA) in long years of fighting against domestic and foreign enemies."

Mao's confidence in his forces' ability to generate local advantages probably reflected more than one consideration. First, he had striven for decades to make the CCP's forces exceptionally flexible and responsive to battlefield conditions. He famously summed up this point of view in a textbook for the Red Army University in 1936: "the enemy advances, we retreat; the enemy camps, we harass; the enemy tires, we attack; the enemy retreats, we pursue."[30] Mao also developed a clear confidence in his forces' capacity for surprise and deception. In fact, he was obsessed with the role of deception in war, and he was particularly fascinated by a tactic he called "luring the enemy in deep" (*you di shen ru*). First articulated in 1930, this practice entailed retreating before stronger forces, which would then become fatigued and less concentrated as they pursued, creating opportunities for the communists to launch surprise counterattacks.[31]

Mao was also clearly impressed with the "will" of the communist troops. Far from taking such dedication for granted, he saw the CCP as playing a crucial role in generating revolutionary fervor through political indoctrination. In fact, Mao became personally involved in training his officers in how to conduct such indoctrination, making it clear how seriously he took this task.[32] The result was to turn the CCP into an impressive ideological mobilization machine, one that produced soldiers of surpassing dedication. This dedication, in Mao's view, was a key element in the communists' victory in the revolution. On more than one occasion in 1947, the CCP leader attributed the communists' mounting successes to his troops' "style of fighting," which he summed up as: "courage in battle, no fear of sacrifice, no fear of fatigue, and continuous fighting (that is, fighting successive battles in a short time without rest)."[33] These remarks were not just for public consumption; Mao also used such language in high-level meetings.[34] Even in private, Mao was fiercely proud of the fighters that his party had produced.

In contrast, Liu's martial confidence never reached the same heights. While Liu may have partly shared Mao's belief in the CCP's capacity

---

[30] "Problems of Strategy in China's Revolutionary War," December 1936, in Stuart R. Schram (ed.), *Mao's Road to Power: Revolutionary Writings 1912–1949* (Armonk: M. E. Sharpe, 1992–), vol. V, p. 499.

[31] For the first articulation, see "Xingguo Investigation," October 1930, in Schram (ed.), *Mao's Road to Power*, vol. III, p. 595.

[32] Zhang, *Mao's Military Romanticism*, pp. 13–16.

[33] For example, see "Strategy for the Second Year of the War of Liberation," in *Selected Works of Mao Tse-tung* (Beijing: Foreign Languages Press, 1961–), vol. IV, p. 145.

[34] "Muqian Xingshi he Women de Renwu," p. 101.

for ideological mobilization, his limited writings on military topics did not usually engage questions of military skill. Moreover, Liu lacked Mao's overall confidence about fighting more powerful adversaries. This became apparent in the fall of 1945, when Liu stood in for Mao at CCP headquarters in Yan'an while Mao was negotiating with Chiang Kai-shek in Chongqing. At the time, both the CCP and the GMD were eager to take control of Manchuria, which Japan had occupied since 1931 but was now vacating. To this end, Liu authorized deployments that brought nearly 100,000 communist troops to areas in and around Manchuria.[35] Once the communist forces began arriving, however, Liu quickly became extremely careful. On September 24, 1945, he ordered CCP forces to disperse into the countryside to conserve strength and take up positions near the borders with Mongolia, Korea, and the Soviet Union.[36] Since it was difficult for newly arrived troops to subsist in such inhospitable areas, local commanders apparently never implemented this order, stationing the soldiers near cities instead. On October 9, Liu repeated his order to disperse troops. To underline his point, he made clear his pessimism about fighting the stronger Nationalist forces in decisive engagements: "At present we should definitely not concentrate our deployments, do not be afraid of being ridiculed for having not thrown off guerrilla warfare concepts. Because we lack planes and artillery, we definitely cannot forsake guerrilla warfare, otherwise we will be wiped out."[37] Liu subsequently urged the CCP's local commanders to focus on increasing their strength by incorporating troops from the defunct Japanese puppet regime.

Mao returned to Yan'an on October 11 and promptly overruled Liu's order. He opted instead to confront the Nationalists in a quick and decisive campaign in hopes of taking control of the northeast's cities as well as its countryside. While Mao did not seek a nationwide war at this point, he clearly had a loftier estimation of what the communist forces could accomplish against the Nationalists than did Liu. In the end, the Nationalists routed the communists in mid-November – a sharp, but temporary, setback for Mao's plans. Liu must have felt vindicated, even if he did not welcome the defeat.[38]

[35] Steven I. Levine, *Anvil of Victory: The Communist Revolution in Manchuria, 1945–1948* (New York: Columbia University Press, 1987), p. 103.
[36] Liu Chongwen and Chen Shaochou (eds.), *Liu Shaoqi Nianpu* [Chronology of Liu Shaoqi] (Beijing: Central Documents Press, 1996), vol. I, p. 502.
[37] Liu and Chen (eds.), *Liu Shaoqi Nianpu*, vol. I, p. 510.
[38] Victor Shiu Chiang Cheng, "China's Madrid in Manchuria: The Communist Military Strategy at the Onset of the Chinese Civil War, 1945–1946," *Modern China* 31 (2005), 82–86.

Overall, the finding that Mao possessed a strong sense of martial prowess – particularly in land warfare – while Liu did not is quite plausible. While the two men became political allies in the late 1930s, they played very different roles in the revolution. Starting in the late 1920s, Mao was deeply involved in the development of the CCP's military strategy, and he played a central role in leading the communists to their ultimate victory in the revolution. In contrast, Liu's work typically revolved around party-building and land reform, and he played much less of a role in military affairs. Indeed, Liu's brief stint as Mao's stand-in in 1945 merely served to reveal his reluctance to confront more powerful adversaries. In short, given their different backgrounds, it is not too surprising that Mao and Liu came to power in 1949 with different senses of what the PLA could accomplish on the battlefield.

China's adventure in Korea

In the early morning hours of June 25, 1950, North Korean troops crossed the 38th parallel and launched a general invasion of the South. In response, US President Harry Truman chose to intervene in the Korean conflict and to "neutralize" the Taiwan Strait with the Seventh Fleet. By late September, US-led UN forces had reversed the tide of the war and were approaching the 38th parallel. On October 1, North Korean leader Kim Il-Sung requested Chinese intervention in the conflict. The same day, Soviet leader Joseph Stalin wrote to encourage China to intervene as well. After debating the matter in the first half of October, China's leaders ultimately chose to join the war.

By challenging the United States in Korea, the Chinese leadership was trying to do far more than China's power line would seem to have allowed. China at mid-century was a country reeling from decades of war and political chaos. Unemployment and inflation were rampant. Between 1936 and 1949, the grain and cotton harvests fell by 22 and 48 percent, respectively. Industry was hit even harder. Total industrial production fell by 50 percent, and heavy industry by 70 percent, over the same period. Years of conflict had also left the main railroads severely damaged. Making matters worse, Mao estimated that more than 400,000 "bandits" still roamed the country as late as mid-1950. The PLA itself was undergoing a demobilization that was designed to leave it with roughly three million soldiers, but these troops were poorly equipped, traveled on foot, and lacked air and naval support.[39] Moreover,

---

[39] Lei Yingfu, "Kangmei Yuanchao Zhanzheng Jige Zhongda Juece de Huiyi [Recalling Several Major Decisions in the War to Resist America and Aid Korea]," *Dang de Wenxian* [Party Documents] 6 (1993), 76.

the PLA had never fought beyond China's borders before, and it lacked the logistics system to supply such an effort.

In contrast, the United States possessed the most modern military in the world. As of 1950, the US military had already amassed 299 atomic warheads and research on the hydrogen bomb had publicly commenced.[40] While the Soviet Union had detonated an atomic device in 1949, Moscow's ability to strike the US homeland was very limited. On the ground, the US Army consisted of ten combat divisions, a figure that doubled as the war proceeded.[41] The army's inventory included more than 3,000 tanks, 27,000 motor vehicles, and an abundance of towed artillery. US ground operations also benefited from tactical air support and from the mobility afforded by the world's most powerful navy. On top of all this, the US military was getting stronger fast: US defense spending jumped from $14 billion to $25 billion after North Korea's invasion, and it would climb by another $17 billion after China intervened.[42] Backing up this rapid rise in military spending was the US economy. US GDP was 27 percent of the world total in 1950, twice that of the Chinese and Soviet economies *combined*.[43]

What role did Mao's sense of martial prowess play in China's decision to challenge such a powerful opponent? The following analysis answers this question in three steps. First, it compares the stances that Mao and Liu took on the question of intervention. If perceptions of martial prowess were important, Mao should have been more willing to join the war than was Liu. As it turns out, this was in fact the case. Second, having assessed Mao and Liu's policy preferences, the analysis asks whether their differing senses of martial prowess played a role in shaping these preferences. As noted above, perceptions of martial prowess should influence the kinds of outcomes that leaders anticipate as they contemplate conflict with stronger adversaries. The evidence indicates that Mao did in fact anticipate more positive outcomes as he contemplated intervention, and that the martial confidence he derived from the revolution underpinned his optimism in this regard. Third, the analysis considers a range of alternative explanations for Mao's belief that China could intervene effectively in Korea.

[40] Information made available to the author by the Office of Public Affairs, National Nuclear Security Administration, US Department of Energy, May 15, 2006.
[41] James Schnabel, *Policy and Direction: The First Year* (Washington, DC: Office of the Chief of Military History, United States Army, 1972), pp. 43–46.
[42] Christensen, *Useful Adversaries*, p. 169.
[43] Angus Maddison, *The World Economy* (Paris: OECD, 2006), vol. I, p. 263.

The decision to intervene

After receiving Kim Il-Sung's request for help on October 1, Mao convened a meeting of the politburo secretariat, which also included Liu Shaoqi, Zhou Enlai, Zhu De, and Ren Bishi.[44] (Ren apparently did not attend due to poor health.) The meeting began that evening and apparently lasted through the night. Mao argued that China should intervene, and he appears to have been supported by Zhou. Zhu, however, was ambivalent, and Liu was more or less opposed.[45] The meeting concluded with a decision to hold an enlarged meeting of the secretariat the next day, attended by military planners.

Liu's opposition at this key moment is worth noting. On September 21, he had sounded willing to intervene while speaking with Soviet ambassador N. V. Roshchin.[46] While the reason for Liu's turnabout remains unclear, Roshchin later speculated that the sharp deterioration of North Korea's position in late September prompted many Chinese leaders to get cold feet.[47] This seems plausible. As of September 21, US forces were exploiting the successful landing at Inchon to break out of Pusan and move north, but neither US nor South Korean troops had approached the 38th parallel. While North Korean forces were in disarray, Pyongyang had kept Beijing in the dark about developments on the battlefield.[48] By October 1, however, Kim Il-Sung was telling Beijing that the situation was "most grave."[49] It thus became clear that China would not be helping North Korea resist the United States, but taking over a war that was going very badly. Under these conditions, Liu was no longer interested in intervening.

[44] The secretariat (*shujichu*) would later be called the standing committee (*zhengzhiju changwei*).

[45] Shen Zhihua, *Mao Zedong, Sidalin, yu Chaoxian Zhanzheng* [Mao Zedong, Stalin, and the Korean War] (Guangzhou: Guangdong People's Press, 2003), p. 228. My understanding of Liu's stance in this meeting has also benefited from conversations with Shen Zhihua.

[46] Shen Zhihua, "Sino-North Korean Conflict and its Resolution during the Korean War," *Cold War International History Project Bulletin* 14/15 (2003/04), 11.

[47] "Luoshen Zhuan Cheng Mao Zedong Guanyu Zan Bu Chubing de Yijian zhi Shidalin Dian [Telegram from Roshchin to Stalin Transmitting Mao Zedong's Opinion on Not Sending Troops for the Moment]," October 3, 1950, in Shen Zhihua (ed.), *Chaoxian Zhanzheng: Eguo Danganguan de Jiemi Wenjian* [The Korean War: Top Secret Documents from the Russian Archives] (Taipei: Modern History Center, Central Research Institute, 2003), vol. II, p. 577. Roshchin also speculated that the United States and Britain were using Indian Prime Minister Jawaharlal Nehru to restrain the PRC.

[48] Shen, "Sino-North Korean Conflict and its Resolution during the Korean War," 10–11.

[49] Quoted in Chen, *China's Road*, p. 172.

Mao began drafting a note to Stalin the following day. Having won support from Zhou the night before, he declared his intention to send troops to Korea: "We have decided to send a part of our armed forces into Korea, under the name of Volunteer Army, to do combat with the forces of America and its running dog Syngman Rhee and to assist our Korean comrades."[50] Mao envisioned Chinese forces relying on mobile warfare to surround and eliminate large numbers of the enemy, just as they had done in the revolution. He also stated that his goal was not restoring the *status quo ante*, but demolishing the US presence in Korea: "[Our troops] must be able to solve the problem; that is, they must be prepared to destroy and expel, within the borders of Korea, the invading armies of America and other countries." Mao was thus focused on total victory as he contemplated intervention at this time, notwithstanding the marked disparity in power between China and the United States.

It now appears this October 2 telegram was never sent. No corresponding copy has been located in the Russian archives, and there is no time of transmission or transmitter's stamp on the original document, as is the case for other telegrams Mao sent that day. This mystery is not hard to understand, however, if we consider what transpired among the Chinese leadership that afternoon.[51]

At 3:00, the enlarged meeting of the secretariat took place as planned. In setting the agenda, Mao tried to skip past the question of intervention entirely, focusing instead on when China should send troops and who would command them. We do not know precisely how the participants in this meeting reacted to Mao's attempt to control the agenda in this way. Yet we do know that Mao produced a very different response to Stalin that day, apparently after the meeting concluded. From this second telegram it is clear that Mao encountered considerable resistance to the idea of intervening.[52] The note began by stating that China had planned to send troops to Korea after the enemy crossed the 38th parallel. However, China's leadership now believed

---

[50] "Guanyu Jueding Pai Jundui Ru Chao Zuozhan Gei Sidalin de Dianbao [Telegram to Stalin on the Decision to Send Troops to Fight in Korea]," October 2, 1950, in *Jianguo Yilai Mao Zedong Wengao* [The Manuscripts of Mao Zedong since the Founding of the Nation] (Beijing: Central Documents Press, 1987–), vol. I, pp. 539–41. Hereafter *MZD Wengao*.

[51] See Shen, *Mao Zedong, Sidalin, yu Chaoxian Zhanzheng*, pp. 227–29.

[52] Ibid., p. 229. This second response was given to Roshchin on October 2 and was then transmitted by Roshchin to Stalin on October 3. While no copy of this telegram has been produced by the Chinese archives, this is not surprising since it was not sent by the Chinese government but by the Soviet embassy.

that "such actions may entail extremely serious consequences." As the note explained:

In the first place, it is very difficult to resolve the Korean question with a few divisions (our troops are extremely poorly equipped, there is no confidence in the success of military operations against American troops), the enemy can force us to retreat. In the second place, it is most likely that this will provoke an open conflict between the USA and China, as a consequence of which the Soviet Union can also be dragged into war ... Many comrades in the central committee of the CCP judge that it is necessary to show caution here.[53]

The note concluded that China would "refrain from sending troops" for the moment. At the same time, it emphasized that this decision was not final.

Based on the optimistic draft Mao had written earlier, the pessimism evident in this note does not seem to have emanated from him. Instead, Mao's comment that "many comrades" were concerned about intervention strongly suggests that he had encountered considerable resistance from his colleagues in the afternoon meeting. Based on Liu's opposition the night before, it is likely that Liu was among those who resisted Mao's push for intervention on October 2 as well. As Mao's apparent successor, Liu's continued opposition could have encouraged others and given Mao reason to pause.

Mao continued to encounter strong resistance to intervention at an expanded politburo meeting on October 4. Chen Jian suggests that almost all members of the politburo, except for Mao, expressed reservations about the intervention in different degrees at this meeting.[54] Shu Ken'ei specifically notes that Liu Shaoqi's attitude was "negative."[55] This accords with the reservations Liu had already expressed, and also with other studies that have examined China's debate over intervention.[56]

The man who would command China's troops in Korea, General Peng Dehuai, arrived at the meeting on the 4th an hour late, having just flown in from Xian. He did not speak during the session, which ended inconclusively, but he later recalled opposing intervention when

[53] For an English translation of this telegram, see Shen Zhihua, "The Discrepancy between the Russian and Chinese Versions of Mao's 2 October 1950 Message to Stalin on China's Entry into the Korean War: A Chinese Scholar's Reply," *Cold War International History Project Bulletin* 8/9 (1996/97), 238.

[54] Chen, *China's Road*, p. 281, fn. 78.

[55] Shu Ken'ei, *Mo Takuto no Chosen Senso: Chugoku ga Oryokko o Wataru Made* [Mao Zedong's Korean War: Up to China's Crossing of the Yalu] (Tokyo: Iwanami Bookstore, 1991), pp. 201–02.

[56] Andrew Scobell, *China's Use of Military Force: Beyond the Great Wall and the Long March* (Cambridge University Press, 2003), p. 84.

Mao first asked for his opinion.[57] In his view, Moscow had "completely washed its hands" (*wanquan xishou*) of the war, and China's armament was "greatly inferior" (*cha de hen yuan*). There was thus no alternative to losing North Korea, as painful as that was. Former aides to Peng believe this conversation probably took place following the inconclusive politburo meeting on October 4.[58]

The politburo met again in enlarged session on the afternoon of October 5. Once again, many of the participants continued to stress the dangers of intervention. The mood changed, however, after Peng and Mao spoke. Peng had wrestled with the question of intervention during the night, and he had come to embrace it as feasible and necessary. Mao followed up by repeating his view that intervention was imperative and noting that Peng would take command of the Chinese troops. After this pair of presentations, opinion swung in favor of intervention, and the group confirmed Peng's appointment as commander. In keeping with this decision, Mao issued an order on October 8 creating "the Chinese People's Volunteers" (CPV) and dispatching this force to Korea.[59]

Up to this point, the PRC leadership had believed that considerable Soviet assistance, including both arms and air cover for Chinese forces in Korea, would be forthcoming if they intervened. They would be greatly disappointed in this regard. According to Shen Zhihua's careful reconstruction of events, Mao learned on October 12 that Soviet air cover would not arrive for at least two months.[60] In response, Mao suspended plans to send troops across the border and called for a politburo meeting the next day. This meeting reaffirmed the decision to intervene, but Peng was apparently so upset that he threatened to resign.[61]

The news from Moscow soon got worse. In particular, it became clear that Soviet air cover would only apply to Chinese territory.[62] Beijing could still count on deliveries of Soviet weaponry and Soviet defense of Chinese airspace, but they would have to make do with their own embryonic air force in Korea. In response, Mao convened another meeting on October 18. In the course of the meeting, Peng reported

[57] Wang Yazhi, "Mao Zedong Juexin Chubing Chaoxian Qian Hou de Yixie Qingkuang [Some Circumstances Before and After Mao Zedong Determined to Send Troops to Korea]," *Dang de Wenxian* [Party Documents] 6 (1995), 87.

[58] Author's interview with Wang Yazhi, Beijing, April 21, 2006.

[59] Zhang Xi, "Peng Dehuai Shouming Shuaishi Kangmei Yuanchao de Qianqian Houhou [Before and After Peng Dehuai's Appointment to Command Troops in Korea]," *Zhonggong Dangshi Ziliao* [Materials on Chinese Communist Party History] 31 (1989), 136–37.

[60] Shen, *Mao Zedong, Sidalin, yu Chaoxian Zhanzheng*, p. 244.

[61] Chen, *China's Road*, pp. 201–02.

[62] Shen, *Mao Zedong, Sidalin, yu Chaoxian Zhanzheng*, p. 247.

that his two vice-commanders had written him to suggest postponing intervention until the spring in light of the lack of air support and the difficulty of constructing fortifications in winter. Mao, however, insisted on proceeding as planned. As a result, Chinese forces began moving into Korea en masse after sunset on October 19.[63]

Taken as a whole, the evidence strongly suggests that China would not have made the same decision had Liu been in Mao's place. Liu apparently supported the idea of intervening in September, when North Korea still appeared a viable ally. Yet at the moment of truth in October, Liu turned much more negative. As noted above, he appears to have argued against sending troops at three vital meetings on October 1, 2, and 4. Of course, Liu ultimately chose to support Mao on October 5, but this is not totally surprising. Mao had invested many hours in attempting to persuade Liu by that point, and Liu may have also worried that continuing to resist Mao would create a dangerous split in the PRC's leadership. Had he been in Mao's place, however, it is hard to see Liu leading the charge into Korea.

Perceptions of martial prowess and the decision

To what degree did Mao's push for intervention, and Liu's resistance in early October, reflect their differing senses of martial prowess? Let us first consider the kinds of outcomes that Mao anticipated in Korea. In the telegram he drafted for Stalin on October 2 (but apparently did not send), Mao focused on the opportunity that the war presented. Ideally, he believed, Chinese forces would be able to destroy the American forces on the peninsula, and the "Korea problem" would be "finished." If so, "the scope of the war will not be very great, and the duration will not be very long." In other words, Mao's best-case scenario was a total victory that would not be very costly to achieve.

In contrast, the "least favorable" outcome Mao foresaw was certainly not the worst that could be imagined. In particular, if Chinese forces were not able to eliminate US troops in large numbers, Mao worried that a prolonged stalemate would ensue. This would likely disrupt China's economic plans and arouse popular discontent with the regime. While this was certainly not an outcome to be welcomed, it was far from the "greatest slaughter" of Chinese forces that MacArthur had forecast for Truman if the PRC intervened.[64] Mao thus seemed to

---

[63] Zhang, "Peng Dehuai Shouming," 157–59.

[64] William Manchester, *American Caesar: Douglas MacArthur, 1880–1964* (Boston: Little, Brown, 1978), p. 592.

dismiss the possibility of total defeat at this juncture, even as many of his colleagues feared just such an outcome.

These optimistic assessments reflected the considerable martial confidence that Mao had derived from the revolution. While Mao did not refer to the revolution directly in the October 2 draft, both Chen Jian and Shen Zhihua have argued that the CCP's stunning successes in the civil war helped inspire his confident calculations at this moment.[65] This assessment is strongly reinforced by the content of a conversation Mao held with Peng Dehuai on the morning of October 5. Meeting privately in his office, Mao told Peng that some of the PRC's leaders were "scared stiff by the planes and artillery of the U.S." Mao then explained why he himself remained unfazed, even as he recognized the seriousness of the challenge. "We have experienced decades of wars," Mao argued. "Didn't we beat enemies with superior equipment in all of them?" Mao's emphasis on the CCP's past military accomplishments at this key moment is worth noting. Peng proceeded to endorse Mao's view and recalled how the communists had prevailed in the revolution even after the Nationalists overran Yan'an in 1947 with 240,000 soldiers armed with American weapons. In response, Mao completely concurred. "Your analysis is absolutely right," he told Peng. "Our minds are on the same track." In short, even in private discussions with his own commander, one can discern the influence of Mao's martial confidence – and the roots of his confidence in past military successes.[66]

There is also evidence that Mao's confidence in the specific components of China's martial proficiency influenced his judgment. In mid-August, Chinese military commanders convened in Shenyang to review war preparations, and the tone of the meeting was strikingly confident. Deng Hua, commander of the 13th Army Corps, reported on studies that he and his staff had conducted concerning how to fight the United States. Deng argued that Chinese forces could rely on their "fine traditions" and "tactical specialties" to contend with superior US firepower. More specifically, he was confident that China's forces would be able to generate local superiority despite the other side's greater firepower. In fact, the CPV could fight just as communist forces had in the revolution: by seeking out weak points in the adversary's lines, encircling them with numerically superior forces, and then destroying them before reinforcements could arrive. Deng also suggested the CPV could catch the enemy off-guard with "sudden, speedy" (*turan, xunsu*) advances.

[65] Chen, *China's Road*, p. 179; Shen, *Mao Zedong, Sidalin, yu Chaoxian Zhanzheng*, p. 351.
[66] Zhang, "Peng Dehuai Shouming," 133–34. Zhang's account of this conversation is based on the notes and recollections of Peng's secretary, Zhang Yangwu.

These would minimize the opportunities for the United States to use its greater firepower, highlighting instead the importance of close-in combat, at which the Chinese forces excelled. In addition, Deng noted several times how the Chinese soldiers' ability to fight "bravely" (*yonggande*) and "boldly" (*dadande*) would allow them to conduct these types of operations against a much better-armed opponent. After Mao received the conference report on August 15, he pronounced its conclusions "correct."[67] In fact, Mao's October 2 draft telegram actually echoed Deng's calculations concerning the forces needed for encirclement operations. This was only fitting, since Deng's analysis had echoed Mao's essays from the revolution.

Mao's confidence did not rest on the assumption that the United States would refrain from using nuclear weapons, as other scholars have noted.[68] Instead, Mao (and some others) seemed to believe that China could handle such attacks. This was partly a function of China's underdevelopment: its industrial base was scattered and only 10 percent of its population lived in cities, offering little in the way of targets. Within Korea itself, the mountainous terrain was seen as limiting the role of nuclear weapons as well. Yet Mao also saw his forces' prowess at guerrilla and mobile warfare as playing a key role. Having mastered the art of dispersal and concealment, China's forces could scatter and hide once on the peninsula, making them difficult to target from the air. When on the attack, their proficiency at close-in combat would make it impossible for the United States to bomb them without hitting American troops. In short, the skills that the communist forces had mastered when fighting against greater firepower in the revolution would serve them well in Korea, too.[69]

It is more difficult to document the kind of outcomes that Liu anticipated in early October with the historical evidence that is available today. The evidence we do have, however, strongly suggests that Liu was not nearly as optimistic as Mao was at this point. In his discussion of the early October meetings, Zhang Xi, a former assistant to Peng Dehuai, has grouped the objections to intervention into five different categories:

1. China's economic plight was too dire for the country to embark on a war.

---

[67] Academy of Military Science Military History Research Department, *Kangmei Yuanchao Zhanzheng Shi* [History of the War to Resist America and Aid Korea] (Beijing: Military Sciences Press, 2000), vol. I, pp. 94–95.

[68] Chen, *China's Road*, pp. 142–44; Zhang, *Mao's Military Romanticism*, p. 63.

[69] Sergei N. Goncharov *et al.*, *Uncertain Partners: Stalin, Mao, and the Korean War* (Stanford University Press, 1993), pp. 165–66.

2. The PRC needed to focus on eliminating the remaining Nationalist troops and liberating outlying areas and offshore islands.
3. Land reform had yet to be implemented in newly liberated areas, so the new revolutionary regimes there were still not solid.
4. The armament of the Chinese military was far inferior to that of the United States, and the PLA lacked the capability to control the air and sea.
5. Many Chinese soldiers longed for peace after many years of fighting.[70]

A discernible theme running through these objections is concern with the PRC's relative lack of material power. Liu must have shared these concerns, given that he was one of the individuals resisting the intervention. Although it is impossible to know precisely which of these concerns was foremost in Liu's mind, it is no stretch to suggest that Liu was concerned about China's ability to compete with the United States militarily. As other scholars have written, "the majority opinion in [early October] was concern about China's capability to win a war against the United States in Korea."[71] As a prominent member of this majority, Liu seems to have been a mirror image of Mao at this point: dwelling on the possibility of defeat and pessimistic about the chance of victory.

Did Mao's optimistic assessment survive Stalin's refusal to provide air support in Korea? Stalin's decision certainly affected Mao's thinking. In fact, one of Mao's secretaries later recalled that intervening in Korea was one of the most difficult strategic decisions that Mao ever had to make.[72] More specifically, after learning that Moscow would not provide air support, Mao appears to have considered the possibility that the CPV might be defeated in Korea.[73] Mao thus no longer dismissed the possibility of defeat, as he seems to have done earlier in the month.

Yet it would be a mistake to underestimate Mao's confidence at this point. Mao did not concede that China would not be able to compete with the United States; instead, he simply recognized that the possibility existed. This was actually a more optimistic point of view than that held by many of Mao's colleagues in early October, when they plainly

---

[70] Zhang, "Peng Dehuai Shouming," 132.
[71] Hao Yufan and Zhai Zhihai, "China's Decision to Enter the Korean War: History Revisited," *The China Quarterly* 121 (1990), 105.
[72] Liao Guoliang *et al.*, *Mao Zedong Junshi Sixiang Fazhanshi* [The Historical Development of Mao Zedong's Military Thought], 2nd edn. (Beijing: PLA Press, 2001), p. 380. Mao is said to have weighed the decision while pacing the floor for *sixty hours* in mid-October, but there is apparently no hard evidence to validate this presumably hyperbolic account. Author's interview with Shen Zhihua, May 29, 2005.
[73] Wang, "Mao Zedong Juexin Chubing Chaoxian," 87.

doubted China's ability to stop the US advance in Korea. In other words, Mao was more optimistic about China's chances in Korea *after* Stalin's refusal to provide air cover than some of his colleagues were *before* that decision had been made.

Moreover, Mao's subsequent correspondence with Peng makes clear that the CCP leader still hoped to win a total victory in Korea, notwithstanding Stalin's decision. Upon learning that US and South Korean forces were moving north faster than expected, Mao focused on the opportunity this presented. Writing to Peng on October 21, Mao noted that UN forces were advancing in two separate lines, which indicated that they remained unaware of the CPV's presence in Korea. Even though Soviet arms shipments had yet to arrive, Mao argued that they could exploit the situation to launch a surprise attack and to begin changing the conflict in China's favor.[74]

Peng sounded a more cautious note when responding on the 22nd. He argued that the CPV should focus on establishing defensive positions in the northernmost parts of Korea over the next six months, making preparations for a large counteroffensive later. Peng also noted that the CPV had no hope of controlling coastal cities in light of the adversary's air and sea superiority. To placate Mao, he assured him that he still hoped to eliminate two or three South Korean divisions in the coming fighting.[75]

Writing back on October 23, Mao conceded that "we should not try to do things we cannot do."[76] He then argued that three questions in particular were critical:

1. Whether the CPV could surprise the enemy;
2. Whether the CPV could operate at night and thus mitigate the effects of the enemy's bombing; and
3. Whether the CPV could eliminate several US divisions through mobile (and some positional) warfare over the next few months before reinforcements arrived.

Mao recognized that these questions might not be answered in China's favor, making the situation "unfavorable to China" (*yu wo bu li*). Even so, he remained hopeful and focused on the opportunity before

[74] "Guanyu Dahao Zhiyuanjun Chuguo Diyi Zhang Gei Peng Dehuai Deng de Dianbao [Telegram on the Volunteer Army Fighting Its First Battle Abroad Well]," October 21, 1950, in *MZD Wengao*, vol. I, pp. 575–76.

[75] *Mao Zedong Junshi Wenxuan (Neibuben)* [Selected Military Writings of Mao Zedong (Internal Edition)] (Beijing: PLA Soldiers' Press, 1981), p. 686, fn. 4.

[76] "Guanyu Chaoxian Zhanju Wenti Gei Peng Dehuai, Gao Gang de Dianbao [Telegram to Peng Dehuai and Gao Gang on the War Situation in Korea]," October 23, 1950, in *MZD Wengao*, vol. I, pp. 588–90.

them. China, he argued, "must do all it can to ensure a satisfactory victory in this campaign." The CPV must inflict substantial losses on the US forces, so that "its reinforcements would not be able to keep up with its losses." This latter point clearly implied continuing preoccupation with the goal of total victory in Korea. If China could deplete American forces faster than the United States could replenish them, it is hard to see how the United States could continue to maintain a presence on the peninsula. In short, while he no longer dismissed the possibility of defeat, Mao continued to play up – and even overestimated – what China could accomplish in Korea.

Alternative perspectives

How well can alternative explanations make sense of Mao's remarkable audacity in Korea? Other scholars have suggested that the intervention was preemptive, claiming that Mao doubted that the United States would stop its advance at the Korean border.[77] If so, one could argue that Mao's confidence level was not very important – he had little choice but to intervene. The evidence makes fairly clear, however, that Mao's motive was *preventive*, not preemptive.[78] In particular, he sought to improve China's long-term position by denying the United States access to Korea, which would allow it to pressure China on an additional front.[79] Mao and Peng stressed this concern – and not the threat of an imminent invasion – when speaking before the politburo on October 5.[80] Subsequently, Mao wrote to Zhou Enlai on October 13 and expressed concern about US troops "pressing up to the Yalu river" (*yazhi yalu jiangbian*), which marked the border between China and North Korea.[81] He did not suggest that these troops were about to invade China, a curious omission if this danger had been driving his thinking. Under these conditions, it is hard to argue that Mao had no choice but to fight.

This is not to say that Mao was not under great pressure to act preventively. In particular, other scholars have stressed that Mao perceived

---

[77] For accounts that stress this point, see Goncharov *et al.*, *Uncertain Partners*, pp. 193–94; Walt, *Revolution and War*, p. 320.

[78] On the distinction between preemptive and preventive attacks, see Dan Reiter, "Exploding the Powder Keg Myth: Preemptive Wars Almost Never Happen," *International Security* 20 (1995), 6–7.

[79] Christensen, *Useful Adversaries*, pp. 160–63.

[80] Zhang, "Peng Dehuai Shouming," 136–37.

[81] "Guanyu Wo Jun Yingdang Ru Chao Canzhan Gei Zhou Enlai de Dianbao [Telegram to Zhou Enlai Explaining that Our Troops Should Enter Korea and Take Part in the War]," October 13, 1950, in *MZD Wengao*, vol. I, p. 556.

a closing "window of opportunity" to evict the United States from Korea in 1950, as well as a growing "window of vulnerability" if the United States dominated the whole peninsula.[82] Yet while this is a compelling view, it cannot be the whole story. The window-of-opportunity logic does not tell us why Mao perceived as much opportunity in Korea as he did – or indeed any opportunity at all. To be sure, Mao's interest in expelling the United States from Korea is not difficult to understand. Not only would it be a blow to American prestige, it would reduce Washington's room to maneuver against Beijing in the future. Nonetheless, desiring a certain outcome and believing that one can achieve that outcome are two separate questions. Similarly, the window of vulnerability logic does not tell us why Mao believed that China could reduce its vulnerability by intervening in the war. After all, it is unclear that China would have been safer if the CPV had been destroyed in Korea. In short, while the windows logic is important, it does not explain why Mao thought that China could compete with the United States in Korea.

One could argue that Mao believed that China could compete with the United States due to contextual considerations, rather than his sense of martial prowess. Earlier studies, for example, have stressed that Mao had only limited goals in Korea, and that he expected support from the Soviet Union, making the intervention appear feasible.[83] Nonetheless, Mao's goals were considerably more ambitious than this explanation recognizes. When deciding to intervene in early October, Mao did not simply seek a fait accompli that would prevent a total defeat of North Korea. Instead, his goals were expansionist: he hoped to drive the United States off the peninsula entirely. This difference is important because Mao's lofty ambitions shaped China's uncompromising approach to the war until it stalemated in mid-1951.

The prospect of Soviet support was undoubtedly an important consideration for Mao. Even so, he was forced to discount Moscow's assistance in important respects when deciding whether to intervene. Most important in this regard was Stalin's unwillingness to provide air cover for Chinese troops in Korea. Moreover, it is not clear how the prospect of Soviet assistance would explain the varying policy preferences within the PRC leadership. Liu was well aware of the Sino-Soviet alliance, and Mao had every reason to tell him how much support he expected from Moscow. Yet Liu was clearly much less willing to intervene in Korea than was Mao.

[82] Christensen, "Windows and War," pp. 54–58.
[83] Paul, *Asymmetric Conflicts*, pp. 86–106.

Mao's ambitions in Korea were clearly bolstered by the sheer number of troops that China could deploy, as well as Korea's geographic proximity to China. In his October 2 draft telegram, Mao planned to dispatch twelve divisions to Korea by October 15, and he expected another twenty-four divisions to be ready by the summer of 1951. As it turned out, the PRC managed to send thirty infantry divisions and three artillery divisions by November 19, totaling more than 400,000 troops.[84] By contrast, UN forces in Korea consisted of roughly 230,000 combat troops at that point, including 103,000 American and 101,000 South Korean soldiers.[85]

Nonetheless, while China's numerical superiority was probably necessary for such a bold intervention, it was far from sufficient. Liu Shaoqi and the rest of the Chinese politburo also knew how many soldiers China could field, and they undoubtedly appreciated the importance of Korea's proximity as well. Yet whereas Mao believed in early October that China could drive the United States from Korea entirely, Liu and others opposed the idea of intervening even in pursuit of more modest goals. In short, China's numerical strength was undoubtedly important, but it alone cannot explain the varying perceptions and policy preferences within the Chinese leadership.

Lastly, one might also ask whether Mao's confidence mainly reflected a belief that the United States was particularly ineffective at warfare for some reason. There is some evidence to support this view. In early September of 1950, for example, Mao had questioned the "combat power" of American troops, suggesting that they did not compare with those of Imperial Japan or Nazi Germany.[86] Mao seems to have changed his tune, however, when considering the actual forces that the CPV would confront in Korea. In particular, his October 2 draft telegram described the US Eighth Army – which he was then planning to destroy – as "an old army with combat effectiveness." Putting ideological bias aside, Mao was clearly trying to be objective in his analysis here. He was undeterred by these tested troops because his confidence did not rest upon the premise of American incompetence. Instead, Mao believed his forces had mastered the art of competing with more powerful opponents on the battlefield.

[84] Zhang, *Mao's Military Romanticism*, pp. 94, 110, 263.
[85] Roy Appleman, *South to the Naktong, North to the Yalu* (Washington, DC: Office of the Chief of Military History, Department of the Army, 1961), p. 606.
[86] "Chaoxian Zhanju he Women de Fangzhen [The War Situation in Korea and Our Guiding Principles]," in *Mao Zedong Wenji* [Mao Zedong's Collected Works] (Beijing: People's Press, 1993), vol. VI, pp. 92–94.

Conclusion

China's intervention in Korea was hardly the only bold military move it made under Mao. Over the next two decades, Mao's China frequently sought to accomplish its goals by resorting to force, even when pitted against the strongest states in the system. In 1954 and 1958, China deliberately sparked two crises in the Taiwan Strait. While China did not attack US naval forces in these crises, as it did not during the Korean War, this restraint is not surprising. The PRC had no navy to speak of in the 1950s, and Mao's sense of martial prowess revolved around land warfare in any case. Subsequently, in response to US escalation in Southeast Asia, China sent more than 320,000 soldiers to North Vietnam between 1965 and 1969, encouraging rather than restraining Hanoi's revolutionary efforts in the South. Chinese records claim that these troops shot down or damaged more than 3,000 US planes, while suffering more than 1,000 battle deaths of their own.[87] In 1969, China ambushed Soviet forces on the Sino-Soviet border, raising tensions with Moscow for years to come. In short, China's intervention in Korea was not an isolated act of audacity, but part of a larger pattern of bold military behavior under Mao.

Mao is not the only prominent historical figure to have sought victory against more powerful opponents, even when his colleagues counseled restraint. When Alexander determined to defeat the more powerful Persian empire at Gaugamela in 331 BC, his most senior general advised him to seek an accommodation.[88] Napoleon chose to fight at Austerlitz against a larger Russian and Austrian force, one that fielded twice as many cannon as the French could, even though his advisers suggested retreating on the eve of battle.[89] When Robert E. Lee ordered Pickett's charge at Gettysburg, General James Longstreet suggested instead maneuvering away from the larger, well-positioned Union force toward more favorable terrain.[90] Future research should explore whether and how perceptions of martial prowess shaped each of these remarkable decisions.

---

[87] Qu Aiguo, "Zhongguo Zhiyuan Budui Zai Yuenan Zhanchang de Junshi Xingdong [Military Operations of China's Volunteer Troops on the Vietnamese Battlefield]," in Li Danhui (ed.), *Zhongguo yu Induzhina Zhanzheng* [China and the Indochina War] (Hong Kong: Cosmos Books, 2000), pp. 92–96.

[88] A. B. Bosworth, *Conquest and Empire: The Reign of Alexander the Great* (Cambridge University Press, 1988), pp. 76–85.

[89] Margaret Scott Chrisawn, *The Emperor's Friend: Marshal Jean Lannes* (Westport: Greenwood Press, 2001), pp. 119–20.

[90] Edwin B. Coddington, *The Gettysburg Campaign: A Study in Command* (New York: Scribner's, 1968), pp. 360–61.

Lastly, these findings have important implications for the study of how leaders relate to the international system. Whereas some leaders are highly sensitive to the balance of power, others seek to rise above their power line and assert themselves despite material disadvantages. There are many variables that could influence such decisions, as discussed above, but the way in which leaders perceive their state's martial prowess seems a vital one. We need not view these kinds of individual differences as unpredictable quirks of history. Instead, this chapter suggests that individuals can hold identifiable beliefs about their state's martial prowess, beliefs which can then shape their military ambitions. Audacity may be idiosyncratic at times, but it need not be unpredictable.

11 The United States' underuse of military power

Ernest R. May

Imagine a gambler willing to bet on conditions a decade in the future. Suppose it is the autumn of 1920, with the Great War of 1914–18 ended in Western Europe just two years ago and fighting still going on in Poland, Russia, and parts of the former Ottoman Empire. In the United States, Republican Warren Harding has just been elected to succeed the Democratic war president, Woodrow Wilson. Our hypothetical gambler is to bet on what will be the posture of the United States in international affairs in the autumn of 1930.

At the moment, the United States is incomparably the strongest power on Earth. Statistics are not kept or reported in today's categories. Gross domestic product will not be measured for another twenty years. Still, in terms of iron and steel production, and energy consumption, the tables on the page opposite show US dominance over the world.

Our hypothetical gambler lacks not only current-style data but also the kind of theoretical writing on international relations that inspires the chapters in this volume. When that theoretical writing does begin to appear, mostly in the United States in the second half of the twentieth century, however, many of the theorists who call themselves realists will cite Thucydides' history of the Peloponnesian Wars as a canonical text. In particular, they will cite the words that he puts in the mouths of Athenian delegates arriving in 416 BCE on the tiny island of Melos to demand its complete submission. In the classic translation by Thomas Hobbes, the Athenians say:

> they that have odds of power exact as much as they can, and the weak yield to such conditions as they can get ... [W]e think ... of men, that for certain by necessity of nature they will every where reign over such as they be too strong for. Neither did we make this law, nor are we the first that use it made: but as we found it, and shall leave it to posterity for ever, so also we use it: knowing that you likewise, and others that should have the same power which we have, would do the same.[1]

---

[1] Thucydides, *The Peloponnesian War*, Book 5, paras. 89 and 105. Quotations are from the 1839 edition of Hobbes's translation, available through the Online Library of Liberty.

Table 11.1. *Iron/steel production of the powers[2] (millions of tons; pig-iron production for 1920)*

Country	1920
United States	42.3
United Kingdom	9.2
Germany	7.6
France	2.7
Russia	0.16
Japan	0.84
Italy	0.73

Table 11.2. *Energy consumption of the powers (in millions of metric tons of coal equivalent)*

Country	1920
United States	694
United Kingdom	212
Germany	159
France	65
Russia	14.3
Japan	34
Italy	14.3

Thucydides probably intended this Melian dialogue to be recognized as statecraft in caricature. He concludes his account by reporting that, when the Melians did eventually yield, "the Athenians ... slew all the men of military age, made slaves of the women and children; and inhabited the place with a colony sent thither afterwards."[3]

To the extent that Thucydides' history offers a general theory of international relations, it is anthropomorphic. His collective

---

[2] Data for Tables 11.1 and 11.2 come from "Correlates of War Printout Data."

[3] Ibid., Book 5, para. 116. Hobbes appended a long footnote, which is worth quoting here:

There is in this an open avowal of the real motives, by which nations universally, and individuals for the most part, are governed in their dealings with each other: stripped indeed of the ordinary disguise of the conventional language of right and justice, in which those motives are usually enveloped. But so far as Thucydides is concerned, it is difficult to say what were the arguments really used on this occasion, if these were not they. As to the Athenians, they were probably as much mistaken in the policy even of the invasion itself, as they most certainly were in the revolting effusion of blood that actors – Athenians, Spartans, Corinthians, Melians, *et al.* – make choices driven by a wide range of human inclinations and appetites, which include folly, pride, anger, trust, mistrust, illusion, and distraction, as well as the arrogance and brutality on display in the dialogue just quoted. But since the realists on whom we focus here cite the Melian dialogue as wisdom for the ages, we can allow our hypothetical gambler to take it as such. For our own heuristic purposes, we can suppose that he or she adopts the Melian-dialogue-like suppositions spun out eight decades after 1920 in John Mearsheimer's *Tragedy of Great Power Politics*, viz:

> [G]reat powers fear each other and always compete with each other for power. The overriding goal of each state is to maximize its share of world power, which means gaining power at the expense of other states ... Their ultimate aim is be the hegemon – that is, the only great power in the system.[4]

On this premise, our gambler would have put money on the year 1930 finding the United States even more dominant than in 1920. The United States would be using its financial and economic leverage to deprive potential rivals of the capability to contest its hegemony. The Harding administration and its successors would not only pursue Wilson's stated objective of having a "navy second to none"; they would have built a fleet so awesome as to discourage any nation from attempting to compete. In ground forces, the United States would not necessarily keep the numerical advantage of 1920. (Mearsheimer explains that sea-protected states such as Britain and the United States have the option of acting as "offshore balancers" – using their own ground forces only when those of clients or satellites do not suffice.) But theory that takes the Melian dialogue as its text would surely tip the betting toward a United States that, as of 1930, would be maintaining an aggressive lead in the technology of ground warfare, staying well ahead of other states in artillery, explosives, military aircraft, tanks, poison gas, etc.

The actual course of events would have left our gambler netting next to nothing. The United States, to be sure, continued to top world economic rankings, even with the domestic slump that started in 1929. Moreover, it earned a reputation as a skinflint, if not a shylock, in consequence of refusing to forgive or even waive interest on loans to its wartime allies. In practice, however, the US Treasury allowed very lenient repayment terms. The US State Department in the meantime

---

followed: which could tend to no other end than to defeat their own object, the security of their empire.

[4] Mearsheimer, *The Tragedy of Great Power Politics*, p. 2.

Table 11.3. *Iron/steel production of
the powers (millions of tons; pig-iron
production for 1930)*

Country	1930
United States	41.3
United Kingdom	7.4
Germany	11.3
France	9.4
Russia	18
Japan	7
Italy	2.3

helped to broker arrangements that eased tension among victors and vanquished. American officials and financiers banded together to pour loans and investments into Western Europe to underwrite economic revival. Dollars even went to bolstering the economies of Fascist Italy and the Communist Soviet Union. Limits on the latter were set in Moscow, not Washington, even though, formally, the US government did not recognize the government of the USSR.

In Asia, the United States meanwhile composed longstanding differences with Japan. US financial and business concerns developed active cooperative relations with Japanese counterparts. Americans and Japanese collaborated in expanding trade and investment in China, even though China, for most of the 1920s, had a government that included Communists.

There were points of friction, to be sure. Throughout the 1920s US and British oil companies were in active competition in parts of the Middle East and Latin America. In Argentina, British railway investors tried unsuccessfully to fight off US companies promoting road-building and trucks and automobiles.

On the whole, nevertheless, the decade 1920–30 can be characterized as one in which the United States actively helped to build up the economies of potential political and military competitors. Compare the 1930 figures in Tables 11.3 and 11.4 with those cited earlier.

The figures in the tables, of course, reflect underlying strength in the various economies. All the belligerents of the Great War were bound to achieve some recovery once they stopped splattering lives and resources on barren battlefields. But the United States, given its relative economic strength as of 1920, could certainly have slowed this recovery. Moreover, the recovery would have proceeded at a much slower pace

Table 11.4. *Energy consumption of the powers (in millions of metric tons of coal equivalent)*

Country	1930
United States	762
United Kingdom	184
Germany	177
France	97.5
Russia	65
Japan	55.8
Italy	24

absent the US money poured into Europe after 1922. By building up opponents, US economic policies and their results were exactly opposite to those that realist theory would have predicted.

The same is glaringly true for the naval and military dimensions of US international relations in the decade 1920–30. As is well known, the Republicans controlling the executive and legislative branches of the US government after 1920 backed away from the naval building program initiated by their Democratic predecessors. The Republican Secretary of State, Charles Evans Hughes, did not abandon the slogan, a "navy second to none," but he deprived it of meaning. At an international conference in Washington in 1922–23, Hughes proposed – and obtained – a five-power treaty providing that the United States, Britain, Japan, France, and Italy all cut back their planned construction of big-gun battleships. The United States and Britain would have fleets of equal size. Japan's would be three-fifths of either. The fleets of France and Italy would each be half the size the Japan's.

In the course of the 1920s, the United States did not build all the ships allowed by the treaty. (Neither did any of the other signatories.) The US Navy did build some smaller vessels and experimental aircraft carriers. But the State Department engaged continuously in negotiations to limit the numbers of these other classes of warships. In Congress, the committees concerned with foreign affairs and appropriations generally overruled those recommending any adventurous naval building.

As for ground forces, the United States rapidly demobilized the army built up to fight the Great War. The same congressional committees that denied funds to the navy took an even more harsh line regarding the army and its nascent air service and research and development activities. American military forces were very small relative to those of Germany, Russia, and France.

Table 11.5. *Military personnel, 1930*

Country	
United States	256,000
United Kingdom	318,000
Germany	114,000
France	411,000
Soviet Union	562,000
Japan	293,000

Not a single prediction flowing from the Melian-dialogue/ Mearsheimer theory would have earned our gambler a penny during the decade 1920–30.

Move forward now a decade and a half. We skip the Great Depression and World War II. Almost nothing in those years could have been predicted on the basis of anything that had ever occurred before. Witness the expectations of Winston Churchill as broadcast in a speech in Canada in 1930. "[T]he outlook for peace has never been better than for fifty years," he said.[5]

Moving to 1945, however, we can reinvent our gambler and pose for him or her the question of how to characterize the likely US posture as of 1955.

The United States in 1945 is even more a colossus than in 1920. The measurements of its relative power are more precise. As Paul Kennedy points out US GDP surged by more than 50 percent during the war, Europe's (minus the Soviet Union) had fallen about 25 percent.[6] The new measure of GNP (Gross National Product) was being recorded and it showed the United States even more dominant in 1950 than it had been in the 1930s.

Now – in 1945 – there is beginning to be a body of realist writing on which our gambler can draw. E. H. Carr's essay, *The Twenty Years' Crisis*, appeared in 1939. It explained why realism required appeasing Nazi Germany. Nevertheless, it laid out the logic of realism in terms lastingly appealing to Anglophone undergraduates. Soon afterward, Hans Morgenthau published his enduringly popular textbook, *Politics among Nations*.

Carr and Morgenthau were, to be sure, more cautious and less dogmatic than later realists. Moreover, Morgenthau wrote as an American advocating realism but acknowledging that, for all its power, it was not

---

[5] Steiner, *The Lights that Failed*, p. 565.
[6] Kennedy, *The Rise and Fall of the Great Powers*, p. 368.

Table 11.6. *Total GNP (1964 $) (in billions)*

Country	1950
United States	381
Soviet Union	126
United Kingdom	71
West Germany	48
Japan	32

necessarily the framework of reasoning for US foreign policy. In a long essay published in 1951, *In Defense of the National Interest*, Morgenthau made two imperfectly consistent arguments. He condemned the United States for not following realist policies. "What passed for [US] foreign policy," he wrote, "was either improvisation or – especially in our century – the invocation of some moral principle in whose image the world was to be made over." At the same time, he described "statesmen who boasted that they were not 'believers in the idea of the balance of power' [as] like a scientist not believing in the law of gravity." He seemed as sure as the Athenians at Melos or Mearsheimer in 2001 that the real world worked as one in which nations maximized their power. "That a new balance of power will rise out of the ruins of an old balance and that nations with political sense will avail themselves of the opportunity to improve their position within it, is a law of politics for whose validity nobody is to blame," he wrote.[7]

For our purpose, it is necessary to suppose once again that the hypothetical gambler adopts a line of reasoning that supposes Thucydides' Melian dialogue to capture essential truth, eventually to be elaborated in works such as Mearsheimer's *Tragedy of Great Power Politics*. In keeping with this version of realism, our gambler should prophesy that, as of 1955, the United States will be holding to non-threatening levels the economic recovery of both the defeated Axis nations and its own former allies. It will maintain its gargantuan advantage in naval and air power. While perhaps reducing its ground forces in anticipation of "offshore balancing," it will retain overawing dominance in all realms of military technology.

Between 1945 and 1950, our gambler would have seen reason to fear a fate exactly like that of the gambler of 1920. The United States, it was true, displayed intention to act henceforth as a world power, not to

---

[7] Hans J. Morgenthau, *In Defense of the National Interest: A Critical Examination of American Foreign Policy* (New York: Alfred A. Knopf, 1951), pp. 4, 32–33.

seem, as earlier, to retreat within a self-protective shell. But the arenas of engagement appeared not to be the rough, open plains of great-power engagement but instead the confines of constitutionally constraining organizations such as the United Nations and the various bodies created by the Bretton Woods conference of 1944 – the International Monetary Fund, the World Bank, etc.

Five years out – in 1950 – the new bet would have looked as dicey as that of 1920. The United States had followed the same course as earlier, pouring dollars across the oceans to renew the sinews of Western European nations, including Germany, and those of Japan. One of the first big steps by the US government was to lend the United Kingdom $3.75 billion. The second was the Marshall Plan announced in 1947 and funded by Congress in 1948, which allowed Europeans to tap a $13 billion pot for recovery projects they designed, the only US stipulations being that the proposals be cooperatively framed in Europe and that US experts deem them feasible. Some of this money eventually went to a provisional German regime. Other money, passed through military-occupation authorities, was earmarked for making Germany and Japan once again strong enough to compete with the United States, at least economically.

Meanwhile, the United States collapsed its military strength just as in the previous postwar period. The army that numbered more than eight million in 1945 was down to less than 600,000 by 1950. The fleets that had controlled the oceans and carried soldiers and marines to Africa, Italy, and France and across the central and southwest Pacific became rusting mothballed hulls. The 50,000-plane air armada ordered up by Franklin Roosevelt mostly turned to scrap. Harry Truman, the vice president elevated to the presidency by Roosevelt's death, won election in his own right in 1948. He installed as the civilian head of his military establishment Louis Johnson, an aggressive and ambitious lobbyist/politician. Truman's mandate to Johnson, which Johnson pursued with zest, was to cut overall US military spending back to levels of the isolationist 1930s.

There were, to be sure, important differences between this postwar period and the last. Though a substantial and weighty minority still thought that prewar isolationism had not been mistaken and that the proper position of the United States would be an independent "Fortress America," the majority of the interested public and of the nation's political leaders accepted instead the proposition that the welfare and safety of Americans required engagement with the rest of the globe. The evident presumption was, however, the reverse of the hard realist's. Engagement itself was taken to be the magic solvent. Participation in international organizations would hold at bay the forces that had produced the terrible wars of the first half of the twentieth century.

Besides US engagement in international organizations, this postwar period was also different because of what columnists came to call the Cold War – the antagonistic relationship with the Soviet Union. Religious beliefs and ideologies that exalted individualism made many Americans intensely hostile to communism and hence to the Soviet Union as sponsor of the international communist movement. This hostility merged with anxiety lest the Great Depression return and restore the allure that communism had had during the 1930s. Anti-communism among the public and members of Congress made it possible, even popular, for Truman publicly to condemn Soviet efforts to whittle off a portion of Iran, to press for concessions from Turkey, and to support communist guerrillas in Greece and communist parties in Italy and France. It enabled him to risk armed conflict over West Berlin, where Americans, British, and French occupied an enclave deep inside the Soviet zone of occupation in Germany. The Soviets tried to freeze the Westerners out by shutting off road and rail access. Truman and British prime minister Clement Attlee responded with a round-the-clock airlift, which preserved the enclave.

In 1949, after Truman's inauguration as president in his own right, Soviet dictator Joseph Stalin called off the Berlin blockade. Truman and many other Americans concluded that Stalin had been taught not to try expanding his sphere by force. All of China had meanwhile come into the communist camp as an outcome of China's long civil war. Truman and his aides regretted that this was the case but saw nothing they could usefully do except to "let the dust settle." Truman was heard to express an expectation that he and "Uncle Joe" would henceforth have a ragged but peaceful relationship.

As a practical matter, the United States has emerged from World War II as a global hegemon. As of June 1950, however, it seemed not to be consolidating this status but instead to be moving briskly toward escaping it, seeking a global environment in which a number of nations would be economic competitors and none – including the United States – would have capability for or inclination toward encroaching on the territory of others.

In June 1950, the United States reversed its posture sufficiently to give at least temporary heart to our hypothetical realist gambler. In secret exchanges that have now become public, Stalin, China's Mao Zedong, and North Korea's "great leader," Kim Il-Sung, agreed that Kim should attempt military conquest of non-communist South Korea and that, against the possibility of a US military reaction, Mao should position forces to back Kim up. (It is interesting to speculate whether a hard realist would have predicted – or could explain in retrospect – this half-lunatic set of decisions.) In any case, the North Koreans acted.

Truman did, indeed, decide to respond with force. During the previous two years, he and his advisers had twice studied South Korea and both times concurred that, in the event of war, it would be a strategic liability. The South Korean regime was authoritarian, corrupt, unpopular, and increasingly under attack from an underground sympathetic to North Korea. Though Truman and his circle did not quite say so, one infers from surviving documents that internal events which made all Korea communist would, like the recent internal events in China, provoke expressions of regret by Washington but little more.

During 1950, retiring diplomat George F. Kennan published lectures on American diplomacy, which he had recently given at the University of Chicago. One of the two most elegant pleaders for an interest-based US foreign policy (the other is Henry Kissinger), Kennan deplored as the actual dominant doctrines "moralism" and "legalism." Truman's decision to fight for South Korea was unquestionably influenced by concern lest the United States be seen as lacking will to fight and lest Stalin be encouraged thereby to make a new move in Germany. But the decision seems to have been inspired even more by a combination of moralism and legalism, for North Korea's attack offended Truman as a violation of the UN Charter, which called to his mind Fascist Italy's attack on Ethiopia in 1935 and the failure of members of the League of Nations to honor their obligations to respond forcefully to any acts of aggression.

Despite the extent to which the United States had stripped away its military strength, call-ups of reservists and de-mothballing of ships and planes made it possible in a matter of months to check the North Korean invasion and send their broken divisions racing home. At this point, the United States made its own half-lunatic decision. Truman allowed the US/UN commander, General Douglas MacArthur, to pursue the fleeing North Koreans and attempt to unify Korea as a non-communist state. Truman's then Secretary of State, Dean Acheson, acknowledges in his memoirs that he, Truman, and Truman's other advisers "sat around like paralyzed rabbits while MacArthur carried out this nightmare."[8] It caused Mao to honor his bargain with Stalin and Kim. Chinese armies entered Korea, drove the Americans back to

---

[8] Dean G. Acheson, *Present at the Creation: My Years at the State Department* (New York: W. W. Norton & Company, 1969), pp. 463–65.

pre-June borders, and pinned them down in murderous fighting that lasted until after the death of Stalin in early 1953.[9]

Meanwhile, Truman did what our realist bettor would have predicted five years earlier. He dumped Louis Johnson and committed himself to building for the United States military forces that, in the language of the key policy document, National Security Council paper number 68,

> can be maintained as long as necessary as a deterrent to Soviet aggression, as indispensable support to our political attitude toward the USSR, as a source of encouragement to nations resisting Soviet political aggression, and as an adequate basis for immediate military commitments and for rapid mobilization should war prove unavoidable.[10]

When Truman left office in early 1953 more than 60 percent of US government spending went to military forces. US combat divisions with supporting air and naval forces were stationed in Western Europe, Japan, and at various points on the periphery of the Soviet Union. Here appeared to be the self-seeking hegemon that the Athenians at Melos and Mearsheimer in 2001 described as natural if not inevitable, given in an international "state of nature."

But in 1955, when our mythical bet would come due, the posture of the United States seemed in many respects to be moving back toward that of the early postwar years. General Dwight Eisenhower had succeeded Truman as president. Outgoing Truman advisers such as Acheson, State Department policy planner Paul Nitze, and foreign aid overseer W. Averell Harriman, pressed on the new administration a policy of "rollback" aimed at gradually depriving the Soviet Union of its satellites. Eisenhower studiously rejected this advice.

Though US combat divisions continued to be deployed to Europe, Eisenhower repeatedly asserted that he intended to pull them out. He pushed the British and French and the now independent West Germans to build up their own ground and air forces. Meanwhile, he vigorously encouraged West Europeans to cooperate in augmenting their collective economic strength. One can perhaps see this as preparation for "offshore balancing." But it is not easy to suppose that a straight-line heir of the Athenians at Melos would have wanted client states working together to strengthen their economic base *and* to act in concert militarily.

Moreover, Eisenhower's policy regarding US military forces was almost exactly the reverse of "offensive realism." Atomic bombs had

---

[9] See Andrew Kennedy's chapter on Mao's hubris.
[10] NSC 68, www.fas.org/irp/offdocs/nsc-hst/nsc-68-cr.htm.

been used to end the Pacific war. The US government had proposed a well-conceived plan for safeguarded international control of the raw material required for such bombs. The USSR, which was a long way toward producing its own atomic bomb, vetoed any such plan. The US laboratories that produced the original bombs discovered ways of mass-producing new types with ever-increasing yields, including hydrogen bombs with unlimited destructive power. In 1949 the Soviet Union was discovered to have successfully tested its own atomic bomb. In the early 1950s, within a year of one another, the United States and the Soviet Union tested hydrogen bombs. The armed forces on both sides meanwhile raced to design and deploy aircraft and rockets capable of intercontinental attacks with these weapons.

Eisenhower made a conscious decision to cut back as sharply as he could the military expansion commenced under Truman. Long-term contractual commitments, together with congressional enthusiasm for contracts beneficial to particular states and districts, set limits to this effort. But Eisenhower made plain to the military establishment, the public, and the world that he had no intention of building or maintaining forces suited even for controlling, let alone for expanding, any kind of American territorial empire.

Eisenhower ruled that US armed forces should be equipped and trained for nuclear war and nothing else. He reasoned *à la* Clausewitz that war had no natural limit and that, if a major war came, nuclear weapons would inevitably be used. He reasoned also that exclusive US reliance on nuclear weapons would serve both to deter any Soviet adventures comparable to those in Korea and, of at least equal importance, to reassure the Soviets that the United States had neither intention nor capacity to interfere militarily in their homeland or their empire. Though US ground forces and tactical air forces were all outfitted with comparatively low-yield nuclear weapons (i.e., weapons resembling those used at Hiroshima and Nagasaki), it was extremely hard for commanders even to develop plans for defensive operations, let alone for operations to seize and take useful possession of any portion of the Soviet empire.

Our hypothetical bettor might have collected some money in 1955. It was not unreasonable to say that, as of this date, the United States retained a hegemonic position in the world. The notion of "offshore balancing" could perhaps excuse the fact that the United States was trying, as in the earlier postwar era, to promote economic development, military preparedness, and mutual cooperation among European states that were potentially America's rivals. The bettor could even claim to be rewarded for the fact that the United States as of 1955 was still spending more than 50 percent of government revenues on its military establishment. Because this establishment was geared for little besides nuclear war, an impartial judge would probably have ruled against the claim. Hegemony through obliteration or mutual suicide? Not very plausible.

Hard realism would have been of no use at all in predicting or explaining US behavior after the Great War. It would have had limited utility for predicting or explaining US behavior in the decade 1945–55.

Let us shift now, however, to the most recent postwar era – that between the end of the Cold War in 1989–91 and the present. In his recent book, *The Return of History and the End of Dreams*, the neoconservative analyst, Robert Kagan, summarizes currents of the George H. W. Bush–Bill Clinton–George W. Bush era as follows:

When the Cold War ended, the United States pressed forward … It began exerting influence in places like Central Asia and the Caucasus, which most Americans did not even know existed before 1989. American power, unchecked by Soviet power, filled vacuums and attempted to establish, where possible, the kind of democratic and free-market capitalist order that Americans prefer. Although the rate of increase in defense spending declined marginally during the 1990s, the technological advances in American weaponry far outstripped the rest of the world and placed the United States more than ever in a special category of military superpower. The natural result was a greater proclivity to employ this force for a wide range of purposes, from humanitarian intervention in Somalia and Kosovo to regime change in Panama and Iraq. Between 1989 and 2001, the United States intervened with force in foreign lands more frequently than at any other time in its history – an average of one significant new military action every 16 months – and far more than any other power in the same stretch of time.[11]

This summation is hard to dispute. Since the end of the Cold War, while the United States has not treated the rest of the world the way the Athenians treated the Melians, it has behaved more or less as realists like Mearsheimer would have predicted or recommended. Not quite, to be sure, for Mearsheimer and like-minded realists would have preferred more "offshore balancing." The second Bush made this more difficult by shouldering aside the UN and NATO in his haste for regime change in Iraq.

But, to return to our original conceit, a gambler who bet in 1990 that by 2005 US foreign policy would comfortably fit the hard realist model would have raked the table. And this despite the fact that many whilom realists had speculated in the early 1990s that, in a new "unipolar" world, military force would have less use and that cooperation with the

---

[11] Robert Kagan, *The Return of History and the End of Dreams* (New York: Alfred A. Knopf, 2008), pp. 49–50.

hegemon, even if reluctant, would become more the rule. (Kagan's title alludes to the notion that the end of the Cold War marked "the end of history.")

So why the difference? Why did the United States depart so far from hard realism in the 1920s and the decade and a half after World War II? Why did it then, from the 1990s forward, become hard realism personified?

My own perhaps idiosyncratic answer borrows from Sir Geoffrey Vickers' 1965 classic, *The Art of Judgment*.[12] I take the foreign policies of almost all nations to be understandable as functions of sets of judgments – about Reality, about Values, and about Action.

Reality judgments concern events. What is going on in the world that demands or offers opportunity for some kind of governmental response?

Value judgments involve calculations, some of which fit the realist canon. How may the observed or supposed realities endanger the nation or create possibilities for making it stronger, safer, or more prosperous? Value judgments may also involve axioms (in the Baconian sense of axioms derived from experience). Americans both of the 1920s and of the period 1945–55 thought it axiomatic that wars were made more likely by international competition for scarce resources and, by the same token, that rising, shared prosperity would equate with peace. Americans of those earlier periods also shared an axiomatic belief in rule of law as the key to maintenance of peace and order both domestically and internationally. Those of 1945–55 believed history to have shown the previous generation to be mistaken in rejecting Wilson's plea for US commitment to collective security. Hence they thought it axiomatic that the United States should abide by the UN charter. It was this, more than any calculations of interest, that inspired Truman's reaction to the events in Korea in 1950.

Action judgments (which Vickers called "instrumental judgments") answer the question: given what is happening and why it matters, either from calculation or axiom, what is the government to do? As Philip Zelikow writes in his seminal 1994 essay, "Foreign Policy Engineering," this breaks into at least four subordinate questions.[13] (1) What would it be useful to do? What objectives would be worth striving for? (2) What *can* be done? What means are available for pursuing the desired objective or objectives? (3) What theory generates a conclusion that the means

[12] Sir Geoffrey Vickers, *The Art of Judgment*, centenary edition (Thousand Oaks, CA: SAGE Publications, 1995).
[13] Philip D. Zelikow, "Foreign Policy Engineering: From Theory to Practice and Back Again," *International Security* 18 (1994), 143–71.

available can be mustered in such a way as to achieve what is hoped for? And (4) what plan for action follows from this theory or theories?

These sets of judgments are continuously interactive. Calculations and axioms inspire attention to events. Before 9/11, most terrorist incidents in the world passed unnoticed by any except a handful of US officials. Since then, almost any terrorist bomb anywhere captures attention in the US news media and takes precious time from the calendars of presidents, congressional leaders, and their highest aides. The mix of questions about possible courses of action ping back and forth with questions about events and conditions in the world and about calculations and axioms.

Key differences between the United States of today and the periods immediately after the two World Wars lie in these realms of judgment, particularly regarding actions and values. One essential truth about the United States before the late twentieth century was captured by the great political scientist, Samuel P. Huntington, in his 1957 book, *The Soldier and the State*.[14] Huntington portrayed the professional military as socially and intellectually isolated from, almost at odds with, the rest of American society. In a follow-on book of 1961, *The Common Defense*, Huntington analyzed the extent to which the build-up of armed forces following upon Truman's adoption of NSC 68 transformed American politics not so much by changing relations between the professional military and civilians as by making military expenditures a major element in the federal budget and hence a preoccupation for large numbers of public officials, including senators, representatives, governors, mayors, and their constituents.[15]

Richard Nixon was one of the few mainstream politicians to proclaim himself a Keynesian.[16] In fact, however, almost every American political leader privately assumed that prosperity depended in some degree on government spending. For conservatives this came most comfortably in the guise of spending for "national security." Eisenhower, fearful of the possible malign influence of a "military-industrial complex," offered as a substitute a huge interstate highway program. Lyndon Johnson diverted spending to health care and welfare. In most years, most stimulative spending went to high-technology weaponry.

[14] Samuel P. Huntington, *The Soldier and the State: The Theory and Politics of Civil–Military Relations* (Cambridge, MA: Harvard University Press, 1957).
[15] Samuel P. Huntington, *The Common Defense: Strategic Programs in National Politics* (New York: Columbia University Press, 1961).
[16] See John H. Taylor, "Newly Keen on Keynes," October 24, 2008, http://thenewnixon.org.

Partly because of the new centrality of military spending but partly for other reasons, the professional military became more integrated into the lager society. Robert McNamara, US Secretary of Defense during the 1960s, packed his office with high-caliber scientists, social scientists, and lawyers. They developed ways of testing the cost-effectiveness of alternative approaches to satisfying military mission requirements. In self-defense, the uniformed military made themselves masters of the relevant analytic skills. McNamara's civilians discovered meanwhile that the training and experience of the uniformed military made them operational planners with almost no peers anywhere else in the government. By the end of the 1960s, McNamara's civilian "whiz-kids" and military staff officers combined to dominate US foreign-policy planning.

President Richard Nixon and his National Security Adviser, Henry Kissinger, followed by President Jimmy Carter and his adviser, Zbigniew Brzezinski, moved analysis and planning away from the Pentagon and toward the White House. They, too, however, found themselves relying on the skill sets of McNamara's former "whiz-kids" and staff officers from the armed services. They diluted the mix in some degree by finding Foreign Service officers like Lawrence Eagleburger and Robert Blackwill and CIA careerists like William Hyland and Robert Gates, who could learn from and match the men and women who had worked for McNamara. With some ups and downs this remained the case through the 1980s.

The United States as a result entered the post-Cold War era with processes for identifying, analyzing, and coping with foreign-policy problems that tended not only to imitate military processes but also to involve men and women with a lot of experience either in uniform or as civilians in the military establishment. These individuals did not necessarily bring with them a bias toward use of military force. Indeed, senior military professionals, such as Brent Scowcroft and Colin Powell, were among those most cautious in this respect. But the process had an inherent bias captured in the warning reportedly given to his aides by General Marshall when Secretary of State – that political problems, if discussed in military terms, were all too apt to *become* military problems.

Working in tandem with this bias in action judgments were value judgments resting on axioms derived from experience of the late Cold War.

The Reagan administration had flaunted a build-up in the most advanced military technologies – space weapons, missiles designed to intercept other missiles, super-quiet submarines, etc. – to make the

Soviet government recognize its systemic inferiority. When the Soviet empire splintered and the Soviet Union itself dissolved, a large proportion of the US elite came away believing that this happy ending for the Cold War demonstrated that the United States could exercise moral suasion on the rest of the world by virtue simply of manifesting military capability.[17]

A second axiom flowed similarly from the ending of the Cold War. From the earliest days of the republic, Americans had been prone to believe that all humans hungered to escape tyranny and to enjoy liberties such as those protected by American constitutions. The largely non-violent overthrow in Eastern Europe of the dictatorships imposed and supported by Moscow seemed new examples of this "self-evident truth." The first Bush, Clinton, and the second Bush all gave voice to this axiom, the latter with particular frequency and force. George W. Bush's "freedom agenda" had as its foundation the assertion that opens his 2006 *National Security Strategy*: "It is the policy of the United States to seek and support democratic movements and institutions in every nation and culture, with the ultimate goal of ending tyranny in our world."[18]

A third axiom came from the Gulf War. In 1990 as in 1950 the United States went to war to resist aggression that violated the UN charter – in this case aggression by Saddam Hussein's Iraq against the kingdom of Kuwait. President George H. W. Bush and his National Security Adviser, Scowcroft, had much in mind the example of 1950. They were determined not to make Truman's mistake but to limit themselves, for practical purposes, to restoring the *status quo ante*. Given this objective, the war achieved brisk success. The chief debate afterward had to do with whether it would have been almost as easy to press on to Baghdad and depose Saddam. The lesson seemed to be, in any case, that, if the United States did use military force, it could, indeed, be awesomely effective.

The fact that the United States acted for a while after the Cold War much as hard realism would have predicted scarcely testifies that the theory has enduring utility for analyzing US foreign policy.[19] It is scarcely to be taken for granted that, in the aftermath of the painful wars in Afghanistan and Iraq, action judgments in the US government will continue to gravitate toward use of military force. Nor is it

[17] That this was not true is strongly suggested by Larson and Shevchenko.
[18] NSS 2006, www.whitehouse.gov/nsc/nss/2006.
[19] Rob Litwak argues below that President G. W. Bush veered toward overuse of US power, again undermining the Mearsheimer thesis.

to be taken for granted that the calculations and axioms prevailing in 1990–2005 will prevail in future.

To conclude this chapter as it began, I invite the reader to think as might a gambler contemplating a bet on the distant future. Ask yourself how much of your own money you would be prepared to risk on a bet that, as of 2025, the international posture of the United States will be that which would be predicted by the propositions of John Mearsheimer quoted earlier.

12   The overuse of American power

Robert S. Litwak

The end of the Cold War and the demise of the Soviet Union left the United States the sole remaining superpower and inaugurated an era of American primacy.[1] America's global dominance prompted popular references to a latter-day Roman Empire. Transcending the Cold War rubric of "superpower," "hyperpower" entered the political lexicon to convey the magnitude of the United States' paramount international status.[2] Scholars described the international system as "unipolar" and debated whether such a structure would be stable or not. As US defense spending approximates that of all other countries in the world combined, the international system remains unipolar, with respect to that single military dimension of hard power. But that unprecedented power did not translate into security for America. The mass-casualty attacks by Osama bin Laden's Al Qaeda network on 9/11 ushered in a new age of American vulnerability more dangerously unpredictable than the Cold War.

On the morning after the September 11, 2001 terrorist attacks on New York and Washington, international solidarity with the United States was dramatically conveyed in the *Le Monde* headline, "Nous sommes tous Américains!" That sentiment, however, soon eroded when the Bush administration pressed to extend the "global war on terrorism" from Al Qaeda's stronghold in Afghanistan into Iraq, an action that France, Germany, Russia, and others regarded as an ill-advised "war of choice." Five years after 9/11, a plurality of West Europeans, according to a public-opinion poll, judged the United States to be "the

---

[1] This chapter draws on Robert S. Litwak, *Regime Change: US Strategy through the Prism of 9/11* (Baltimore and Washington, DC: Johns Hopkins University Press and Wilson Center Press, 2007). An earlier version of this chapter was presented at the conference, "After the Unipolar Moment: Clarifying the Purposes of US Hard Power," sponsored by the Stanley Foundation and the International Institute for Strategic Studies, April 26–27, 2007.

[2] French Foreign Minister Hubert Védrine coined this neologism in 1998.

246

greatest threat to global stability."[3] This changed perception of the United States – from victim to rogue superpower – was the result of Washington's sharp departure from past policies and its new assertive unilateralism. The reason for this shift was suggested by President George W. Bush at the US–EU summit in June 2006, when he declared, "For Europe, September the 11th was a moment; for us, it was a change of thinking."[4]

This chapter explores the relationship between unipolarity and American unilateralism – the unchecked application of US power. The mere existence of unipolarity in the initial post-Cold War era did not precipitate the balance-of-power response to American hard power that realist theory would have predicted. Political scientist John Ikenberry has persuasively argued that the reason why a coalition to counter American hyperpower did not emerge was the embedding of US power in international security and economic institutions. That channeling of American power made it more legitimate and less threatening to other states. This strategic restraint fostered the perception of the United States as a benign superpower.[5] The United States advanced its national interests even as it operated below its "power line" as defined by America's paramount ranking in the international power hierarchy.[6] By contrast to the quiescent international reaction to the advent of unipolarity, the unilateral application and overuse of US hard power after 9/11, most glaringly manifested in the Bush administration's launching of a preventive war in Iraq to topple the Saddam Hussein regime, did trigger major opposition from other major powers in the UN Security Council.[7]

Unipolarity vs. unilateralism (the overuse of power)

The advent of a new era of vulnerability after 9/11 powerfully influenced the Bush administration's perception of the United States' role within the international system. A generation ago, French political theorist Raymond Aron's classic work, *The Imperial Republic*, aptly

---

[3] The results of this *Financial Times*/Harris Poll were published on September 25, 2006, www.harrisinteractive.com/news/allnewsbydate.asp?NewsID=1097. Among perceived threats, the United States was at the top with 34 percent; Iran was second with 25 percent.

[4] White House, Office of the Press Secretary, "President Bush Participates in Press Availability at 2006 U.S.–EU Summit," Vienna, Austria, June 21, 2006, www. whitehouse.gov/news/releases/2006/06/20060621-6.html.

[5] G. John Ikenberry, *After Victory: Institutions, Strategic Restraint, and the Rebuilding of Order after Major Wars* (Princeton University Press, 2001), pp. 246–56.

[6] See the chapter by Ernest May in this volume.

[7] Beginning, thereby, the overuse of American power.

characterized America's competing twin identities. The United States fulfills an "imperial" function as the dominant power maintaining order in an international system forged after World War II through indispensable American leadership and power. At the same time, America is a "republic" – a sovereign state with its own parochial national interests. The inherent tension between the two identities was successfully managed during the Cold War through the immersion of US power in international security and economic institutions, which made the exercise of American power more legitimate and less threatening, fostering the perception among other states of the United States as a benign superpower, while advancing American national interests. This unique identity was the key to America's international success in the post-World War II era – the creation of an unprecedented democratic community of security and wealth. In this sense the underuse of US power also explains why the demise of the Soviet Union and the end of the bipolar Cold War system did not trigger the rise of a coalition of states to balance American power, as realist political theory would have predicted.

Neither the George H. W. Bush nor Clinton administrations took up conservative columnist Charles Krauthammer's call to seize "the unipolar moment" and "unashamedly lay down the rules of world order and be prepared to enforce them." The Clinton-era formulation was that the United States would act multilaterally when possible but unilaterally when necessary. That said, despite the international rancor over the George W. Bush administration's assertive unilateralism and overuse of power, one should not overlook the episodes in the 1990s when US behavior (as during the Kosovo war and the August 1998 bombing of Sudan), provoked strong criticism in many foreign capitals.

The United States' turn to unilateralism and the beginnings of overuse of power came in response to the 9/11 terrorist attacks. President Bush's conviction that the urgent threats posed by rogue regimes and terrorist groups could necessitate unilateral US action outside the structure of international institutions and norms – a sentiment captured in the blunt formulation that he did not require the UN Security Council's "permission" to defend America – had major implications, both for how the United States perceived itself and for how it was perceived abroad. Before 9/11, Richard Haass, head of the State Department's Policy Planning Staff, characterized the Bush administration's policy stance as "a la carte multilateralism."[8] Yet post-9/11 events indicated that the administration had essentially reversed the terms of the Clinton

---

[8] Thom Shanker, "White House Says the U.S. Is Not a Loner, Just Choosy," *New York Times*, July 31, 2001, p. A1.

formulation by making clear its preference for unilateralism when possible and multilateralism when necessary. The combination of assertive unilateralism (later coupled with the proselytizing Wilsonian emphasis on democratization) fed the perception of the United States as a "revisionist hegemon."[9]

The 9/11 attacks exposed the susceptibility of the United States and other Western societies to non-state terrorism, but the attacks (however horrific and psychologically searing) did not alter the structure of international relations. Indeed, Russia and China viewed the Al Qaeda attacks on the iconic World Trade Center towers as an assault on the global economic system into which they were increasingly integrating themselves. The acquiescence (unthinkable a decade earlier) of America's former Cold War adversaries to the establishment of US bases in Central Asia to conduct military operations in Afghanistan was testimony to their shared perception of, and unified response to, the events of 9/11. In the eyes of the international community, the US military intervention in Afghanistan against Al Qaeda and the Taliban regime that had abetted the 9/11 attacks was a "war of necessity" – a legitimate and proportionate application of the inherent right of self-defense codified in the UN Charter. But that international solidarity with the United States collapsed when the Bush administration pressed to extend its "global war on terrorism" into Iraq.

The hallmark of the post-9/11 era of vulnerability, in the Bush administration's phrase, is "the nexus of terrorism and Weapons of Mass Destruction" – that is, the link between a terrorist group's millennial political *intentions* and its potential access to *capabilities* for inflicting horrific mass-casualty attacks with weapons of mass destruction (WMD). The 9/11 suicide terrorism revealed the unprecedented danger posed by the availability of the means of mass violence to an "undeterrable" non-state actor such as Al Qaeda. Equally significant for US national security policy, the 9/11 terrorist attacks also starkly recast the debate about state actors – most notably, the countries designated by the Bush administration as "rogue states." President George W. Bush has asserted that the threat posed by rogue regimes derives from "their true nature."[10] During the 2000 presidential campaign, Condoleezza Rice, then an adviser to candidate Bush, had written that the United

[9] Robert Jervis, "The Remaking of a Unipolar World," *Washington Quarterly* 29 (2006), 17.
[10] White House, Office of the Press Secretary, "President Delivers State of the Union Address," January 29, 2002, www.whitehouse.gov/news/releases/2002/01/20020129-11. html.

States' "first line of defense [with rogue states] should be a clear and classical statement of deterrence."[11]

In striking contrast, after 9/11, the administration explicitly declared that the United States could no longer rely on the traditional strategic concepts of deterrence and containment to meet the "new deadly challenges" because of the *character* of its adversaries – terrorist groups and rogue states. In its comprehensive *National Security Strategy* report of September 2002, the Bush administration maintained that a *strategy of deterrence* based on punishment is "less likely to work against leaders of rogue states [who are] more willing to take risks" and more prone than an orthodox great-power rival (such as the Soviet Union during the Cold War, or contemporary China) to use WMD.[12]

In branding Iraq, Iran, and North Korea – the core group of rogue states – as the "axis of evil," President George W. Bush explicitly pointed to the threat that a state sponsor might transfer a weapon of mass destruction to a terrorist group, thus "giving them the means to match their hatred." A sense of urgency and a baldly stated commitment flowed from this analysis of the threat: "[T]ime is not on our side. I will not wait on events, while dangers gather ... The United States of America will not permit the world's most dangerous regimes to threaten us with the world's most destructive weapons."[13] The challenge to international order posed by these "rogue states" with respect to proliferation and terrorism pre-dated September 11, but the president made clear that their actions and perceived intentions would now be viewed through a post-9/11 lens.

In the 2002 *National Security Strategy* document, the Bush administration elevated the option of military preemption against "rogue states" and terrorist groups in US doctrine. Press reports characterized that element of the "Bush Doctrine" as the most revolutionary change in American strategy since the forging of US nuclear deterrence policy in the 1950s. Preemption was said to be supplanting the outdated Cold War concepts of deterrence and containment. Proponents of American unilateralism embraced the shift, arguing that pre-9/11 constraints on the use of force, such as the international legal prohibition against "anticipatory self-defense," are nonsensical in an age when Osama bin Laden has said that obtaining nuclear weapons is a moral duty – and when he certainly has no compunction about using them

---

[11] Condoleezza Rice, "Promoting the National Interest," *Foreign Affairs* (January/February 2000), 60–61.

[12] White House, *The National Security Strategy of the United States of America*, September 17, 2002, pp. 13–14, www.whitehouse.gov/nsc/nss.html.

[13] White House, "President Delivers State of the Union Address," January 29, 2002.

against the United States. But the public presentation of the *National Security Strategy* generated controversy and apprehension, particularly among America's European allies, over whether the new emphasis on preemption would erode international norms governing the use of force. US officials maintained that although preemption has gained heightened status as an understandable response to the advent of qualitatively new threats, such as Al Qaeda, it remained part of a continuum of means, including non-military instruments, which the United States would continue to employ.

Confusion about the new preemption policy arose from several issues that have been misleadingly conflated in the American debate, beginning with the important analytical and policy distinction between "preemption" and "prevention." Preemption, in this context, pertains narrowly to military action when actual WMD use by an adversary is imminent, whereas prevention refers to the broader repertoire of military and non-military policy instruments to forestall WMD acquisition. Because the threat from Saddam Hussein's regime did not meet the criterion of imminence, Iraq was an instance of preventive war and not of preemption. Another misleading conflation of issues – driven by the assumption that a "rogue state" might be motivated to transfer WMD capabilities to a terrorist group – linked the terrorism and proliferation agendas. Military action against a non-state terrorist group bent on mass-casualty attacks enjoyed broad international legitimacy, but that consensus broke down over the use of force against a *state* violating nonproliferation norms. Finally, confusion has stemmed from the political conflation of the preemption option in US strategy with the debate over Iraq in 2002. The Bush administration was ostensibly unveiling a *general* doctrine of preemption, to be undertaken unilaterally when necessary, just as it was making the *specific* case for multilateral military action against a state – Iraq – that had flouted UN Security Council resolutions for over a decade.

The controversy over preemption fed into the acrimonious UN debate leading up to the 2003 Iraq War. While the US preemption doctrine generated friction between the United States and its allies over the appropriate *means* to address security threats in the post-9/11 era, Iraq opened a political chasm over the *ends* of the Bush administration's "global war on terrorism." The fall 2001 military action in Afghanistan had won broad international support to deny Al Qaeda's unfettered ability to use that state as a base from which to mount its terrorist activities. In British strategist Lawrence Freedman's fitting play on State Department terminology, Afghanistan under the Taliban regime was less a state sponsor of terrorism than a "terrorist-sponsored state."[14] That international consensus broke down over Iraq, when nations differed over continued containment versus externally imposed regime change. Looking through the prism of 9/11, the Bush administration maintained that Iraq was not a "war of choice," but one of necessity.

The UN Security Council crisis that began in late 2002 as a debate about Iraq and Saddam Hussein ended in March 2003 in a criticism of the illegitimate exercise of American power. On opposite sides of the Atlantic, a parallel debate played out. In the United States, two approaches to Iraq were articulated in back-to-back speeches by Vice President Cheney and President Bush. Cheney's highly publicized speech to the Veterans of Foreign Wars in August 2002 stated that Saddam Hussein constituted an unacceptable threat in a post-9/11 world. Cheney rejected the status quo policy of containment and characterized the proposed resumption of UN weapons inspections in Iraq as a dangerous illusion. He advocated instead a strategy of regime change, which was later characterized as an application of the administration's new preemption doctrine. In contrast to the Cheney speech, Bush's address to the UN General Assembly in September 2002 suggested that intervention in Iraq was to enforce Security Council resolutions – on WMD – which had been routinely flouted by Saddam Hussein.

To be sure, the issue for the Bush administration was not *whether* to intervene in Iraq as part of its global war on terrorism. That strategic decision had reportedly been made no later than winter 2001–02, after the toppling of the Taliban regime in Afghanistan. Rather, the question was *how* that decision should be implemented – whether US military action should be framed in terms of the preemption doctrine, which had just been articulated, or as an operation to enforce UN Security Council resolutions. The administration emphasized the WMD rationale because it provided a legitimate, defensible basis for military action. Among the several rationales, the WMD issue was, in the words of then Deputy Secretary of Defense Paul Wolfowitz, "the one issue that everyone could agree on."[15] In Europe, British prime minister Tony Blair echoed the internationalist case of Bush's UN speech. But the opposition of France, Germany, and Russia to military action was less a response to the Bush speech than to the unilateralist line laid down in the Cheney speech. These alternative perspectives created a transatlantic rift that threatened to become a political chasm.

[14] Lawrence Freedman, "The Third World War?" *Survival* 43 (2001), 74.
[15] Department of Defense, Deputy Secretary Wolfowitz interview with Sam Tannenhaus of *Vanity Fair*, May 9, 2003, www.defenselink.mil/transcripts/2003/tr20030509-depsecdef0223.html.

Underlying the dispute were contending perspectives on the core issue of Iraqi sovereignty. President George H. W. Bush faced a far easier task assembling an international coalition for a showdown with Iraq than his son did twelve years later. In the 1991 Gulf War, Security Council authorization and the forging of a broad multinational coalition to liberate Kuwait were diplomatically possible because Saddam Hussein had violated a universally supported international norm: the protection of state sovereignty from external aggression. (As one observer colorfully put it, one state should not be permitted to murder another.) By contrast, in the bitter 2003 UN debate, Security Council approval for military action was inherently bound to rouse strong opposition for the very same reason. If the UN compelled Iraqi WMD disarmament through externally imposed regime change – even if undertaken to enforce a Security Council resolution – it would represent a precedent-setting attack on state sovereignty.

Bush's effort to reconcile the contradiction between the US determination to remove Saddam and UN Security Council resolutions that made no mention of regime change produced the tortured formulation: "[T]he policy of our government ... is regime change – because we don't believe [Saddam Hussein] is going to change. However, if he were to meet all the conditions of the United Nations ... that in itself will signal the regime has changed."[16] One could argue that the threat of regime change could have provided effective coercive leverage with Saddam, but that would also have required a credible commitment to lift that threat if the Iraqi leader came into compliance with the UN Security Council resolutions. In the case of Iraq, it was clear that the Bush administration was not prepared to take "yes" for an answer.

As historian John Lewis Gaddis observed, "The rush to war in Iraq in the absence of a 'first shot' or 'smoking gun' left ... a growing sense throughout the world there could be nothing worse than American hegemony if it was to be used in this way."[17] In withholding its imprimatur for the 2003 war, the United Nations was saying, in essence, that the international community considered the precedent of a US-imposed regime change in Baghdad *worse* than leaving the Iraqi dictator in power. The perception of the United States as a rogue superpower, which had arrogated an unfettered right of military preemption,

---

[16] White House, Office of the Press Secretary, "President Discusses Foreign Policy Matters with NATO Secretary," October 21, 2002, www.whitehouse.gov/news/releases/2002/10/20021021–8.html.

[17] John Gaddis, *Surprise, Security, and the American Experience* (Cambridge, MA: Harvard University Press, 2004), p. 101.

prompted a de facto effort by France, Germany, and Russia to block this unilateral application of US power.

This development was most clearly manifested in the French diplomatic campaign in early March 2003 to mobilize opposition to the Anglo-American proposal for a final UN Security Council resolution with an ultimatum to trigger the use of force. President Jacques Chirac expounded the French aspiration for a "multipolar" international system (presumably with a French-led European Union as one pole) that went far beyond the familiar calls for increased US multilateralism. Whether or not this constituted "balancing" is debated by political scientists.[18] But in the aftermath of the divisive debate over Iraq, strong incentives pushed both parties to heal the rift: in France, a recognition that the creation of a nineteenth-century-style multipolar system is illusory in a globalized twenty-first-century world; in the United States, a renewed appreciation (born of the hard experience of essentially going it alone, along with Britain, in Iraq) of the utility of multilateralism in conferring political legitimacy and the tangible assistance of allies. This recognition was only re-emphasized by the incoming Obama administration.

The transatlantic dispute over Iraq highlighted the misleading conflation of the terms "unipolar" and "unilateral" in policy discussions. The historical record reveals no axiomatic relationship between the emergence of a unipolar structure after the Cold War and US unilateral behavior.[19] The greatest impulse for US unilateralism was not American hyperpower, but the increased sense of vulnerability arising from the 9/11 attacks. The elevation of military preemption as an option in the 2002 *National Security Strategy* was a reflection of that change.

The challenge for Bush policy-makers contrasted sharply with that of the Cold War era, when the shared perception of the Soviet threat was NATO's strategic glue. The attempt to forge a common strategy was difficult in circumstances where the US administration felt compelled to take actions that the Europeans regarded as potentially increasing their vulnerability. For example, after the March 11, 2004, bombing in Madrid, some Europeans spoke openly of distancing themselves from the United States to reduce the motivation for Al Qaeda to

---

[18] For a discussion of "soft balancing" and the broader issue of international reactions to the unilateral exercise of US hyperpower see Robert A. Pape, "Soft Balancing against the United States," *International Security* 30 (2005), 7–44. A contrary view is offered by Keir A. Lieber and Gerard Alexander in "Waiting for Balancing: Why the World Is Not Pushing Back," *International Security* 30 (2005), 109–39, who argue that soft balancing is synonymous with "normal diplomatic friction."

[19] John Van Oudenaren, "Unipolar versus Unilateral," *Policy Review* 124 (April/May 2004), www.policyreview.org/apr04/oudenaren.html.

target them. But such differences in perception were ultimately illusory. As French political scientist Pierre Hassner observed, "both are at war with Al Qaeda because [it] is at war with them ... The Europeans tend to underestimate the gravity of the war on terrorism ... [while] the Americans tend to overlook the danger of it becom[ing] a 'clash of civilizations'."[20]

The failure to discover WMD stocks and the Bush administration's shifting rationales frustrated the US effort to legitimize the war after the fact. In Henry Kissinger's words, the United States utterly failed to convince "the rest of the world that our first preemptive war has been imposed by necessity and that we seek the world's interests, not exclusively our own."[21] Policy analyst Robert Kagan argued that the United States' international legitimacy was essential, but that it would prove elusive in the absence of a consensus on the character of the threat and on the appropriate strategy, including military means when necessary, to address it.[22] That gap existed not only between Washington and other foreign capitals, but within America itself. During the Cold War, notwithstanding the major trauma over Vietnam, a remarkably durable public consensus existed on both the threat (Soviet expansionism) and the strategy (containment and deterrence). The Bush administration was unable to build similar broad support around the central organizing concept for a post-9/11 strategy: the nexus between proliferation and terrorism, and between states and non-state actors. That goal was undercut by the failure to find WMD stocks in Iraq, the 9/11 Commission's refutation of administration claims of an operational link between Iraq and Al Qaeda, and the costly persisting insurgency in Iraq. A core consensus exists in American society on the imperative of eliminating the Al Qaeda network through all necessary means, including the preemptive use of force. But that consensus breaks down over rogue states.

After the toppling of the Saddam Hussein regime in Iraq in spring 2003, the Bush administration faced escalating nuclear-proliferation crises with the other two charter members of the "axis of evil" – North Korea and Iran. Major constraints on the ability of the United States to bring about regime change in Pyongyang and Tehran, as well as the political fallout over the WMD intelligence debacle in Iraq, prompted the administration's pragmatic turn toward multilateral diplomacy.

---

[20] Pierre Hassner, "The United States: The Empire of Force or the Force of Empire," *Chaillot Papers* 54 (Paris: Institute for Security Studies, 2002), 48–49.
[21] Quoted in Robert Kagan, "A Tougher War for the U.S. Is One of Legitimacy," *New York Times*, January 24, 2004, p. B7.
[22] Ibid.

It pursued this diplomatic course with North Korea, directly, and with Iran, indirectly. The Obama administration has continued both efforts.

Dissuasion or persuasion?

Since the end of the Cold War, a major US foreign-policy goal has been to preserve American global primacy – and prevent the rise of a "peer competitor"; it would use "dissuasion" to prevent the rise of a new challenger. Before 9/11, particular attention was accorded China, characterized as a rising, revisionist power that rejected the "status quo" and aspired to alter the Asian balance of power in its favor. Presidential candidate Bush referred to China as a "competitor" and rejected the previous view of the Clinton administration that the Beijing regime could become America's "strategic partner."[23] Underlying the Bush administration's pre-9/11 attitude toward China and, to a lesser extent, Russia was the realist tenet that a post-Cold War liberal international order would not bring an end to great-power rivalry.

Within this context, the term *dissuasion* entered the US strategic lexicon and generated controversy over its policy application. The 2001 *Quadrennial Defense Report* and the January 2002 *Nuclear Posture Review* cited dissuasion as one of four US strategic objectives – along with the *assurance* of allies, the *deterrence* of adversaries, and the *defeat* of adversary forces in the event of overt conflict.[24] The Bush administration's September 2002 *National Security Strategy* stated simply that a major function of US military forces is to "dissuade future military competition."[25] Secretary of Defense Donald Rumsfeld asserted, "[W]e need to find ways to influence the decision-makers of potential adversaries to deter them not only from using existing weapons but to the extent possible try to dissuade them from building dangerous new capabilities in the first place ... [W]e must develop capabilities that merely our possessing them will dissuade adversaries from trying to compete."[26] While these major policy pronouncements highlighted the new concept, it has not been fully developed conceptually or in policy terms.

---

[23] Bush, "A Distinctly American Internationalism."
[24] Department of Defense, *Quadrennial Defense Review Report*, September 30, 2001, www. defenselink.mil/pubs/qdr2001.pdf; Department of Defense, "Special Briefing on the Nuclear Posture Review," January 9, 2002, www.defenselink.mil/transcripts/2002/t01092002_t0109npr.html.
[25] White House, *National Security Strategy of the United States*, p. 32.
[26] Remarks as delivered by Secretary of Defense Donald Rumsfeld, National Defense University, Washington, DC, January 31, 2002, www.defenselink.mil/speeches/speech.aspx?speechid=183.

The Bush administration's public presentation of dissuasion lacked clarity on two central issues. The first was whether dissuasion was aimed at preventing the acquisition of military capabilities (such as WMD or ballistic missiles) or at forestalling foreign policy objectionable behavior. The second was whether the policy was directed at potential peer competitors (not currently adversaries) or at "rogue states" (with which the United States did have an adversarial relationship). Notwithstanding these questions, the apparent impetus behind the dissuasion strategy was to leverage American hard power to forestall the rise of a potential peer competitor and to foster an international milieu consonant with American interests and values – in short, to impose an American pattern of stability. Underpinning this strategic approach was the assumption that the United States' asymmetrical advantage in military capabilities, both offensive and defensive, would affect a potential rival's intention to compete in that sphere.

Yet with China the dissuasion explanation confused consequence and cause. One could attribute the Chinese decision in the early 1980s to cap their intercontinental ballistic missile (ICBM) program at a relatively low number to the dissuasion effect of American nuclear superiority. Beijing certainly had the ability to develop much larger strategic forces. (Indeed, the United States itself has relied on Chinese ballistic missiles to launch US commercial satellites.) But the alternative, more plausible explanation is that the Chinese concluded that such an ICBM build-up was unnecessary and indeed ran contrary to their burgeoning economic interests, which relied upon the increased integration of the PRC into the liberal international economic order. Indeed, the Clinton administration's strategy of engagement and enlargement was premised on that process of integrating former Cold War adversaries into the system.

With potential peer competitors, China and Russia, Washington made clear that the US objective was behavior change (in areas such as nonproliferation and human rights) and not regime change. Under those circumstances, the Beijing regime saw no reason to match US strategic forces and move beyond a minimum nuclear deterrent. It is plausible that the Chinese leadership concluded that to do so – thereby presenting itself as a full-fledged strategic competitor to the United States – would undermine a bilateral economic relationship that is one of the major drivers of the Chinese economy (yielding a $120 billion trade surplus). The Chinese were also reportedly influenced by the Soviet experience in which excessive military spending was a major factor responsible for the long-term weakening of the regime. Political scientist Avery Goldstein argues that a rough consensus emerged within the Chinese leadership that constitutes a "de facto grand strategy":

> The grand strategy aims to engineer China's rise to great power status within the constraints of a unipolar international system that the United States dominates. It is designed to sustain the conditions necessary for continuing China's program of economic and military modernization, as well as to minimize the risk that others, most importantly the peerless United States, will view the ongoing increases in China's capabilities as an unacceptably dangerous threat that must be parried or perhaps even forestalled. China's grand strategy, in short, aims to increase the country's international clout without triggering a counterbalancing reaction.[27]

The converse of dissuasion – "persuasion" – is a more plausible explanation for improved Chinese behavior – abstention from serious military competition with the United States and improved compliance with international norms (e.g., nonproliferation).[28] A 2007 Council on Foreign Relations Task Force found "no evidence to support the notion that China will become a peer military competitor of the United States."[29] Indeed, a US Naval War College study characterized the ongoing Chinese military modernization program as a "hedging strategy," motivated in part by Beijing's perception (in the words of a Chinese analyst) of Washington's "wild ambition" and drive to build an American "empire."[30] While experts debate the future trajectory of China's strategic nuclear forces, the salient point in this context is that the restraint reflected in its minimum deterrent posture can not be plausibly attributed to the dissuasive effect of US hard power. Nor is it clear that China will remain satisfied with a minimum deterrent over the long term.

In the case of "rogue states," the Bush administration's policy toward Iran and North Korea, the two remaining members of the "axis of evil," was undercut by an unresolved tension over whether the objective was regime change or behavior change. As with potential peer competitors like China, the focal point of US policy needed to be the target state's

---

[27] Avery Goldstein, *Rising to the Challenge: China's Grand Strategy and International Security* (Stanford University Press, 2005), p. 12.

[28] Thomas C. Schelling in *Arms and Influence* drew on the distinction introduced by J. David Singer between the terms *persuasion*, where the subject is desired to "act," and *dissuasion*, where the subject is desired to abstain. Discussed in Gregory F. Treverton, *Framing Compellent Strategies* (Santa Monica: RAND Corporation, 2000), p. 5, www.rand.org/publications/MR/MR1240.

[29] Council on Foreign Relations Task Force, *U.S.–China Relations: An Affirmative Agenda, A Responsible Course* (New York: Council on Foreign Relations, 2007), p. 50.

[30] Andrew Erickson and Lyle Goldstein, "Hoping for the Best, Preparing for the Worst: China's Response to US Hegemony," *Journal of Strategic Studies* 29 (2006), 961.

intention – as that is the lead proliferation indicator and the key determinant of foreign-policy behavior more broadly. Dissuasion cannot
affect intention (inhibiting the development of unconventional military
capabilities and promoting responsible regional behavior) when the
objective remains regime change. Indeed, the target state's motivation,
most particularly with respect to WMD acquisition, cuts in precisely
the opposite direction: US dissuasion will lead opponent regimes to
acquire a nuclear capability to deter an American attack and ensure
regime survival. In so doing, the US effort to exploit its asymmetrical
relationship with the target state by leveraging American hyperpower
may well prompt an asymmetrical response from the "rogue state"
(such as the use of terrorism or the effort to develop WMD) to level the
playing field.[31]

Regime change or behavior change?

After 9/11, the fundamental issue was, and remains, whether the US
objective toward rogue states should be to change their ruling regimes
(thereby eliminating the source of the threat), or to change their foreign-policy behavior (thereby mitigating the threat). Administration
hardliners argued that mere behavior change would no longer suffice
because the bad behavior was intimately linked to the character of the
regimes.

The Bush administration emphasized regime change after 9/11.
In response to the new perception of vulnerability, the administration elevated military preemption. The United States would use force
preemptively against imminent threats (which is a usage consistent with
international law), but would also act *preventively* against "emerging
threats" before they could act. This controversial shift in perspective
and policy was captured in Secretary of Defense Rumsfeld's telling
acknowledgment that the Bush administration's change from containment to a rollback strategy in Iraq arose not from new information

---

[31] Richard Kugler, "Dissuasion as a Strategic Concept," *Strategic Forum* (Institute for
National Security Studies, National Defense University), December 2002, p. 5, www.
ndu.edu/inss/strforum/SF196/sf196.htm. Kugler argues:

> As the United States seeks … benefits through the use of military power and other
> instruments, it will need to recognize the chief risk of dissuasion: if it is pursued in
> heavy-handed ways, it can be counterproductive. It can help intensify regional polar-
> ization and militarization, motivate countries to pursue asymmetric strategies aimed
> at negating U.S. strengths, alienate allies, and trigger the formation of coalitions
> against the United States.

about the threat posed by Saddam Hussein, but from viewing the old Iraq data "through the prism of 9/11."

President Bush asserted that the United States was "redefining war" through its ability, demonstrated in Iraq, to decapitate a regime without inflicting unacceptable collateral damage on the civilian population. On the heels of Saddam's toppling, Defense Secretary Rumsfeld reportedly sent a memorandum to the White House recommending that the United States enlist Chinese assistance to oust the Kim Jong-Il regime. Ironically, Washington's regime-change emphasis in the heady weeks of spring 2003 signified the high-water mark of the Bush Doctrine as Iraq descended into a Sunni-dominated insurgency against US occupation and the post-Saddam government in Iraq.

In contrast to the Iraqi case of nonproliferation through a change *of* regime, Libya offered the contrasting precedent of change *in* a regime. When Qaddafi announced that Libya was voluntarily terminating its covert WMD programs and submitting to intrusive international inspections to certify compliance, President Bush declared that the surprise disarmament move, which followed the Tripoli regime's financial settlement of the Pan Am 103 bombing case, would permit Libya to "rejoin the international community." The Bush administration and its supporters claimed Libya as a dividend of the Iraq War. In their narrative, Qaddafi had been "scared straight" (as one analyst put it) by the demonstration effect of the regime-change precedent. The alternative explanation, put forward by former Clinton administration officials involved in negotiations with Libya, was that the decision represented the culmination of a decade-long effort by Qaddafi to shed Libya's pariah status and reintegrate into the global system in response to mounting domestic economic pressures.

Both explanations address Libyan motivations, but neither speaks to the central issue of regime intention. A historical analysis of cases in which states decided either to acquire or to forgo nuclear weapons clearly reveals that the lead proliferation indicator is regime intention and not regime type. The centerpiece of the Libyan deal was a tacit bargain entailing the Bush administration's assurance of security for the regime: in essence, if Qaddafi halted his objectionable external behavior with respect to terrorism and proliferation, Washington would not press for a change of regime in Tripoli. Without such a credible security assurance, Qaddafi would have had no incentive to relinquish his WMD arsenal; to the contrary, the belief that he was targeted by the US administration after Iraq would have created a powerful incentive for him to accelerate his regime's efforts to acquire unconventional weapons as a strategic deterrent. The contrasting precedents set in Iraq and Libya have important implications for the ongoing nuclear crises with North Korea and Iran.

The Bush administration's characterization of the war to oust Saddam Hussein as a model of nonproliferation, linking the *National Security Strategy*'s preemption doctrine to the Iraq regime-change precedent, affects the US ability to conduct coercive diplomacy – that is, to marshal the credible threat of force in support of diplomatic efforts to resolve the twin nuclear crises with North Korea and Iran. The Bush White House remained unclear whether the objective of US policy was to change the countries' regimes or to change the regimes' objectionable external behavior. To the leaderships in Pyongyang and Tehran, "counterproliferation" strikes on their WMD assets would likely be perceived not as limited actions but as indistinguishable from a broader US military campaign to topple their regimes. This dynamic was evident during the Iraq War when the movement of US aircraft to South Korea to bolster deterrence prompted Kim Jong-Il to disappear into his bunker, evidently fearing that the deployment was a prelude to decapitating, regime-changing air strikes.

In fashioning effective strategies for North Korea and Iran, the Bush administration was caught between the Iraq and Libya precedents. The administration's aspiration for a change of regimes (through collapse in North Korea and a popular uprising in Iran) was not an immediate prospect, while its hard-line rhetoric (Vice President Cheney's emblematic declaration, "We don't negotiate with evil, we defeat it") undercut its ability to offer the assurances of regime security that, in the Libyan case, were critical to Qaddafi's strategic decision to terminate his WMD programs. Optimists among US specialists believed that agreements were attainable and the challenge was to identify acceptable terms. Skeptics discounted the possibility of negotiated settlements because they believed Pyongyang and Tehran were determined to acquire nuclear weapons, no matter what.

Have North Korea and Iran made *irreversible* decisions to "go nuclear"? The North Korean weapons test in 2006 and Iranian diplomatic intransigence support the affirmative. But because no one outside the regimes knows for certain, their nuclear intentions need to be tested through direct negotiations, as the Obama administration seems likely to do. The Pyongyang and Tehran regimes should be presented with the tangible benefits of behavior change and not be threatened with regime change. As in the case of Libya, a credible US assurance of regime security would be central. The new administration could affect nuclear intentions in both North Korea and Iran by removing the United States as a reason (or pretext) for these states' weapons programs.

Resolving the core contradiction in Washington over the objective of US policy (regime change versus behavior change) would shift the political onus to Pyongyang and Tehran. As with Iraq, the perception by Russia, China, and others that the US objective is to change the ruling regimes in North Korea and Iran undercuts Washington's ability to win multilateral support for meaningful coercive measures to bring those states into compliance with their obligations under the Nuclear Non-Proliferation Treaty (NPT).

Not surprisingly, North Korea and Iran seek to avoid a structured choice imposed from outside. Their objective is to obtain the tangible benefits of contact with the external world while not relinquishing their nuclear weapons option and, above all else, ensuring regime survival. The Pyongyang and Tehran leaderships face the mirror image of the dilemma in Washington. They too are caught between precedents: on the one hand, refusing to accept transparent WMD disarmament, like Libya; and on the other, facing strong international resistance to their aspiration of becoming overt nuclear weapons states, like Pakistan. Between these two poles of choice, North Korea and Iran may pursue a third option: cultivating ambiguity about their intentions and the status of their nuclear capabilities for as long as they can.

Saddam Hussein cultivated ambiguity about his WMD capabilities in an effort to deter a US attack, though he failed. For North Korea, the option would maintain Pyongyang's sole source of bargaining leverage, provide a degree of deterrence as a hedge against hostile US intentions, and not further antagonize China through additional weapons testing. For Iran, ambiguity would frustrate the ability of the United States to develop a consensus for collective action. The default position of Russia and China was to interpret Iranian behavior (including uranium-enrichment activities) as consistent with Iran's obligations under the NPT. This reinforced US and EU pressure to curb the nuclear program, though it could be interpreted by Russia and China as a discriminatory effort by the West to deny Iran advanced technology.

A long-term element of US strategy in dealing with current hard cases will be deterrence. Contrary to the characterization in the Bush White House, historical experience indicates that the leaders of rogue states are not inherently irrational and "undeterrable." But they do miscalculate – hence the need for clear and consistent communication from Washington to avert the failure of deterrence. The North Korean nuclear case illustrates the difficulty of enforcing a red line to prevent the crossing of a key technological or production threshold along the path to nuclear weaponization. Though obligated to live with ambiguity about the nuclear capabilities and intentions of North Korea and Iran for the foreseeable future, US officials must unambiguously lay down a deterrent red line – the threat of a regime-changing US counter-response if a state transfers nuclear materials or capabilities to a non-state terrorist group, such as Al Qaeda. For the target states, a US declaratory policy combining *deterrence* (linked to a clear red line) and *reassurance* of non-hostile US intentions would create a new calculus of decision for their ruling regimes.

The contrasting precedents set in Iraq and Libya have important implications for the nuclear crises with North Korea and Iran, but they also raise a fundamental question about the meaning of a term that has been central to the US foreign-policy debate: "regime change." The Iraq War reinforced the widespread but misleading connotation of regime change as a sharp split between old and new, and as something brought about by outsiders rather than insiders. The term is better viewed as embodying a dynamic process along a continuum. Total change – through war (Germany and Japan) or revolution (China and Iran) – that not only removes a regime's leadership but also transforms governmental institutions is rare. More commonly, the degree of change is limited, as when a newly elected political party makes a significant policy shift, or when one leader supplants another in an authoritarian regime. Leadership is perhaps the key determinant of change, affecting its pace and extent, or indeed influencing whether it will be undertaken at all.

The most important instance of regime change in the latter half of the twentieth century was accomplished in the Soviet Union under President Mikhail Gorbachev through neither revolution nor war. In 1989, diplomat George Kennan correctly declared an end to the Cold War, arguing that the Soviet Union under Gorbachev had evolved from a revolutionary expansionist state into an orthodox great power. Gorbachev's grand strategy – which represented a form of purely domestic regime change – was to integrate a transformed Soviet Union into the international order forged after World War II.[32] The complementary US strategy of the post-Cold War era has been to promote the integration of post-Soviet Russia into that international order.

Historically, the periods of greatest turmoil in the modern era have arisen from the emergence of expansionist great powers with unbounded ambition, such as Nazi Germany or Stalin's Soviet Union, seeking the wholesale transformation of the international order. With the demise of

---

[32] See the Larson and Shevchenko chapter in this volume.

the Soviet Union, the defining feature of contemporary international relations has been the absence of competition among the great powers that might bring with it the risk of major war. Although China's meteoric rise and Russia's uncertain political trajectory have prompted balance-of-power realists to question the long-term durability of this current condition, neither great power is mounting a frontal assault on the existing international order. Some commentators declared that Russia's military intervention in Georgia in August 2008 marked the return of the Cold War. This development could alternatively be viewed as the reassertion of traditional Russian national interests. Though a State Department official called Russia a "revisionist" state after its move into Georgia, its revisionism is in the conventional tradition of a great power seeking to create a sphere of influence on its periphery. This stance is closer to the Monroe Doctrine than to the Comintern. To be sure, Russia's new assertiveness carries risks of regional strife and inadvertent military escalation, but in contrast to its behavior during the Cold War, the Kremlin is not advancing an alternative vision of international order.

Conclusion

The Iraq War highlighted the costs, both direct and indirect, of unilateral activism and overuse of hard power. A Gallup poll taken as early as June 2004 indicated that a majority of Americans believe the Bush administration's decision to send military forces to Iraq was a mistake, and that the war has not made the United States safer from terrorism.[33] A Pew poll in November 2005 found that the Iraq War has had a "profound impact" on public attitudes toward America's global role and that isolationist sentiment was at a level not seen since the Vietnam War.[34] The erosion of public confidence in governmental institutions began with the Iraq War (from the WMD intelligence debacle to the incompetent postwar planning) and was compounded by the failure of government at all levels during Hurricane Katrina. As the war's initial "shock and awe" air campaign segued into a bloody counterinsurgency on the ground in Iraq, British scholar Timothy Garton Ash likened the United States' position and public mind-set to that of Britain in the early twentieth century during the Boer War when it too faced the

---

[33] CNN/*USA Today*/Gallup poll cited in CNN, "Poll: Sending Troops to Iraq a Mistake," June 25, 2004, www.cnn.com/2004/ALLPOLITICS/06/24/poll.iraq.

[34] Meg Bortin, "Survey Finds Deep Discontent with American Foreign Policy," *New York Times*, November 18, 2005, p. A12.

dilemmas of imperial overstretch and an intractable guerrilla war in South Africa.[35]

The Bush administration maintained that Iraq was the central front in the global war on terrorism. Critics pointed out that Iraq was not a terrorist haven until the chaotic aftermath of the US invasion, and that the presidential decision to make Iraq the overriding priority after the removal of the Taliban regime in Afghanistan was a colossal strategic blunder, a diversion from the real war on terrorism. They further argued that the exhaustion of the US military in Iraq, as well as the enormous drain on financial and materiel resources that the war has entailed, undercut the US ability to continue that war on terrorism. Even Secretary of Defense Donald Rumsfeld, in a memo to senior aides on "metrics" to assess the global war on terrorism, queried whether US forces were killing more terrorists than the radical clerics were recruiting and deploying against the United States.[36]

Public opinion polls indicate that the Iraq debacle, now compounded by the worst economic crisis since the Great Depression, has dramatically eroded domestic support in the United States for an activist foreign policy. Whether public sentiment will harden into a full-blown "post-Iraq syndrome" that will significantly constrain the use of force, or its threat in support of diplomacy, is unclear. The paradox is that while the United States' "unipolar moment" may have ended in Iraq, the world is still unipolar in terms of hard power, and America remains, in Madeleine Albright's terms, the "indispensable nation." But America will have to use its power more guardedly, making sure that it does not persistently push above its "power line" as it did during the Bush administration. A new administration more reliant on soft power could actually win greater support. This would mean that the world could rally in support of intervention in Darfur or elsewhere to stop mass killings. Other nations may even lament the return of an America that does too little.

Alternatively, the United States might, under the Obama administration, revive its pre-9/11 formula for success – which involved embedding American power in international institutions. This would avoid persistent overuse, by "constitutionalizing" US hard power. The years since 9/11 have eroded the perception of superpower restraint as the United States demonstrated that it could and would break out of institutional

---

[35] Timothy Garton Ash, "Stagger On, Weary Titan," *Guardian* (London), August 25, 2005, www.guardian.co.uk/comment/story/0,3604,1555724,00.html.

[36] The text of Donald Rumsfeld's "war-on-terror memo," dated October 16, 2003, was published in *USA Today*, May 20, 2005, www.usatoday.com/news/washington/executive/rumsfeld-memo.htm.

constraints when threatened, but, as we have seen, only at some loss of both power and influence. The pressing challenge for the United States in the new era of vulnerability is how to tend to its national interest without calling into question its commitment to international norms of order. Under the Obama administration, the United States needs to make greater use of its soft power, diminishing its overuse of hard power.

13   Redrawing the Soviet power line: Gorbachev and the end of the Cold War

Deborah Welch Larson and Alexei Shevchenko

Between 1985 and 1991, the foundation of Soviet foreign policy changed from a Marxist-Leninist view of inevitable conflict between capitalism and socialism to an idealist vision of cooperation between states in solving global problems. Mikhail S. Gorbachev fundamentally altered Soviet foreign-policy theory and practice by adopting the ideals of the New Thinking, including global interdependence, universal human values, the balance of interests, and freedom of choice. Nor was this just rhetoric; he accepted the dismantling of Soviet medium-range missiles in Europe and asymmetric reductions in Soviet conventional forces, withdrew support from communist movements, and helped mediate an end to regional conflicts in the Third World. He applied the principle of freedom of choice to Eastern Europe, culminating in his decision to tolerate the fall of communism and to acquiesce to Germany's unification. The change in Soviet identity, in how the Soviet Union viewed itself in relation to the rest of the world and its mission in international politics, brought an abrupt end to the Cold War. For many observers the most striking aspect of the new Soviet identity was Gorbachev's and his comrades' determination to discard Soviet traditional *Realpolitik* without substituting any moderate, reformed version of realism for it.[1] What explains Gorbachev's adoption of an idealist view of the world and of the Soviet role within it?

Understanding the radical changes in Soviet foreign policy has both theoretical and practical significance. The Gorbachev revolution bears on the question of how states cope with a declining power position. Since the reformulation of Soviet identity was closely accompanied by a set of ideas, the New Thinking, the end of the Cold War has also been viewed as a test case for whether ideas such as the New Thinking are merely tools for pursuit of material interests or have independent causal influence. Some scholars argue that Gorbachev's adoption of the New

---

[1] Vladislav M. Zubok, *A Failed Empire: The Soviet Union in the Cold War from Stalin to Gorbachev* (Chapel Hill: University of North Carolina Press, 2007), pp. 309–10.

Thinking was caused by Soviet geopolitical overextension and economic decline, which provided incentives to reduce overseas involvements, cut defense spending, and conciliate the West. The New Thinking rationalized policies made necessary by material pressures due to the imbalance between Soviet commitments and capabilities, exacerbated by a declining economy.[2] Ideational theorists, on the other hand, maintain that material pressures did not uniquely determine Gorbachev's foreign-policy posture. These scholars have given an important causal role to a variety of ideational variables including cognitive learning, political entrepreneurship, transnational networks, and socialization to Western norms and values.[3] From a policy standpoint, whether the Soviet Union was forced by lagging economic growth rates and strategic overextension to end the Cold War is relevant for dealing with major powers that

[2] William C. Wohlforth, "Realism and the End of the Cold War," *International Security* 19 (1994/95), 91–129; Dale Copeland, "Trade Expectations and the Outbreak of Peace: Détente 1970–1974, and the End of the Cold War, 1985–1991," *Security Studies* 9 (1999/2000), 15–59; Stephen G. Brooks and William C. Wohlforth, "Power, Globalization and the End of the Cold War: Evaluating a Landmark Case for Ideas," *International Security* 25 (2000/01), 5–53; Randall L. Schweller and William C. Wohlforth, "Power Test: Evaluating Realism in Response to the End of the Cold War," *Security Studies* 9 (2001), 60–107; William C. Wohlforth, "The End of the Cold War as a Hard Case for Ideas," *Journal of Cold War Studies* 7 (2005), 165–73.

[3] Jeffrey T. Checkel, "Ideas, Institutions, and the Gorbachev Foreign Policy Revolution," *World Politics* 45 (1993), 271–300; Jeffrey T. Checkel, *Ideas and International Political Change: Soviet/Russian Behavior and the End of the Cold War* (New Haven: Yale University Press, 1997); Sarah Mendelson, "Internal Battles and External Wars: Politics, Learning, and the Soviet Withdrawal from Afghanistan," *World Politics* 45 (1993), 327–60; Sarah Mendelson, *Changing Course: Ideas, Politics, and the Soviet Withdrawal from Afghanistan* (Princeton University Press, 1998); Richard Ned Lebow, "The Long Peace, the End of the Cold War, and the Failure of Realism," *International Organization* 48 (1994), 249–78; Thomas Risse-Kappen, "Ideas Do Not Float Freely: Transnational Coalitions, Domestic Structures, and the End of the Cold War," *International Organization* 48 (1994), 185–214; Robert Herman, "Identity, Norms, and National Security: The Soviet Foreign Policy Revolution and the End of the Cold War," in Peter J. Katzenstein (ed.), *The Culture of National Security* (New York: Columbia University Press, 1996), pp. 271–316; Matthew Evangelista, "The Paradox of State Strength: Transnational Relations, Domestic Structures, and Security Policy in Russia and the Soviet Union," *International Organization* 49 (1995), 1–38; Matthew Evangelista, *Unarmed Forces: The Transnational Movement to End the Cold War* (Ithaca: Cornell University Press, 1999); Matthew Evangelista, "Norms, Heresthetics and the End of the Cold War," *Journal of Cold War Studies* 3 (2001), 5–35; Andrew Bennett, *Condemned to Repetition? The Rise, Fall, and Reprise of Soviet-Russian Military Interventionism, 1973–1996* (Cambridge, MA: MIT Press, 1999); Robert D. English, *Russia and the Idea of the West: Gorbachev, Intellectuals, and the End of the Cold War* (New York: Columbia University Press, 2000); Robert D. English, "Power, Ideas, and New Evidence on the Cold War's End: A Reply to Brooks and Wohlforth," *International Security* 26 (2002), 70–92; Robert D. English, "The Sociology of New Thinking: Elites, Identity Change, and the End of the Cold War," *Journal of Cold War Studies* 7 (2005), 43–80.

might challenge the West in contemporary international politics, for if hard-line policies led to Soviet accommodation, then a similar stance might be useful today. On the other hand, if the Soviet identity transformation was not predetermined by material and geopolitical pressures, then more sophisticated approaches are needed.

While illuminating the external context of Gorbachev's reforms and the intellectual sources of many of his innovations, neither materialist analyses nor ideational accounts explain why Gorbachev adopted the radical New Thinking instead of more conventional alternatives that would have led to different foreign policies. Material pressures are insufficient to explain why Gorbachev went so dramatically beyond *Realpolitik* retrenchment from areas where Soviet power was overextended instead of opting for some new version of the Soviet détente policy of the 1970s. Ideational explanations, on the other hand, do not identify the precise mechanism driving the selection of particular ideas, which could account for the appeal of the New Thinking ideas to Gorbachev and his advisers.[4]

We argue that Gorbachev and like-minded associates chose the idealistic New Thinking over competing foreign-policy programs because it offered a new global mission that would enhance Soviet international status while preserving a distinctive national identity. In the early 1980s, the Soviet Union possessed all the conventional elements of power – a sizable nuclear arsenal, huge conventional forces, and a territorial empire in Eastern Europe – but still was not accepted as a diplomatic or political equal by the United States and other advanced Western industrial powers. Recognizing that military power alone did not confer political influence or acceptance, Gorbachev and his advisers sought to attain a new status for the Soviet Union as the moral and political leader of a new international order, shaped according to the principles of the New Thinking. This new identity based on "soft power"[5] would have allowed the Soviet Union (and Russia) to achieve the status of a great power without first attaining a level of economic and technological development comparable to that of the United States; it was a shortcut to greatness.

Our explanation for the Soviet foreign-policy revolution draws on social identity theory (SIT) from social psychology.[6] By grounding

---

[4] For a recent promising attempt to overcome this problem see English, "The Sociology of New Thinking."

[5] Joseph S. Nye, *Bound to Lead: The Changing Nature of American Power* (New York: Basic Books, 1990) and *Soft Power: The Means to Success in World Politics* (New York: Public Affairs, 2004).

[6] Seminal works on social identity theory include Henri Tajfel (ed.), *Differentiation between Social Groups: Studies in the Social Psychology of Intergroup Relations* (London: Academic

our argument in SIT, we are able to draw on a well-established theoretical framework that has been tested in numerous experiments and field studies. Social identity theory holds that people form part of their image of who they are from their membership in social groups. The group's achievements reflect back on individual members, providing them with self-esteem. Accordingly, people prefer to belong to higher-status groups. Groups may deal with potential threats to their identity by pursuing any of several strategies: (1) trying to join the higher-status group (social mobility); (2) competing for status with the superior group (social competition); or (3) finding a new domain in which to be preeminent (social creativity). Becoming a "soft power" fits the third strategy.

This chapter is a "plausibility probe"[7] to determine whether it might be worthwhile to apply SIT with its focus on identity and status concerns to other cases in which states' foreign policies are either more ambitious or more cautious than would be expected given their relative power position. SIT implies that a state's foreign policy is influenced by its image of itself and of where it should stand in the global power hierarchy. Because status is subjective and dynamic, and because status-seeking behavior aims to achieve positive recognition from others, material benefits are important only insofar as they affect others' perceptions and evaluations. Material power and status thus should not be conflated as they are in most realist writings, and status-seeking actions should be distinguished from the search for raw-material power. Consequently, foreign policies of a state searching for enhanced international status recognition can diverge dramatically from the logic of realist paradigm "power lines" mandated by national material capabilities.

Our argument proceeds as follows. First, we consider what realist theory would predict for Gorbachev's foreign policy in light of Soviet economic decline and strategic overextension. We argue that material factors would predict unilateral retrenchment or diplomatic Realpolitik rather than the ambitious effort by Gorbachev to reshape the norms

---

Press, 1978); Henri Tajfel and John C. Turner, "An Integrative Theory of Intergroup Conflict," in William G. Austin and Stephen Worchel (eds.), *The Social Psychology of Intergroup Relations* (Monterey, CA: Brooks/Cole, 1979), pp. 33–47; and Henri Tajfel, *Human Groups and Social Categories* (Cambridge University Press, 1981). For applications of social identity theory to international relations, see Jonathan Mercer, "Anarchy and Identity," *International Organization* 49 (1995), 299–52; Deborah Welch Larson and Alexei Shevchenko, "Shortcut to Greatness: The New Thinking and the Revolution in Soviet Foreign Policy," *International Organization* 57 (2003), 77–109.

[7] Harry Eckstein, "Case Study and Theory in Political Science," in Fred I. Greenstein and Nelson W. Polsby (eds.), *Handbook of Political Science*, vol. VII, *Strategies of Inquiry* (Reading, MA: Addison Wesley Press, 1975), pp. 79–137.

underlying the international system represented by the "New Thinking." Second, we present an interrelated set of hypotheses from SIT on the strategies that disadvantaged groups have used to achieve a more positive social identity. Third, we use these hypotheses to explain the New Thinking as an effort to enhance Soviet prestige and standing in the world despite the Soviet Union's relative inferiority in economic growth rates and technological development. We argue that the New Thinking is part of a historic pattern in which Russian rulers sought great-power status despite their country's relative backwardness by taking shortcuts to development and reevaluating deficiencies as a source of strength. In the conclusions, we draw out implications of our argument for the debate over the relative influence of material and non-material factors in bringing about the revolution in Soviet foreign policy. We also propose that concern for identity and status continues to play an important role in the foreign policies of rising and declining powers, one that should be addressed by the international community.

Realistic power line and Gorbachev's foreign policy

The Soviet Union's declining power position

According to an influential materialist interpretation, Gorbachev adopted the New Thinking in response to Moscow's deteriorating geopolitical position and economic decline. The Reagan administration's heavy arms spending and stepped-up covert operations in the Third World threatened to undermine the hard-won achievement of Soviet parity.[8] The Soviet Union not only could not match US defense increases, but it was having a hard time holding on to its empire. The rate of Soviet economic growth had begun to decline in 1960 and dropped precipitously beginning in the mid-1970s, which meant that military expenditures consumed an increasing proportion of the gross national product (GNP). The burden of subsidizing Soviet allies in Eastern Europe and propping up unreliable Third World clients was increasing when the Soviet economy could no longer support such expenditures without some strain.[9] Compounding the decline in the Soviets' position relative to the West was their failure to participate in the most recent

[8] Wohlforth, "Realism and the End of the Cold War"; Robert G. Patman, "Reagan, Gorbachev and the Emergence of 'New Political Thinking,'" *Review of International Studies* 25 (1999), 577–601.
[9] Hannes Adomeit, *Imperial Overstretch: Germany in Soviet Policy from Stalin to Gorbachev* (Baden-Baden: Nomos Verlagsgesellschaft, 1998), pp. 145, 147–48; Schweller and Wohlforth, "Power Test," 86–87; Brooks and Wohlforth, "Power, Globalization and the End of the Cold War," 16–17, 22–23.

scientific-technological revolution in information and microelectron-
ics, a lag that also impaired the competitiveness of the Soviets' military
sector.[10] The budgetary costs of maintaining the foreign-policy status
quo – the arms race, regional conflicts in the Third World, and the
Soviet sphere of influence in Eastern Europe – exceeded income by a
growing margin.[11]

To improve economic productivity and use resources more efficiently,
the Soviet Union needed to become more fully integrated into the world
economy, reduce defense spending, and acquire advanced technology
from the West.[12] Gorbachev supposedly adopted the New Thinking to
rationalize policies of retrenchment and accommodation of the West to
domestic and foreign audiences. Just as the "Old Thinking" image of
a world divided into capitalist and socialist camps rationalized policies
of economic autarky and military mobilization, so the ideals of interdependence and the priority of universal values supported policies of
economic openness and détente with the West.[13] Promoting such ideas
as common security and interdependence would also establish a more
benign image for the Soviet Union in the West, undermine Western
unity, and induce the United States to allow more trade and technology
exchanges.[14]

It is important to realize that such explanations of the end of the
Cold War are based in large measure on the post-1988 Soviet steep
economic decline which, materialists argue, was pre-ordained by
structural deficiencies of the Soviet economy. Materialist explanations are also powerfully shaped by the Soviet Union's subsequent
collapse, a fact which generates a powerful "certainty of hindsight
bias" – a false sense of inevitability produced by the knowledge of the
outcome.[15] A key flaw of such logic is that it ignores the possibility

---

[10] Brooks and Wohlforth, "Power, Globalization and the End of the Cold War," 26–27.
[11] Wohlforth, "Realism and the End of the Cold War," 113–14; Schweller and Wohlforth, "Power Test," 88–89.
[12] Jack Snyder, "The Gorbachev Revolution: A Waning of Soviet Expansionism?" *International Security* 21 (1987/88), 109–17; Snyder, *Myths of Empire*, pp. 250–54; Brooks and Wohlforth, "Power, Globalization and the End of the Cold War," 32–33, 37–42; Copeland, "Trade Expectations and the Outbreak of Peace."
[13] Snyder, "The Gorbachev Revolution," 109–10, 115–16; Snyder, *Myths of Empire*, pp. 250–54; Mendelson, *Changing Course*.
[14] Wohlforth, "Realism and the End of the Cold War," 111; Brooks and Wohlforth, "Power, Globalization and the End of the Cold War," 32, 40; Schweller and Wohlforth, "Power Test," 91.
[15] See Richard Ned Lebow and Janice Gross Stein, "Understanding the End of the Cold War as a Non-Linear Confluence," in Richard K. Herrmann and Richard Ned Lebow (eds.), *Ending the Cold War: Interpretations, Causation, and the Study of International Relations* (New York: Palgrave Macmillan, 2004), pp. 189–218 and English, "Power, Ideas, and New Evidence on the Cold War's End," 88, fn. 61.

that the Soviets' rapid decline was caused primarily by contingent and idiosyncratic factors, such as Gorbachev's misguided domestic choices. It also fails to consider what the potential alternatives to the Soviets' 1985–88 domestic policies could have yielded.[16]

For example, there is some evidence that a policy of Chinese-style reforms combining marketization with strong authoritarian political and macroeconomic controls was a viable (and, probably, the most sensible) scenario for Soviet economic reforms.[17] By the time Gorbachev came to power Chinese reforms were having remarkable success, and the Soviet leaders could not ignore their demonstration effect. As earlier Eastern European reforms, the Chinese experience demonstrated that reforming the service and agricultural sectors was much simpler than implementing meaningful industrial reforms, and that such measures quickly delivered benefits for the population. It would have been logical for the Soviet reform to start in a similar manner. For example, the potential benefit of quick and efficient reform of agricultural production was clearly suggested by the impressive record of the tiny "individual plots" of land belonging to Soviet residents.[18] Equally important, Chinese-style fiscal decentralization would have drastically changed the Soviet bureaucracy's incentive structure by playing to the interests of the regional party and state cadres who were heavily dominated by Moscow ministries and had no independent taxing or money-allocation powers.[19] Some of the active participants in Soviet politics in the 1970s and 1980s suggest in their memoirs that there was a chance that the Soviet Union would adopt elements of the Chinese reform model. For example, based on his meetings with Yuri Andropov (the man who promoted Gorbachev to the top of the Soviet power ladder) during his tenure as General Secretary (1982–84), Nikolai Ryzhkov (at that time Central Committee secretary in charge of the Economic Department) was confident that, had Andropov lived for five more years, he would have introduced "something close to the Chinese variant with, of course, Russian specifics ... a model in which the fundamental problems are under government control and the market system

---

[16] For a similar criticism see English, "The Sociology of New Thinking," 70.

[17] For an early analysis pointing to Gorbachev's (and Yeltsin's) lost opportunities for adopting Chinese-style reform measures see Marshall I. Goldman, *Lost Opportunity: Why Economic Reforms in Russia Have Not Worked* (New York: W. W. Norton, 1994), pp. 190–212. See also Jerry Hough, *Democratization and Revolution in the USSR, 1985–1991* (Washington, DC: Brookings Institution Press, 1997).

[18] Alexander Shubin, *Istoki Perestroiki, 1978–1984* [The Origins of Perestroika, 1978–1984] (Moscow, 1997), vol. I, p. 62.

[19] Cameron Ross, *Local Government in the Soviet Union: Problems of Implementation and Control* (New York: St. Martin's Press, 1987), chps. 4 and 5.

spins around it."[20] Andropov was also well known for his sympathy and support for Janos Kadar's successful partial market economic reforms in Hungary.

Gorbachev's unwillingness to implement Chinese-style reforms ultimately doomed the system he intended to refurbish, not to destroy. After the program of "acceleration" failed due to the weakened mobilizational capacity of the Soviet regime, Gorbachev and his team made a fatal mistake of not providing clear-cut economic incentives for party–state officials to embrace a packet of relatively modest market reforms (perestroika). To make matters even worse for the fortunes of the Soviet system, instead of attempting to come up with a more efficient incentive structure for his agents, Gorbachev began to interpret their lack of enthusiasm for his reforms as organized "direct sabotage" of perestroika policies.[21] Gorbachev's disillusionment with the Soviet bureaucracy ultimately led to political and administrative reforms undermining Soviet centralized controls. Unfortunately, with the party's and branch ministries' withdrawal from economic management and decision-making Gorbachev and his allies successively lost control over revenues and spending, state enterprises, the banking system, foreign trade, credit, money, and wages. Once the Soviet system for economic coordination and correction of economic blunders was undermined, the Gorbachev team's numerous economic mistakes (such as policies that led to severe monetary imbalances)[22] created a vicious circle from which the Soviet economy never managed to escape. Successful application of the Chinese-style reform program, a less cavalier attitude toward macroeconomic controls, and lack of the confusion about the lines of political authority in the Soviet system would have almost certainly produced dramatically different results.

So would a selection of a more conservative top party leader in 1985, such as Gorbachev's close rivals for the post of the Communist Party of the Soviet Union (CPSU) General Secretary, Moscow party boss Victor Grishin or the CPSU Central Committee military industry secretary Grigory Romanov, who were likely at best only to tinker with the Soviet economic system. In the absence of significant positive economic developments (but also without the severe organizational

---

[20] Nikolai I. Ryzhkov, *Ia iz Partii po Imeni "Rossiya"* [I Am from the Party Named "Russia"] (Moscow: Obosrevatel', 1995), pp. 314–15. See also Nikolai Ryzhkov, *Desiat' Let Velikikh Potryasenii* [Ten Years of Major Shocks] (Moscow: Assotsiatsiya Kniga, Prosveshenie, Miloserdie, 1995), p. 50.

[21] Mikhail Gorbachev, *Zhizn' i Reformy* [Life and Reforms] (Moscow: Novosti, 1995), vol. I, pp. 297–98, 305–06.

[22] Anders Aslund, *Gorbachev's Struggle for Economic Reform* (Ithaca: Cornell University Press, 1991).

shocks dealt by Gorbachev's reforms), the post-1985 USSR could have continued to muddle through for at least a decade before economic stagnation jeopardized the system.[23] Even then, the Soviet economy could have stayed afloat for a protracted period by relying on energy resources and raw materials. The experience of post-Soviet Russia, which only in 2006 reached the GDP level attained before the onset of Gorbachev's reforms[24] and in significant measure relies on exports of natural resources for its economic livelihood, provides further evidence that a "getting-by" scenario was viable.

Materialists argue that Gorbachev moved to more radical foreign-policy reforms and unilateral concessions in 1988–89 after he embraced more radical domestic reforms to save the Soviet economy from imminent collapse,[25] but this assertion, which is crucial for the "power-line" paradigm, ignores substantial evidence that Gorbachev adopted the New Thinking before Soviet elites recognized the seriousness of Soviet economic problems.[26] In fact, Gorbachev presented its basic tenets in 1986–87, when his domestic economic policies were still in the traditional "command-administrative" framework and Soviet policy-makers had not yet accepted more radical economic ideas.[27] In that sense, it is difficult to explain Gorbachev's foreign-policy initiatives as driven by Soviet economic decline. While the Soviet leadership was certainly aware by the mid-1980s that Soviet economic growth rates had declined,[28] Gorbachev and his colleagues did not believe that the

[23] Vladimir Kontorovich, "The Economic Fallacy," *The National Interest* (1993), 35–45.

[24] Stefan Hedlund, "Such a Beautiful Dream: How Russia Did *Not* Become a Market Economy," *The Russian Review* 67 (2008), 187–208.

[25] Schweller and Wohlforth, "Power Test," 90; Brooks and Wohlforth, "Power, Globalization and the End of the Cold War," 31; Stephen G. Brooks and William C. Wohlforth, "Economic Constraints and the End of the Cold War," in William C. Wohlforth (ed.), *Cold War Endgame: Oral History, Analysis, Debates* (University Park: Pennsylvania State University Press, 2003), p. 285.

[26] For thoughtful criticism of materialist explanations see English, "The Sociology of New Thinking," 68–71 and "Power, Ideas, and New Evidence on the Cold War's End."

[27] The new General Secretary's first major strategy announcement was the neo-Andropovian "acceleration" of economic growth, to be achieved by a massive shift of investment into the machine-building sector, the standard policy for a centrally planned economy since Stalin's industrialization. The 1986–90 Five Year Plan gave priority to investment in high-technology sectors, which in the Soviet economy were administratively subordinated to the military and provided their needs. Acceleration was supposed to be accompanied by tightening work discipline and a strict anti-alcoholism campaign.

[28] For evidence from the declassified transcripts of CPSU Politburo meetings in the early to mid-1980s, see Mark Kramer, "Ideology and the Cold War," *Review of International Studies* 25 (1999), 539–76.

problems with the Soviet economy had reached crisis proportions.[29] Describing the beginning of the reforms in his memoirs, Gorbachev admitted that neither he nor his colleagues attributed the country's economic problems to "inherent properties of the system."[30] In a February 1987 memo to Gorbachev, New Thinker Alexander Yakovlev criticized the "grave miscalculation of American Sovietology" in assuming either that the Soviet economy was "approaching the brink of an avalanche-like crisis" or that increasing "economic, scientific-technological, and social backwardness" would cause the loss of the Soviet Union's "material prospects for development as a world power."[31]

It is certainly possible that the Soviet top officials would have been more humble had they not been misled by phony official statistics that overstated Soviet economic growth rates in the 1970s and 1980s.[32] Nevertheless, relative power considerations can only influence policy decisions if they are perceived and taken into consideration by political elites. Moreover, while providing a much bleaker picture than the official Soviet estimates at the time, Central Intelligence Agency (CIA) and Soviet Gorbachev-era estimates demonstrate that the now popular perception of the Soviet Union as being on the verge of crisis in the mid-1980s is largely exaggerated. The data indicate that the most dramatic drop in the Soviet growth rate occurred during the first half of the 1970s. By contrast, the decline from then up to the beginning of the Gorbachev period was less dramatic.[33]

While aware of many deficiencies of the Soviet economy, Gorbachev was bullish about Soviet economic possibilities as demonstrated by his ambitious economic policies that coincided with the adoption of the New Thinking ideas. The Soviet economy entered the 1980s bearing

---

[29] Michael Ellman and Vladimir Kontorovich, "The Collapse of the Soviet System and the Memoir Literature," *Europe–Asia Studies* 49 (1997), 262; Checkel, *Ideas and International Political Change*, p. 79.

[30] Mikhail Gorbachev, *Memoirs* (New York: Doubleday, 1995), p. 250; Evangelista, *Unarmed Forces*, p. 255.

[31] Alexander Yakovlev, Memorandum for Gorbachev, "Toward an Analysis of the Fact of the Visit of Prominent American Political Leaders to the USSR (Kissinger, Vance, Kirkpatrick, Brown, and others)," February 25, 1987, NSA Briefing Book No. 238, www.gwu.edu/~nsarchiv/NSAEVV/NSAEVV238/index.htm.

[32] Michael Ellman and Vladimir Kontorovich (eds.), *The Destruction of the Soviet Economic System: An Insider's History* (Armonk, NY: M. E. Sharpe, 1998), pp. 70–76.

[33] For example, according to the estimates of prominent economist Gregory Khanin (whose work with the Soviet economic statistics produced much *lower* estimates than the CIA's for the period of the 1970s and early 1980s), the national income growth rate swung from –2 percent a year in 1981–82 to 1.8 percent in 1983–88. Income per capita was growing in 1983–88 at an annual rate of 0.8 percent. Gregory Khanin, "Economic Growth in the 1980s," in Michael Ellman and Valdimir Kontorovich (eds.), *The Disintegration of the Soviet Economic System* (London: Routledge, 1992).

a heavy burden of unresolved problems, including the quality of labor; the quality of goods; the wasteful utilization of resources; a huge number of unfinished construction projects; backward agriculture; exports heavily skewed toward a few raw materials; and strong dependence on the import of grain, consumer goods, and technology. It was also clear that the oil price boom was over and world fuel prices were likely to drop. That pushed the Soviet economic bureaucracy to favor a very cautious scenario for the country's development during the Twelfth Five Year Plan (1986–90) and up to 2000. This, however, was too slow and unimpressive for Gorbachev. Taking a page from Khrushchev's book, Gorbachev insisted on a 2.5-fold growth of labor productivity in 1986–2000, which meant attaining by the end of the century the US labor productivity of the early 1980s. Gorbachev also seriously believed in the possibility of catching up with the United States in industrial production output by 2000.[34]

Arguments emphasizing the Cold War geopolitical challenges ignore the fact that considerable Western pressure on the Soviet Union had been present since the last stages of the Brezhnev regime, yet his successors prior to Gorbachev opted for a belligerent response to the US hard-line strategy. Under Andropov and Chernenko, Moscow not only left the negotiating table in 1983 but also accelerated the production and deployment of new nuclear weapons.[35] In fact, Soviet hard-liners' influence was actually bolstered by Reagan's "full court press" on the Soviet Union in the 1980s, and this complicated the political ascent of the young and inexperienced Gorbachev whom conservatives distrusted and feared.[36] The US Strategic Defensive Initiative (SDI), though potentially troubling to

---

[34] The first version of the "Concept of Economic and Social Development to the Year 2000" sent to the Soviet leadership in September 1984 projected the average annual growth rate of national income as 2.8–3.2 percent for 1986–2000. The growth of investment for each five-year period was estimated at no more than 7–9 percent. Converting these figures to the methods used by the CIA would imply a rate of GNP growth no higher than 1.5 percent per year for 1986–2000. When Gorbachev came to power he almost immediately insisted on increasing planned investment growth to 12–15 then 20–22 percent. GNP growth was projected at 5 percent by 2000. See Gennady Zoteev, "The View from Gosplan: Growth to the Year 2000," in Ellman and Kontorovich (eds.), *The Destruction of the Soviet Economic System*, pp. 85–94 and Vitaly Vorotnikov, *A Bylo Eto Tak ... iz Dnevnika Chlena Politbyuro TsK KPSS* [That's How It Happened ... From the Diary of the Member of the CC of the CPSU] (Moscow: Soviet Veteranov Knigoizdaniya, 1995), p. 28.

[35] Ted Hopf, "Peripheral Visions: Brezhnev and Gorbachev Meet the Reagan Doctrine," in George W. Breslauer and Philip E. Tetlock (eds.), *Learning in U.S. and Soviet Foreign Policy* (Boulder: Westview Press, 1991), pp. 586–629; Michael McGwire, *Perestroika and Soviet National Security* (Washington, DC: Brookings Institution, 1991), chps. 5 and 10.

[36] English, "The Sociology of New Thinking," 54. On the relationship between Gorbachev and the conservative old guard in Soviet leadership, see Valery Boldin, *Ten*

the Soviets in a military sense, remained largely a political issue through-out the 1980s. In addition, the majority of Soviet scientists and military strategists considered an asymmetrical (cheap and not technologically sophisticated) response to the SDI to be quite viable.[37]

Overall, it is clear that the selection of the new Soviet leader in March 1985 was based almost exclusively on Soviet domestic political consid-erations, not on the need to select an overseer of Soviet geopolitical retrenchment.[38] Consistent with a lack of urgency, Gorbachev initially did not alter the traditional priority given to the military and heavy industry in Soviet economic planning and investment, despite the unusually high toll that defense spending exacted on the Soviet econ-omy.[39] He did not reduce Soviet military research and development and production, or force deployments.[40] He did not launch a policy of cut-ting military expenditures to facilitate perestroika until the Politburo meeting of November 3, 1988, on the eve of his historic address to the United Nations.[41] The Soviet Union also did not reduce its costly for-eign and military assistance programs to Third World clients such as Syria, Ethiopia, and Nicaragua until 1990.[42]

Another problem with materialist explanations is that, in general, Gorbachev's foreign policy was not well-suited for alleviating Soviet economic problems and was far too ambitious in scope for a power in relative decline. Gorbachev actively promoted a set of norms to reori-ent the international system from ideological rivalry and geopolitical competition to common human values and international cooperation in addressing global problems. The disarmament initiatives and pol-itical concessions made by Gorbachev did not address the Soviet Union's excessive defense spending and overseas involvements. Nuclear

---

Years That Shook the World: The Gorbachev Era as Witnessed by His Chief of Staff (New York: Basic Books, 1994), p. 53.

[37] See Roald Sagdeev, *The Making of a Soviet Scientist: My Adventures in Nuclear Fusion and Space from Stalin to Star Wars* (New York: Wiley, 1994), p. 268.

[38] Archie Brown, *The Gorbachev Factor* (Oxford University Press, 1996) and "Gorbachev and the End of the Cold War," in Herrmann and Lebow (eds.), *Ending the Cold War*, pp. 31–58.

[39] Around 15–20 percent of GDP in the early 1980s. See Noel E. Firth and James H. Noren, *Soviet Defense Spending: A History of CIA Estimates* (Houston: Texas A & M University Press, 1998); Clifford Gaddy, *The Price of the Past* (Washington, DC: Brookings Institution Press, 1997).

[40] Robert M. Gates, *From the Shadows* (New York: Simon & Schuster, 1996), pp. 335–36.

[41] Anatoly Chernyaev, *Shest' Let s Gorbachevym: Po Dnevnikovym Zapisiam* [Six Years with Gorbachev] (Moscow: Kultura nyaev, 1993), pp. 255–56; Evangelista, *Unarmed Forces*, p. 255.

[42] Odd Arne Westad, *The Global Cold War: Third World Interventions and the Making of Our Times* (Cambridge University Press, 2005), p. 384; Zubok, *Failed Empire*, pp. 299, 308.

weapons – the focus of Gorbachev's disarmament initiatives in the first part of his tenure – were a relatively small component of the overall Soviet defense budget and at least in the short term, dismantling existing weapons and verification cost more than maintaining them. Gorbachev wanted to avert a new arms race over the US SDI, but heading off future competition did nothing to reduce current defense spending.

If Gorbachev's foreign policy did not seem to be motivated by the need for retrenchment, neither were his efforts at accommodation. Contrary to what one might expect if Soviet foreign policy was motivated by economic need, Gorbachev did not use his arms-control initiatives and flexible diplomacy to induce the United States to relax its policy of economic containment. While Gorbachev sometimes complained about discriminatory US trade policies, in making critical decisions paving the road to the end of the Cold War, he did not bargain for economic *quid pro quo* such as technological assistance, trade concessions, or membership of economic institutions in return for arms control and other political concessions.[43]

We do not, of course, deny that Gorbachev's foreign policy was influenced by his desire to reform the economy so that it could support the Soviet Union's aspirations to be a great power. Soviet reformers themselves have frequently stated that they needed a more tranquil international environment in order to carry out domestic economic restructuring in the Soviet Union. But achieving this objective did not require Gorbachev and his advisers to choose radical ideas over others that would have led to very different foreign policies. Perhaps the best evidence that Gorbachev did not have to adopt the New Thinking in response to geopolitical and economic pressures is that he considered and ultimately rejected plausible alternative foreign-policy ideas that would have facilitated his domestic economic reforms.

New Thinking and its alternatives

More in line with the Soviet Union's relative power position were two alternatives that Gorbachev considered and rejected.[44] There was also

---

[43] Thomas Risse, "The Cold War's Endgame and German Unification (A Review Essay)," *International Security* 21 (1997), 167–68. After a meeting with Helmut Kohl in February 1990 at which Gorbachev conceded German unity, Horst Teltschik, Kohl's chief foreign policy adviser, commented in his diary, "Gorbachev does not commit himself to a specific solution; no demand of a price, and certainly no threat. What a meeting!" Quoted in Adomeit, *Imperial Overstretch*, p. 488.

[44] For an in-depth analysis of potential alternatives to the New Thinking, see Robert Herman, *Ideas, Identity and Redefinition of Interests: The Political and Intellectual Origins of the Soviet Foreign Policy Revolution*, unpublished Ph.D. dissertation,

considerable support for a return to Soviet hard-line policies, despite unfavorable economic trends. The first alternative, a *détente-plus* strategy,[45] favored reducing defense spending and overseas commitments somewhat until the Soviet Union had recovered its power, then resuming expansion. Such a strategy could have enabled Gorbachev to carry out cautious domestic economic reforms without endangering the Soviet empire. A prudent conservative leader could have improved the Soviet economic situation substantially without making major changes in foreign-policy priorities by cutting defense spending sharply – by 10–20 percent or, reasonably, much more – and seeking an expansion of East–West trade and technological cooperation. Deep Soviet arms cuts need not have worsened the Soviet security position, because even a minimum number of nuclear weapons would have guaranteed the state's territorial integrity. Unilateral arms cuts quite possibly would have induced comparable cuts in Western spending, as actually happened under Gorbachev in 1989. Soviet retrenchment from the Third World could have been justified with a few doctrinal modifications, as had been done repeatedly and relatively painlessly in the history of the USSR.[46] Deputy Director of the CIA Robert Gates believed that Gorbachev was pursuing such a strategy, seeking a "breathing space" in which to make the Soviet Union a "more competitive and stronger adversary in the years ahead."[47]

Adjusting Soviet foreign policy in accordance with a *détente-plus* power line was not only a sensible response to Soviet international woes, but also a genuinely popular idea among the Soviet elite.[48] It was associated with the modest program of domestic economic reforms inaugurated during the brief tenure of Yuri Andropov (November 1982–February 1984) as the Soviet top leader. Since Gorbachev was closely associated with Andropov – having been promoted by him into the senior leadership and blessed as heir-apparent – the *détente-plus* scenario was in fact what the Soviet top leaders expected Gorbachev to implement when

---

Cornell University (1996). See also English, *Russia and the Idea of the West*, pp. 229–30.

[45] The term *"détente plus"* is used by Herman in "Identity, Norms and National Security."

[46] Ellman and Kontorovich, "The Collapse of the Soviet System and the Memoir Literature," 265; Westad, *The Global Cold War*, pp. 380–81.

[47] Robert M. Gates, Memorandum for the President, "Gorbachev's Gameplan: The Long View," November 24, 1987, in Svetlana Savranskaya and Thomas Blanton (eds.), *National Security Archive (NSA), Electronic Briefing Book (EBB) No. 238*, www.gwu8. edu/~nsarchiv/NSAEBB/NSAEBB238.index.htm.

[48] The *détente-plus* strategy was very influential among members of the Gorbachev Politburo. See Yegor Ligachev, *Inside Gorbachev's Kremlin* (New York: Random House, 1993).

they selected him as General Secretary. That Gorbachev's nomination was supported by Foreign Minister Andrei Gromyko, the ultimate gate-keeper of Soviet post-Stalin foreign policy, support which was crucial for Gorbachev's election to the post of General Secretary, is a sure indication that top Soviet leadership did not contemplate radical changes in Soviet foreign policy in early 1985. Not surprisingly, with the progress of the New Thinking revolution many of Gorbachev's early supporters would complain of Gorbachev's "betrayal" of their trust.[49]

A second vision of Soviet foreign policy criticized the traditional Soviet ideological approach to foreign policy as inefficient; it wasted valuable resources on weak Third World allies and provoked the emergence of an unprecedented threat from the antagonized West. These critics advocated abandoning Marxist-Leninist ideology as a guide to Soviet foreign policy in favor of a traditional Realpolitik interpretation of Soviet/Russian interests. Realpolitikers proposed such actions as swift rapprochement with the People's Republic of China (PRC), playing Western Europe off against the United States, negotiating territorial solutions with Japan in order to gain its assistance in solving problems in the Soviet economy, and withdrawal from Afghanistan.[50] The Soviets could have radically shifted their policy toward Japan – the key technological giant in the Western bloc – and negotiated for significant technological and economic assistance and investments in exchange for conceding the Kurile Islands.[51]

A third alternative differed from both *détente plus* and Realpolitik options in projecting a much harder power line for the Soviet Union. Leaders of the Soviet military-industrial complex, some of the top leadership of the KGB, and the neo-Stalinist wing within the CPSU favored increased defense expenditures with a focus on high-tech military technologies (including a Soviet version of the US "Star Wars" system) and an assertive neo-Stalinist anti-Western foreign policy. Contradicting expectations of the materialist arguments emphasizing the Soviet geopolitical predicament of the early 1980s, this group

---

[49] As one of the former Politburo supporters of Gorbachev, Geidar Aliev, complained later, "He did not turn out to be the man we'd voted for." Andrei Karaulov, *Vokrug Kremlya: Kniga Politicheskikh Dialogov* [Around the Kremlin: The Book of Political Dialogues] (Moscow: Novosti, 1990), vol. I, p. 268. Cited in English, "The Sociology of New Thinking," 55.

[50] These are the main points of an early April 1985 memo for Gorbachev authored by Georgy Arbatov, the leading specialist on the United States in the Soviet academic establishment. Quoted in Chernyaev, *Shest' Let s Gorbachevym*, p. 41. See also Herman, "Identity, Norms and National Security," p. 274.

[51] Thomas Forsberg, "Power, Interests and Trust: Explaining Gorbachev's Choices and the End of the Cold War," *Review of International Studies* 25 (1999), 603–21.

became especially powerful following the resumption of the Cold War confrontation under Reagan, utilizing the vacuum of power at the top of the Soviet political system in the wake of Andropov's death. As mentioned before, one of its preferred candidates from the younger generation of the Soviet leaders, Grigory Romanov, was a serious contender for the General Secretary post.[52]

A fourth vision, the New Thinking, while accepting some of the *détente plus* and Realpolitik criticisms of past Soviet foreign policy, advocated more far-reaching changes. The initial group of New Thinkers included Alexander Yakovlev, Georgy Shakhnazarov, Anatoly Chernyaev, Alexander Bovin, Evgeny Primakov, Vadim Zagladin, Alexei Arbatov, Oleg Bogomolov, Vyacheslav Dashichev, and other members of academic institutes (such as physicists Roald Sagdeev and Evgeny Velikhov), as well as the International Department of the Central Committee of the CPSU.[53] Future New Thinkers no longer saw the West as a political-ideological or geostrategic adversary. While differing on many specific points, the New Thinkers rejected the inevitability of conflict between capitalism and socialism and the class-based nature of international relations.[54] The New Thinking argued that the world was complex and interdependent. States had to cooperate in solving global problems such as the growing gap between rich and poor nations, nuclear war, and ecological disasters; universal values should have priority over class interests. Security was indivisible and could only be attained by political means. A comprehensive international security system should

---

[52] See English, "The Sociology of New Thinking," 51, 69. For some of the examples of the hardliner's views of foreign affairs, see recollections of the members of the senior Soviet military command cited in Ellman and Kontorovich (eds.), *The Destruction of the Soviet Economic System*, pp. 61–63.

[53] Views of this camp were espoused by such publications as *Moscow News*, *Ogonek*, *Novoye Vremya* [New Times], and foreign-policy specialist journals *MEiMO*, *SShA*, and *Mezhdunarodnaya Zhizn'* [International Affairs]. For detailed analysis of the institutions and development of the New Thinking in the Soviet Union, see Herman, *Ideas, Identity and Redefinition of Interests*; Checkel, *Ideas and International Political Change*; English, *Russia and the Idea of the West*.

[54] On the origins and development of New Thinking by some of its architects, see Mikhail Gorbachev, *Perestroika: New Thinking for Our Country and the World* (New York: Harper & Row, 1987); Gorbachev, *Memoirs*; Eduard Shevardnadze, *The Future Belongs to Freedom* (New York: Free Press, 1991); Chernyaev, *Shest' Let s Gorbachevym*; Georgy Shakhnazarov, *Tsena Svobody: Reformatsiya Gorbacheva Glazami Ego Pomosh'nika* [The Price of Freedom: Gorbachev's Reformation as Witnessed by His Aide] (Moscow: Rossika-Zevs, 1993); Evgeny Primakov, *Gody v Bol'shoi Politike* [Years inside Big Politics] (Moscow: Sovershenno Sekretno, 1999). For summaries of the New Thinking, see Bruce Parrott, "Soviet National Security under Gorbachev," *Problems of Communism* 37 (1988), 1–36; Stephen M. Meyer, "The Sources and Prospects of Gorbachev's New Political Thinking on Security," *International Security* 13 (1988), 124–63; Robert Legvold, "The Revolution in Soviet Foreign Policy," *Foreign Affairs* 68 (1988/89), 82–98; David Holloway, "Gorbachev's New Thinking,"

be created, one that would address states' economic, ecological, and humanitarian as well as political and military needs. Smaller states had to choose their own path of social development, while great powers no longer had the right to dictate to others how they should live. To achieve this new world order, the New Thinkers believed that the Soviet Union would have to act in a tutorial role, exercising moral leadership in persuading the West to abandon its "old" thinking and behavior.[55]

In summary, Gorbachev was presented with at least four distinct programs for his foreign policy. The radical version of the New Thinking to which Gorbachev and his followers eventually subscribed was not the most likely outcome of the Soviet foreign-policy transition given power realities, but triumphed against the odds and a majority of Soviet elite opinion.[56] Only a relative minority of the Soviet intelligentsia, its liberal-reformist wing of academia and foreign-policy experts, supported the global-integrationist outlook of the New Thinking.[57]

Materialist explanations also significantly understate the extent of the hard-line conservative opposition to Gorbachev's foreign-policy choices throughout his tenure in office. The "Old Thinkers," conservative members of the military and central party apparatus, attacked New Thinking ideas privately and publicly, delayed and obstructed negotiations with the US, attempted to upset Soviet–American relations, systematically exaggerated the Western threat, and opposed Gorbachev's military cuts. Given the centralized nature of Soviet politics and sheer scope of Gorbachev's personal power as the General Secretary, the degree of opposition to New Thinking was nothing short of remarkable, culminating in the anti-Gorbachev coup attempt in August 1991.[58]

Foreign Affairs 68 (1988/89), 66–81; V. Kubálková and A. A. Cruickshank, *Thinking New About Soviet "New Thinking"* (Berkeley: Institute of International Studies, University of California, 1989); Adomeit, *Imperial Overstretch*, p. 194.

[55] Kubálková and Cruickshank, *Thinking New*, pp. 30–31, 61; Herman, "Identity, Norms, and National Security," pp. 310–11; Lévesque, *The Enigma of 1989: The USSR and the Liberation of Eastern Europe* (Berkeley: University of California Press, 1997), p. 36, translated from French by Keith Martin.

[56] Raymond L. Garthoff, *The Great Transition: American–Soviet Relations and the End of the Cold War* (Washington, DC: Brookings Institution Press, 1994), pp. 773–74; English, *Russia and the Idea of the West*, pp. 13–14.

[57] Robert Legvold, "Soviet Learning in the 1980s," in Breslauer and Tetlock (eds.), *Learning in U.S. and Soviet Foreign Policy*, p. 704; Kubálková and Cruickshank, *Thinking New*, pp. 36–37; English, *Russia and the Idea of the West*, pp. 10, 235.

[58] For an excellent analysis and examples, see English, "Power, Ideas, and New Evidence on the Cold War's End." For multiple examples of opposition to the New Thinking, see William E. Odom, *The Collapse of the Soviet Military* (New Haven: Yale University Press, 1998); Shakhnazarov, *Tsena Svobody*; Chernyaev, *Shest' Let s Gorbachevym*; Georgy Kornienko, *Kholodnaya Voina. Svidetel'stvo ee Uchastnika* [The Cold War. Testimony of a Participant] (Moscow: Mezhdunarodnye Otnoshennia, 1994); and Jack F. Matlock, Jr., *Autopsy on an Empire: The American Ambassador's Account of the Collapse of the Soviet Union* (New York: Random House, 1995).

The presence of plausible alternatives and opposition to Gorbachev's policies prove that geopolitical and economic factors were not powerful enough to establish the elite's consensus on Soviet foreign policy.[59] The idea that almost any Soviet leader selected in 1985 would have pursued policies similar to Gorbachev, which is essentially what the "power-line" interpretation of the end of the Cold War claims, is thus not persuasive. In fact, it is almost inconceivable that any of Gorbachev's serious rivals in 1985 would have replicated his most important foreign-policy choices or conducted his liberalizing political domestic reforms. Serious consideration of counterfactual scenarios is a welcome and long overdue correction to the analytical shortcomings of the materialist interpretation of the end of the Cold War.[60]

In what follows we move beyond the power-line approach by incorporating ideational factors normally ignored by materialist explanations, such as Soviet international identity and status concerns. We argue that the crucial reason for the appeal of the New Thinking to Gorbachev and his advisers was that it would allow the Soviet Union to finally resolve its persistent status predicament in international politics and establish a positive international identity as a leader in constructing a new world order while at the same time creating a more benign international atmosphere for domestic reform. We now turn to social identity theory to show how status considerations shape identity and foreign policy.

Identity and status

People define part of their identity, their conception of who they are, by their membership of social groups, whether based on gender, ethnicity, nationality, religion, or occupation. A social identity is "that part of an individual's self-concept which derives from his knowledge of his membership of a social group (or groups) together with the value and emotional significance attached to that membership."[61]

Cognitive processes of categorization and social comparison encourage people to identify with their social group. In order to simplify reality,

---

[59] For evidence of the lack of consensus on the extent of Soviet economic decline, see testimonies of former Soviet officials quoted in Ellman and Kontorovich, (eds.), *The Destruction of the Soviet Economic System.*

[60] Robert English, "The Road(s) Not Taken: Causality and Contingency in Analysis of the Cold War's End," in Wohlforth (ed.), *Cold War Endgame*, pp. 243–72; Brown, "Gorbachev and the End of the Cold War"; and George W. Breslauer and Richard Ned Lebow, "Leadership and the End of the Cold War: A Counterfactual Thought Experiment," in Herrmann and Lebow (eds.), *Ending the Cold War*, pp. 161–88.

[61] Henri Tajfel, "The Psychological Structure of Intergroup Relations," in Tajfel (ed.), *Differentiation between Social Groups*, p. 63.

we perceive the world and partition experience in terms of categories, whether objects or groups. Social categorization helps define the individual's place within society; it furnishes expectations about the traits that others are likely to attribute to the person as well as how others will respond. To reduce the flood of outside information, people tend to overemphasize similarities within categories and exaggerate differences between categories, which means that they exaggerate the homogeneity of their own group and its distinctiveness from other groups. Categorization therefore tends to sharpen intergroup boundaries and to produce stereotyping, favoritism, and prejudice, even without any objective conflict of interest.[62]

Social comparisons provide a way for people to evaluate their group identity. The attributes of a group derive meaning from being compared to those of other groups. Overall, social groups – whether professions, jobs, races, universities, or ethnic groups – may be arrayed on a status hierarchy.[63] People generally choose to evaluate themselves and their group relative to similar or slightly higher reference groups.[64] India measures its economic development relative to Pakistan or China rather than Bangladesh. Similarly, Russia has long compared itself to European rather than Asian powers because Europe was perceived to be at a higher level of development. The Soviets also aspired to become a full-fledged member of the Western community of nations.[65] When Gorbachev traveled to Italy, France, Belgium, and the Federal Republic of Germany in the 1970s, his faith in the "superiority of socialist democracy" was shaken as he observed the functioning of civil society. He was most impressed that the people of Europe lived in better conditions and were better off than in the Soviet Union. "The question haunted

---

[62] Tajfel, "Psychological Structure of Intergroup Relations," pp. 63–64; Tajfel and Turner, "An Integrative Theory of Intergroup Conflict," p. 40; Michael A. Hogg and Dominic Abrams, *Social Identifications: A Social Psychology of Intergroup Relations and Group Processes* (London: Routledge, 1988), pp. 17, 19–20; Ad F. M. van Knippenberg, "Intergroup Differences in Group Perceptions," in Henri Tajfel (ed.), *The Social Dimension: European Developments in Social Psychology*, vol. II, ed. (Cambridge University Press, 1984), p. 561.

[63] Hogg and Abrams, *Social Identifications*, pp. 14, 26–27; Ad F. M. van Knippenberg and Naomi Ellemers, "Strategies in Intergroup Relations," in Michael A. Hogg and Dominic Abrams (eds.), *Group Motivation: Social Psychological Perspectives* (New York: Harvester Wheatsheaf, 1993), pp. 20–21.

[64] Tajfel, "Psychological Structure of Intergroup Relations," pp. 66–67; Rupert Brown and Gabi Haeger, "'Compared to What?' Comparison Choice in an Internation Context," *European Journal of Social Psychology* 29 (1999), 31–42.

[65] In contrast, Gorbachev's vision of the Asia-Pacific region as outlined at Vladivostok in July 1986 and Krasnoyarsk in September 1988 did not invoke the shared values of a "common home" theme. See Herman, "Identity, Norms, and National Security," p. 309, fn. 121.

me: why was the standard of living in our country lower than in other developed countries?"[66]

Social identity theory posits that groups strive for positive distinctiveness.[67] People prefer to belong to higher-status groups and they are reluctant to be identified with lower-status ones.[68] This is illustrated by a field study in which students were more likely to wear their university's clothes after their football team had won a game than when they had lost. When their school won, students referred to the team as "we," but as "they" when their team lost.[69] For committed group members, being distinctive from other groups is also important.[70] Applied to international relations, in an era of globalization where cultural differences are homogenized by economic competition, diffusion of technology, and global production, states still try to retain their national identities.

Members of disadvantaged groups may adopt any of three strategies to improve their position: social mobility, social competition, or social creativity, depending on whether group boundaries are perceived as permeable and the status hierarchy is regarded as stable and legitimate.[71] If the higher-status group's boundaries are open, individuals may strive for social mobility, to join the more privileged group by emulating its members. The ideal of social mobility through hard work is an ideal of Western culture, as in the man of humble origins who is elected president of the United States.[72]

When boundaries of the higher-status group are impermeable, and the status hierarchy is regarded as unstable or illegitimate, members of the inferior group may try to improve their status through social competition.[73] Denied recognition by the West as a major power despite

[66] Gorbachev, *Memoirs*, pp. 102–03.
[67] Tajfel and Turner, "An Integrative Theory of Intergroup Conflict," p. 40; van Knippenberg, "Intergroup Differences in Group Perceptions," p. 8.
[68] van Knippenberg and Ellemers, "Strategies in Intergroup Relations," p. 21.
[69] Robert B. Cialdini, R. J. Borden, A. Thorne, M. R. Walker, S. Freeman, and L. R. Sloan, "Basking in Reflected Glory: Three (Football) Field Studies," *Journal of Personality and Social Psychology* 34 (1976), 366–75.
[70] Naomi Ellemers, Russell Spears, and Bertjan Doosje, "Self and Social Identity," *Annual Review of Psychology* 53 (2002), 178.
[71] Tajfel, "Psychological Structure of Intergroup Relations"; Tajfel and Turner, "An Integrative Theory of Intergroup Conflict."
[72] Dominic Abrams and Michael A. Hogg, "An Introduction to the Social Identity Approach," in Michael A. Hogg (ed.), *Social Identity Theory: Constructive and Critical Advances* (New York: Harvester Wheatsheaf, 1990), pp. 4–5; Naomi Ellemers, Ad F. M. van Knippenberg, and Henk Wilke, "The Influence of Permeability of Group Boundaries and Stability of Group Status on Strategies of Individual Mobility and Social Change," *British Journal of Social Psychology* 29 (1993), 766–78.
[73] Tajfel, "Psychological Structure of Intergroup Relations," pp. 51–52; Tajfel and Turner, "An Integrative Theory of Intergroup Conflict"; John C. Turner, "Social

having adopted Western diplomatic, political, and economic institutions, in the early twentieth century Japan chose to compete with Western powers for imperial possessions, a major component of great-power status.[74]

But the status hierarchy may be stable and based on legitimate criteria. Under such conditions, groups whose identity is threatened by unfavorable comparisons may still maintain a positive self-image by taking a different perspective on their situation, thereby exercising social creativity.[75] Groups can redefine the value of what was considered to be a negative characteristic, as in the "gay pride" movement. One of the first uses of Japan's name, "land of the rising sun," is found in a letter dated 632 from the Japanese emperor to his Chinese counterpart, addressed to the "emperor of the land of the setting sun." Japan could turn its relative backwardness into an asset by portraying itself as a rising power that would eventually pass China.[76]

Alternatively, group members may find a new dimension on which their group excels. For example, a losing soccer team may console itself by saying "we are better sports" or "we played better as a team."[77] In a field study, Dutch students pursuing a practical technical education acknowledged that science students would have greater prestige and higher wages, but argued that their own group rated higher on human-relations qualities, such as being friendly, modest, and cooperative.[78]

Comparison and Social Identity: Some Prospects for Intergroup Behavior," *European Journal of Social Psychology* 5 (1975), 5–34; John C. Turner and Roger J. Brown, "Social Status, Cognitive Alternatives, and Intergroup Relations," in Tajfel (ed.), *Differentiation between Social Groups*, pp. 201–34; and Naomi Ellemers, Henk Wilke, and Ad F. M. van Knippenberg, "Effects of the Legitimacy of Low Group or Individual Status on Individual and Collective Status-Enhancement Strategies," *Journal of Personality and Social Psychology* 64 (1993), 766–78.

[74] Tadashi Anno, "Collective Identity as an 'Emotional Investment Portfolio': An Economic Analogy to a Psychological Process," in Rudra Sil and Eileen M. Doherty (eds.), *Beyond Boundaries? Disciplines, Paradigms, and Theoretical Integration in International Studies* (Albany: State University of New York Press, 2000), p. 129.

[75] Gerard Lemaine, "Social Differentiation and Social Originality," *European Journal of Social Psychology* 4 (1974), 17–52; Tajfel, "Psychological Structure of Intergroup Relations," pp. 93–94; Tajfel and Turner, "An Integrative Theory of Intergroup Conflict"; Hogg and Abrams, *Social Identifications*, pp. 28–29; Ellemers *et al.*, "Effects of the Legitimacy of Low Group Status"; Steve Hinkle, Laurie A. Taylor, Lee Fox-Cardamone, and Pamela G. Ely, "Social Identity and Aspects of Social Creativity: Shifting to New Dimensions of Intergroup Comparison," in Stephen Worchel, J. Francisco Morales, Daril Paez, and Jean-Claude Deschamps (eds.), *Social Identity: International Perspectives* (Thousand Oaks, CA: Sage, 1998), pp. 166–79.

[76] Anno, "Collective Identity," p. 138n.

[77] Richard N. LaLonde, "The Dynamics of Group Differentiation in the Face of Defeat," *Personality and Social Psychology Bulletin* 18 (1992), 336–42.

[78] van Knippenberg, "Intergroup Differences in Group Perceptions," p. 571.

Historically, one consequence of Russia's relative backwardness, insecurity, unsettled identity, and sense of not belonging to the West has been an obsession with international status, great-power standing, and "catching up" with the advanced nations. As Robert Legvold notes in his recent sweeping historical analysis of Russian foreign policy, when Russia's great-power status is called into question, Russian elites sink into preoccupation with their country's decline. There is even a special Russian word for the phenomenon, *derzhavnost*, which connotes a preoccupation with great-power standing regardless of whether the country has the military and economic wherewithal or not.[79]

To defuse a threat to its positive identity, the Russian elite sought to attain great-power status quickly, through accelerated, often superficial means rather than a slower, more organic development of political and economic institutions that would eventually redress Russia's relative backwardness in administration, finances, transportation, education, and technology. Russian elites rationalized that their country's backwardness provided advantages in competing with more advanced Western societies, recasting Russia's weakness as a source of strength using a strategy of social creativity.[80] In this sense, Lenin and the Bolsheviks were only the most recent in a line of reformers who provided a shortcut – a theory and organization that would allow Russia to skip an entire stage of Western development (capitalism) and proceed directly to a type of society superior to the West (socialism/communism). In a sweeping act of social creativity, the Bolsheviks pronounced the industrial backwardness of Russia and the rudimentary character of its capitalism to be not liabilities but great assets for the social revolution.[81] Soviet "New Thinkers" also found a way to reframe their country's innate characteristics as distinct from the West and positive by developing a messianic ideology that would reshape the world and ensure positive recognition of the Soviet Union by the West.

[79] Robert Legvold, "Russian Foreign Policy during Periods of Great State Transformation," in Robert Legvold (ed.), *Russian Foreign Policy in the Twenty-First Century and the Shadow of the Past* (New York: Columbia University Press, 2007), p. 114.

[80] Dominic Lieven, *Empire: The Russian Empire and its Rivals* (New Haven: Yale University Press, 2000), pp. 299–300; Legvold, "Russian Foreign Policy during Periods of Great State Transformation"; and David McDonald, "Domestic Conjunctures, the Russian State, and the World Outside, 1700–2006," in Legvold (ed.), *Russian Foreign Policy in the Twenty-First Century*, pp. 92–99, 149–51, 167–69.

[81] Nikolai Berdyaev, *Origin of Russian Communism* (Ann Arbor: University of Michigan Press, 1960); George Konrad and Ivan Szelenyi, *The Intellectuals on the Road to Class Power* (New York: Harcourt Brace Jovanovich, 1979).

The Soviet Union and soft power

Social identity theory and the New Thinking

Until Gorbachev, postwar Soviet diplomacy assumed that achievement of strategic military parity with the West would entitle the USSR to be treated as a political-diplomatic equal as well, validating its arrival as a major player on the international scene. The Soviet Union opted for a strategy of social competition, waging geopolitical and ideological competition to replace the United States as the dominant power and political regime. At the same time, Soviet leaders valued even symbolic indicators of equality, validating the Soviet Union's arrival as "the other superpower." As Henry Kissinger noted, "it has always been one of the paradoxes of Bolshevik behavior that their leaders have yearned to be treated as equals by the people they consider doomed."[82]

The Soviets' drive for acceptance as an equal power accelerated with Nikita Khrushchev's optimistic effort to reach the American level of nuclear capability (or at least to deceive the West about the strength of Soviet nuclear delivery capacity), based on the conviction that an altered military balance would translate into enhanced political status for the Soviet Union.[83] The humiliation of the Cuban missile crisis and Western exposure of Khrushchev's bluffs stimulated Soviet leaders to try to overcome their inferior power-projection capabilities. The Brezhnev leadership retained the strategy of social competition, but concentrated on achieving a real strategic balance with the United States rather than an image based in part on deception and bluster. By the end of the 1960s, the Soviet effort was visible and impressive: the Soviets had matched and in some respects even surpassed American nuclear deployments quantitatively while retaining their conventional force superiority. The Soviets attributed détente in the 1970s to the

---

[82] "Memorandum from the President's Assistant for National Security Affairs (Kissinger) to President Nixon," (undated), US Department of State, *Foreign Relations of the United States, 1969–1976*, vol. XII, *Soviet Union, January 1969–October 1970* (Washington, DC: Government Printing Office, 2006), p. 603.

[83] To Khrushchev's great disappointment, Kennedy's acknowledgement of Soviet military parity at the 1961 Vienna summit did not extend to the political and diplomatic sphere. The United States continued to want the USSR "to sit like a schoolboy with its hands on the desk." Cited in William Taubman, *Khrushchev: The Man and His Era* (New York: W. W. Norton & Company, 2003), p. 497. In an October 27, 1962 letter to Kennedy during the missile crisis, Khrushchev revealed his consternation: "How then does the admission of our equal military capabilities tally with such unequal relations between our great states? They cannot be made to tally in any way." Cited in William C. Wohlforth, *The Elusive Balance: Power and Perceptions during the Cold War* (Ithaca: Cornell University Press, 1993), pp. 177–78.

failure of the United States to achieve strategic hegemony, and thought that it signified recognition of Soviet–American equality and the increasing safety of the superpower rivalry.[84] Moscow's interpretation of détente as an "equal right to meddle" in the different corners of the world and the belief that the growing Soviet influence ensured US interest in cooperation quickly clashed with Washington's continuing unwillingness to grant the Soviets equal political status and parity on most crucial issues. Soviet leaders accused the United States of practicing double standards and denying Moscow what Washington did on a routine basis – expanding in the Third World, establishing military bases around the world, becoming a power broker in the Middle East. As Robert Jervis notes, détente broke down in part over disagreements over whether the Soviets could emulate American behavior.[85]

As a result, the Soviet Union entered the 1980s with even less political and diplomatic influence in the world than at the beginning of détente, in a position of international isolation. Soviet foreign-policy specialists concluded that expansion of territorial control and acquisition of weapons did not confer increased prestige and influence in international relations.[86] Instead, Soviet military power increased the "enemy image" in neighboring countries, while that military strength was increasingly endangered by the lagging Soviet economy. The Soviet economic model was losing much of its appeal to the Third World. This precipitous decline in the Soviet Union's international status, combined with the succession of a new leader, Mikhail Gorbachev, created conditions conducive to rethinking the Soviet identity.

From SIT, we can deduce more specific expectations about Gorbachev's probable reaction to the decline in Soviet international status. First, social identity theory would predict that Soviet elites would be motivated to find a new domain in which to be preeminent. The existing status hierarchy appeared to be unchangeable. The Soviets' impressive coercive capabilities had not persuaded Western states to accept the Soviet Union as a political and moral equal (in fact, as a new

---

[84] See Brezhnev's statement in *Pravda*, June 14, 1975, p. 1; Holloway, "Gorbachev's New Thinking," 66–67. Georgy Shakhnazarov recalled that Yury Andropov, who was chief of the Central Committee Department on Liaisons with Communist and Worker Parties in the 1960s, commented, "We and the Americans hold each other at a distance based on mutual respect ... The struggle shifted to the areas where both sides can wage it without directly harming themselves." Shakhnazarov, *Tsena Svobody*, pp. 25–26.

[85] Robert Jervis, "Identity and the Cold War," in Melvyn P. Leffler and Odd Arne Westad (eds.), *The Cambridge History of the Cold War, Volume 2: Conflicts and Crises, 1962–1975* (Cambridge University Press); See also Westad, *The Global Cold War*, p. 283.

[86] Adomeit, *Imperial Overstretch*, p. 142.

round of Cold War unfolded, the Reagan administration accused the
Kremlin of barbarism and incivility, labeling it an "evil empire" and
in the wake of the KAL 007 accident accusing it of having basic disre-
gard for humanitarian values[87]), and the Soviets could not reasonably
expect to catch up with the United States in economic production or
technology in the near future. Having reached the limits of mobility in
the international system and having understood the futility of competition for geopolitical power, the Soviet leadership could be expected
to try a social-creativity strategy. In this case, one avenue open to the
Soviets was to seek "soft power" – exercising influence by means of the
attraction of its culture, values, norms, or ideals rather than military or
economic power.[88]

Second, since SIT predicts that groups will combine the pursuit of
increased status with efforts at preserving distinctiveness, we would
expect Gorbachev and New Thinkers not to be content with simply
joining the club of "civilized" states by meeting Western conditions or
merely borrowing and rehashing Western ideas. On the contrary, we
might expect them to put forward norms and ideas that would underscore Soviet uniqueness, moral superiority, and originality. Evidence of
a strategy of social creativity would include, for example, elite charac-
terizations of the Soviet Union as an innovator or creator of principles
underlying a new world order.

Third, because a social identity depends on others' recognition,
Gorbachev should have sought opportunities to perform on a world
stage as well as promote acceptance of new ideas and norms in private
meetings with foreign leaders. We would also expect him to play to
groups who could give the Soviet Union higher status – Western power
brokers and public-opinion makers – and to have much less interest in
audiences in the Third World or Eastern Europe.

Fourth, since persuading others to accept the new Soviet identity
required maintaining consistency between words and deeds, Gorbachev
would have been under pressure to follow the New Thinking principles
in his own foreign policy. Lack of interest in how Soviet actions were
perceived by the world would be inconsistent with the expectations that
SIT generates for this case.

Finally, once Gorbachev was committed to a soft-power strategy,
we would expect him to avoid bargaining hard for *quid pro quo* (such
as requesting economic aid, technological assistance, or geopolitical

---

[87] President Reagan's remarks to reporters, September 2, 1983 in *Presidential Documents*,
vol. XIX (September 5, 1983), p. 1193.
[88] On the projection of "soft power" see Nye, *Bound to Lead*, pp. 31–33.

concessions from the West), which would have undercut the image he was trying to establish as creator of a new, more cooperative international order. According to SIT, status concerns may overwhelm material calculations. People may accept lower material benefits in order to improve their group's position relative to the outgroup. In the same vein, Gorbachev might be expected to discount the importance of traditional material symbols of Soviet power such as large arms arsenals and control over satellite regimes and to be willing to sacrifice them for improved status.

Below, we assess whether these expectations fit the pattern of Soviet foreign policy, following the congruence method for imputing causality in a single case.[89] We may now address the puzzle introduced earlier of why Gorbachev chose the New Thinking over more "realistic" and conventional foreign-policy strategies.

The Soviet Union as moral, visionary leader

Despite their popularity among the Soviet elite, the problem with both the Realpolitik and *détente-plus* strategies was that their cautious and incremental suggestions did not offer any means of halting the erosion in the Soviet Union's relative power and prestige. In striking contrast to its rivals, however, the New Thinking promised not to manage the USSR's accelerating decline[90] but to arrest and reverse it. As a former Soviet official put it, "from the outset Gorbachev dreamed of the empire surging ahead, rather than merely surviving."[91] The radical New Thinkers' intellectual breakthrough was in realizing that to transform their country into a real and not just a "one-dimensional" great power, they had to reject military might as a criterion of international influence in the contemporary world. By adopting the New Thinking, Gorbachev and his advisers could pursue indirect or cooptive "soft" power in the international system based on the attraction and influence of Soviet ideas and norms that would underlie a new, cooperative international system.[92]

---

[89] Alexander L. George and Andrew Bennett, *Case Studies and Theory Development in the Social Sciences* (Cambridge, MA: MIT Press, 2005), pp. 181–204.

[90] Stephen Sestanovich, "Gorbachev's Foreign Policy: A Diplomacy of Decline," *Problems of Communism* 37 (1988), 1–15.

[91] Zoteev, "The View from Gosplan," p. 92.

[92] Kubálková and Cruickshank, *Thinking New*, pp. 68, 105. Others have commented on this feature of Gorbachev's foreign policy. For example, Ambassador to Moscow Jack Matlock argued that the Soviet peace offensive, unilateral arms cuts, and defensive military strategy were "designed to maintain Moscow's great power status and influence during a period of military and economic retrenchment." Matlock to Baker and

The social-creativity hypothesis suggests that Gorbachev adopted the New Thinking to establish a new dimension on which the Soviet Union could excel in the world arena. This strategy promised a short-cut to achieving truly prominent status in the international system and political equality vis-à-vis the West. Moral visionary leadership thus became the new criterion for Soviet "greatness." As Foreign Minister Eduard Shevardnadze would state in April 1990:

> The belief that we are a great country and that we should be respected for this is deeply ingrained in me, as in everyone. But great in what? Territory? Population? Quantity of arms? Or the People's troubles? The individual's lack of rights? In what do we, who have virtually the highest infant mortality rate on our planet, take pride? It is not easy to answer these questions: Who are you and what do you wish to be? A country which is feared or a country which is respected? A country of power or a country of kindness?[93]

In adopting the ideas of the New Thinking, Gorbachev declared nothing less than his commitment to bridging "the gap between political practice and universal moral and ethical standards."[94] In his report to the 27th CPSU Congress in February 1986, Gorbachev argued that "global problems affecting all humanity" required states to cooperate.

Scowcroft, February 13, 1989 and February 11, 1989, *End of the Cold War Collection, NSA*, quoted in Melvyn P. Leffler, *For the Soul of Mankind* (New York: Hill and Wang, 2007), p. 425. Daniel Deudney and John Ikenberry state that the New Thinking "can be understood as an attempt to refurbish the Soviet state's ideological appeal in the world." See Daniel Deudney and John Ikenberry, "The International Sources of Soviet Change," *International Security* 16 (1991/92), 106. In "Identity, Norms, and National Security," Herman observes that "foreign policy radicals had a very different conception of what it meant to be a great power." Their goal was for the Soviet Union to "return to a position of visionary leadership" (pp. 310–11). Jacques Lévesque emphasizes the "messianic, innovative character" of Gorbachev's international policy and his conviction that he could give the USSR "a new political and moral leadership role in international affairs." See *Enigma of 1989*, pp. 23, 27. Similarly, Vladislav Zubok argues in *Failed Empire* (pp. 309–10) that Gorbachev replaced "one messianic revolutionary-imperial idea that had guided Soviet foreign policy with another messianic idea" – that Soviet perestroika was part of a new world moral order.

[93] *FBIS-SOV*, April 26, 1990, cited in Don Oberdorfer, *The Turn: From the Cold War to a New Era: United States and the Soviet Union, 1983–1990* (New York: Poseidon Press, 1991), p. 438. Similar ideas were evident as early as January 1987, when, after his visit to Afghanistan, Shevardnadze acknowledged in his report to the Politburo that Soviet actions there were not compatible with "the moral image of our country." Anatoly Chernyaev, A. Veber, and Vadim Medvedev (eds.), *V Politburo TsK KPSS. Po Zapisyam Anatoliya Chernyaeva, Vadima Medvedeva, Georgiya Shakhnazarova (1985–1991)* [Inside the Politburo of the CPSU CC. According to the Diaries of Anatoly Chernyaev, Vadim Medvedev, Georgy Shakhnazarov (1985–1991)] (Moscow: Al'pina Biznes Buks, 2006), p. 136. On Shevardnadze's concern with international public opinion, see ibid., p. 150.

[94] Speech by CPSU General Secretary Mikhail Gorbachev at the Forum "For a Nuclear-Free World, for the Survival of Mankind," Moscow, *FBIS-SOV*, February 27, 1987, AA20.

An "interdependent and in many ways integral world" was emerging.[95] Security, stressed Gorbachev, could only be obtained by political means and must be mutual.[96] Disrupting the foundations of the Cold War Realpolitik calculus, Gorbachev contrasted militarism and the balance of power with a "balance of interests," that is, voluntary agreement among states.[97] Finally, Gorbachev advocated the establishment of a "comprehensive international security system" that would guarantee states' economic, political, and humanitarian as well as military needs. For example, there should be an end to economic sanctions and discrimination, effective measures to prevent international terrorism, cooperation in the peaceful use of outer space and in resolving global problems, and efforts to reunite divided families.[98]

In a well-received September 1987 article in *Pravda*, "The Reality and Guarantees of a Secure World," timed to coincide with the opening of the 42nd meeting of the UN General Assembly, Gorbachev elaborated his vision of a comprehensive international-security system built on a strengthened United Nations. Gorbachev charged that it was "immoral" to ignore regional wars in the Third World and urged that more extensive use be made of UN observers and peacekeeping forces in "disengaging the troops of warring sides, observing ceasefires and armistice agreements."[99] He suggested that the permanent members of the Security Council renounce the use or threat of force, practices that often fanned regional conflicts. Other proposals included creation of a world space agency, a tribunal to investigate and prosecute incidents of terrorism, and international monitoring of arms control and confidence-building agreements.[100]

Ideational theorists have attributed Gorbachev's adoption of the New Thinking to a variety of factors, including cognitive learning, policy entrepreneurship, transnational networks, and socialization to the norms and values of the West. Some theorists credit the Soviet foreign-policy revolution to cognitive learning by members of academic institutes, the Ministry of Foreign Affairs, and the International Department of the Central Committee.[101] By the early 1980s, some foreign-policy specialists concluded that the Brezhnev regime's

[95] Gorbachev, "Political Report of the CPSU Central Committee at the 27th CPSU Congress," February 25, 1986, reprinted in *Mikhail Gorbachev: Selected Speeches and Articles*, 2nd edn. (Moscow: Progress Publishers), pp. 362, 364.

[96] Ibid., pp. 419–21.   [97] Ibid., p. 422.   [98] Ibid., pp. 432–33.

[99] Mikhail Gorbachev, "The Reality and Guarantees of a Secure World," *Pravda*, September 17, 1987, pp. 1–2, in *FBIS-SOV*, September 17, 1987, pp. 23–28.

[100] Ibid., pp. 25, 27.

[101] For learning interpretations of Soviet foreign policy, see George Breslauer, "Ideology and Learning in Soviet Third World Policy," *World Politics* 39 (1987), 429–48; Joseph

decision to install SS-20s had threatened Western Europeans and contributed to the enemy image held by many in the West. In the mid-1980s, many specialists also inferred that most Third World countries were not ripe for communist revolution, and that Soviet assistance to national-liberation movements had impeded Soviet economic development.[102] Other scholars emphasize domestic politics – the role of policy entrepreneurs in taking advantage of windows of opportunity to promote new ideas as solutions to political problems.[103] But policy entrepreneurs or expert communities would not gain a favorable hearing if political elites were not disposed to consider their ideas. Why did Gorbachev find the ideas of the New Thinking more compelling than alternatives?

Some theorists have traced the origins of particular New Thinking ideas to international contacts between arms controllers and scientists in the Pugwash and Dartmouth movements and in the conferences and discussions sponsored by Western European social democrats such as the Palme Commission, named after the Swedish prime minister Olaf Palme.[104] Gorbachev read widely in European

S. Nye, Jr., "Nuclear Learning and U.S.–Soviet Security Regimes," *International Organization* 41 (1987), 371–402; Emanuel Adler, "Cognitive Evolution: A Dynamic Approach for the Study of International Relations and Their Progress," in Emanuel Adler and Beverly Crawford (eds.), *Progress in Postwar International Relations* (New York: Columbia University Press, 1991), 48–88; Franklin Griffiths, "Attempted Learning: Soviet Policy Toward the United States in Brezhnev Era," in Breslauer and Tetlock (eds.), *Learning in U.S. and Soviet Foreign Policy*, pp. 630–84; Legvold, "Soviet Learning in the 1980s," pp. 684–734; Janice Gross Stein, "Political Learning by Doing: Gorbachev as Uncommitted Thinker and Motivated Learning," *International Organization* 48 (1994), 155–83; Andrew Bennett, *Condemned to Repetition?*.

[102] Legvold, "Soviet Learning in the 1980s."

[103] Checkel, "Ideas, Institutions"; Checkel, *Ideas and International Political Change*; Mendelson, "Internal Battles and External Wars"; Mendelson, *Changing Course*; Matthew Evangelista, "Sources of Moderation in Soviet Security Policy," in Philip E. Tetlock, Jo Husbands, Robert Jervis, Paul Stern, and Charles Tilly (eds.), *Behavior, Society, and Nuclear War*, vol. II (New York: Oxford University Press, 1991), pp. 254–354; Evangelista, *Unarmed Forces*.

[104] Risse-Kappen, "Ideas Do Not Float Freely," 185–214; Evangelista, "The Paradox of State Strength"; Evangelista, *Unarmed Forces*, pp. 187–88, 190–91, 305–15; Georgy Arbatov, *The System* (New York: Random House, 1992), pp. 211, 310–12; Gorbachev, *Perestroika*, pp. 196, 206–07; Georgy Arbatov, "America Also Needs Perestroika," in Stephen F. Cohen and Katrina Vanden Heuvel (eds.), *Voices of Glasnost* (New York: W. W. Norton & Company, 1989), p. 315; Timothy Garton Ash, *In Europe's Name: Germany and the Divided Continent* (New York: Random House, 1993), pp. 119, 313, 320. Among the most important international institutions introducing Soviet researchers to several New Thinking concepts were the Bradford University (UK) group on alternative defense, Frankfurt Peace Research Institute, Stockholm International Peace Research Institute, and the Institute for Defense and Disarmament Studies (US). For scientific exchanges, in addition to the Pugwash and Dartmouth conferences, there were the International Physicians for

social-democratic thought and was influenced by their foreign-policy ideas as well.[105] Others have attributed the New Thinking to the influence of a "Westernizing" academic elite who wanted the Soviet Union to become part of the West rather than opposing it.[106] On the other hand, although the New Thinkers borrowed freely from Western academic as well as leftist writings, they not only wanted to join but to educate the West to adopt new modes of international conduct.[107] While indispensable in their correction of the deterministic bias of materialist explanations, constructivist interpretations thus tend not to recognize sufficiently the Soviets' need for a unique identity that would maintain their status as a great power.

The New Thinkers combined elements of different strands of Western thought with Soviet academicians' ideas to create an eclectic synthesis. For each concept ostensibly borrowed from the West, Soviet writers could cite a parallel Soviet or Marxist idea or antecedent.[108] The New Thinking was a philosophy of humanistic universalism that also drew on Soviet foreign-policy experience in the Khrushchev thaw and the détente period of the 1970s, further undermining the materialist argument that the ideas were endogenous to Soviet economic decline.[109] In an influential 1968 *samizdat* memorandum, Soviet nuclear physicist and dissident Andrei Sakharov argued that global problems such as the environment, human rights, and overpopulation made the division of the world into capitalist and socialist systems increasingly dangerous

the Prevention of Nuclear War, the Federation of American Scientists, Physicians for Social Responsibility, Union of Concerned Scientists, Natural Resources Defense Council, the Atlantic Council, and the National Academy of Sciences Committee on International Security and Arms Control (CISAC).

[105] Gorbachev, *Perestroika*, pp. 196, 206–07; Gorbachev, *Memoirs*, pp. 159–60, 676–77; Risse-Kappen, "Ideas Do Not Float Freely," 210; Brown, *The Gorbachev Factor*, pp. 116–17; English, *Russia and the Idea of the West*, pp. 212–13, 330; Garton Ash, *In Europe's Name*, pp. 119, 320; Lévesque, *The Enigma of 1989*, pp. 35–36, 252–53; Evangelista, *Unarmed Forces*, pp. 306–07.

[106] Herman, "Identity, Norms, and National Security"; English, *Russia and the Idea of the West*.

[107] Kubálková and Cruickshank, *Thinking New*, pp. 30–31; Lévesque, *The Enigma of 1989*, pp. 4, 26–27, 34.

[108] Kubálková and Cruickshank, *Thinking New*, p. 29.

[109] Ibid., pp. 23, 26–27; Legvold, "Soviet Learning in the 1980s," p. 711; Arbatov, *The System*, p. 211; Garthoff, *The Great Transition*, p. 261; English, *Russia and the Idea of the West*, pp. 2–3, 100–15, 127–36. Three major academic institutes are usually given credit for early versions of New Thinking: the Institute of World Economy and International Relations (IMEMO), Institute of the USA and Canada (ISKAN), and Institute of Economics of the World Socialist System (IEMSS). On the role of IMEMO in developing early versions of the New Thinking beginning in the 1960s and 1970s, see Checkel, "Ideas, Institutions"; Checkel, *Ideas and International Political Change*. For other academic institutes, see Herman, "Identity, Norms, and National Security."

and anachronistic.[110] The principles of "freedom of choice" and non-interference in internal affairs were not inspired by contacts with European social democrats or liberal arms controllers, but grew out of the New Thinkers' disillusionment with the 1968 Soviet invasion of Czechoslovakia.[111]

Gorbachev was not satisfied with merely assimilating foreign-policy ideas held by Western European social-democratic politicians and peace researchers. As SIT leads us to expect, the New Thinkers aimed not just at tearing down the "iron curtain" and achieving integration in the community of advanced industrial nations. They aspired to preserve the distinctiveness of the new Soviet identity while radically transforming the international system according to the principles of the New Thinking. Gorbachev writes that in today's interdependent world "a country can develop its full potential only by interacting with other societies, yet without giving up its own identity."[112] At an April 1988 Politburo meeting, Anatoly Chernyaev scoffed at Shakhnazarov's statement that the Soviet Union should claim to be the "same as everybody else" in order to enter the world community, saying that the Americans would ask, "excuse me, if you are the same as us, tell us – how many personal computers do you have per capita? Oh, 48 times less than we do! Then say goodbye to the place of a superpower." "We are a power-house of modern world development of morality and justice," Chernyaev argued vehemently. "This is our strength."[113]

Exuberance over success in creating a new distinct role for the Soviet Union as moral leader is visible in Chernyaev's description of Gorbachev's meeting with Helmut Kohl in late October 1988. Chernyaev noted in his diary that he "felt physically that we were entering a new world, where class struggle, ideology, and, in general, polarity and enmity are no longer decisive. And something all-human is taking the upper hand … No wonder that the world is stunned and full of admiration."[114]

---

[110] English, *Russia and the Idea of the West*, pp. 107–08, 129–30.
[111] Evangelista, *Unarmed Forces*, p. 316. In 1969, when Gorbachev visited Czechoslovakia he observed that, contrary to the Soviet government's claims that the intervention was in defense of working-class interests, the Czechoslovak communists did not dare introduce the visiting Soviet delegation to workers collectives. "We felt viscerally, deep down, that this action was indignantly rejected by the people." Gorbachev, *Memoirs*, p. 100.
[112] Gorbachev, *Memoirs*, pp. 402–03.
[113] Chernyaev Diary – 1988, April 26, 1988, NSA EBB, No. 250, www.gwu.edu/~nsarchiv/NSAEBB/NSAEBB250/index.htm.
[114] Chernyaev Diary – 1988, October 28, 1988, quoted in Vladislav M. Zubok, "New Evidence on the 'Soviet Factor' in the Peaceful Revolutions of 1989," *Cold War International History Project Bulletin* 12–13 (2001), 5–23.

Nor did Gorbachev accommodate to the Western power-holders' worldview. One of the striking features of the New Thinking is that it advocated security and humanitarian norms that challenged the views of Ronald Reagan, Helmut Kohl, and Margaret Thatcher, who maintained a Hobbesian approach to international relations.[115] In private meetings as well as his public speeches, Gorbachev tried to convert conservative Western power brokers to his new faith, for example, by subscribing to norms of nuclear disarmament and non-use of force. During heated polemics with Thatcher, Gorbachev argued that nuclear weapons were an "absolute evil" and that it was necessary to "get liberated from the mode of thinking of the 1940s."[116] At Reykjavik in 1986, Gorbachev tried to push Reagan to agree to mutual renunciation of nuclear weapons. At his meeting with Reagan in Moscow in July 1988, Gorbachev proposed a communiqué that would enshrine the norms of non-use of force and non-intervention in the internal affairs of other states. After Reagan's advisers objected to the statement, Gorbachev bitterly lamented that an "opportunity to take a big stride in shaping civilized international relations has been missed."[117]

Shevardnadze emphasized at the time that "Soviet diplomacy has a clear goal before it – to materialize the concept of the new political thinking in international-legal norms and principles."[118] When Gorbachev and his team were preparing for the most impressive display of the New Thinking before a world audience, his December 1988 address to the UN General Assembly, Gorbachev told his advisers that he wanted his speech to be a bold reply to Churchill's "Iron Curtain" speech at Fulton, Missouri in March 1946. It "should be anti-Fulton – Fulton in reverse," he said. "We should stress the process of demilitarization and humanization of our thinking."[119] Gorbachev's UN address advocated overturning the principles that had ordered the world for at least four decades – deterrence, spheres of influence, and the balance of power. Gorbachev ruled out "force or the threat of force" as an instrument of foreign policy and called for freeing international relations from the influence of ideology. For the Soviet Union, he said, "freedom of choice is a universal principle to which there should be no exceptions."[120] Similar to previous

[115] Risse-Kappen, "Ideas Do Not Float Freely," 191–92.
[116] Chernyaev, *Shest' Let s Gorbachevym*, pp. 137–39.
[117] Garthoff, *The Great Transition*, pp. 354–56.
[118] Shevardnadze's June 1987 statement is quoted in John van Oudenaren, *The Role of Shevardnadze and the Ministry of Foreign Affairs in the Making of Soviet Defense and Arms Control Policy* (Santa Monica: RAND, 1990).
[119] Chernyaev Notes, October 31, 1988, quoted in Zubok, "New Evidence," 9.
[120] M. S. Gorbachev's United Nations Address, *Pravda*, December 8, 1988, pp. 1–2, translated in *FBIS-SOV*, December 8, 1988, p. 13.

Russian leaders such as Tsar Alexander I and foreign ministers who, conscious of their country's weakness and vulnerability, had proposed pan-European security structures, Gorbachev and Shevardnadze pursued this vision of a new international order based on mutual security and universal values.[121] New Thinkers promoted principles that would underlie a new international system in which states would submerge their ideological differences in order to cooperate in solving global problems such as the threat of nuclear catastrophe, poverty, pollution, terrorism, and underdevelopment. In short, they were not only "norm-takers" but norm entrepreneurs as well.

Implementation of the New Thinking

The radicalization of Soviet foreign policy proceeded apace as Gorbachev worked through the practical implications of the New Thinking ideas. These norms were not just rhetorical window-dressing; Gorbachev and his advisers often referred to the need to match words with deeds and to implement the principles of the New Thinking. Beginning in July 1985, Gorbachev carried out an eighteen-month unilateral moratorium on nuclear testing. On January 15, 1986 he proposed to eliminate nuclear weapons by the year 2000 as well as other arms-control measures. This was followed by the Stockholm 1986 Agreement to on-site inspection and confidence-building measures in Europe, and the December 1987 treaty to eliminate medium- and shorter-range missiles from Europe.[122] Alexander Yakovlev had recommended delinking an agreement limiting medium-range missiles from restraints on the SDI to serve as a "practical expression of our new thinking, the unity of words and deeds."[123] "The new thinking is the bridging of the gap between the word and the deed, and we embarked on practical deeds," Gorbachev wrote. "In all these issues the Soviet Union is a pioneer."[124]

In line with his proposal for a comprehensive security system, Gorbachev argued for an increased role for the United Nations and worked for cooperative solutions to regional conflicts. In October 1987, the Soviet government paid the United Nations $200 million in accumulated arrears for peacekeeping operations that the Soviets had declined to support since 1973.[125] From 1988 to 1991 the Soviet

---

[121] Geoffrey Hosking, *Russia and the Russians: A History* (Cambridge, MA: Harvard University Press, 2001), p. 573.
[122] Garthoff, *The Great Transition*, pp. 252–53, 284, 326–28.
[123] Yakovlev, Memorandum for Gorbachev, February 25, 1987, NSA EBB, No. 238, www.gwu.edu/~nsarchiv/NSAEVV/NSAEVV238/index.htm.
[124] Gorbachev, "Reality and Guarantees," p. 23.
[125] *New York Times*, October 16, 1987, p. A1; October 18, 1987, p. A2.

leadership contributed to a comprehensive international-security system by mediating political resolution of conflicts in Ethiopia, Angola, Namibia, Cambodia, Nicaragua, and El Salvador. The Soviets disengaged from occupation of Afghanistan, encouraged the Cubans to pull out their military forces from Ethiopia and Angola, urged the Vietnamese to withdraw from Cambodia, persuaded the Nicaraguans to agree to free elections even if it meant loss of power for the Sandinistas, and promoted a solution to the Salvadorean civil war.[126] Gorbachev's foreign policy went beyond elimination of costly commitments, as the Soviets could simply have withdrawn their troops and advisers from Afghanistan, Angola, and Mozambique.

In his December 1988 UN address, Gorbachev announced that the Soviet Union would unilaterally cut its army by 500,000 and reduce its military forces in Eastern Europe by 50,000 troops and 5,000 tanks.[127] While one of the reasons Gorbachev decided to make unilateral reductions was that perestroika could not succeed so long as the army received "the best scientific-technical forces, the best production funds, reliable supplies," the credibility of the New Thinking principles was also an important concern. If we publish "that we spend over twice as much as the US on military needs, if we let the scope of our expenses be known," Gorbachev exclaimed at one point, "all our new thinking and our new foreign policy will go to hell."[128]

The need to make principles of the New Thinking credible to the West was a principal motivation for Gorbachev's embrace of Western liberal-democratic values, as evidenced in his address to the Soviet Foreign Ministry conference in May 1986 where he called for rejection of an outdated approach to human rights issues as "part of the process of building trust" with the West. In the same vein, Gorbachev recollects that post-Reykjavik discussions with Thatcher convinced him of a link between democratization at home and trust abroad.[129]

Conforming to another prediction derived from SIT, with their efforts focused on winning over key Western power brokers and opinion makers, Gorbachev and the New Thinkers paid much less little attention to traditional Soviet reference groups such as Eastern European "fraternal" parties managing the Soviet sphere of influence. According to the testimony of Gorbachev's advisers, he was frustrated with the

---

[126] Garthoff, *Great Transition*, pp. 735–44.
[127] *New York Times*, December 8, 1988; *Washington Post*, December 8, 1988; Gorbachev, *Memoirs*, p. 460.
[128] Chernyaev Diary – 1988, November 3, 1988, NSA EBB No. 250, www.gwu. edu/~nsarchiv/NSAEBB/NSAEBB250/index.htm.
[129] Cited in English, "The Sociology of New Thinking," 62, 66.

small-mindedness and conservatism of Eastern European communist leaders such as Zhivkov, Ceausescu, or Honecker. They were too far beneath him to deserve consideration.[130] At an important March 1988 Politburo meeting which started the debate on the future of Eastern Europe, Shevardnadze went so far as to question the Eastern bloc's relevance to the future of socialism: "Take for instance Bulgaria, take the old leadership of Poland, take the current situation in German Democratic Republic, in Romania. Is it socialism?"[131] As the New Thinkers struggled to implement their understanding of true greatness on the world stage, they tended to perceive the Eastern European regimes not as prized possessions but as embarrassing reminders of Stalinism. The New Thinkers' lack of interest in Eastern European affairs is also evidenced by the lack of a coherent new policy for the region, apart from Gorbachev's strategy of "meticulous non-interference" in these countries' domestic affairs.[132]

The imperative to back words with deeds was another force that shaped Gorbachev's policy toward Soviet satellites. Gorbachev, with remarkable consistency, affirmed freedom of choice as a universal principle and key concept of relations with Eastern Europe.[133] His adviser in Eastern European affairs Shakhnazarov recalls that Gorbachev "thought that changes were entirely the subject of sovereign choices of the parties and peoples."[134] Gorbachev's refusal to interfere in the internal affairs of Eastern European countries was not motivated by concern about the costs of maintaining the Soviet bloc,[135] but by his belief in the principle of freedom of choice. To avoid popular unrest that might force the Soviet Union to intervene, beginning in late 1988 Gorbachev encouraged Eastern European elites to enact reforms.[136] In a July 1989 speech to the Council of Europe in Strasbourg, Gorbachev declared "any interference in domestic affairs and any attempts to restrict the sovereignty of states – friends, allies or any others – are inadmissible." Acknowledging that "social and political orders in one country or another changed in the past and may change in the future," Gorbachev affirmed that such changes were the "exclusive affair of

---

[130] Zubok, "New Evidence," 8.

[131] Chernyaev's notes from Politburo meeting, March 24–25, 1988, quoted in Zubok, "New Evidence," 9.

[132] Zubok, "New Evidence," 8 (quotation); Zubok, *Failed Empire*, pp. 321–22.

[133] *Pravda*, February 26, 1986; *Vestnik, Ministry of Foreign Affairs* August 5, 1987, pp. 4–6; *Pravda*, June 28, 1988; Gorbachev's United Nations Address, 13; *Pravda*, February 24, 1989.

[134] Shakhnazarov, *Tsena Svobody*, p. 100.

[135] Brooks and Wohlforth, "Economic Constraints," p. 291.

[136] Mark Kramer, "The Collapse of East European Communism and the Repercussions within the Soviet Union (Part I)," *Journal of Cold War Studies* 5 (2003), 186–90.

the people in that country" and "their choice."[137] In the context of
the recent Polish election and the possibility of a Solidarity-led government, Gorbachev's comments were viewed as a deliberate signal to
Polish authorities that the Soviet military would not save them and that
they should allow the formation of a non-communist government.[138]
Gorbachev's comment during a trip to Helsinki in late October 1989
that the USSR did not have the "moral and political right" to interfere in the affairs of Warsaw Pact allies confirmed the demise of the
Brezhnev Doctrine.[139]

Adherence to the principles of freedom of choice and non-
interference in the internal affairs of other countries culminated in the
Soviet decision not to prop up foundering communist regimes in the
Warsaw Pact alliance.[140] According to Chernyaev, "if you presented
Gorbachev with the question: would you sacrifice the freedom that
you had given to the countries of Eastern Europe ... in the name of
preserving the imperial image, of great power status in the old Soviet
meaning of the word, he would say that the question for him was
absurd."[141] While Gorbachev did not originally anticipate or envision
that Eastern European countries would abandon socialism, he was
prepared to accept loss of the Soviet security zone rather than undermine the New Thinkers' grand design for a cooperative world order.[142]
While Soviet reformers had learned that the use of force was costly
and counterproductive, this did not imply that they should grant the
Eastern Europeans freedom to choose their own social systems; the
Soviet Union could have easily maintained its hegemony in Eastern
Europe by means of the implied threat of intervention, made credible
by the Soviet invasions of Hungary in 1956 and of Czechoslovakia in
1968. Eastern European leaders kept waiting for the Soviet Union to
signal that it would send troops if necessary, but instead Gorbachev
encouraged the reformers.[143]

The crucial test of Gorbachev's adherence to the freedom-of-choice
idea was posed by independence movements within the USSR itself.

---

[137] *New York Times*, July 7, 1989, p. A1.
[138] Kramer, "Collapse of East European Communism (Part I)," 196–97.
[139] Ronald Asmus, J. F. Brown, and Keith Crane, *Soviet Foreign Policy and the Revolutions of 1989 in Eastern Europe* (Santa Monica: RAND Corporation, 1991); Robert Hutchings, *American Diplomacy and the End of the Cold War* (Washington, DC: Woodrow Wilson Center Press, 1997).
[140] Lévesque, *The Enigma of 1989*, p. 54.
[141] Zubok, "New Evidence," 8.
[142] Levesque, *The Enigma of 1989*, p. 3; Adomeit, *Imperial Overstretch*, p. 274.
[143] Kramer, "Collapse of East European Communism (Part I)," 197–201; Brown, "Gorbachev and the End of the Cold War," pp. 38–39.

Yet, even faced with a nightmare of national dissolution and an offensive of conservative forces at home, the New Thinkers by and large managed to rule out resorting to force. As Shevardnadze explained to his American counterpart, James Baker, following the April 1989 unrest in Georgia: "If we were to use force then … It would be the end of any hope for the future, the end of everything we are trying to do, which is to create a new system based on humane values … We cannot go back."[144] Even if Eastern Europe had lost its significance for Soviet security, East Germany might have been placed in a different category; its pro-Soviet regime was perhaps the most important strategic gain from the Soviets' hard-fought victory in World War II. Nevertheless, while he did not favor German reunification at first, once he had articulated the New Thinking, Gorbachev was constrained to apply these principles to his own foreign policy, which meant allowing the East Germans freedom of choice. To make an exception for Germany would have contravened his identity as a "norm entrepreneur" and undermined the Soviet Union's newly obtained and distinctive status as a moral and political leader on the international stage. In the June 1989 joint Soviet–West German declaration, Gorbachev acknowledged "the right of all peoples and states freely to determine their destiny," language that had previously referred to the East German peoples' right to free elections.[145] During a February 1990 meeting with West German chancellor Helmut Kohl in Moscow, Gorbachev formally approved German reunification by acknowledging that "the Germans in the Federal Republic and in the GDR themselves have to know what road they want to take."[146]

Gorbachev's consent to Germany's membership of NATO was influenced by American invocation of the freedom-of-choice principle. Initially, Gorbachev was "genuinely and adamantly opposed" to a unified Germany's joining the Atlantic alliance.[147] During the Soviet–American summit of May–June 1990 President Bush remarked that all nations had the right to choose their own alliances. He then asked Gorbachev whether Germany, too, had the right to decide for itself which alliance to join,[148] forcing the Soviet leader to acknowledge that "the matter of alliance membership is, in accordance with the Helsinki

---

[144] Michael Beschloss and Strobe Talbott, *At the Highest Levels: The Inside Story of the End of the Cold War* (Boston: Little, Brown, 1993), p. 96.

[145] *Izvestiya*, June 15, 1989.

[146] Adomeit, *Imperial Overstretch*, p. 487. See also Garton Ash, *In Europe's Name*, p. 351.

[147] Adomeit, *Imperial Overstretch*, p. 508.

[148] Philip Zelikow and Condoleezza Rice, *Germany Unified and Europe Transformed: A Study in Statecraft* (Cambridge, MA: Harvard University Press, 1995), p. 277.

Final Act, a matter for the Germans to decide."[149] Bush recalled that "the dismay in the Soviet team was palpable. [Marshal] Akhromeyev's eyes flashed angrily." His National Security Adviser Brent Scowcroft concurred that "I could scarcely believe what I was witnessing." It was obvious that Gorbachev "had created a firestorm in his delegation and faced bitter opposition."[150]

Social identity theory might help to explain why Gorbachev's drive for world recognition and acceptance seemingly took precedence over material considerations, as he agreed to German reunification and membership of NATO without gaining anything tangible in return. Despite the critical state of the Soviet economy, the Soviet leadership did not establish a firm *quid pro quo* between Soviet consent on the NATO issue and large-scale West German economic and financial aid.[151] According to Chernyaev, Gorbachev considered "undignified" the attachment of stringent economic conditions to unified Germany's NATO membership.[152] Even if the Soviet domestic economic crisis had weakened Gorbachev's bargaining position by this time,[153] he made no attempt to play his remaining card, the presence of 300,000 Soviet troops in East Germany.[154] If for former Soviet Foreign Minister Andrei Gromyko, the epitome of the Stalin–Brezhnev tradition, it was a mystery "why Gorbachev and his friends ... cannot comprehend how to use force and pressure for defending their state interests,"[155] for the New Thinkers Gromyko's "realist" calculus based on coercion and the balance of power was not only immoral, but "absurd" and inefficient as a means of attaining true superpower status. After Gorbachev was criticized by conservatives for giving up Eastern Europe to Western penetration, in a 1991 interview with *Izvestia*, Yakovlev said that he was "perplexed" by the "ultra-hardliners in our country who insist that the country's prestige has been undermined" by political changes in Eastern Europe. He wondered what the "loudmouths who are clamoring for national greatness" would "include in their conception of 'great

---

[149] Zelikow and Rice, *Germany Unified*, p. 281. For an explanation of this episode as a case of argumentative rationality, see Thomas Risse, "'Let's Argue!': Communicative Action in World Politics," *International Organization* 48 (2000), 1–40.

[150] George Bush and Brent Scowcroft, *A World Transformed* (New York: Alfred A. Knopf, 1998), pp. 282–83.

[151] Adomeit, *Imperial Overstretch*, p. 548.

[152] Adomeit's interview with Chernyaev. Adomeit, *Imperial Overstretch*, p. 556.

[153] Brooks and Wohlforth, "Economic Constraints," p. 301.

[154] Zubok, *Failed Empire*, p. 330.

[155] Anatoly Gromyko, *Andrei Gromyko v Labirintakh Kremlya: Vospominaniya i Razmishleniya Syna* [Andrei Gromyko in the Kremlin Labyrinth: His Son's Recollections and Reflections] (Moscow: IPO "Avtor," 1997), p. 184.

power' – the use of force?" That sort of approach had been used by Joseph Stalin, Nikita Khrushchev, and Leonid Brezhnev, but it would have been "foolish and insane" for Gorbachev to continue their policies. "A power's 'greatness,'" Yakovlev emphasized, "should be assessed by different criteria nowadays – by the criteria of morality, peaceableness, a desire to cooperate, and so forth."[156]

Gorbachev's disarmament and conflict-resolution initiatives not only helped to end the Cold War but enhanced Soviet international prestige. Ironically for Gorbachev and the other New Thinkers, Soviet success in projecting "soft power" internationally coincided with the collapse of the Soviet Union from within. Emboldened by his international success and acceptance, Gorbachev until the last moment was hoping to reverse Soviet internal fortunes and save the Union and perestroika. As one of Gorbachev's aides put it, "He [Gorbachev] had become so good at convincing the rest of the world of his ability to perform political miracles that perhaps he eventually believed it himself."[157] Yet, it was much harder to convince domestic political forces of Gorbachev's ability to perform economic miracles. The moment of Soviet triumph as a multidimensional superpower was sweet but extremely short-lived.

Conclusion

The Gorbachev revolution is a recent example of Russian efforts to obtain Western recognition as a great power despite its relative backwardness. Soviet foreign-policy thinkers realized that the Soviet Union was lagging behind the United States economically and militarily, but were unwilling to give up great-power status. Consistent with SIT, Gorbachev and the other New Thinkers sought a new domain in which to compete with the United States – promoting new international norms and ideas. Gorbachev found the New Thinking more attractive than alternative foreign-policy programs because it offered a new role for the Soviet Union as a norm entrepreneur and a distinctive status as the author of principles underlying a new world order. In public and private, he pointed out that the Soviet Union was a pioneer, the first to implement the New Thinking principles in deeds as well as words, evidencing use of social creativity to attain a desired status. That the Soviet Union would promote a new world order based on universal

---

[156] Quoted in Mark Kramer, "The Collapse of East European Communism and the Repercussions within the Soviet Union (Part III)," *Journal of Cold War Studies* 7 (2005), 57.

[157] The phrase belongs to Gorbachev's spokesman, Andrei Grachev, after the August 1991 coup attempt. Quoted in Lévesque, *The Enigma of 1989*, p. 20.

human values and international cooperation could not have been predicted from its relative decline in the economic basis of power.

As SIT would lead us to predict, Gorbachev enacted the Soviet Union's new role on a world stage, culminating with his highly publicized and widely acclaimed December 1988 speech to the United Nations. Also in line with SIT, Gorbachev sought recognition from powerful Western leaders, whom he regarded as his reference group, rather than his "fraternal" socialist allies. He promoted the New Thinking in public speeches, private meetings with conservative leaders, and published writings. To persuade Western elites to accept the Soviet Union's new identity as moral leader, he matched words with deeds by supporting UN peacekeeping operations, working for a multilateral solution to regional conflicts, and refraining from interference when Soviet satellites abandoned communism.

Realism would predict that the Soviet Union would either pursue a policy of unilateral retrenchment until it had recovered its power, or use balance-of-power diplomacy to play off its rivals against each other. It is difficult to explain from a realist perspective why Gorbachev allowed former Soviet satellites to abandon communism and their alliance with the Soviet Union, actions that brought the West to Soviet borders and brought about the end of the Soviet empire. The Soviets were motivated not just by material pressures that favored retrenchment but by the desire to be recognized as a great power and to be a member of the club. The New Thinking was premised on the belief that international influence could be derived not from military power but rather the power of example.

Realism is correct that a state's identity is shaped by its geographic location and ability to compete in the struggle for power. But material factors alone do not determine a state's identity. History, tradition, and ideology also influence the role that political elites believe that their state should play in world politics. A strategy of social creativity – i.e., leaders' ability to find a new dimension on which their state is superior – can compensate to some extent for inferiority on standard power indices in achieving international recognition. Status is based on others' recognition, and is therefore more subjective than power. We need to understand how aspiring powers can achieve status by means other than geopolitical competition, thereby attaining a positive identity without infringing on the interests of the established states.

14 Shared sovereignty in the European Union: Germany's economic governance

Sherrill Brown Wells and Samuel F. Wells, Jr.

This chapter explores the question of why West Germany, with the most powerful economy within the European Union (EU), chose to give up its stable, highly prized deutsche mark to join the European Monetary Union (EMU) and accept significant constraints on its fiscal and monetary policies. The answer for Germany lies in a series of historical stages after 1945, each reflecting an increasing acceptance of the need to abandon balance-of-power politics for a multiple-level shared sovereignty through economic and political integration with other EU member states. In domestic policy, West Germany developed a "social partnership" in which power and decision-making was shared among major interest groups. In foreign policy, the parallel system was called a "security partnership" with major and minor powers in Europe and North America. As a result, Germany based its international actions on multilateral institutions such as the United Nations, the North Atlantic Treaty Organization, the Council of Europe, the Conference on Security and Cooperation in Europe, and the European Community (later European Union). Internally this approach ensured that no major interest, neither big business nor labor, would dominate. Internationally the multilateral policy encouraged other states to accept Germany's increasing economic strength without fearing it would be harnessed to national political ambitions. The ultimate proof of the wisdom of this approach was the relative ease with which Germany's neighbors, allies, and rivals accepted the unification of the Federal Republic of Germany and the German Democratic Republic. This system evolved gradually with occasional reversals and not without guidance and sometimes pressure from allies and partners.[1]

Such an interpretation of West German behavior runs directly counter to the theory of offensive realism as argued most prominently

---

[1] Peter Katzenstein, "Taming of Power: German Unification, 1989–1990," in Meredith Woo-Cumings and Michael Loriaux (eds.), *Past as Prelude: History in the Making of a New World Order* (Boulder: Westview Press, 1993), pp. 59–81.

by John J. Mearsheimer in *The Tragedy of Great Power Politics* and earlier articles. In an anarchic international system in which states can never know the intentions of their rivals, Mearsheimer contends that each state must seek to maximize its share of world power. "A state's ultimate goal," he asserts, "is to be the hegemon of the system." In this theory, international institutions such as the UN or EU are not significant actors. Only states wield actual power.[2]

This chapter will show how West German policy was shaped by a very different calculus than that advanced by Professor Mearsheimer. Determined not to repeat the mistakes that led to defeat in two world wars, German leaders after 1945 developed a new concept of the state. The power of the state was to be essentially economic, and military strength was to be kept limited, focused on defensive capabilities, and embedded in multilateral organizations for any operations outside German territory. This is a dramatically different power line than that advanced by the theory of offensive realism. And this chapter will show that Germany was even willing to subordinate its main element of power to a union of European states. The intellectual and political origins of this policy began before 1945 and were initially shaped by leaders of Germany's traditional enemy France.

The Schuman Plan: the first step in shared sovereignty

The most innovative proponent of shared sovereignty was Jean Monnet, a French businessman and international administrator who together with the French foreign minister Robert Schuman developed the first significant initiative in the process of European integration. Monnet's concept of shared sovereignty, the heart of the Schuman Plan, brought this idea to the forefront of a wide range of proposals for European integration circulating in the period after 1945. The idea of pooling the coal and steel resources of France, Germany, and other European nations had been discussed among European political circles for several decades. Monnet's specific ideas of pooling sovereignty arose from his belief that rampant unchecked nationalism was one of the most significant causes of the two world wars. He had also experienced as an official of the League of Nations that the intergovernmentalism of the league made it ineffective as an international body in maintaining peace, because its member nations could veto any plan for action.

---

[2] Mearsheimer, *The Tragedy of Great Power Politics*, p. 21. Also see John J. Mearsheimer, "Why We Will Soon Miss the Cold War," *Atlantic* (August 1990), 35–50; and Mearsheimer, "Back to the Future," 5–56.

Monnet's idea of shared sovereignty developed not through any theoretical analysis but from his experience as an economist and civil servant working on allied economic coordination in World War I and as Deputy Director General of the League of Nations. For him shared sovereignty was a means to achieving several of his principal goals. Foremost he wanted to bring lasting peace and an end to the wars that had dominated Europe for two centuries. He also sought to restore Europe's economic and political power as well as its international influence by uniting the principal nations of Europe through the political and economic leadership of France. And finally his long-range goal was to change the relationship between states in a manner that would revolutionize international relations.[3]

Monnet set forth some of his ideas in an article in the August 1944 issue of *Fortune* magazine. In order to establish lasting peace, he asserted there would have to be "a true yielding of sovereignty" to "some kind of central union." He favored a large European market without customs barriers to prevent nationalism, which he characterized as "the curse of the modern world."[4] By the late 1940s Monnet expressed his ideas more broadly. He understood that peaceful intentions and treaties were not enough to guarantee peace because the nation state was not reined in by laws or institutions. He therefore wanted a new kind of international institution which would require nations to transfer "to a common authority the powers which they can no longer exercise separately for the benefit of each of our countries." The only way to prevent a "coalition of governments acting to the detriment to one of the partners," he stated, was "the delegation of some part of the powers of the States to a common authority, that is, to a federal institution whose members are the representatives of all participating countries."[5]

In April 1950 Monnet explained his proposal to Robert Schuman. He emphasized the need to tie an expanding Germany economy to France and pointed out that American officials were preparing to remove the restrictions placed by the occupying powers on industrial activity. Already a proponent of French–German reconciliation, Schuman persuaded his government to adopt Monnet's proposal and announce the plan on May 9, 1950. Two weeks later Monnet traveled to Bonn to present the Schuman Plan to the German chancellor, Konrad

---

[3] Sherrill Brown Wells, *Pioneers of European Integration and Peace, 1945–1963* (Boston: Bedford/St. Martin's, 2007), pp. 6–10.
[4] Quoted in François Duchêne, *Jean Monnet: The First Statesman of Interdependence* (New York: W. W. Norton & Company, 1994), p. 183.
[5] Jean Monnet, interview in *Le Monde*, June 16, 1955, quoted in Wells, *Pioneers of European Integration*, p. 116.

Adenauer. The German leader proved a very receptive listener, because he strongly believed that the way to rebuild Germany without arousing anxiety among its neighbors was to integrate its economic and political systems firmly in European multilateral institutions. At the end of their meeting Adenauer told Monnet that "he considered the implementation of the French proposal to be the most important mission falling to him. If he succeeded in reaching the proper resolution, he would feel that he had not wasted his life."[6]

Many Germans did not share Adenauer's vision. Opposition to the Schuman Plan was especially strong within the Social Democratic Party (SPD), whose leaders attacked the proposal on nationalistic and ideological grounds. Kurt Schumacher, leader of the SPD, sharply criticized the plan as putting the Germany economy "in the service of French diplomacy" and placing heavy industry under private control, thus preventing the creation of a social-democratic Europe. For different reasons, most West European industrialists also opposed the plan as destroying the cartels that protected their vested interests.[7]

During negotiations, French support for the plan was challenged by the issue of German rearmament. The outbreak of the Korean War, widely thought to be inspired by Moscow, raised fears in the United States of increased Soviet threats to Western Europe. To ease such threats, leaders in the Truman administration wanted a strengthened European defense built around a rearmed Germany. Again Jean Monnet produced a plan to deal with this problem through further European integration. His solution was a gradual rearmament of Germany with the units to be merged into a larger European army under a supranational European Defense Community (EDC) with a European minister of defense. Endorsed by the French National Assembly in October 1950, this proposal was called the Pleven Plan, after the French prime pinister René Pleven.[8]

Pressure from the US high commissioner for West Germany, John J. McCloy, persuaded Adenauer to overcome the opposition to the Schuman Plan and sign the treaty creating the European Coal and Steel Community (ECSC) on April 18, 1951. This treaty established a supranational community with the goal of creating a common market in

---

[6] Duchêne, *Monnet*, pp. 190–207; Hans-Peter Schwarz, *Konrad Adenauer*, vol. I (Providence, RI: Berghahn Books, 1995), pp. 608–18; French summary of Adenauer–Monnet meeting, Bonn, May 23, 1950, quoted in Wells, *Pioneers of European Integration*, p. 95.

[7] Thomas A. Schwartz, *America's Germany: John J. McCloy and the Federal Republic of Germany* (Cambridge, MA: Harvard University Press, 1991), pp. 105–12; Wells, *Pioneers of European Integration*, p. 12; Schwarz, *Adenauer*, vol. I, p. 608.

[8] Duchêne, *Monnet*, pp. 207–29.

coal and steel, without customs duties or other trade restrictions. It was ratified by six nations: France, West Germany, Italy, the Netherlands, Belgium, and Luxembourg. In the summer of 1952 after ratification the new supranational community was established by a nine-member High Authority which named Jean Monnet as its president.[9]

Established national priorities and special interests in economic and defense policies created insurmountable problems for both the EDC and the ECSC. After many negotiated changes to the original Pleven Plan, the EDC Treaty was signed in May 1952. But many doubts remained, especially in France, and in August 1954 the French National Assembly rejected the treaty and put the EDC to rest. Meanwhile, the High Authority of the ECSC had extensive discussions with national ministers, unions, and industrialists about eliminating tariffs and production quotas on coal and steel. But they found it impossible to persuade these groups to remove the barriers to free trade, and they had to accept that they lacked the authority to order them to do so. While the ECSC created some improved communication and understanding on industrial cooperation and rule-making among old enemies, it ultimately was deadlocked in its attempt to create a free-trade area in coal and steel.[10]

The deepening Cold War overshadowed the tentative steps toward integration as Soviet pressure on West Germany emphasized the need for improved European defense and German rearmament. At British initiative in 1954, the six members of the Brussels Pact (a March 1948 security treaty) agreed to end the occupation in Germany, add Germany and Italy as members, and create the Western European Union for common defense activities as part of NATO. This ultimately brought Germany into the Atlantic alliance, kept US forces in Europe, and created a widely accepted European defense organization. With the participation of Britain and the United States, an important step was achieved in strengthening European defense and in making Germany an equal member of the alliance. Adenauer declared at the signing of the agreement in Paris that October 23, 1954 was "the day of reconciliation with France."[11]

[9] Jean Monnet, *Memoirs* (Garden City, NY: Doubleday, 1978), pp. 345–50; Duchêne, *Monnet*, pp. 207–35; Schwarz, *Adenauer*, vol. I, pp. 598–99.

[10] Ibid., pp. 598–627; Desmond Dinan, *Europe Recast: A History of European Integration* (Boulder: Lynne Rienner, 2004), pp. 55–64; Jean-Pierre Rioux, *The Fourth Republic, 1944–1958* (Cambridge University Press, 1987), pp. 224–31; John Gillingham, *Coal, Steel, and the Rebirth of Europe, 1945–1955* (Cambridge University Press, 1991), pp. 319–48; Duchêne, *Monnet*, pp. 226–57.

[11] Anthony Eden, *Full Circle: The Memoirs of Sir Anthony Eden* (London: Cassell, 1960), pp. 165–71; Schwarz, *Adenauer*, vol. II, pp. 94–132; Rioux, *Fourth Republic*, pp. 231–33;

Germany and the Rome treaties

Along with improved security in Western Europe, sustained economic growth and further steps in French–German cooperation stimulated new efforts to improve sovereignty and advance integration of the six European economies. A referendum on the future of the Saar region in October 1955 saw the residents vote overwhelmingly to return to Germany. The peaceful reunion of the Saar with West Germany was an important measure in building confidence and improved relations between Bonn and Paris. Spurred by the failure of the EDC, Monnet and Spaak began to exchange ideas in the fall of 1954 about new initiatives for integration. During 1955–56 the six foreign ministers gathered at conferences in Messina and Venice to discuss these concepts in depth.[12]

By the summer of 1956 these discussions were sufficiently advanced to convene an intergovernmental conference in Brussels chaired by Paul-Henri Spaak. The negotiators confronted many difficulties, with the main obstacle being French protectionism driven by fear of the power of a resurgent German economy. Konrad Adenauer played a key role in bringing to a successful conclusion the difficult negotiations for what became the Rome treaties. He worked closely with Spaak and showed himself willing to compromise on key issues that were important for the further integration of West Germany into Europe. Adenauer strongly believed that a united Europe would further Franco-German reconciliation, strengthen Europe against the Soviet Union, improve relations with the United States, and benefit West Germany's economy through market liberalization. In a memorandum to the members of his cabinet on January 19, 1956, Adenauer demanded that in the forthcoming negotiations his ministers demonstrate a "clear, positive German attitude toward European integration." He asserted: "if integration is successful we can add the weight of a united Europe as an important new element into the balance of the negotiations on security as well as reunification." The parties achieved agreement due to concessions to France on two key points: French overseas territories would be included in the new common market, and a new organization to promote the peaceful uses of atomic energy would be created by the six nations.[13]

Ernest R. May, "The American Commitment to Germany, 1949–1955," in Lawrence S. Kaplan (ed.), *American Historians and the Atlantic Alliance* (Kent, OH: Kent State University Press, 1991), pp. 52–80.

[12] Dinan, *Europe Recast*, pp. 63–70; Moravcsik, *The Choice for Europe*, pp. 86–122; Mark Gilbert, *Surpassing Realism: The Politics of European Integration since 1945* (Lanham, MD: Rowman & Littlefield, 2003), pp. 62–66.

[13] Gilbert, *Surpassing Realism*, pp. 65–83; Dinan, *Europe Recast*, pp. 66–77; Adenauer's directive of January 19, 1956, quoted in Wells, *Pioneers of European Integration*, pp. 124–25.

The six nations signed the two treaties of Rome on March 25, 1957. The European Atomic Energy Community (Euratom) would exploit the peaceful uses of atomic energy through research, development of safety measures, supervision of nuclear materials, and creation of a common market for specialized materials, capital, jobs, and equipment. The European Economic Community (EEC), a more important agreement, created a customs union to move toward a common market, a goal that would not be achieved until the early 1990s. The EEC worked through a Council of Ministers representing heads of government, a Commission of high civil servants, a Parliament, and a Court of Justice. The treaties were ratified by the end of 1957 and went into effect on January 1, 1958. Europe now consisted of three communities: the European Coal and Steel Community, the European Economic Community, and the European Atomic Energy Community.[14]

With these treaties the leaders of Europe put aside old rivalries and, while protecting many basic national interests, compromised on others in order to achieve peace, economic growth, and political stability. In particular, in accepting Euratom Germany agreed to significant constraints on its uses of nuclear technology, and by entering a customs union tied its economic prospects to the common future of the six members. In return Italy and Germany gained acceptance of their political rehabilitation and returned to membership in the European family of states. Overall these agreements were a unique step in the long history of conflict among European nation-states as six members agreed to limit but not totally transfer national sovereignty in economic policy to a set of common institutions.

The European Monetary System

The period from 1957 to 1978 saw many developments in Europe but only gradual evolution of the institutions of the European communities. Charles de Gaulle as president of France from 1958 to 1969 took significant steps to establish the Common Agricultural Policy (CAP) by a key agreement with Germany and to strengthen cooperation with Bonn through the Elysée Treaty of 1963. But de Gaulle's opposition to shared sovereignty slowed development of European institutions beyond the creation of a customs union. Meanwhile, the decline in utility of the ECSC and Euratom led to the merger of their executive functions with the EEC in 1967, creating a single European Community (EC). The six member states realized significant economic growth for most of this

---

[14] Derek W. Urwin, *The Community of Europe: A History of European Integration Since 1945* (London: Longman, 1991), pp. 75–84; Dinan, *Europe Recast*, pp. 76–77.

period until the Arab oil embargo of 1973. This event, along with turbulence in financial markets following the abandonment of the gold standard and the adoption of floating currencies, also in 1973, led to worldwide inflation and recession in the following year. The EC also expanded its membership with the addition of Britain, Ireland, and Denmark in 1973.[15]

By 1978 European leaders were ready to take action to establish effective European regional cooperation in monetary policy. Advocates of closer European integration had long wanted to add monetary cooperation to the market coordination that had developed, but it took several years of oil-price-driven inflation and fluctuating currency markets to persuade politicians to move. The creation of the European Monetary System (EMS) was a result of cooperation and creative leadership by Roy Jenkins, president of the European Commission, who conceived of the idea in 1977, President Valéry Giscard d'Estaing of France, who strongly supported it, and German chancellor Helmut Schmidt, who was the driving force behind it. After initially ignoring the proposal, Schmidt moved in early 1978 to propose the creation of a new monetary system because the persistent depreciation of the dollar and a corresponding appreciation of the deutsche mark reduced the competitiveness of West German exports and threatened its jobs. The United States appeared to be recovering from a global economic crisis at the expense of West Germany's prudence and prosperity. Schmidt was incensed by the foreign policy of Jimmy Carter's administration and what he saw as its cavalier approach to international monetary matters, and he was determined to respond to the impact of these policies on Germany. He wanted to cushion West Germany from the impact of ill-advised US policies by establishing a Europe-wide monetary system to demonstrate to Washington that the Europeans were able and willing to respond to poor US leadership in economic affairs.[16]

The Franco-German proposal was thrashed out and finally approved at the European Council summit in Brussels in December 1978. The EMS, which began operation in March 1979, established an exchange-rate mechanism using a parity grid and a divergence indicator based on the European currency unit (ECU), an artificial unit of account made

[15] Wells, *Pioneers of European Integration*, pp. 30–42; Desmond Dinan, "Building Europe: The European Community and the Bonn–Paris–Washington Relationship, 1958–1963," in Helga Haftendorn *et al.* (eds.), *The Strategic Triangle: France, Germany, and the United States in the Shaping of the New Europe* (Washington, DC: Woodrow Wilson Center Press, 2006), pp. 29–51; Michael Kreile, "The Search for a New Monetary System: Germany's Balancing Act," in Haftendorn *et al.* (eds.), *Strategic Triangle*, pp. 149–63.
[16] Gilbert, *Surpassing Realism*, pp. 139–43; Dinan, *Europe Recast*, pp. 173–75.

up of a basket of participating currencies weighted according to their values. Currencies were allowed to fluctuate against each other within a band of plus or minus 2.5 percent of their value. Finance ministers and central bankers would have to agree on changes in parity.[17]

The primary purpose of the EMS was, according to Andrew Moravcsik, "to dampen DM appreciation by helping weak currency countries impose macroeconomic discipline rather than either devalue or impose trade restrictions." Schmidt argued to skeptics that they should view EMS "in the political context of the next fifteen to twenty years." For Schmidt and Giscard d'Estaing, the EMS was laying the foundation of a European economy that would be less vulnerable to outside shocks. They hoped that the new system would enable Germany to stem the tendency of the mark to overshoot in value and that it would provide the franc with a potential frame for austerity. If it served these purposes, it would be useful economically and politically.[18]

The Single European Act

By 1985 most governments in the EC wanted to expand economic integration to revitalize the organization. The EMS had achieved some success in coordinating monetary policy, but the leaders of all governments recognized that it needed to be extended to a full monetary union to be effective. The obvious next step was deeper market integration to complete the common market that had been the stated goal of the 1957 ECC Treaty. At this point, Jacques Delors was appointed president of the European Commission in January 1985 to activate a program of deeper integration. The former finance minister of France, Delors was a master bureaucrat with a vision for an activist Europe. For him the single market was a step toward full monetary union, a reformed budget, and a broad charter of social rights. In March the European Council agreed in principle to the creation of a single market, and in December it agreed on the text of the Single European Act amending the Treaty of Rome.[19]

The Single European Act committed the member states to create a fully integrated internal market by the end of 1992. The nine states of the EC would become an area "in which persons, goods and capital shall move freely under conditions identical to those obtaining within a Member State." The removal of all barriers to trade would create

[17] Dinan, *Europe Recast*, pp. 174–75.
[18] Moravcsik, *Choice for Europe*, p. 253; Gilbert, *Surpassing Realism*, pp. 140–45.
[19] Kenneth Dyson and Kevin Featherstone, *The Road to Maastricht: Negotiating Economic and Monetary Union* (Oxford University Press, 1999), pp. 691–745; Dinan,

economies of scale and cheaper goods for consumers inside the community. The same efficiencies would make EC products more competitive in external trade. The Act called in general terms for expanded political coordination and institutional reform, and it strongly implied the creation of a monetary union as a complementary step. Most significantly, it extended qualified majority voting in the Council of Ministers so that it would require a minimum of three states to block a proposal. This action promised to speed up the decision-making process and represented a major increase in shared sovereignty.[20]

German leaders played a crucial role in shaping the Single European Act. The EMS had basically committed German policy-makers to creating a single economic space in a Europe based on mutually contingent, parallel macroeconomic management. Hans-Dietrich Genscher, the foreign minister in various coalition governments from 1974–92, was a steadfast advocate of increased European integration as an essential means of achieving the related goals of German and Western European prosperity and security and ultimately German and European reunification. Helmut Kohl became German chancellor in October 1982 and reestablished European integration as his country's central priority. By presenting himself as "Adenauer's grandson," Kohl reunited his party and coalition government behind the legacy of the postwar chancellor who had championed reconciliation with France and German integration with Europe. Genscher and Kohl, along with Italian leaders, showed "a strong propensity to test the limits of European integration and push for significant renunciations of national sovereignty to Community institutions," argues Mark Gilbert. "Germany, moreover, backed her rhetoric with hard cash. By allowing France to devalue the franc within the EMS and paying for the British budget rebate, Germany prevented these two more acrimonious partners from wrecking the Community altogether."[21]

Toward economic and monetary union

As the detailed process of revising the laws and regulations to implement the Single European Act began in July 1987, significant political

Europe Recast, pp. 206–07; Derek W. Urwin, *The Community of Europe*, 2nd edn. (London: Longman, 1995), pp. 226–30, 270–71.

[20] Urwin, *Community of Europe*, 2nd edn., pp. 230–33.

[21] Carl Lankowski, "Germany: Transforming Its Role," in E. E. Zeff and E. B. Pirro (eds.), *The European Union and the Member States* (Boulder: Lynne Rienner, 2006), pp. 35–38; Desmond Dinan on Genscher and Wilie Paterson on Kohl in Desmond Dinan (ed.), *Encyclopedia of the European Union* (Boulder: Lynne Rienner, 1998), pp. 251, 318; Dyson and Featherstone, *Road to Maastricht*, pp. 256–60; Gilbert, *Surpassing Realism*, p. 183.

changes unfolded on the continent. The Cold War was winding down. Mikhail Gorbachev's reforms were opening Soviet society, and his negotiations with the Western alliance started to produce results with the signing of the Intermediate-range Nuclear Forces Treaty on December 8, 1987. The Berlin Wall fell in November 1989, and the communist regimes of Eastern Europe collapsed in the following months. With these transformations in Central Europe, the unification of Germany became a pressing issue for the two German states and their four occupying powers.[22]

Meanwhile pressure to create a monetary union to complement the single market began to build among business and political leaders in France, Italy, and Germany. Both parties in the governing coalition in Germany, the Social Democrats and the Free Democrats, had advocated monetary union in their platforms since the 1970s. German business associations and trade unions also supported stronger monetary coordination. Former chancellor Helmut Schmidt and Valéry Giscard d'Estaing had formed the Association for the Monetary Union of Europe in 1986 to lobby for the cause among bankers and business leaders. By 1987 French and Italian officials and business executives were pushing for monetary union because of the domestic costs of shadowing the deutsche mark within the EMS.[23]

In Bonn Kohl and Genscher wanted to create monetary union, but they needed to avoid a public fight with the highly respected governing board of the Bundesbank, the German central bank led by its president Karl-Otto Pöhl. Bundesbank leaders and other German economists had traditionally followed an "economist approach" toward monetary union which called for a long gradual convergence of EC economies along with steps toward political union before monetary union should be established. An alternative school was the "monetarist approach" led by French central bank and treasury officials and by Jacques Delors and many of the Commission economists. This group argued that a new EC institution such as a common central bank could bring about economic convergence among members by changing market behavior. Based on the French experience in using the exchange-rate mechanism to deal with currency fluctuations after the oil embargo and other financial shocks, the monetarists persuaded the leaders of the Bundesbank to

---

[22] Samuel F. Wells, Jr., "From Euromissiles to Maastricht: The Policies of Reagan–Bush and Mitterrand," in Haftendorn et al. (ed.), Strategic Triangle, pp. 297–304; Dinan, Europe Recast, pp. 233–34.

[23] Markus Jachtenfuchs, "Germany and Relaunching Europe," in Haftendorn et al. (ed.), Strategic Triangle, pp. 312–15, 323; Dinan, Europe Recast, pp. 234–49; Gilbert, Surpassing Realism, p. 190.

back an early move toward EMU. By the summer of 1988 the main forces were aligned to advance the case for monetary union.[24]

Commission president Jacques Delors played the key role in shaping the way in which monetary union would be established. For some time Delors had believed that a common European currency was essential for the single market to function properly. He lobbied hard for monetary union by attending the monthly meetings of the committee of central bank governors, by courting and winning the support of Karl-Otto Pöhl of the Bundesbank, and by attending the meetings of the ministers of economics and finance of the EC as well as the meetings of the European Council. With strong support from Helmut Kohl, the European Council in June 1988 created a special committee to explore the timing and form of economic and monetary union and named Delors to head this committee. The Delors Committee was composed of the heads of the central banks, one commissioner from the European Commission, and three independent experts all acting in personal capacities. The group analyzed prior studies of monetary union such as the Werner Report of 1970, and their final product contained many of its recommendations. In April 1989 the committee presented the Delors Report which proposed a three-staged approach to monetary union and argued that such union was needed in order to prevent currency fluctuations from undermining market unification. Their deeper, implied argument was political: by pooling sovereignty in economic areas, European monetary union would create a huge leap forward in integration within the EC. The Madrid summit of June 1989 endorsed the Delors Report as a blueprint for action, and it became the document over which the intergovernmental conference would negotiate in shaping the Maastricht Treaty. With this accomplishment Delors had made his most important contribution to the process of economic and monetary union, and in the process he had incorporated the goals of the Bundesbank and the German model of monetary policy into the proposals of the Delors Committee.[25]

---

[24] Dyson and Featherstone, *Road to Maastricht*, pp. 29–31.

[25] Amy Verdun, "A Historical Institutionalist Analysis of the Road to Economic and Monetary Union: A Journey with Many Crossroads," in Sophie Meunier and Kathleen R. McNamara (eds.), *Making History: European Integration and Institutional Change at Fifty* (Oxford University Press, 2007), p. 203; Gilbert, *Surpassing Realism*, p. 189; George Ross, "Jacques Delors," in Dinan (ed.), *Encyclopedia of the European Union*, p. 126; Amy Verdun, *European Responses to Globalization and Financial Market Integration: Perceptions of Economic and Monetary Union in Britain, France, and Germany* (Basingstoke: Macmillan, 2000), pp. 80–82; Dyson and Featherstone, *Road to Maastricht*, pp. 172–201, 315–50, 691–745.

The Maastricht Treaty and EMU

After the acceptance of the Delors Report in mid-1989, rapid changes swept Europe. During the fall Western observers saw the collapse of the Berlin Wall followed by replacement of the communist governments across Eastern Europe. After intense "two plus four" negotiations among the two German states and the occupying powers, German unification occurred in October 1990. Soon thereafter new countries – ranging from Finland and Austria among the neutrals to Cyprus and Malta in the Mediterranean – applied for EC membership. The leaders of the EC agreed that it was necessary to move quickly to strengthen integration before considering adding new members, especially those from former command economies. But mindful of the uncertain future facing Europe, many other leaders wanted to move cautiously on any steps that required giving up national sovereignty.[26]

The heads of government of the EC member states met in the Dutch city of Maastricht in December 1991 to consider reports from the two intergovernmental conferences which had been working for a year shaping recommendations on political union and economic and monetary union respectively. During the course of the intense and wide-ranging negotiations at the summit, the recommendations on political union were greatly watered down. At British insistence all references to federalism were removed as was the social charter setting out regulations for labor and human rights. Several other states joined Britain in insisting on putting the recommendations on foreign and security policy as well as those on justice and home affairs outside the normal EC decision structure in separate pillars for intergovernmental decision, i.e. decision by the heads of government meeting as the European Council.[27]

For the advocates of increased European integration such as Helmut Kohl of Germany and François Mitterrand of France the painful concessions made on political union made it all the more important to achieve effective economic and monetary union. This was essentially accomplished as the leaders agreed to create a monetary union through stages that would lead to the creation of a single currency and a central bank. Progress toward these goals would be determined by the speed with which a majority of states met four strict criteria of economic performance on inflation, government deficits, overall debt, and currency stability. The final implementation of economic and monetary union was projected for January 1999.[28]

[26] Urwin, *Community of Europe*, 2nd edn., pp. 241–52.
[27] Ibid., pp. 252–55.   [28] Ibid., pp. 255–56.

Despite the compromises made, the general tone at the conclusion of the Maastricht summit was positive. While the advocates of deeper European union were disappointed by what they had been able to achieve on the political side, they were pleased with their accomplishments on monetary union. Even then it must be noted that the terms of EMU were not what economic theorists had projected as their goal during the 1950s and 1960s. This union, called an economic and monetary union, was in fact confined to monetary policy and did not cover budgetary or fiscal policies. The leaders of the member states were not prepared to sacrifice control over budgets or tax policy just as they were not prepared to give up control over foreign and security policy or justice and home affairs. In today's world, this asymmetrical EMU – supranational monetary policy and national fiscal and budgetary policy – seems "still to offer an acceptable half-way house between national sovereignty and European supranational sovereignty over economic and monetary matters." But for a group of nations which fifty years before had just concluded a long war stretching across several continents, monetary union remained a significant accomplishment.[29]

Conclusion

Recent scholarship has put to rest the widely accepted interpretation from the 1990s that German unification came about as a result of a "high-politics bargain" in which Kohl "accepted the abolition of the deutsche mark and the end of Bundesbank autonomy in exchange for Britain's and France's acceptance of Germany's unification."[30] As this chapter has shown, German leaders, political parties, business associations, and labor unions accepted the logic and desirability of economic and monetary union by the mid-1980s. What remained to be negotiated were the criteria and the timing, and these were worked out in the Delors Report of April 1989, some months before German unification became an immediate issue. "The German government did not give away the deutsche mark," argues Markus Jachtenfuchs, "but it advocated EMU because it corresponded to its political vision of the European Union and at the same time served German business interests."[31]

---

[29] Verdun, "A Historical Institutionalist Analysis," pp. 208–09.

[30] Jachtenfuchs, "Germany and Relaunching Europe," p. 311; see also Joseph M. Grieco, "State Interests and Institutional Rule Trajectories: A Neorealist Interpretation of the Maastricht Treaty and European Economic and Monetary Union," in Benjamin Frankel (ed.), *Realism: Restatements and Renewal* (London: Frank Cass, 1996), pp. 261–306.

[31] Jachtenfuchs, "Germany and Relaunching Europe," pp. 311–15; Jeffrey Legro and Andrew Moravcsik, "Is Anybody Still a Realist?" Working Papers (Cambridge,

This chapter has focused on Germany and its most important element of national power, its strong export-driven economy. From the creation of the Federal Republic of Germany in 1949 German leaders understood that their nation's future prospects were tied to its development of close ties with its western neighbors. With the creation of the European Coal and Steel Community and the approval of the Treaties of Rome, Konrad Adenauer and his successors knew that their nation's future lay with the European Community. By the 1970s Germany wanted economic coordination with Europe to move beyond a customs union and was prepared to take the lead with French leaders in creating the European Monetary System.

German commitment to deeper European integration came during the 1980s. The shared vision of Helmut Kohl and François Mitterrand for expanded integration drove Europe forward after a period of institutional stasis. The presence of Jacques Delors as the concert master at the head of the European Commission made certain that preparations for EMU and political union would be made carefully and thoroughly. Reform in the Soviet Union and the end of the Cold War accelerated progress.

At Maastricht and beyond German leaders wanted deeper political union than their partners would accept, and they were prepared to go much further in sharing sovereignty in foreign and security policy, justice and home affairs, and provide increased power to the European parliament.[32] Germany by the time of unification had fully cast its lot in a security partnership with its EU partners and with the United States, and the primary focus of its economic and political policies operated through the European Union in Brussels. By pooling its sovereignty in European economic and, to a lesser degree, political institutions, Germany has followed a very different road from the one predicted by any form of realist theory. The Federal Republic had performed much below any predicted military or even economic power line. It had charted a new course with a new unprecedented form of multinational institution, the European Union.

---

[32] Simon J. Bulmer, "Shaping the Rules? The Constitutive Politics of the European Union and German Power," in Peter J. Katzenstein (ed.), *Tamed Power: Germany in Europe* (Ithaca: Cornell University Press, 1997), pp. 76–79.

15   John Mearsheimer's "elementary geometry of power": Euclidean moment or an intellectual blind alley?

Jonathan Haslam

"There will always be some anomalies."[1]

John Mearsheimer of Chicago, quondam soldier, US Air Force officer, and unmasker of the brilliant but flawed military theorist Sir Basil Liddell Hart – "the most famous and widely advanced military historian and theorist in the world"[2] – is himself an *enfant terrible*. "I don't like authority," Mearsheimer confesses.[3] An odd remark is this to come from a West Point graduate: clearly no facile mind; indeed, an engaging intellectual, a gifted teacher and debater, the genial host, Mearsheimer is also the compulsive contrarian, courting controversy among liberals while complaining that the doors of Harvard are closed to him because of their intolerance.[4] The latest example is an onslaught against the Israeli lobby in US foreign policy, which cuts directly across Mearsheimer's extensively articulated notion that domestic politics play a subordinate if not insubstantial role determining international relations.[5]

Mearsheimer made a name for himself after the end of the Cold War with a merciless onslaught against "The False Promise of International

The phrase in the chapter title, 'elementary geometry of power', is taken from Mearsheimer, "Why We Will Soon Miss the Cold War."

[1] "Conversations in International Relations: Interview with John J. Mearsheimer (Part 1)," *International Relations* 20 (2006), 105–23.

[2] John Mearsheimer, *Liddell Hart and the Weight of History* (Ithaca: Cornell University Press, 1989), p. 1.

[3] Interview by Harry Kreisler, http://globetrotter.berkeley.edu/people2/Mearsheimer/mearsheimer-con2.html.

[4] In private and in public: "it is worth noting," he writes, "that despite realism's widely acknowledged dominance of the intellectual agenda in international relations, Harvard's government department has not employed a realist theorist since Henry Kissinger left in 1969. Moreover, it made no effort to hire either Morgenthau or Waltz, the two most influential international relations scholars of the past fifty years." See Michael Brecher and Frank P. Harvey (eds.), *Realism and Institutionalism in International Studies* (Ann Arbor: University of Michigan Press, 2002), p. 30.

[5] John Mearsheimer and Stephen Walt, "The Israeli Lobby," *London Review of Books* 28 (March 23, 2006); "Letters: The Israeli Lobby," *London Review of Books* 28 (May 11, 2006) and Mearsheimer and Walt, *The Israeli Lobby in U.S. Foreign Policy* (Farrar, Straus and Giroux 2008).

322

Institutions." Following a decade of disillusion after heightened expectations the United Nations was in no condition to meet, the polemic has withstood well the test of time and a barrage of attacks from fervent liberal internationalists.[6] A magnum opus, *The Tragedy of Great Power Politics*, takes the assault to higher ground and outlines an entire model of international relations. Here Mearsheimer asserts that "[t]he main causes of war are located in the architecture of the international system."[7] On this view the great powers, because of their mutual fear, have as "their ultimate aim ... to gain a position of dominant power over others ... States facing this incentive are fated to clash as each competes for advantage over the others. This is a tragic situation, but there is no escaping it unless the states that make up the system agree to form a world government."[8]

A proposition of this simplicity suggests a degree of determinism difficult if not impossible to escape. If domestic politics matter so little, and Mearsheimer is consistent, to attack the Israeli lobby is quixotic. Such a striking inconsistency in the thrust of Mearsheimer's thought is not, however, unique. An article in *Foreign Affairs* acknowledges that although "powerful structural imperatives of the international system" would "probably force the United States" to act in a certain way, "states occasionally ignore signals from the anarchic world in which they operate, choosing instead to pursue strategies that contradict straightforward balance-of-power logic."[9] The irresistible question arises: what separates "occasional" from "normal"? Mearsheimer says "that any time a state behaves in a strategically foolish fashion, it counts as a clear contradiction of my theory."[10] In his writings, however, the United States never quite acts as a great power should, so a convenient caveat has been created to allow for the difference: it is represented as insular, primarily a sea power. Indeed, the author admits that the example of the United States, and Britain beforehand, "might appear to provide the strongest evidence against my claim that great powers are dedicated to maximising their share of world power."[11] Doubts are hard to suppress when an entire theory seeking to explain great-power behavior in international relations then finds that the world's only superpower, the greatest great power, does not fit the model. Furthermore, events

---

[6] Mearsheimer, "The False Promise of International Institutions," 5–49.
[7] Mearsheimer, *The Tragedy of Great Power Politics*.
[8] Ibid., pp. xi–xii.
[9] John Mearsheimer, "The Future of the American Pacifier," *Foreign Affairs* 80 (September/October 2001), 61.
[10] "Conversations in International Relations: Interview with John J. Mearsheimer (Part I)," 112.
[11] Mearsheimer, *The Tragedy of Great Power Politics*, p. 234.

almost immediately belied Mearsheimer's implicitly benign interpretation of US policy. First came the "option of preemptive actions" formulated in the *National Security Strategy* of September 17, 2002,[12] then the war launched against Iraq on March 18, 2003 with the flimsiest of justifications, bolstering the suspicion that Washington sought hegemony over the Middle Eastern region – to the evident consternation of the author.[13]

Using insularity as an explanation for the absence of hegemonic expansion in turn creates another major problem accounting for one of the most aggressive powers from 1895 to 1945 – imperial Japan: no less insular than Britain; certainly no less insular than the United States. "The Japanese attack against the United States at Pearl Harbor in December 1941 might appear to be another exception to this rule," Mearsheimer acknowledges, "since Japan is an insular state, and it struck first against another great power."[14] Yet the model does not say that great powers will attack only other great powers; preemption against the territory of lesser powers likely to be friendly to the adversary makes some kind of strategic sense given Mearsheimer's presuppositions. Moreover, Japan did attack Russia, a great power, in 1904, and to imply that because Japan did not actually invade Russia, this was somehow not major aggression is at odds with the facts. The defeat of the Russian fleet at Tsushima delivered a devastating blow to St. Petersburg that prompted a revolution in 1905.

Moreover, Mearsheimer's assertion that the Japanese did "not even think about conquering" the Soviet Union in 1939 may be technically correct but is substantially misleading. Had Japan won the battle at Khalkhin-Gol in September – and the purge of the Soviet Far Eastern Army made this a distinct possibility – who is to say what Tokyo would have done? This much is evident from discussions at the highest level early in 1941. From 1932 to 1935 General Araki, as War Minister, was actually planning on the basis of war with Moscow. One only has to read his speeches to see that this was on his mind. Furthermore, the Russians obtained surreptitious access to plans for the invasion of Siberia. This was why a war scare broke out in Moscow concerning Japan in late 1933, why the Americans then assumed overt conflict was on the cards, and why the French refused to include Japan in the mutual-assistance pact concluded with the Soviet Union in 1935. It was these fears that had forced the pace of Soviet rearmament, not Hitler's rise to power, which it

---

[12] For the full text see www.whitehouse.gov/nsc/nss.html.
[13] John Mearsheimer and Stephen Walt, "An Unnecessary War," *Foreign Policy* (January/February 2003), 50–59.
[14] Mearsheimer, *The Tragedy of Great Power Politics*, p. 136.

preceded. And through to the German invasion in June 1941 the Japanese leadership regularly considered the option of moving against the Soviet Union. All this has been extensively documented.[15] The option of war to the West fell away finally only with the Battle of Kursk in July 1943, when the tide of war in Europe turned. Furthermore, the claim that attacking across into Asia for Japan was very different from attacking across into Europe for Britain and the United States begs the question of motive, a factor which Mearsheimer refuses to consider outside his system-oriented model.[16] The entire line of reasoning on Japan is severely undermined by the author's failure fully to account for the brutal occupation of China from 1931 through to the attack on Pearl Harbor in 1941.[17] Above all Japanese behavior requires a domestic as well as an international explanation – both constitutional and economic (top-heavy industrialization with no internal natural resources under an emperor with divine right and the senior flag officer as War Minister) – which Mearsheimer is unwilling to acknowledge. This instance raises a further question about Mearsheimer's work. Just how seriously does he take History?

For now, however, let us return to statements on policy. Inevitably these raise awkward questions about Mearsheimer's steadfast commitment to a deterministic doctrine so trenchantly canvassed and so resolutely defended against all-comers. For Mearsheimer, academic theory does not suffice: he aims at "the body politic for the purpose of influencing the public debate and particular policies in important ways."[18] Yet if one believes with him that the conduct of international relations is a "tragedy" in which the great powers are condemned to follow a path laid out before them – that is certainly what the ancient Greeks meant by the term – what is the purpose of focusing on policy? It is puzzling and, indeed, more than a little unfortunate for an academic who eschews serious treatment of ideas generating the conduct of international relations over two entire centuries, even in the motivation of revolutionary France or Soviet Russia, to make a public spectacle of an issue in foreign policy so loaded ideologically as well as ethnically. Here the brusque dismissal of "irrational" factors in Nazi behavior – most notably the obsession with the master race that drove Hitler eastward – is perhaps the most striking and, doubtless to anyone who has not met the author, more than a little disconcerting.[19]

---

[15] See Jonathan Haslam, *The Soviet Union and the Threat from the East, 1933–1941: Moscow, Tokyo, and the Prelude to the Pacific War* (London: Macmillan, 1992).
[16] Mearsheimer, *The Tragedy of Great Power Politics*, pp. 264–65.
[17] Ibid., pp. 136–37. [18] Interviewed by Harry Kreisler.
[19] Mearsheimer, *The Tragedy of Great Power Politics*, pp. 216–17.

What has driven Mearsheimer's search for simplistic interpretations of world politics? Academic work, including choice of discipline, is arguably a vocation. A discipline, which Political Science could just about claim to be but International Relations self-evidently is not (in spite of the long search for legitimacy), defines itself by method as well as subject matter.[20] A given method unquestionably holds special appeal to a particular cast of mind. Mearsheimer readily concurs. He believes "I[nternational] R[elations] theorists, are born, not created. I think you either have an instinct for creating theories or you don't."[21] He has accordingly expressed an insatiable appetite for "simple theories that address important issues."[22] By the same token and from the absence of any archival research in *The Tragedy of Great Power Politics*, we can assume that Mearsheimer is not interested in historical accuracy for its own sake. Curiosity about the past and an aptitude for archives and foreign languages are vital in that pursuit. He thus resembles many political scientists in International Relations; including, to a limited degree, its most distinguished, neorealist Kenneth Waltz, with whom he is loosely identified.[23] Thereafter, however, sharp differences emerge that throw Mearsheimer's approach into stark relief. The urge to simplify irrevocably highlights differences even with fellow thinkers rather than shading alternatives into mere nuance.

Mearsheimer is proud to call himself "a realist." But this realism is *sui generis*. Crucially he is "an offensive realist who believes that war is a legitimate instrument of statecraft and that states should maximize their relative power."[24] He asserts "that states seek hegemony."[25] Mearsheimer's position is like that of Waltz: both see behavior determined by the nature of the states system rather than the internal composition of society. This doctrine is known as "neorealism" or "structural realism" rather than "realism" per se. Mearsheimer is, however, distinct from Waltz the liberal. Mearsheimer dismisses Waltz's neorealism as "defensive realism." Waltz's realism went hand in hand with strong reservations about the militarization of US Cold

---

[20] Mearsheimer believes International Relations to be a discipline: "Realism, the Real World, and the Academy," in Brecher and Harvey (eds.), *Realism and Institutionalism in International Studies*, pp. 23–33, fn. 4.

[21] Interviewed by Harry Kreisler.

[22] "Conversations in International Relations: Interview with John J. Mearsheimer (Part 1)."

[23] Waltz, of course, has native German and working French but is proud of the fact that International Relations theory does not require their use.

[24] "Conversations in International Relations: Interview with John J. Mearsheimer (Part 1)."

[25] Interviewed by Harry Kreisler.

War policy: not for him justification of the accumulation of armaments which Mearsheimer logically sees as inevitable.

Mearsheimer differs from Waltz in other key respects. Waltz follows the disciplinary pattern of Natural Science adopted by Economics in structuring a model that is explicitly an artificial construct, the components of which are not necessarily in themselves proven facts. Its value lies in the potential to explain and predict reality, not mirror the constituents of realty in its various parts. This has an inestimable advantage tactically because it insulates the model from attacks by historians claiming that the components of the model are inaccurate when judged against the known evidence. But it also elevates International Relations theorizing to a status not dissimilar to Economics and the Natural Sciences. The conscientious critic is therefore restricted to attacking the model only with respect to its explanatory or predictive capacity, not the failure of its foundations to conform to established historical fact.

When he embarked on his odyssey in 1990 Mearsheimer wisely argued that because the historical record of international relations was "inconclusive," he would make the case "chiefly on deduction."[26] He has since decided it to be more conclusive than he thought. In the meantime a friend, Stephen Walt of Harvard, whose painstakingly accurate exploitation of the historical record is most unusual among political scientists, had persuaded him to take History more seriously;[27] though, as the reader will see, not seriously enough. The *Tragedy* thus presents a model explicitly built on what Mearsheimer calls "the empirical database"[28] in illustrating his argument from the course of international relations over the previous two centuries. The structure is therefore vulnerable to demolition at its base if it fails tests of proof long established among professional historians. In responding to Stephen Walt, Mearsheimer thereby unwittingly opened up a flank that Kenneth Waltz never had to defend, while simultaneously leaving himself exposed to attack on lines similar to those delivered against Waltz as to the model's explanatory and predictive capacities.

The third way in which Mearsheimer differs from Waltz breaches a further rampart in defenses now under siege. Whereas Waltz never assumed states to be entirely rational in the pursuit of their aims, Mearsheimer insists they are. The "key difference between us," he says,

is that I have a rational actor assumption in my theory and he does not. If you assume that states are strategic calculators, as I do, then your theory has to

---

[26] Mearsheimer, "Why We Will Soon Miss the Cold War."
[27] In conversation with Walt.   [28] Interviewed by Harry Kreisler.

account for foreign policy behavior as well as for international outcomes. After all, your theory expects states to act rationally; and if they don't act rationally your theory has a problem.[29]

On this measure Mearsheimer certainly has one, if not more. He has inadvertently loaded a-none-too-sturdy wagon well beyond its carrying capacity.

Insistence on assumed rationality goes entirely against the grain of realism as traditionally understood. It does, however, reveal a great deal about mind-set and education. At a time when economists such as Kenneth Arrow of Stanford and the Chicago School of behavioral finance were seriously questioning assumed rationality, political scientists discovered and appropriated it as their own. Assiduous readers of History and political practitioners do not readily leap to the rash assumption that governments know what they are doing; that they pursue goals in a manner that makes sense given their intentions regardless of domestic pressure, whether personal, commercial, bureaucratic, or party political. This is an assumption comforting liberal and economistic internationalists such as Robert Keohane, for whom it verges on dogma.[30] Whereas Mearsheimer assumes, correctly, that security is vital to a state's purpose, survival within the domestic political system leads politicians to jeopardize the interests of the state to ensure continuation in office. Democratic governments do this all the time; the United States more than most. The two goals are by no means compatible, however, and the conflict between them presents a serious obstacle to those who place their emphasis on the influence of the international states system in the making of foreign policy.

An essay by distinguished former US diplomat George Kennan (1904–2005) has cast the irresponsibility of office-seeking at the expense of the national interest within democracies in the most cynical terms.[31] Kennan was, of course, a deeply engrained individualist at odds with the nature of US government and uncomfortable in American society. In an earlier incarnation, he was also one of the most astute Sovietologists only too familiar with the same phenomenon under dictatorship. At its most extreme, Stalin's Great Terror from 1936 to 1939 is the best example of a statesman willfully sacrificing the national interest – not least the lives

---

[29] "Conversations in International Relations: Interview with John J. Mearsheimer (Part 1)."

[30] As I discovered during a bruising encounter at a conference in Santa Barbara organized by Michael Fry in the late 1980s when presenting a paper on the persistence of irrationality in Soviet decision-making on Japan.

[31] George F. Kennan, *Around the Cragged Hill: A Personal and Political Philosophy* (New York: W. W. Norton & Company, 1993), chp. 3.

of half his officer corps on the eve of war – for obsessive personal need. And it was precisely to forestall such behavior that the realists of the sixteenth century devised the concept *ragion di stato* (reason or reasons of state), to straitjacket foreign-policy-making for the purpose solely of serving state interests, the interests of society, rather than the selfish or, worse still, perhaps, in terms of resources expended and blood shed, the high-minded purposes of its rulers.[32] From Giovanni Botero to Henry St. John, Viscount Bolingbroke, the working assumption was that the "passions" would dictate policy unless a conscious effort were made to counter their impact. But Mearsheimer, alas, knows nothing of this.

A short spell in Washington, not merely in government, would cure most of this delusion. Only an armchair observer, a political scientist, perhaps, at great remove from the exercise of power, would be so fool-hardy as to assume rationality, an economistic fallacy in the world of politics. David Stockman, who headed the US Office of Management and Budget under Ronald Reagan, arrived stricken with this agreeable malady only to be rapidly and brutally disabused of its validity. "Governance was not a realm of pure reason, analysis, and the clash of ideologies," he discovered. "It really did involve the brute force of personality, the effrontery of bloated egos, the raw will-to-power."[33] The assumption of rationality does, of course, make modeling so much easier. Undoubtedly this explains its continued attraction to the unworldly political scientist. Yet at what cost? Mearsheimer has painted himself into yet another corner. "Unlike defensive realism," he confesses, "my theory cannot tolerate much non-strategic behavior."[34] In fact his theory cannot tolerate any significant "non-strategic behavior" given the absolute form in which it has been expressed.

A further point is warranted. Common to many realists, Mearsheimer confuses the elementary distinction between "ought" and "is." Immanuel Kant long ago argued that statements expressing fact and statements expressing preferences should not be conflated. Inevitability is a tempting line of argument in the heat of debate but it lays a trap for the unwary. If states are obliged by both their inherent rationality and the pressures of the states system to act in certain predictable ways, then it is entirely contradictory to argue that they should be doing so, since, according to theory, they are already doing so and have no choice

---

[32] The great historian of political thought Rodolfo de Mattei has charted this story best: Jonathan Haslam, *No Virtue Like Necessity: Realist Thought in International Relations since Machiavelli* (New Haven: Yale University Press, 2002).

[33] David Allen Stockman, *The Triumph of Politics: Why the Reagan Revolution Failed* (New York: Avon Books, 1987), p. 263.

[34] Haslam, *No Virtue Like Necessity*.

in the matter. "I argue," writes Mearsheimer, "that states should and do seek to maximize relative power; they should and they do pursue hegemony in my story."[35] Realists of any stripe are unlikely to convince doubters of their case if realism in any form, however desirable, is represented as a description of reality rather than a normative doctrine. Realism is fundamentally an issue of preference. That much is clear from the conduct of international relations over the centuries, in which idealists have see-sawed with realists.[36] A glance merely at the history of US foreign policy in the twentieth century – Woodrow Wilson versus Warren Harding; Franklin Roosevelt versus Herbert Hoover; Jimmy Carter versus Richard Nixon – one provides evidence enough.

For some strange reason, political scientists in the field of International Relations are expected to be great experts on current affairs; yet they read just the same newspapers as we do and, absent direct and personal contacts with those in power, they stand in no better position to understand the contemporary world than does the jobbing journalist or, indeed, the historian. In Mearsheimer's case his understanding of contemporary Europe is plainly unsound. His grasp of post-Cold War Germany is so far from reality as to undermine his credibility entirely. A country that restricts the dispatch of its soldiers even on UN missions to minuscule numbers and in such a way as to keep them out of the direct line of fire to the great annoyance of its allies hardly meets Mearsheimer's expectations of a new Reich. And why does it do so? Because the Greens (junior partner in the governing coalition from 1998 to 2005) and the left Social Democrats would not have it otherwise. No great power is so constricted in the conduct of foreign and defense policy (or indeed internal security) than today's Germany, and for obvious reasons of history.

Yet Mearsheimer never sees constitutional structure, however constricting, or past events, however traumatic, as exerting any influence on the behavior of states. That, after all, would be difficult to model since it partakes of the organic nature of states and society, a realm far distant from the proclivity of American political scientists for seeing the world in terms of machinery. This leaves out a great deal that we need to know. Although human beings all too frequently fail to learn from the past, they do at least have the capacity to do so. Britain's withdrawal from the allied intervention to destroy Bolshevism in Russia was, as we know, based on prime minister David Lloyd George's understanding of

---

[35] "Conversations in International Relations: Interview with John J. Mearsheimer (Part II)," *International Relations* 20 (2006), 231–43.

[36] Haslam, *No Virtue Like Necessity.*

what caused the Napoleonic Wars.[37] France's debacle in Indochina led President Charles de Gaulle to warn the Americans against repeating old mistakes. The US government decided not to listen. And the folly of war and occupation in Iraq was foreseeable by most attentive and knowledgeable observers, even within the US government, on the basis of past experience. Ironically, but to his credit, Mearsheimer could be counted amidst their number.[38]

After the Cold War Mearsheimer expected "that the new Europe will involve a return to the multipolar distribution of power that characterized the European state system from its founding, with the Peace of Westphalia, in 1648, until 1945." Europe, he claimed, "is reverting to a state system that created powerful incentives for aggression in the past." This system, Mearsheimer continues, "was plagued by war from first to last."[39] Yet the notion that the states of Western Europe have learnt absolutely nothing from the past and that they are fortresses armed against the encroachments of one another is archaic. A decade later Mearsheimer effectively admitted he had got it wrong. "I think there's no question that there was less conflict among the great powers during the 1990s than there was during the rest of the twentieth century," he acknowledged. But he claimed this was all due to a continued US troop presence in Europe.[40]

But why had Mearsheimer not foreseen a continued US presence in Europe when he confidently predicted the return of the multipolar order from 1648 to 1945? Furthermore, the idea that the presence of US troops kept the great powers of Europe – presumably Germany, France, Britain, and Russia – from one another's throats is surely an Americocentric delusion. It amounts to an escape clause contrived to avoid reference to the fact that, in return for German reunification, Chancellor Helmut Kohl promised France he would speed up the political integration in Europe and the adoption of the single currency.[41] And this brings us to part of Mearsheimer's problem in that he sees power almost entirely in military terms. "When you talk about the balance

[37] Richard Ullman, *Anglo-Soviet Relations 1917–1921: Vol. 2: Britain and the Russian Civil War: November 1918–February 1920*; *Vol. 3: The Anglo-Soviet Accord* (Princeton University Press, 1968; 1972).

[38] "A Case Study of Iraq – Analogous to Vietnam," in Christian Hacke, Gottfried-Karl Kindermann, and Kai Schellhorn (eds.), *The Heritage, Challenge, and Future of Realism* (Göttingen: Bonne University Press, 2005), pp. 139–48.

[39] "Conversations in International Relations: Interview with John J. Mearsheimer (Part 1)."

[40] Interviewed by Harry Kreisler.

[41] This much is apparent from the diaries of Jacques Attali, quoted in Haslam, *No Virtue Like Necessity*, pp. 247–48.

of power," he insists, "you're really talking about military power and the use of military force."[42] But the power and the balance in Western Europe has long been almost entirely economic in character. Here the Franco-German axis has held the European Community in place: more than that, it has driven forward the process of integration at a far greater pace than any imagined. That is why the purchasing power of Britain's nuclear-weapons system, for example, is nil on the very sub-continent where wars usually emerged.

Here an understanding of economic matters is also wanting. The assumption that unproductive investment by government in the accumulation of military capability has no deleterious effect long-term sapping the vitality of an economy flies in the face of reason. The Soviet Union is a prime example, well attested from the diplomatic as well as the economic record. This high-handed dismissal of economic laws fits, however, with a disdain for welfare as against warfare. "States," Mearsheimer asserts, "are not primarily motivated by the desire to achieve prosperity."[43] Yet if there is one feature that strikes the eye about Western Europe since the war it is precisely the pursuit of prosperity that has above all motivated those in office. And was this not invariably the core motivation in pursuit of empire? It was why the United States had such a problem getting Europe to rearm in the 1950s and again in the 1980s. Notoriously foreign policy does not win elections. Wars most certainly lose them if they go badly. Why else did Roosevelt stand on a peace ticket in 1940? Did not Vietnam and the fate of Lyndon Johnson demonstrate this to every American? And George Bush senior actually won his war in the Gulf. But then the statesman as victor failed in his attempt at a second term under the merciless jibe from the Democrats: "It's the economy, stupid."

Mearsheimer claims the absence of "systematic evidence demonstrating that Europeans believe war is obsolete."[44] But this is misleading. First of all, absence of evidence is not evidence of absence. Second, the governments of Western Europe can and do believe that war between one another is obsolete without necessarily believing that war in general is obsolete. Why should they believe war is obsolete outside Europe when it is so frequent in areas such as the Middle East upon which the European Union is so energy-dependent? From this emerges a striking characteristic in that Mearsheimer steadfastly refuses to see any maturation of foreign-policy behavior as a consequence of democratization

---

[42] Interviewed by Harry Kreisler.
[43] Mearsheimer, "Why We Will Soon Miss the Cold War."
[44] Ibid.

or industrialization. It is as though we are living still in 1648. One does not have to subscribe to the deluded notion that democracies invariably eschew war as an option – since belied by Bush and Blair – to see that the option of war is more difficult for representative government than a dictatorship. Thus for Mearsheimer the Germany of the post-Cold War era is essentially no different from that of the Kaiser. "Is it not possible," he asks, "for example, that German thinking about the benefits of controlling Eastern Europe will change markedly once American forces are withdrawn from Central Europe and the Germans are left to provide for their own security?"[45] Possible, yes; likely, surely no.

Having staked out a position on the field far forward of the main body of evidence, extending lines of communication to breaking point across enemy territory, Mearsheimer has been driven to impasse by contrarian urges harnessed to relentless logic. Its most bizarre manifestation appeared just after the fall of the Berlin Wall: "The West ... has an interest in the continuing Cold War confrontation," he insisted. "The Cold War antagonism could be continued at lower levels of East–West tension than have prevailed in the past, but a complete end to the Cold War would create more problems than it would solve."[46] This view is no accident. The assumption that the developed industrial democracies of Western Europe view one another with the same degree of hostility and fear as do states in the Third World, that, in short, the international states system drives all, regardless of type, into identical behavior is central to Mearsheimer's reasoning. And it is this that prompts the prudent navigator guided by a great tradition from the sixteenth century to jump ship at the first port of call.

A further point needs be made. "For the purpose of developing sound theories, which is the essence of our enterprise," Mearsheimer asserts, "we need to be deeply engaged with the real world, and to be constantly thinking about how well our theories explain what is happening in the world around us."[47] But there are only three means of direct access to the "real world" of political action conducted largely in secret: direct participation in government – the revolving door in and out of Washington that lands some academics in the White House; working as an historian in government archives, which affords a bird's eye view of decision-making on the part of bureaucracies abroad as well as at home; or jobbing as a journalist with insider access to the processes of power. All open the way to what the political scientist never

---

[45] Ibid. [46] Ibid.
[47] "Conversations in International Relations: Interview with John J. Mearsheimer (Part II)."

normally sees. Would it be presumptive to suggest that a better intuitive sense of power is more likely to be found among former practitioners, diplomatic historians, or journalists than amidst self-described realists at great remove from these realities?

Mearsheimer's worldview thus suffers troubling inconsistencies not least because of the urge to advocate policy while preserving the status of purist objectivity and its blind adherence to assumed rationality. It also suffers from a weak historical foundation, entirely at odds with his recommendation that students "constantly" run "all those different theories that they've studied up against the historical record to determine for themselves which theories they think best explain the world."[48] He also contradicts the dubious assertion that "you have to know a lot of history to be an IR theorist of some consequence."[49] Another confusion between "ought" and "is": most prominent political scientists in international relations know very little History indeed. And this is not surprising: in leading American universities it can cost one appointment to a Political Science department where a facility with numbers is prized more highly than an acquaintance with the past. A background in Economics has for some time been regarded as more relevant than a background in History. The problem for the political scientist is, of course, that "a lot of history" merely taken from other people's books is insufficient to establish the truth of events without sense of what archival research is and how dubious most history books are. The historical record is not some agreed consensus, a reliable database (to use social science jargon), relying upon the same degree of discovery for each major historical event. It is an uneven mass of interpretation. That does not, however, mean that all interpretations are equally well verified. And how is the political scientist, now out of his depth, to know which interpretation is likely to be the more reliable? A degree of humility is therefore advisable.

Doubtful evidence has been adduced to illustrate Mearsheimer's model. To some extent this is inevitable. Illustration culled from two centuries is bound to contain lapses in accuracy, particularly when patched together by research assistants. But there looms a larger methodological problem in choosing which facts to highlight, which to ignore. The temptation is for the political scientist modeling international relations to select from the historical record solely in support of an argument laid out in abstract, and in so doing to omit evidence that contradicts his views and to distort interpretation of events to fit the model. Indeed,

---

[48] Interviewed by Harry Kreisler.   [49] Ibid.

Mearsheimer openly acknowledges the need to make the argument that Imperial Germany, Imperial Japan, and Nazi Germany acted aggressively "on rational calculations, not domestic political considerations ... otherwise my theory would fall apart."[50] Because, as he acknowledges elsewhere, "any time a state behaves in a strategically foolish fashion, it counts as a clear contradiction of my theory."[51] Unfortunately this militates against wholehearted detachment and the precision necessary to locating evidence. The model-builder's muse is in this case the serpent and Mearsheimer shows every sign of having succumbed to the serpent's guile and eaten of the apple.

What use does Mearsheimer make of the historical record? It is not hard to find minor errors of fact. References to the "Soviet Union" withdrawing from World War I look peculiar to anyone vaguely familiar with the period.[52] The belief that "all territory west of Moscow ... was prime real estate" will strike anyone who has traveled the Mozhaisk highway as utterly bizarre: in the United States much of this desolate and largely unproductive land would merit more the description of "badlands."[53] Every student of English history learns early on that the British avoided large armies not because of the difficulty of crossing the Channel so much as to resist the creation of a standing army because of the unpleasant experience of Cromwell's military dictatorship.[54] But these peccadilloes pale in comparison with Mearsheimer's treatment of major world events.

Cast an eye at his treatment of the Soviet Union and its relations with the capitalist world. Consistent with the beliefs underlying his model, Mearsheimer plays down the terrifying force of ideas emerging with the October Revolution and its disruptive impact on the stability of the states system at a time when the Bolsheviks had little else in their arsenal other than propaganda. It is illustrative that the word "revolution" nowhere appears in the book's index under "Russia." Of course, if ideas are a significant form of power, power cannot then be defined – as Mearsheimer has done – in purely military terms. Although the Soviet Union emerged into being with no armed forces worthy of the name and no independent military industries at all, it never ceased to be an object of fear from powers much weightier than itself – most notably the British Empire. It then stood up to them stiffened by fanatical

[50] "Conversations in International Relations: Interview with John J. Mearsheimer (Part 1)," 113.
[51] Ibid., 112.
[52] Mearsheimer, *The Tragedy of Great Power Politics*, p. 155.
[53] Ibid., p. 79.   [54] Ibid., p. 77.

conviction, demonstrating that moral power can outweigh the power of arms in situations short of war. Mearsheimer, of course, underrates this for "realist logic."[55]

Whereas it is true that Lenin was a great practitioner of *Realpolitik*, the application of force and political duplicity where necessary, he was most emphatically not a believer in Reasons of State: the priority of the interests of Russian society over the larger interest in world socialism. Policy naturally did not preclude what Lenin called tactical "zigzags" to the larger goal. *Realpolitik* was a necessary and unscrupulous tool by which socialism could be preserved in Russian embryo until it could be achieved globally after taking Berlin. To present Lenin in the same mode as Bismarck is thus misleading. It is, moreover, doubtful even to present Stalin in such terms. Mearsheimer, however, goes a step further and certainly one step too far in suggesting that "ideology mattered little for Stalin's successors."[56] Boris Ponomarev of the Soviet leadership scolded his East German opposite number for discounting prospects in Western Europe as late as 1976. Although a classic revolution was not on the cards, he readily conceded, "objectively you have a great deal of inflammable material. We have said to the Italian communist party: you stand on the threshold of important events; but so much depends upon you."[57] Indeed, "The Soviet Union," KGB chief Yuri Andropov told Pham Hung from North Vietnam in October 1980, "is not merely talking about world revolution but is actually helping to bring it about."[58] *Hic sunt leones.* Given the Soviet Union's importance in the second half of the twentieth century, one would have expected an exceptional degree of circumspection in investigating the subject before issuing conclusions *urbi et orbi*. Citing the non-specialist sociologist Barrington Moore on Soviet foreign policy, for example, is puzzling and curiously archaic. One suspects that Barrington Moore's assertions just happen to fit Mearsheimer's argument, on the age-old principle: any port in a storm.

Tucked away in a footnote is the statement that "For an offensive realist, neither side can be blamed for starting the Cold War; it was the international system itself that caused the intense security competition between the superpowers."[59] It takes more than one to be a warrior, as Plato (and Stalin) said. But that is a different proposition

[55] Ibid., p. 190.   [56] Ibid., p. 191.

[57] Meeting between Axen, head of the SED International Department, and counterpart Ponomarev, October 20, 1976 in *Bundesarchiv. SAPMO. DY/30/IV B 2/20. 157.*

[58] Quoted in Christopher M. Andrew, *The Mitrokhin Archive II: The KGB and the World* (London: Allen Lane, 2005), p. 471.

[59] Mearsheimer, *The Tragedy of Great Power Politics,* p. 513, fn. 132.

from suggesting that both are or neither is equally at fault for a conflict emerging. If one believes, as E. H. Carr did and as Marc Trachtenberg does, that the Soviet Union was a normal state like Tsarist Russia, the United States, and the rest, then seeking ideological explanations for the origins of the Cold War makes no sense. Yet the evidence against Mearsheimer's position is substantial and is not properly considered in researching the subject. Even on geopolitics, Mearsheimer appears much weaker with respect to the Soviet Union than one has a right to expect given the breadth and significance of his model. The Soviet Union was, after all, second only to the United States as a great power from 1945. A grievous example is the ill-judged claim that at the end of the Pacific War the Soviet Union was "the most powerful state in Northeast Asia," which certainly does not fit with Stalin's view at the time, trenchantly expressed in a secret telegram to Molotov and reiterated *ad nauseum* to Averell Harriman.[60] Indeed, one of the major reasons why the Kremlin did not give full support to Mao Zedong in the Chinese civil war that resumed soon thereafter was concern lest he provoke the Americans, the dominant power in the area, engulfing the Pacific with ground troops in China, holding the Marshall Islands and in unilateral military occupation of Japan.

Another important dimension to taking the past seriously is the history of ideas. Those seeking to construct models of political behavior would be well advised first to take more than a polite glance at the history of political and economic thought. The obvious danger ever present is that, otherwise and embarrassingly, apparent novelty turns out to be nothing of the sort. But this is not just a matter of due diligence. An opportunity also exists at little cost to take ideas from the past and develop them to their fullest extent. Bear in mind the sustained intensity with which our predecessors – many engaged in the business – tried to make sense of international relations. Mearsheimer, however, takes no account of this whatever. His knowledge appears to reach no further back than the turn of the twentieth century: hence the otherwise baffling obsession with Lowes Dickinson, whose ideas are at best a shallow derivative from earlier times of which Mearsheimer seems to know little. The idea that the states system was anarchic and that anarchy generated war was, of course, first articulated in the modern era by Thomas Hobbes: "during the time men live without a common power to keep them all in awe, they are in that condition which is called war," which "consisteth not in battle only, or the act

---

[60] Ibid., p. 322. See "Soyuzniki nazhimayut na tebya dlya togo, shtoby slomit' u tebya volyu ..." *Istochnik* 2 (1999).

of fighting, but in a tract of time wherein the will to contend by battle is sufficiently known." This was a description of society in a state of nature. His model for society as a whole, however, was drawn from international relations:

> in all times kings and persons of sovereign authority, because of their independency, are in continual jealousies and in the state and posture of gladiators, having their weapons pointing and their eyes fixed on one another, that is, their forts, garrisons, and guns upon the frontiers of their kingdoms, and continual spies upon their neighbors, which is a posture of war.[61]

Can one find a more articulate explanation than this?

Mearsheimer's ignorance of such texts is equally evident from an unsustainable assertion that "realism has dominated the international relations discourse for the past seven centuries or more."[62] On the contrary, entire monographs exist on the significant idealist conceptions of international relations, covering those self-same centuries, that Mearsheimer seems entirely unaware of.[63] The core notion in realist thought – namely the idea of *ragion di stato* – arose to ensure rational policy-making. It emerged on the assumption that if nothing were done then policy would be corrupted by petty politics, venality, personal ambition, and the like, but also by emotion or "the passions," as they were called. Pufendorf expressed it best:

> those who have the Supreme Administration of Affairs, are oftentimes not sufficiently instructed concerning the Interest both of their own State, as also that of their Neighbours; and yet being fond of their own Sentiments, will not follow the Advice of Understanding & faithful Ministers. Sometimes they are misguided by their Passions, or by Time-serving Ministers & Favourites. But where the Administration of the Government is committed to the Care of Ministers of State, it may happen, that these are not capable of discerning it, or else, being divided into Factions, they are more concern'd to ruin their Rivals, than to follow the dictates of Reason.

He also pointed out how critical a factor this could be in determining the ultimate status of any power: "it frequently happens, That a state, which in it self consider'd, is but weak, is made to become very considerable by the good Conduct & Valour of its Governors; whereas a

---

[61] Haslam, *No Virtue Like Necessity*, pp. 53–54.
[62] Mearsheimer, *The Tragedy of Great Power Politics*, p. 369.
[63] Tuck, *The Rights of War and Peace*; F. H. Hinsley, *Power and the Pursuit of Peace: Theory and Practice in the History of Relations between States* (Cambridge University Press, 1963); A. Beales, *The History of Peace: A Short Account of the Organised Movements for International Peace* (New York: Dial Press, 1931).

powerful State, by the ill management of those that sit at the Helm, oftentimes suffers considerably."[64]

A crucial function served by *ragion di stato* was also that of countering hitherto dominant universalist ideas. Dante Alighieri was not alone in seeing the state as merely a transient phenomenon prompted by the failure of universal empire backed by a universal church. Established after the failure of the universal church and with the Holy Roman Empire no longer holy, Roman, nor an empire, reasons of state had still to meet and counter the challenge of universal empire under a secular banner: the Spanish scholastics (Francisco de Vitoria, Francisco Suárez, Luis de Molina) who established the bases of what became international law under Hugo Grotius; the liberalism of Adam Smith, which foresaw the extinction of the state and created the first sustained challenge even to so settled a notion as the Balance of Power as the regulator of the European states system, or Marxism, predicting and working to the same end, until superseded by Leninism. All envisaged a set of values that demanded higher authority over reasons of state, whether as universal religion, universal humanitarianism, the world market, or international socialism. One could plausibly claim that the practice of diplomacy was dominated more by realist assumptions, though never so prevalent as some would have us believe; but certainly not the discourse.[65]

How useful, then, is Mearsheimer's theory? Any theory stands or falls by its capacity to explain against the known facts. Knowing those facts is vital for accurate judgment. Yet the theorist by temperament and thus by vocation is normally averse to detail. The danger was pointed out by Lord Maliquist, a character in Tom Stoppard's only novel:

Nothing is the history of the world viewed from a suitable distance. Revolution is a trivial shift in the emphasis of suffering; the capacity for self-indulgence changes hands. But the world does not alter its shape or course. The seasons are inexorable, the elements consistent. Against such vast immutability the human struggle takes place on the same scale as the insect movements in the grass and carnage in the streets is no more than the spider sucked husk of a fly on a dusty window-sill.[66]

Certainly Mearsheimer affords some useful insights into closely defined situations – notably the rough and tumble in the Third World rather than the tough-talking and wheeler-dealing at the negotiating

---

[64] Haslam, *No Virtue Like Necessity*, pp. 66–67.
[65] Ibid., passim.
[66] Quoted in Kathleen Tynan and Ernie Eban (eds.), Kenneth Tynan, *Profiles* (London: Hern Books, 2000), pp. 300–01.

tables of Europe; but these insights come at too high a price because of his insistence on generalizing to cover almost every instance of great-power rivalry. Moreover, a key assumption is the rationality of decision-making; an assumption realists have always abjured. And for good reason: insistence on assumed rationality defies common sense and accumulated experience.

To the extent that the model pivots on historical fact, it wobbles on an unstable axis. To the degree that it ignores the long tradition of thought in international relations, it risks reinventing the wheel; though here Mearsheimer could plea bargain that he is in this respect no different than most of his colleagues. Even if these failings are deemed marginal by the political scientist, other requirements are not met. The structure contrived is too lopsided in its emphasis on the states system to carry conviction. Theorists of international relations frequently claim that their models can provide effective explanations of state behavior. But in this they compete with not merely thinkers from the distant past of which they are barely conscious, but also from counterparts among historians. At Yale, for instance, in a department replete with chairs in International Relations, the visitor is told that the only distinguished authorities on international relations in the university are Donald Kagan and Paul Kennedy, both historians. Should we really be that surprised? Is the one explanation – that of the political scientist – really any advance on the other – that of the historian? Historians, however, are not usually in the business of the future, unless they become pundits. Here, one might expect the political scientists to have the advantage. Unfortunately, as soon as prediction is required, the elaborate structure of this political scientist crumbles: Mearsheimer has to look to the unit and not the system. As he acknowledges with respect to the two most troublesome powers he has identified, "nobody can predict with any degree of certainty what Chinese or German foreign policy goals will be in 2020."[67] This suggests that one has to address domestic factors rather than the architecture of the states system to seek an answer to who will be at war by then. If so, what value Mearsheimer's much-vaunted model?

---

[67] Mearsheimer, *The Tragedy of Great Power Politics*, p. 363.

Richard Rosecrance and Zara Steiner

No scholar, historian, or policy-maker wishes to dispute the role that power plays in foreign affairs. From Thucydides to modern international politics, the power of a state has influenced its position and success in dealing with other countries. But the calculus of "power" is not the be-all and end-all of national policy in international relations. Countries are prompted to act as a result of their economic circumstances, their moral codes, and their institutional setting (reinforced by domestic politics) as much as by their position in the power hierarchy. Leaders frequently have ambitions that range beyond the limits that power technically permits. Sometimes, decision-makers also minimize their involvements owing to the pressures of internal factors. Sustained by such pressures, inter-national institutions, ideologies, and recognized legitimacies temper and channel the pursuit of influence. Sometimes leaders strive to protect their own position against domestic opponents, even when their country might lose a war in consequence.[1] The definition of the state's situation in foreign affairs also conditions outcomes: is the state rising or declin-ing? Does action have to be taken to prevent further decline?[2] In regard to each of these factors, the authors of this volume have shown in case after case that countries do not restrict their policies to what their "power line" apparently mandates – the relative position they occupy vis-à-vis other major nations in the power hierarchy. Instead they chart their own course – influenced by external pressures, but not determined by them.

Power is a Protean term, embodying many facets. Neorealism in the sense used in this volume is a theory in which external power relation-ships determine (ultimately) the policy of a state. There is a *Primat der Aussenpolitik*.[3] Accepting this view, so-called "defensive realism" does

---

[1] See particularly H. E. Goemans, *War and Punishment* (Princeton University Press, 2000).

[2] See Kahneman and Tversky, "Prospect Theory."

[3] Michael Doyle sums up "structural realism" in the following way:

competition and socialization under anarchy select for power-seeking ends and rational decision-making processes the way a competitive market selects for profit

not specify what states will or must do.[4] Countries may balance or not; they may seek to augment or merely maintain their power. They may form alliances or desert them. Diplomacy can perform an important and even facilitative role in such a system. The one thing that is inconsistent with defensive realism, however, is the domestic determination of a state's international policy.[5] Realism is a theory of the third image, not the second.[6] If countries' actions are routinely determined by leaders, ideology, regime changes, political conflicts, bureaucratic politics, or other internally generated factors, they transgress the normal confines of defensive realism.[7]

Even more specifically, "offensive realism" requires major countries to increase their power and to seek at least regional hegemony. Such states will not overlook opportunities to expand their power.[8] Yet, the entire corpus of this volume demonstrates that countries frequently do not do what their relative power requires. Under persuasive leaders, for instance, they rashly depart from their "power lines" and may even sometimes risk the nation with a single throw of the dice.

There is a third form of realist theory which might be called "ecumenical Realism." It conjoins the behavior of individuals with domestic politics to produce international anarchy: individuals struggle for power; the organizational units which they form create similar struggles within the state, and states themselves contend for power. Briefly stated, this is the argument of Hans Morgenthau.[9] In his theory, nothing is extraneous; all is included in the universal drive for power, at the individual, societal, and international levels. If action originates in domestic ideology, or the musings of a charismatic leader, it is equally power-driven. If a state accentuates or diminishes its interventions as a result, the outcome comports with ecumenical realism. Morgenthau

maximization. States that do not operate according to these standards of power maximization will simply be eliminated; we should thus assume that complex political and moral choices are irrelevant. States naturally balance power against power, rather than "bandwagon" toward the powerful. They fight when they think they can win.

See Doyle, *Ways of War and Peace*, p. 70.

[4] See Waltz, *Theory of International Politics*.

[5] Waltz regards this as an erroneous "reductionism." In their book on the "Israel Lobby," John Mearsheimer and Stephen Walt acknowledge that the Israel Lobby is an exception to realist theory because it illustrates how strongly a domestic pressure group can influence policy.

[6] The first image is human nature; the second is domestic politics; the third is the international system.

[7] See particularly Waltz, *Theory of International Politics*; Morgenthau, *Politics among Nations* 1st edn. (New York: Alfred A. Knopf, 1948); and Snyder, *Myths of Empire*.

[8] See Mearsheimer, *The Tragedy of Great Power Politics*.

[9] See Morgenthau, *Politics among Nations* (New York: Alfred A. Knopf, 1954).

was prone to criticize the United States for failing to pursue its national interests vigorously enough,[10] but he did not deny that the pursuit of power ultimately drives its policy.

The problem with this third and more general form of realism, however, is that there is no action or occurrence which actually or hypothetically (if it occurred) could prove that the theory is false. Isolationism, aggrandizement, the misguided pursuit of ethical norms or professed adherence to institutions – all are comprehended within the ambit of power policies, however mistaken they might be.[11] Ecumenical realism thus fails to satisfy the "falsifiability criterion." If no imaginable state of affairs contradicts the theory's predictions, then the theory can predict nothing.[12] A country could be on or off its "power line" but that outcome could not raise questions about the validity of realism.

The main focus in this book, therefore, has been on offensive and defensive realism. Though broader in reference and implications than offensive realism, defensive realism clearly is falsifiable.[13] In contradistinction to its theoretical claims, the authors of this book claim that domestic politics can dominate international policy. Economic interdependence can theoretically at least govern international ambitions. Bipolarity can foment instability (as Athens and Sparta proved during the Peloponnesian War). Such outcomes do not accord with the predictions of defensive realism. If countries persistently depart from their "power lines," the result is devastating to such a theory. Yet, the present volume shows that such deviations occur frequently and in very important cases.

Chapter conclusions

In his chapter on the United States, Ernest May tests the conclusions of the Melian dialogue – the argument that the goal of each state is to maximize its power at the expense of other states – in recent American history. He shows that during the 1920s when the supremely strong United States might have pushed forward its claims to international

---

[10] See Morgenthau, *In Defense of the National Interest*.

[11] See also George F. Kennan, *American Diplomacy, 1900–1950* (New York: New American Library, 1951).

[12] See also Richard Rosecrance, "Categories, Concepts and Reasoning in the Study of International Relations," *Behavioral Science* 6 (1961), 222–31.

[13] Michael Doyle writes: "structural inferences, such as the hypothesized stability of a bipolar world, the instability of multipolarity, and the weaknesses of transnational restraints, are deduced from the model..." Structuralism offers the promise of regularities which can be falsified or confirmed." See Doyle, *Ways of War and Peace*, p. 47.

hegemony, Republican administrations did the reverse. The United States acted below its power line, helping possible rivals to recover financially, cutting back its military power, and refusing to intervene abroad. Again in 1945 an even stronger United States did not try to maximize power in competition with others but instead held back. Through Marshall Plan aid, the United States put Britain, Germany, and Japan back on their feet while cutting American military expenditure. Then in the Korean War it vastly increased defense spending and concluded a range of important alliances, including NATO. Under Eisenhower, the United States sought to meet its obligations more cheaply, relying on its nuclear deterrent; the president returned to negotiations, and reduced the defense burden. It was only in the 1980s and 1990s that American power was fully utilized. The campaigns in Afghanistan and Iraq showed what the United States could accomplish, both positively and negatively, acting mainly by itself. In the future, given their results, however, American presidents will likely be more hesitant and more multilateral in their employment of military force. If this happens, Mearsheimer's thesis may no longer prove an adequate guide to explaining America's international strategy, as the United States will most likely operate below its power line.

Niall Ferguson illustrates a similar deviance from the power line, in the case of Nazi Germany. After 1933 Hitler repeatedly overexercised German power (as Britain underused its power in response). Hitler sought the Greatest Possible Reich and not just one based on German self-determination. This would include the largest number of Germans, and go well beyond the borders of pre-1914 Germany. The result would be to exterminate Jews and Soviet communists on Germany's frontiers. Theoretically, this Reich could become a Great Empire which would rival that of Great Britain. Given the success of large continental and imperial agglomerations of power, it was not surprising that Hitler wanted the Reich to join their number. To create such a vast realm, however, Hitler needed far greater space and food to nourish the German population, a well equipped army, the industrial base to equip the army, and the raw materials needed for war, including oil, rubber, copper, lead, and a host of other rare minerals that could be found only in the British and French empires, the United States, and the Soviet Union. German expansion to acquire these resources could be achieved only through war. The question was when? In 1938 German rearmament was already becoming too costly for the country to sustain but Germany did not have the means to become self-sufficient. Hitler needed an early and successful short war to acquire the food and raw materials required for the larger full-scale contest with the Western powers or, his ultimate objective, the Soviet Union. When Hitler pressed forward in 1938, however, he did not have the means to engage in the larger contest. Britain and France stood in his way. They should have fought instead of yielding to his demands at Munich. The fact that Hitler was willing to go to war in 1938 shows how far he had deviated from his power line. Ferguson believes the attack on Russia was an understandable extension of Hitler's (failed) vision, but it did not reflect the likely cost and dubious benefit of such a strategy. In addition, Hitler's war with the United States in 1941 was a catastrophic departure from the constraints of German power.

Michael Barnhart describes a Japan that was aggressive because of an absence of coordinated leadership. Japan was virtually a headless state. Though the emperor was sovereign over all matters of foreign and military policy, he would be advised by the army and navy. If the two services disagreed, there were no constitutional remedies. After the Meiji Restoration, Japan embraced Alfred Thayer Mahan's "navalism" and built a great navy. It was inevitable that this would lead to a clash with the Imperial Army, which considered itself the backbone of the state. The two services fought it out in the legislature, seeking greater funds. Barnhart shows how interservice rivalry determined Japan's entry into the Great War and how that intervention further sharpened their differences. After the First World War Japan briefly accepted the Washington Treaty because it could not match the US naval-building program. The younger officers successfully ousted the "treaty-faction" admirals in the 1930s. Thereafter the navy wanted to move south to acquire the needed resources and undermine the British, Dutch, and French possessions that were put in jeopardy by the Nazi gains in Europe. The army, however, wanted to move north (against the Soviet Union) but was briefly deterred by the 1939–41 peace between Germany and Russia. In July 1941, however, when the United States cut off all oil and raw-material shipments to Japan, Japan could no longer afford to move north; it had to move south in order to secure oil if it were to act at all. The army grudgingly accepted the naval action and offered only limited support. To expand southward, however, the navy had to neutralize the American Fleet, hence the decision to attack Pearl Harbor. This attack, however, as Admiral Yamamoto presciently foresaw, would bring on a US naval-building program which Japan could not match. Nonetheless, Emperor Hirohito would not bow to the Americans until the dropping of the atomic bombs. Japan acted above its power line because it could neither quash nor rise above the interservice rivalries which had determined its policy for fifty years.

Zara Steiner sees Great Britain as both under- and overusing its power. It did not act in 1938 when power realities (see also Niall Ferguson) would have favored its military opposition to Germany. In 1939 it did act when power realities (though not normative and political ones) should have counseled caution and hesitation. Britain did not possess the power to attack Germany, nor could it count on assistance from other foreign countries, above all, the United States. In the past much emphasis has been placed on Britain's unpreparedness in 1938 for war against Germany. A closer look suggests that it was Hitler's Germany which was most at risk from such a conflict. Hitler's most important advisers warned him that Germany could not fight a war against Britain and France which would probably result in America supplying the Allies with the material they needed. Even if the German army crushed Czechoslovakia quickly, it could not have mounted an offensive against France. Thus Chamberlain's concession at Munich saved Hitler and Germany from a disastrous defeat. In 1939, however, the military balance edged in favor of Germany even though Britain had made important preparations in its air defense. But the public mood had changed after Munich; the German takeover of Prague on March 15 acted as a catalyst to the rising opposition to any further concessions to Hitler. Many Britons, both within and outside the cabinet, became convinced that Hitler's aims were unlimited and that he would have to be stopped by war. Once the Poles decided to resist, the die was cast. British leaders, however, did not have a short-term strategy to defeat Germany. And the Treasury warned that Britain would not win the long war of attrition unless the United States came to the Allies' rescue. The decision for war was made despite an existing and future balance of power tipped against Britain. In going to war in 1939 "Bulldog Britain" acted above its actual power line.

Andrew Kennedy observes that leaders may choose different options when confronted by crisis. He focuses on the contrasting responses of Mao Zedong and Liu Shaoqi when Kim Il-Sung, the North Korean leader, asked for Chinese help in the Korean War in October 1950. From the start Mao was an enthusiastic supporter of intervention. He believed that the Chinese army, tutored in battle with the Kuomintang and the Japanese, could hold its own and even succeed against superior American forces. He held to this view even when Stalin did not offer air support to Chinese troops in Korea. Mao's faith in Chinese military prowess was undiminished; he believed that Chinese "volunteers" could eject American forces from the Korean peninsula. Even after the tide of battle turned against China, Mao persisted in his optimism. Liu, like most of the Politburo, opposed intervention, fearing defeat by the US-led forces. It was not until the American spring offensive of May 1951 and the receipt of Stalin's rebuke that Mao agreed to enter negotiations and scale down the war. Mao's leadership was critical to the Chinese military response, going well above China's modest power line.

Sam Williamson's chapter contends that from 1867 on, Austria-Hungary's policy was defensive and dictated by the need for survival, given the restiveness of its subject nationalities. The only possible exception was the annexation of Bosnia-Herzegovina which merely turned de facto into de jure control. Every foreign-policy decision had domestic repercussions, and Austrian leaders were sensitive to their internal constituencies up to and including the July Crisis. The decision to go to war against Serbia was taken in Vienna, though it rested on the German "blank check" which was supposed to neutralize Russian opposition. The Austrians believed it was essential to punish Serbia to ensure the survival of the Dual Monarchy and to maintain Austria's claim to be a great power. The decision was not taken for the purposes of territorial expansion. In fact, Tisza, the Hungarian prime minister, insisted that no substantive territory should be taken from Serbia and that no more Slavs should be incorporated into the Austro-Hungarian empire. Williamson also denies that Germany's hegemonic ambitions were the primary cause of the war. The acceleration of the Russian mobilization, given Germany's need to respond quickly, left Berlin few other options. Austrian actions in July thus conform to the dictates of "defensive" but not "offensive" realism.

Paul Schroeder shows that even in the disorderly and war-prone seventeenth century, there was a quest for order alongside the struggle for power; both were responses to the fundamental problem of international anarchy. To underscore his thesis, he points to the new relations between the state and religion, the improved instruments of diplomacy, the creation of alliances, however temporary, the triumph of the balance of power over that of "universal monarchy," and even the beginning of notions of a European family of nations. These did not make international life more peaceful but they made it more orderly and rational. States took greater authority over colonial trade and independent chartered companies, and the law of the sea was developed. The establishment of military monarchies led to conflict during the Thirty Years War, but the rehabilitation of the Holy Roman Empire represented an attempt to provide security among its units and prevent war and conflict between them.

Schroeder does not deny that some changes during the seventeenth century contributed to a struggle for power, and that the problem of dynastic succession was never addressed. But whereas Mearsheimer insists that the struggle for power is cyclical, Schroeder sees a positive linear development. Great wars and the French Revolutionary and Napoleonic struggles overthrew the existing international order but led to the creation of a more durable one. Schroeder's arguments underline the importance of change over time and the vital importance of non-power (institutional and normative) factors in establishing enduring patterns in international affairs. He claims that the quest for order is as fundamental a response to the problem of anarchy as is the struggle for power. As a consequence, the Concert of Europe system emerged in the first part of the nineteenth century, and further efforts to contain international violence continue today.

Jonathan Haslam offers a broader critique of realist theory. Devoting himself to Mearsheimer's work, he singles out two major assertions which he believes are questionable. The first proposition is that the main causes of war are located in the architecture of the international system. The second is that great powers, because of their mutual fear, seek to gain a position of dominance over others. The United States and Great Britain do not quite fit this model (as Mearsheimer himself admits), perhaps because they are sea powers. But then, Japan was also a sea power and that did not restrain her desires for regional hegemony. Haslam also questions the assumption of rationality that is supposed, at least in Mearsheimer's work, to govern state behavior. History abounds with examples where this is simply not true. Statesmen are often willing to sacrifice national interest for personal needs. Stalin's Great Terror and the purge of the Red Army is a case in point. In addition, the rejection of ideological and domestic influences invalidates Mearsheimer's approach. Marxism-Leninism was central to both Lenin's and Stalin's thinking and that of their successors. Stalin feared a deal between Churchill and Hitler (at Soviet expense) because he erroneously believed class interests would take priority over national interests. Again Stalin believed Soviet military entry into Germany would provoke communist revolutions throughout Europe, an idle speculation. Because even latterly Soviet leaders still believed in Marxism, the Cold War did not in fact end until Shevardnadze's abandonment of the notion of class war and Gorbachev's adoption of a new line of policy. These, not the fall of the Soviet Union in 1991, marked the end of the Cold War. Such ideological changes have no place in a theory which emphasizes power interests above all else. Haslam finds the stress upon the state system and military power far too narrow to account for past or future state behavior. An examination of domestic factors is needed to provide an understanding of the possibilities of future war.

Deborah Larson and Alexei Shevchenko contend that Mikhail Gorbachev underused Soviet power. This was not because he was not aware of Soviet strength. He could easily have intervened to put down the vestigial revolutions in the Baltic countries. He decided not to do so and also opened the Hungarian border to East Germans seeking to migrate to Austria and the West. He did not act to reinforce the Berlin Wall when it was breached on November 9, 1989. As an observer of the Czech revolution (and Soviet intervention) in August 1968, Gorbachev resolved not to use force to decide political outcomes, even inside the bloc. Rather, in accordance with social identity theory (in which subjects seek to excel in new realms that will be lauded in their social networks) Gorbachev sought to recast Russia as a "modern nation," gaining a new international status and claiming the respect of all the other leading nations. In this way Moscow could represent itself as an innovative great power without having to use force or to equal the West economically.

Rob Litwak points out that American president George W. Bush never convinced his allies to support the American invasion of Iraq. The United States had the power to invade Iraq by itself, but it did not enjoy the legitimacy to stay in Baghdad or to run Iraq. Former allies (including China and Russia) did not actively subvert it by aiding the Iraqi insurgency, but they did withhold support, leaving the United States isolated. As Litwak observes, it was not only its military action but also US doctrines of preemption and dissuasion – keeping rivals down – which led others to believe the United States was beginning to act like a rogue nation, that is, seeking to wield authority far above its actual power line. This contrasted with its behavior after 1945 when the American use of its power was accepted because its actions were not unilateral but embedded in multilateral institutions.

Robert Keohane and Lisa Martin contend that the realist argument against institutionalism (that institutions are simply the expression of the national interests of their members) neglects the role of "agency" and "delegation" in modern institutions. It is true that in past centuries and even in the 1920s and 1930s, international organizations had little leeway. But since 1945, institutions have acted as "agents" for their so-called "principals" and have acquired a degree of independence in proposing and fashioning solutions to international problems. The European Commission operates with authority delegated to it by its members. The Soviet Union was hesitant about Basket Three of the Helsinki agreement, but Gorbachev heeded its strictures in reforming Soviet practice and ending the Cold War. Modern international institutions have wielded greater influence than those in the past and this has allowed state members to operate below their typical power lines.

John Owen argues that domestic politics can alter foreign policy as a result of three possible changes: (1) a change of regime; (2) a change of government; or (3) a change of the degree of coherence in domestic politics. Any of these can alter government objectives in foreign relations. Napoleon did not pursue the same policy as Louis XVI, nor did the Bolsheviks carry on the policies of the Tsars. Hitler did not simply implement the foreign policies of his predecessors. The effects of internal influences can be charted by observing a nation's power before and immediately after a domestic change. If the policy shifts, it presumably cannot be because of change in power. Equally if power grows, but policy remains the same, the result cannot be due to the influence of power. In all these instances domestic institutions, ideologies, and the amount of popular support condition policy in decisive ways. There is a presumption that democratic states behave differently from autocratic countries. If this is true, nations may act below or above their power line (or band) because of changes in the domestic sphere.

Sherill and Sam Wells argue that the institutions of the European Union allow states to transfer their sovereignty and to act (as nation-states) below the level of the power they could otherwise dispose. In particular, West Germany settled for a role which was much diminished from its nineteenth-century or interwar stature. It did so in order to rebuild its status as a respected actor and an acceptable member of the West European community. Even before the question of German unification arose, Chancellor Kohl and Jacques Delors were equally committed to submerging the German mark into the euro in order to tie Germany even more firmly into European institutions. As a result, German unification was accepted by its neighbors. Germany proved to be in advance of many other states, including Britain, in its willingness to accept diminished sovereignty through the creation and support of European institutions. At Maastricht, though Germany did not get all it wanted, the Treaty was seen by the German leadership as a positive step toward the strengthening of the European Union.

Richard Rosecrance depicts a world in which nations do not merely rise above or below their contours of power, but where the constituents of power are themselves changed. These changes have been approximated in the past, only to fail at the last minute. The possibilities of peace were sacrificed with the French Revolution in the late eighteenth century which engendered a nationalist response. They were again neglected in the late nineteenth century, as tariffs rose and empires beckoned. But the major change since then has been the widespread recognition that the attempt to conquer vast new territories no longer adds to a nation's strength. This is not only because the local inhabitants will resist or quash those attempts but because nations can achieve economic growth intensively and globally, without military and imperial expansion. In future, therefore, countries, and particularly great powers, could move from their power line to new lines more reflective of the needs for technological and economic strength.

Factors that influence national position on or off the power line

1. International power

Aside from the movement of the power lines themselves, four major factors appear broadly to be associated with nations charting their position in international affairs. The first and perhaps most important is "power" itself, however defined but always a relative term. The policy of other great states and the strength they dispose will always be important in international politics. Wars have sometimes occurred, or been avoided, because of power variables alone as assessed by rationally calculating adversaries. Ideological claims have been trimmed or objectives elevated by the recognition of the power of any state in respect to other states. As nations rise and decline, their influence in international politics varies, though not always in direct proportion to the change in their position. It is probably true that some degree of opposition would have occurred between the two greatest victors of World War II after 1945 even had the two superpowers not been the United States and the Soviet Union. Power, therefore, has to be accorded a major explanatory role in the framing of national policy.

2. Domestic politics and ideology

As John Owen shows, the domestic politics of a country also determine, and even overshadow the overarching power realities. Countries sometimes go to war when they should not do so, pressed as they might be by leaders, ideologies, domestic pressures, and other internal influences. A regime in danger of losing power or a country facing widespread discontent may risk ventures that a more satisfied government would not. Economic downturns or prevailing inequities capture the minds of the unemployed and dispossessed, perhaps readying them and their leaders for adventures abroad. Revolutionary change – even where power vis-à-vis foreign counterparts remains the same – may predispose a government to action or sometimes to isolation. Citizens of democracies may have special affinity for other democratic states and show hostility to authoritarian regimes, modifying the national response to purely power relationships. In the case studies reviewed above, domestic factors were central in British, Austrian, and to some degree Japanese decision-making, leading governments to be less or more demanding than they otherwise would have been. American public opinion was certainly a factor in contributing to the country's isolation in the 1930s and the support for containment after 1949–50. The European Union was strongly supported by citizens in member states in the 1950s because many believed that the Franco-German tension had to be brought to an end if the European peace was to be maintained. Public support, of course, may sometimes represent the necessary but not the sufficient condition to take particular actions. Leadership may be necessary to mobilize and direct public support.

Domestic ideology or religious zeal are often critical to departures from the power line. Nations will sometimes decide to take action in the fervor of ideological moments that they would not do after further consideration and thought. Some countries appear almost willing to sacrifice themselves on behalf of their ideological attachments as France nearly did under Danton in 1792–93.[14] Others seek isolation or neutrality because of historically conditioned ideological assumptions. The United States did from the 1920s to 1937 and the Netherlands and Switzerland did during the later 1930s. At the other end of the spectrum, revolutionary states may backtrack if they face huge threats when implementing their ideologies. The Bolsheviks curbed their revolutionary tactics but not their goals in the 1920s. Saddam Hussein should have backed down twice, once in 1990 and the other, fatally, in 2003, but he did neither. In each of these cases, ideological and even perhaps psychological incentives operated to divert national leaders from their appropriate power lines.

Finally, domestic politics recognizes the limits imposed by the norms and institutions of the international system. Nations consider the range of justifiable international behavior when they make their calculations.[15] The Thirty Years War (1618–48) was one the most rapacious in modern European history, but as Paul Schroeder shows, even seventeenth-century countries sought to find a new regulatory principle to promote order when the old hierarchical ones could no longer be

---

[14] Some psycho-biologists stress the influence of the left amygdala in the generation of emotions and risk-taking behavior.

[15] See Arthur Stein, "The Justifying State: Why Anarchy Doesn't Mean No Excuses," in Mueller (ed.), *Peace, Prosperity, and Politics*.

sustained. When Hitler took the rest of Czechoslovakia on March 15, 1939, violating the principle of national self-determination, it became obvious to many that the Nazi dictator harbored unlimited ambitions, and some governments drew the appropriate conclusion that they had to act to prevent further aggression. When George H. W. Bush – under UN pressure – went into Somalia to restore domestic peace in 1989, no power theory could explain his action. Pressed by Kofi Annan to act, President Bush was motivated by institutional and normative considerations sustained by domestic politics. When the country of Kuwait was obliterated in August 1990, other nations were affected, some grievously. They acted to restore the emir and his government to power even when their immediate and geographic interests did not necessarily dictate action. Nations as remote as Japan and Germany assisted in this process.

3. International leadership

Leadership is one of the most important factors in determining how states use their power in the international arena. The nature of the government, regime change, and domestic opinion may influence decision-making but do not always shape or determine the leader's response. Chamberlain was backed by the British public when he set out to appease Germany during 1938, but subsequently had to acknowledge the changing public mood without being willing to abandon his former policies. Without Winston Churchill at the helm of British politics in June 1940, Britain might have sought a negotiated peace.[16] Hitler's policies were not those of his Weimar predecessors, nor would most of the Nazi leaders, with the exception of Ribbentrop, have embarked on such dangerous policies as the Führer initiated in 1938 or 1939 or sought to enlarge the war in the autumn of 1940.[17] In Japan the leaders of the army and navy charted the nation's course with little involvement by the emperor. They assassinated officials or politicians who did not agree with them. Ultimately, only the emperor's decision to sacrifice himself could bring the war to an end.

Mikhail Gorbachev proved a unique figure in Soviet politics. His policy DNA had been bred in the petri-dish of Andropov's Politburo when it became clear that the Soviet Union was lagging in the "scientific and technical revolution." Gorbachev wanted a new burst of

---

[16] See Hugh Trevor-Roper's Inaugural Lecture, University of Oxford (1957).

[17] See John Mueller's view, supported by historians, that few other German leaders, for instance, Göring, would have risked war in 1938 or followed Hitler's aggressive military path.

"acceleration" in Soviet economic growth and proposed glasnost and perestroika to achieve it. Few other Kremlin leaders and certainly not Grigory Romanov would have moved so drastically and directly to make the Soviet Union a more modern nation. As Larson and Shevchenko show, Gorbachev launched the New Thinking despite the opposition of many of his colleagues. They question whether the Cold War would have come to an end without the dominant role of Gorbachev in the Kremlin. In case after case, one must take into account the powerful and decisive role of such statesmen as Bismarck, Napoleon, Hitler, Chamberlain, Churchill, Mao, and Gorbachev as well as military men and some civilian advisers who change the direction of state policy. Without subscribing to the Great Man theory of international politics, to ignore the role of individuals is to do violence to the historical record.

4. Domains of loss or gain

Finally, as many of our historical episodes suggest, most great powers faced either placid pastures or angry seas. Countries in the "zone of loss" were willing to take more risks to redeem the nation than those eyeing pleasant vistas. In the "zone of gain" little needed to be done; one could rest on the foreign-policy oars and drift with the current. The United States has felt this for long periods and underperformed in power terms as a result. The United Kingdom found in its so-called "splendid isolation" a successful strategy for a period of time.[18] Since the eighteenth century the Scandinavian states have believed they were sufficiently distant from the arena of immediate contestation that they did not have to increase or demonstrate their power. A Canadian once told the League of Nations: "we live in a fireproof house, far from flammable materials," underestimating, perhaps, the advantages of having a peaceful great-power neighbor. Many EU states today are content to spend less than 1–2 percent of their GDP on armaments, believing they do not face a major threat to their security. Smaller nations tend to spend a much lower percentage of their Gross National Product on arms than bigger ones. Geography or alliances have enabled them to reside in the interstices or edges of the system, provoking no enemies.[19] Sometimes "ostrich-like behavior" brings retaliation against which small states have no defense as with Belgium and the Netherlands in 1940.

[18] See Kennedy, *Strategy and Diplomacy*.
[19] See Lake, "Escape from the State of Nature."

Countries facing greater losses will tend to take greater risks, elevating their position above the power line. This prospect confronted parties just prior to the First World War. Both Austria-Hungary and Russia, in fear of Germany, operated in the domain of loss, and neither was prepared to back down.[20] From the 1950s to the 1970s the Soviet Union and the United States found themselves atop the international pyramid. They tended to avoid risks to change the situation. Mutual destruction would have been a high price to pay for hegemony. In the 1980s Gorbachev could compromise precisely because Russia had not fallen irretrievably into the domain of loss and therefore felt he could risk an innovative policy. In the Cuban Crisis of October 1962, however, both the United States and the Soviet Union faced a deteriorating situation.[21] The United States was able to persevere because Russia's missile base in Cuba had not yet been fully incorporated into the Russian "definition of the situation." Russia had not yet assimilated its position in Cuba into a new psychological status quo from which it would be impossible to retreat.[22] President Kennedy assisted that compromise by making important concessions of his own. As Ernest May demonstrates, the United States, for at least part of the Cold War era, could underuse its great power because of prior gains. It was only toward the end of the Cold War era that it felt called upon to exercise a greater proportion of its available strength.

Other cases also show the importance of zones of loss or gain. In the 1930s Japan had already come to regard its territorial position in China as part of the imperial status quo. When Roosevelt and Secretary of State Hull asked Konoye or Matsuoka to compromise, they would not concede what they had come to regard as their own empire. Nagano, the Japanese naval minister, said Japan was like a dying man on an operating table. If one did not operate, death was certain. If one did act, his survival was at best uncertain, but the doctor still had to go ahead. The emperor agreed, believing honor demanded that Japan resist the American ultimatum.[23] Roosevelt, however, did not think that Japan

---

[20] See Jack S. Levy, "Loss Aversion, Framing and Bargaining: The Implications of Prospect Theory for International Conflict," *International Political Science Review* 17 (1996), 179–95; as well as Daniel Kahneman and Amos Tversky, "The Framing of Decision and the Psychology of Choice," *Science* 211 (1981), 453–58.

[21] See the magisterial account in Ernest May and Philip Zelikow (eds.), *The Kennedy Tapes: Inside the White House during the Cuban Missile Crisis* (New York: W. W. Norton & Company, 2002).

[22] See Gitty Amini, "Prelude to a War: Superpower Mediation in the Shadow of Coercion," American Political Science Association Paper (2004).

[23] See Robert J. C. Butow, *Tojo and the Coming of the War* (Princeton University Press, 1961).

had fully consolidated its position in China; he believed, correctly as it turned out, that Tokyo would never subdue China and thus expected Japan to retreat.[24] Japan's perception of a deteriorating situation provides a possible explanation for the hesitancy of both the army and the navy to compromise.

The result: The interaction of leadership, international power, domain of loss/gain, and domestic politics/ ideology

All the factors we have considered briefly above can be comprised into a single conspectus of four determinants: leadership, the definition of the situation (the domain of gain or loss), domestic politics (including ideology, normative and institutional concerns), and international power.

We can summarize incentives or disincentives to use force in terms of *plus* or *minus*. If the international situation facilitates the use of force, a Plus (+) would accrue on its account. If "leadership" strongly propounds military or aggressive action, a Plus (+) would be affixed to its box. If the state's situation in terms of gain or loss favors the status quo a Minus (−) would be applied. If domestic politics is hesitant or restrictive about the use of force, a Minus (−) would again be affixed in its column. Sixteen cases are viewed from this perspective.

Table 16.1. *Action–restraint under the impulsions of the international system, leadership, situation, and domestic politics*

Case	International system	Leadership	Situation (Gain or Loss)	Domestic politics
1	+	+	+	+
2	+	+	+	−
3	+	+	−	+
4	+	−	−	−
5	−	−	−	−
6	−	−	−	+
7	−	−	+	+
8	−	+	+	+
9	+	−	+	−
10	+	+	−	+

[24] See Waldo Heinrichs, *Threshold of War: Franklin D. Roosevelt and American Entry into World War II* (Oxford University Press, 1990), as well as Barnhart's chapter in this volume.

Case	International system	Leadership	Situation (Gain or Loss)	Domestic politics
11	+	−	−	+
12	+	−	+	+
13	−	+	−	+
14	−	−	+	−
15	−	+	+	−
16	−	+	−	−

(I) Coincidence with the power line:

>   Under Case (1) all systems are "go." The international system, leadership, the domain of gain/loss, and domestic politics are aligned together, and all facilitate action; the country is likely to act accordingly.

>   Under Case (5), all systems are "stop," and the country is likely to hold back and remain on its power line. In each case (of action or non-action) the country remains on its power-dictated course of action.

(II) Divergence from the power line:

>   In Case (8) international power dictates restraint, but domestic politics, leadership, and an unfavorable domain ("loss") press for action.

>   Under Case (4) the international power balance favors action, but domestic politics, leadership, and the definition of the situation ("gain") counsel restraint. These cases will represent divergence, leading to shifts either above or below the power line.

If, in international history, most cases are like (1) and (5), neorealist theories are vindicated. If the reverse is true and cases are like (8) and (4), deviations from realism are chronic and lead to questions about the theory.

The final applicability of neorealism rests on cases where the incentives to violate one's power line or to stay on it are mixed. The action then taken would test the range of validity of neorealist theory.

(III) Mixed Cases:

>   In Case (2) and Case (6), we examine the importance of domestic politics. If countries violate their power lines in these two cases, it can only be because of domestic politics.

In Cases (12) and (16), we test the importance of leadership. If countries violate their power lines in these instances, it can only be because of leadership.

In Cases (10) and (14), we examine the importance of the definition of the situation. Since all other factors point the opposite way, if a nation violates its power line in these two cases, it can only be because of the overriding importance of the definition of the situation.

The record: In Case (8), Japan and Germany acted when they should not have done so.

In Case (4), the United States and Britain failed to act when they could or should have intervened.

In Case (7), Britain faced great military and economic limitations when it decided in 1939 to make a stand over Poland. Britain did not possess the military means to make such a commitment, but the British definition of the situation, its future movement into the zone of loss, pressed the government to take action. Whatever his hesitancy, the deteriorating status quo and domestic pressure forced Chamberlain to try to stop Nazi Germany.

In Case (2) in 1919–20, Woodrow Wilson was checked by domestic politics in his attempt (facilitated by the international system and by a favorable definition of the situation) to bring the United States into the League of Nations and the Treaty of Guarantee with Britain and France. Franklin Roosevelt was ready to make a commitment against Germany in the fall of 1938, but he was well in advance of domestic political sentiment, and could not carry out his policy.[25, 26] Both the international balance and the definition of the situation (loss), however, would have favored action.

In Case (12) both Harding and, later, Hoover should (and could) have acted to buttress the international economy and to take action against rising international instability. They failed to take the necessary action. Their leadership was decisive against variables – including international power – which pressed in favor of action.

In Case (15) Mao exercised his leadership to intervene in the Korean War but was opposed by important domestic colleagues. He exaggerated what the Chinese army could accomplish, but China had not yet moved irretrievably into the zone of loss.

[25] See William L. Langer and S. Everett Gleason, *Challenge to Isolation: The World Crisis of 1937–1940 and American Foreign Policy* (New York: Harper & Row, 1952).
[26] See Jean Edward Smith, *FDR* (New York: Random House, 2008), p. 429.

In the Soviet case (Case 9) Gorbachev forwent action in the Baltic countries when he could easily have intervened. The unfavorable definition of the situation (confronting longer-term Soviet loss) also might have dictated action. He was, for a brief period, supported by Russian domestic politics. Yet, the Soviet leader did not follow the impulsions of power in his refusal to act.

Arrogation of case studies: historical cases

Austrian Case – Leadership favored action, definition of situation favored action, domestic politics was unclear. It is not certain that Austria could sustain its position as a great power if it did not defeat Serbia. (L (favored action+), D (definition of situation favored action+), DP (domestic politics was uncertain 0), Power (power variable ambiguous+,−)) AUSTRIA ACTED

British Cases – In the first (1938) case, leadership favored non-action and so did domestic politics. The actual distribution of power, though not properly perceived, favored action, as did a definition of the situation (Britain in domain of loss). (L−, D+, DP0, Power+) BRITAIN DID NOT ACT

In the second (1939), domestic politics favored action and so did the definition of the situation, but power variables and leadership were more questionable. (L+,−, D+, DP+, Power−) BRITAIN ACTED

German Cases – In 1938 German leadership almost took action when the balance was against it. Domestic politics was divided and Germany was not in a zone of loss. (L+, D0, DP−, Power−) GERMANY READY TO ACT

In 1939–41 German leadership favored action, but domestic politics did not. The definition of the situation was favorable. German power, however, could not sustain a war against both Russia and the United States. (L+, D0, DP0, Power−) GERMANY ACTED

Japan – Leadership (army and navy) prompted action; domestic politics was not a major factor though the population was strongly nationalist and militarist. Japan perceived that it existed in a domain of loss, but it did not have the power really to act. (L+, D+, DP0, Power−) JAPAN ACTED

China, Mao 1950 – Leadership moved to act, though this was not justified by international power or domestic politics. Only a stretched interpretation of zones of gain or loss could regard China as residing in a domain of loss. (L+, D+,−, DP0, Power−) CHINA ACTED

United States, early record (1920–80) – Leadership for the most part favored a moderate policy underusing US power. Domestic politics also favored restraint or later multilateral action. Power was available. (L0, D0, DP0, Power+) UNITED STATES DID NOT ACT

US–Cuban Crisis (1962) – Leadership, domestic politics, and the definition of the situation favored action. It is not clear that US power could fully justify it. (L+, D+, DP+, Power+,–) UNITED STATES ACTED

United States, 1980s – Reagan used more power, with some domestic support. The definition of the situation did not fully require it. (L+, D0, DP+, power+) UNITED STATES ACTED

United States, 2000–08 – In the second Bush administration, leadership dictated action that was not fully supported by domestic politics, and also not fully supported by international power. No zone of loss dictated action. (L+ D0, DP0, Power+,–) UNITED STATES ACTED

Soviet Union – It was Gorbachev's leadership, not domestic politics, that dictated policy. None the less, the definition of the situation was turning unfavorable. International power would have acceded to action against Baltics and satellites, but Gorbachev did not use it. (L–, D0, DP0, Power+) SOVIET UNION DID NOT ACT

Institutions – derive their support from domestic politics in many countries, sometimes against the leadership and contrary to patterns of international power (note, for example, the humbling of postwar Germany). (L0, D0 DP+, Power–) GOVERNMENTS RESTRICT ACTION

European Union – Most European leaders, domestic politics, and a feeling of loss of influence (due to World War II) brought the creation of the European Union. Member nations proved willing to restrict their sovereignty when they need not have done so. (L–, D–, DP–, Power+) GOVERNMENTS RESTRICT ACTION

Seventeenth and eighteenth centuries – It is difficult to sum up Schroeder's findings in terms of the four categories sketched above. During the seventeenth and eighteenth centuries, hierarchical influences are diminished (the role of the Church) and the absolutist princes gain standing. Wars are still devastating, but new mechanisms – alliances, concerts, balance of power, and regular stationing of diplomats in each other's countries – emerge to provide a degree of greater order among states. Leaders did not explicitly seek this outcome; nor did their publics. Still, there was a consciousness of the need for order and a dissatisfaction with the prior system. (L+, D–, DP0, Power+) GOVERNMENTS PARTLY HELD BACK TO GAIN ORDER

Arrogating cases, we have the following tentative results for fourteen different instances:

1. When governments took action (in eight cases), despite their power limits, the definition of the situation favored action in six cases; domestic politics favored action in four cases; leadership favored action in eight cases.
2. When governments held back in six cases, despite power availabilities, the definition of the situation favored restraint in four cases; domestic politics favored restraints in six cases; leadership favored restraint in six cases.

Thus when nations violated their power lines, leadership was involved in thirteen cases; domestic politics was correlated with action/inaction in seven cases.

What does this suggest? In the important cases we have studied, leadership, domestic politics, and the contours of the situation (smaller-scale variables) appear to be as important as the international system of power in determining national policy. Major wars occurred or expansive action was taken when power variables would appear to have ruled them out. Weak or futile responses to international challenge were often dictated by supine or indecisive leaders or by domestic politics when the actual power to act existed. Nations did not always perceive that they were moving into a "domain of loss" and when they did, they frequently acted precipitately and out of accord with their actual power. Nations frequently exceeded or slid off their "power lines." It seems highly likely that they will do so in the future as well. Given these circumstances, the amount of power in terms of traditional definitions that a nation possesses does not allow one to predict what it will do.

Redefinitions of power?

For much of international history, nations have operated on essentially short-term horizons, given the opacity of the future. But there were historical moments in which they changed perspectives to address the longer term. These occurred particularly when military expansion had reached apparent limits. Britain was prepared to give up imperial and territorial expansion when the British colonial experiment failed in America in 1783. Again, at the end of the nineteenth century, territory had already been divided up, further attempts to pursue it could only lead to conflict. While France, Britain, and the United States had become relatively satisfied powers, anxious to preserve the status quo, Germany and Japan felt left out. In an age of empire, they were effectively slighted or bereft of colonies. Such dissatisfied countries renounced intensive (economic) expansion and returned to extensive or territorial expansion. Changes in the concept of power caused some states to leave their previous power lines while others returned to earlier definitions and pursued aggressive policies.

Paul Schroeder contends that historic change has favored a greater containment of national policy over time. New legal, institutional, and normative usages – sustained by domestic politics – have been created to limit previous conflicts.[27] It is indubitable that the concept of power has changed throughout history and is still in flux today. Each of the two world wars lent a greater importance to economic factors in constructing the balance of power. Today a monopoly of any scarce but essential raw material or commodity gives a country, without military power, a special role in the hierarchy of nations. The case of Kurdistan, weak in every other respect but rich in oil, is an outstanding example, as are some of the Gulf states. Possession of an atomic bomb can alter the power balance; the North Korean threat to the stability of East Asia derives not only from Kim Jong-Il's unstable leadership, but also from Pyongyang's possession of nuclear weapons. There have been times in the past where the possession of an atomic bomb acts to stabilize the system. The fact that India and Pakistan both have nuclear weapons has capped their willingness to go to war against each other. In recent years, too, we have seen the new importance of people power: the ability of the masses, without weapons, to unsettle governments and bring about regime change. We are accustomed to thinking of domestic changes in democratic governments as reasons for international action or inaction but rarely have we considered what can happen in dictatorships or ideologically driven nations. Even where regimes are not toppled, "people power" exerts a real constraint over policy. Growing modernism makes even more inexplicable Hitler's crude, dangerous, and destructive policies in a culturally sophisticated and advanced country like Weimar Germany.

Renouncing such policies, countries have discovered new means of improving their position and increasing the welfare of their populations without recourse to war. Economic (intensive) growth has become the alternative to lateral (extensive) expansion.[28] As long as the economic system remained open, intensive gain was possible; when it closed down,

---

[27] See also Hedley Bull, *The Anarchical Society: A Study of Order in World Politics* (New York: Columbia University Press, 1979).
[28] See Mueller (ed.), *Peace, Prosperity and Politics*.

however, nations resumed lateral aggrandizement to acquire what they could no longer obtain through trade.[29] Globalization today raises the same questions. Economic crisis and the "great recession" of 2008–09 queried the continuance of openness. Countries were tempted to adopt tariffs or subsidies to protect their industries from foreign competition. Foreign direct investment, however, still reinforced the links between economies, compensating for tariff barriers. New IMF resources could aid countries in trouble, obviating their need to put on customs restrictions against foreign competitors. It also could diminish the demand for trade surpluses to gain foreign exchange to weather the next crisis. As the world economy revives, openness might re-emerge and countries could once again gain access to foreign markets and raw materials without having to resort to military expansion.

Various proposals have been made to render this reliance more effective for debtor countries. New international regulation of banks and hedge funds offered an alternative to the discredited prior efforts of national legislation. The European Union, in particular, emerged as an arena in which the measured march toward a common currency reduced fluctuations and indebtedness among its members, thereby attracting new states to join. Ireland – a member of the euro area – did much better than Iceland which saw its currency collapse. The common currency could be extended to new members, diminishing difficulties in repaying their external debts. A gradual but progressive institutional development through delegation can foster greater relaxation for small countries and perhaps also for larger ones, reducing the need to stay on one's power line.

Over time historic change could potentially offer a redefinition of what constitutes "power." In the past, the old definition was restricted to armed forces, natural resources, and the size of the economy and population.[30] But in the new age of high technology, a revised definition of power would have to include intellectual capital and the strength of educational systems as well as traditional measures of military and demographic achievement.[31] Flexibility and the ability to garner knowledge quickly and deeply were more important than in the past. In dealing with the problem of terrorism, for instance, major powers had to

---

[29] See John Kroll, *Closure in International Politics: The Impact of Strategy, Blocs, and Empires* (Boulder: Westview Press, 1982).

[30] See Brooks Emeny, *The Great Powers in World Politics: International Relations and Economic Nationalism* (New York: American Book Company, 1935); Morgenthau, *Politics among Nations*. See also Charles F. Doran, *Systems in Crisis: New Imperatives of High Politics at Century's End* (Cambridge University Press, 2008).

[31] See Richard Rosecrance in Chapter 2 of this volume.

concert their efforts and keep in touch, providing intelligence to each other. This change meant that the danger of internal conflict (though internationally organized) could bring countries closer together to combat it. In the past, secrecy was the order of the day among contending great powers who believed that the main danger was external. They believed in the inevitability of great-power war. That inevitability is no longer accepted today,[32] and nations focus more centrally on the problem of micro-conflicts within the state.

In the end, the factors of leadership, domestic policy, and definition of the situation were frequently joined to change a state's international strategy. If the three were aligned together, they might bring about a massive change in direction as Gorbachev did, or as Hitler negatively did. The calculus of power is and continues to be important to relations among states. But its dictates can be modified and even overthrown by ideological regimes which achieve leadership. North Korea and Iran are two present examples of countries seeking to act above their power lines. North Vietnam did so in the 1960s and early 1970s. Indeed, even the Western focus on "regime change" reflects the new importance placed on domestic politics, often unsupported by strict power relationships. Neorealists may bewail the fact or declare that the emphasis upon domestic politics or leadership predilections is reductionist, but it is in this contested arena, more than in narrowly defined power relations, that international outcomes are likely in the end to be charted.

Hedgehog or fox?

What does this tell us? Philip Tetlock has done a magisterial survey of social scientists' predictions in key international and historical policy episodes that illuminate this question.[33] Using Isaiah Berlin's definitions (hedgehogs know one big thing; foxes know a lot of little things), Tetlock finds that "foxes" are more often right than "hedgehogs." Realism is one big thing, as is, of course, unalloyed economic liberalism. Tetlock demonstrates that analysts who acclimated themselves to new features of any given situation were better predictors of outcomes than those who proffered single-factor theories to account for reality. This book falls into the "Foxian" tradition; the authors believe a series of smaller-scale variables is more likely to account for variations in policy than one single all-embracing insight. This does not mean

---

[32] See the comments of Paul Kennedy in the 1984 International Security symposium dealing with World War I.

[33] Philip E. Tetlock, *Expert Political Judgment: How Good Is It? How Can We Know?* (Princeton University Press, 2005).

that "realism" is wrong. It is one factor in what is essentially a broader regression equation. Perhaps power coefficients are higher than certain other variables, but taken alone, power cannot predict what goes on in the complex field of international relations. It is only by broadening the canvas that we can either explain the past or make any predictions about the future.

Index